ROYAL ARMADA
400 YEARS

© 1988 MANORIAL RESEARCH (ARMADA) LTD
104 Kennington Road, London SE11 6RE
Telephone 01-582 1588
Registered in London No. 1768040

ISBN 0 9513128 0 4

Distributed by Seymour, 334 Brixton Road, London SW9 7AG

Production, including typesetting and colour separations by Alphaprint, 3 Spicers, Ashdell Park, Alton, Hants GU34 2SJ.

Designed by Colin S. Lewis and Associates, 92 Church Street, Weybridge, Surrey KT13 8DL

Printed by McCorquodale Varnicote Ltd, Pershore, Worcs WR10 2DN

CONTENTS

Previous visitors include the Romans, the Moors and the Christians. Now it's your turn.

Peñíscola (Castellón).

Vélez Blanco (Almería).

Jadraque (Guadalajara).

Loarre (Huesca).

Tossa de Mar (Gerona).

The occupancy of a Spanish castle has changed hands so many times it's difficult to remember who hasn't been there.

The thing is, none of them seemed able to move on without undertaking their own building programme.

Which is why the Spanish castle you see today can have as many as four or five different architectural styles.

The number of castles to visit is equally breathtaking; 2,500 at the last count.

But if this still isn't enough for you, there are even some castles you can stay in.

They're called Paradores and every effort has been made to keep them as original as possible yet at the same time providing a high level of comfort.

Something which the Romans, the Moors and the Christians only dreamt about.

ESPAÑA

Spain. Everything under the sun.

ACKNOWLEDGEMENTS

MANORIAL Research would like to thank the Chairman, Admiral of the Fleet The Lord Lewin KG GCB MVO DSC, and the Trustees of the National Maritime Museum, Greenwich, for their support and help in preparing and promoting *Royal Armada*. Particular thanks are due to Richard Ormond, Director, John Palmer, Head of Marketing, Stephen Deuchar, Keeper of Pictures and Exhibition Organizer, Commander Roger Payne, and Hélène Mitchell.

The Foreign Secretary, Sir Geoffrey Howe QC MP, HE The Spanish Ambassador, Senor José Don J Puig de la Bellacasa GCVO, The Duke of Wellington, Viscount Blakenham, Sir Ronald Lindsay, and David Ratford CMG of the Foreign and Commonwealth Office rolled up their sleeves and got involved last December in the cut and thrust of commercialism at a media party for *Royal Armada* and the Exhibition. I am grateful to them.

Numerous libraries have assisted with photographs and these are credited in our captions.

But not another moment can pass without my recording my profound gratitude to some of this country's most eminent 16th century historians who have contributed handsomely to this collection of essays, bringing to tens of thousands of people new insights into one of our most glorious periods and demystifying some of the myths. The commercial backing we have received from our advertisers has made it possible to produce a workmanlike and readable publication at an affordable price.

On the Manorial Research side, I would like to thank my directors, consultants, and other colleagues who are in no particular order: Nirj Deva DL, J H Smith CBE FCA, Trisha Wilson, Ros White, Kate Allen (Managing Editor), Jane Ramella (Advertising Director), Helen Garrett (Media Sales Executive), Mary King (Picture Research), Chris Anderson (Production), Colin Lewis (Design), Peter Brown, Trisha Comrie, Desmond de Silva QC CStJ, Baron Bert E Grove, Lord Sudeley, Michael Petry, and Nick Clavel.

A publication of this sort does not emerge from thin air. It needs financial backing and this has come unstintingly from Michael Montague, Chairman of Yale and Valor PLC, and members of the Manorial Society of Great Britain.

Manorial Research's principal other occupation is the sale of lordships of the manor, historical and heraldic research, manorial legal advice, family history, manorial documents, and estate acquisition and sale. Many of *Royal Armada's* backers are lords or ladies of the manor who also supported Manorial Research in the promotion and realization of the Domesday ninth centenary with the Public Record Office in 1986. I thank them for helping to make possible another national celebration in 1988.

Robert A Smith
Chairman and Managing Director

"*This fascinating publication chronicles one of the most spectacular periods of European and, in fact, world history.*

In 1988 some 700,000 or more people will see the Armada exhibitions in London and Belfast, and hundreds of thousands more will see and participate in Fire Over England, when 600 Armada bonfires will be recreated around the country.

Pageantry, a sense of history, colour and excitement will be generated during 1988 by the exhibition and the host of events being organized to mark the Quarter-centenary of the Spanish Armada.

This souvenir brochure allows us to enter into that historic time, and bring to life for the many overseas visitors events they have only previously known of from dusty history books.

At Yale and Valor Plc we are concerned with world-wide trade in the form of security and comfort. Our employees, both in Britain and in Spain, are proud to be associated with this excellent publication and to be reminded of the cultural and commercial ties which link our two great nations."

MICHAEL MONTAGUE CBE
CHAIRMAN, YALE & VALOR PLC

300 *years before*
the Masthead...

The Financial Times

Drake's strategy stops take-over bid

"*While most historians agree that the defeat of the Armada was one of the more decisive events in world history, there is perhaps less agreement on precisely what it decided. To me, and I am not an historian, it was the perceived change in the balance of maritime power and the confidence that this gave to the English people that probably altered the course of history.*

By the middle of the 16th century the professional skill of the English seafarer was well acknowledged, schooled as he was in treacherous coastal waters, used to coping with wind, tide and fog; but the successful expeditions of a few like Hawkins and Drake had not been enough to encourage a widespread expansion of maritime trade. The outcome of the Armada campaign not only reduced the threat from the Spanish Fleet, it enhanced the reputation of the English mariner. Merchants were now more prepared to invest in overseas trading ventures with the assurance that they would see a good return.

The half century after the Armada saw a dramatic expansion in volume and extent of overseas trade and the great Trading Companies flourished. To protect this growing merchant fleet it was necessary to maintain a Navy, and a prosperous Nation could afford to pay for it. Out of this sense of national self-confidence created by the events of 1588, there grew not only the Royal Navy but also the British Empire. This is what makes the Armada so well worth remembering in its 400th anniversary year."

**ADMIRAL OF THE FLEET
LORD LEWIN**

ALFEX ✚ SWISS
Quality by Design ...

ALFEX ✚ SWISS

... it takes time
to reach perfection

...se necesita tiempo para llegar a la perfección

● Members of the Armada Exhibition Honour Committee (from left): Admiral of the Fleet Lord Lewin KG; H.E. the Spanish Ambassador Don José J. Puig de la Bellacasa GCVO; and the Foreign Secretary Rt. Hon. Sir Geoffrey Howe QC, MP.

One of the most surprising causes for Anglo-Spanish con-celebration has to be the quatercentenary which is being commemorated during 1988, namely that of the great Spanish Armada, which set sail for England in 1588. The National Maritime Museum in Greenwich, London, are mounting their largest ever exhibition in the refurbished East Wing, generously sponsored by Pearson plc. The Armada Exhibition will be opened by HRH The Prince of Wales, and runs from 20 April onwards.

Spanish involvement was manifest from the very beginning of the Armada Exhibition project. As well as many priceless treasures, in the form of jewellery and art, coming on loan from Spain for the period of the Exhibition, a strong Spanish support was demonstrated by the members of the Committee of Honour, formed by the Trustees of the National Maritime Museum for Armada 1588-1988. Committee members include His Excellency Don José J. Puig de la Bellacasa, Spanish Ambassador to London, and the Anglo-Spanish Society's own Chairman and Vice-Chairman, the Duke of Wellington and Sir Ronald Lindsay, respectively. With the British Foreign Secretary, Sir Geoffrey Howe, and revered historians of the calibre of Professor Sir Geoffrey Elton

also on the Committee, the presentation of Armada as something more than an English naval victory which gave rise to myths and folk-heroes had the strongest of factual and moral support.

Dr Stephen Deuchar of the National Maritime Museum has been at pains to establish the truth about Armada and Drake's so-called heroic rôle in the proceedings. Whilst Plymouth has remained steadfastly loyal to the reputation of one of its most famous sons, the Armada Exhibition has been developed around a broader theme, depicting the courts of Phillip II and Elizabeth I, Anglo-Spanish relations before 1588 and life at sea for both Spanish and English sailors of the 16th Century. The final section of the Exhibition surveys the propaganda campaign launched by England in the wake of the Armada's return and looks at the renewed naval conflicts which preceded the Anglo-Spanish peace treaty in 1604. In short, it is an Exhibition set in an international context which examines the background and effects of the conflict on two great naval countries of that time.

Armada will be forming the theme for many exciting activities around the country this year. Not least of these will be the Thurrock, Essex, Armada Pageant, which will re-enact Elizabeth I's journey down the

Thames from Lambeth to rally the troops at Tilbury Fort, and the Fire Over England project which will, literally, see the country lit up on July 19th. Fire Over England is the brainchild of organiser Bruno Peek, who has committed phenomenal amounts of time and energy to establishing beacons around the country (wherever possible on ancient beacon sites), to be lit simultaneously on the anniversary of the day Armada was first sited. The first beacon, sponsored by British Telecom International, will be lit on the Lizard in Cornwall, the point upon which it is popularly believed that the fleet was first spotted heading up the Channel.

Armada 1588-1988 is not only an exceptional anniversary because of its interesting maritime aspect or the fascinating characters who feature in its annals.

As Robert Smith, Managing Director of Manorial Research and the Armada Group puts it: "It is exceptional in its international implications, and especially its Anglo-Spanish expression of a joint look-back in present day peace and European unity to a unique event that severed, temporarily, the friendship between the two great 16th Century sea-powers".

Jane Ramella,
courtesy of the Anglo-Spanish Review.

Europe 1588

TSARDOM OF RUSSIA
● Moscow

SCOT-LAND

SWEDEN

KINGDOM OF DENMARK

● Edinburgh

NORTH SEA

IRELAND

Dublin ●

York ●

Berlin ●

HOLY ROMAN EMPIRE

TEUTONIC KNIGHTS

Warsaw ●

KINGDOM OF POLAND

ENGLAND
London ●
Exeter ●

Calais

NETHER-LANDS

ATLANTIC OCEAN

Plymouth ●

CHANNEL

Brussels ●

LUXEMBOURG

AUSTRIA

R. Vistula

Krakow ●

Rouen ●
R. Seine
Paris ●

Burgandy

GERMANY

SWITZERLAND

Vienna ●

Budapest ●

ROMANIA

Brittany

HUNGARY

R. Danube

BULGARIA

BISCAY

FRANCE

Milan ●
Pavia ●

VENICE

Genoa ●

Dalmatia (to Venice)

OTTOMAN (TURKISH) EMPIRE

BLACK SEA

PORTUGAL

Barcelona ●

CORSICA

Tuscany

Rome ●

PAPAL STATES

Naples ●

Constantinople ●

SPAIN
● Madrid

Aragon

Lisbon ●

Castile

SARDINIA

GREECE

Cadiz ●

Granada ●

KINGDOM OF TWO SICILIES

Athens ●

MEDITERRANEAN SEA

CRETE (TO VENICE)

LEGEND

● Main cities

Elizabeth I's domain

Phillip II's dominions (Spanish Habsburgs)

Area of direct rule by Austrian Habsburgs, Holy Roman Emperors

Venetian possessions

Boundary of Holy Roman Empire, comprizing 300 independent or semi-independent states, mostly in Germany

Kingdom of France

Direct rule by the Pope in Rome

Ottoman (Turkish) Empire, ruled by the Sultan in Constantinople

Janet Tanner

400 years after the Armada Queen Elizabeth I still epitomises the British spirit.

ACTUAL SIZE: 8¾"

Colibri have contributed for more than 60 years to the country's record for fine workmanship and have played a major role in the technological and design development of luxurious personal accessories. Today, Colibri is recognised by the discerning throughout the world as one of the finest fashion accessory houses offering a choice of desirable and prestigious gifts that are as rewarding to give as to receive.

● Queen Elizabeth I, the 'Rainbow' portrait, attributed to Isaac Oliver c.1600 (detail).

● King Phillip II of Spain by Alonso Sanchez Coello (detail).

A customer arriving by seaplane.

rubber bands onto his deck, in e
change for the whisky. Hot meals we
provided for any buyer who admitt
to hunger, and every buyer receiv
a free good-will case of whisky.

Bill soon had a reputation, a

not just for generosity. The whisky
sold was purchased in Nassau fro
our agent. Highly impressed with
fine quality, Bill's customers call
it "the real McCoy": genuine Sco
whisky blended with a pleasingly hi

HOW BILL McCOY GAVE SMUGGLING A GOOD NAME

Captain Bill McCoy didn't want to be a smuggler. After twenty years at sea, he had finally settled down to run a boatbuilding-cum-ferry business in Florida.

It turned out to be a more peaceful retirement than he'd planned: he went bankrupt. And he couldn't drown his sorrows, as Prohibition had started.

Then, a once-destitute acquaintance reappeared, having grown rich smuggling whisky. For McCoy, it seemed a way to kill three birds with one stone: he'd have the sea, adventure and money.

At that time, smuggling was a pretty casual affair. Bill would anchor his schooner just off the coast, and people would row out to throw rolls of cash wrapped in proportion of mildly peated ma and matured in light oak cas

In 1925, Bill McCoy returr to Florida and obscurity, havi salted away over $1,000,000.

You could say Cutty Sa made his fortune.

And when you ta it, you'll know why.

CUTTY SARK
THE
REAL McCOY

CUTTY SARK
SCOTS WHISKY
FROM Scotland's best Distilleries
Matured for many years in wood

Photos courtesy of The British Museum.

● Her Majesty Queen Elizabeth II by Pietro Annigoni (detail).
FISHMONGERS HALL, PHOTO MICHAEL HOLFORD

● His Majesty King Juan Carlos I of Spain.
COURTESY OF THE SPANISH EMBASSY, LONDON

DRAKE THE MAN

Joyce Youings assesses the hero and "pirate"

*L*OW OF stature, of strong limbs, broad-breasted, round-headed, brown hair, full-bearded, his eyes round, large and clear, well- favoured, fair, and of a cheerful countenance.

The truth of this description of Sir Francis Drake by Edmund Howes is amply borne out by contemporary portraits.

Born in about 1541, of solid farming stock, not far from Plymouth, the young Drake could expect no inheritance. His own father was a younger son who (if he was indeed Edmund Drake, shearman) obtained a pardon in 1548 for committing highway robbery, perhaps his eldest son's first lesson in aggressive self-help. At some stage, the boy must have had some schooling from which to develop that fluency of tongue and pen which was almost as much the mark of the man as his undoubted excellence in practical seamanship. By the 1560s, he was employed as a mariner by his Hawkins kinsmen, and in 1569 had his first experience of the Court when, having brought the *Judith* safely back to Plymouth after a near-disastrous encounter with some Spaniards on the coast of Mexico, he was sent post haste to London to report the incident at first hand.

Of the many exploits which followed, surely the highlight was Drake's

● Buckland Abbey.   NATIONAL TRUST.

circumnavigation of the world in 1577-80. Not only was it a superb feat of ship handling, but it presaged a new style of command. The young gentlemen who, as was usual, travelled aboard the *Golden Hind*, were required to "haul and draw" with the seamen. Drake himself, as reported by his prisoners, surrounded like a prince by his council, dined off silver dishes to the sound of music. The knighthood which followed at Deptford merely added the Queen's approval, especially of the incredible return on her investment.

With part of his own share of the spoils, Drake paid handsomely for the former abbey church of Buckland, already converted by Sir Richard Grenville into a splendid residence and within

easy reach of the port of Plymouth. Between voyages, he played his part as a country gentleman, even sitting in parliament. Since his boyhood, he had moved largely in extreme Protestant circles. As a young seaman, he had preached novel doctrines to his shipmates, encouraging them to put their faith in a very personal relationship with an all-powerful God, a faith he himself continually proclaimed even when corresponding with those in high places. But his was no religious war. Always an opportunist, he would deal harshly with anyone who flouted his authority, but be magnanimous to a fault with those of his prisoners with whom he could enjoy mutual respect.

Neither Mary Newman, the daughter of a shipmate, nor his second wife, Elizabeth Sydenham, a Somersetshire heiress, bore him any children. But the descendants of his brother, Thomas, cherished many of his most valuable possessions, not least the Drum which, in an age of celestial voyaging, may yet awaken his spirit across the oceans to come to the aid of his countrymen in their hour of need.

● OPPOSITE: Sir Francis Drake. Attributed to Jodocus Hondius. NATIONAL PORTRAIT GALLERY, LONDON.

FRANCIS
DRAECK

17

the GREAT Armada '88

PAGEANT

6th & 7th August

Tilbury Fort & Parsonage Common, Essex

Celebrating the 400th ANNIVERSARY of the GREAT ARMADA of 1588

England's largest Tudor Pageant. Two full days of entertainment and revelry around the Tudor Army's encampments, beginning at 10 am and continuing late into the night.

Elizabethan Fayre with Pig and Ox Roasts.

Fire Eaters, Jugglers, Stilt-Walkers, and Mediaeval Jousting.

Ale Tents.

Falconry.

Grand Firework Display.

Children's Rides and Fun Fair.

Elizabethan Side Shows.

Over 1000 costumed participants. Join in the fun, why not come in costume too?

THURROCK LEADS THE WAY

Please reserve me the following seats at the Pageant:

Saturday 6th August, **Grand Review Stands** on Procession Route	...seats @ £5 = £
Saturday 6th August, **Spectator Stands** at Parsonage Common	...seats @ £6 = £
Sunday 7th August, **Spectator Stands** at Parsonage Common	...seats @ £5 = £_____
	£
Deduct 10% for Party Bookings of 20 seats and over	£_____
I enclose my cheque made out to Thurrock Borough Council for the sum of	£_____

My name and address is ....

....

....

To book your seat/s at the Pageant please send your cheque and this form to:-
Bruno Peek, Pageant Master & Grand Marshall
Advance Booking Office, Thurrock Armada '88
5 Officers Quarters, TILBURY FORT, Essex RM18 7NR

HERESY AND REFORM

John Fines traces the powder trail that led to Henry VIII's explosive break with Rome

*O*N THE EVE of his 14th birthday, the year of his majority as a man, on June 27, 1505, the Prince of Wales slipped quietly away from the state apartments at Richmond and, accompanied by the Bishop of Winchester, a notary, and a few selected courtiers, went downstairs to a windowless room below the kitchen and there rehearsed aloud and signed a most secret document.

Henry declared that he had contracted to marry Catherine of Aragon, his elder brother's widow in his minority under pressure, but now he denounced that contract. No doubt his father, the King, had ordered this as a useful piece of insurance in case Catherine's father, the equally wily Ferdinand (well known for letting down all and sundry in his own interests), should fail to send the second half of the dowry. Indeed, there might well be better fish in the sea - a Burgundian marriage could well be promoted. The document, about which nobody needed to know if all went well, could be handy, brought out of the archives later on to prove a point.

In this seedy piece of chicanery, so typical of Tudor politics, lies the start of a long story which was to reach its culmination in the agonizing death of the great Spanish fleet in the North Sea, on the rocky shores of Scotland, the Northern Isles and Ireland. The story would have many constituents: most notably England's relationship with Spain, the Tudor dynasty and its anxieties about succession, the fast-changing relationship of developing nation states with that medieval notion of Christendom, new ways of looking at government and, above all, religion, a religion that had to choose in the context of fast developing thought between the state and the papacy.

England had been closely tied to Christendom and to its arbiter, the papacy, throughout the Middle Ages. In the great contest between Henry II and Thomas Becket in the 1160s, it was the murdered saint who won (a point Henry VIII was not to forget - he ordered the very name of Becket to be abolished throughout the land, as manuscripts with heavy erasures testify to this day). Henry II's younest son, King John, was finally forced to resign his crown to Pope Innocent III in 1213 and receive it back as a papal fief (a condition that lasted in England for 150 years). Equally, Henry VIII looked back to King John with warm sympathy and affection, and the Protestant writer, John Bale, made a good name for himself with his play on the subject: "King John appeared as an earnest, pious, and divinely appointed monarch who had been undermined by an international Romish conspiracy..."

England had also been loyal in terms of religion itself: before the outbreak of Lollardy in the late 14th century, the incidence of heresy had been so rare that little provision had been made for dealing with it other than on an *ad hoc* basis. Some 12 cases are noted in the 14th century before 1370, and so bishops and the Crown had little reason to be worried.

The Inquisition had only once entered English territory, during the suppression of the Knights Templar in 1308, when one is pleased to note that no one could be found to torture the prisoners and the inquisitors meditated importing torturers from abroad.

There were problems, however, *vis-à-vis* the Church itself. The reign of Edward III saw the beginning of a long attack on papal power to fill English benefices (provisions) and on the rights of English litigants to use papal courts in cases of first instance (*praemunire*). There was a general feeling that the papacy represented a drain on English finances, and this could most clearly be seen in the alien priories, with English rents of a substantial order being sent directly abroad. In a world whose economics regarded wealth as finite, the English could look forward to a day when all their wealth would have gone.

These early pieces of legislation restricting English subjection to the controls of a papal Church set up a series of precedents about the cutting of papal power, about restraining the outflow of capital and legal decisions (a further financial drain as legal decision involved fines), and about the power of the state to intervene decisively in the affairs of monastic orders. These precedents were to be eagerly examined in the 1530s when much greater strides were meditated.

It was not all a matter of finances. The removal of the papacy from Rome to Avignon in 1305 had signalled a break-

● Coronation of Henry VIII and Catherine of Aragon.

down of major proportions. Petrarch (keenly anxious for a return of the papacy to Rome, but nonetheless an honest observer) wrote of the Eternal City as "the impious Babylon, the hell on earth, the sink of vice, the sewer of the world. There is neither faith, nor charity, nor religion, nor the fear of God, nor shame, nothing that is true, nothing that is holy..." In 1378, the world saw the beginnings of the Great Schism, with two contending popes. By 1415, two years before the end of the Schism, there were three popes, and a great council met to solve the embarrassing problem. Two popes were charged with a great range of crimes, the chief being John XXIII who was accused, among other things, of fornication, adultery, incest, sodomy, poisoning the previous pope, and denying the immortality of the soul (and considering his many crimes one can well understand his last belief).

There was plenty to be critical about, and in England plenty of critics, most

obviously William Langland and Geoffrey Chaucer, but as was pointed out long ago, it was the established clergy in this country who gave in their sermons the most pointed criticism of the Church. Take John Bromyard, a Dominican, writing well before the Great Schism, and in the early days of the Avignon papacy how he hears the people saying "'Why should I give tithes to a rector who keeps a concubine ... How should I lead a clean life when I have so many foul examples before me' ... It would be better" (adds Bromyard) "that the church should have no minister at all ... 'Woe, woe upon my sanctuary, because it is profaned!'"

Into this critical arena backed the extraordinary figure of John Wyclif. An Oxford scholar, testy and arrogant in controversy, he was no model in his own behaviour as a priest or as an ordinary Christian; his rowdy insistence on his own righteousness surely disqualifies him for the title of "Morning Star of the Reformation". Yet he came at the right

time with fertile ideas which had a deep and abiding influence on the history of the English Church.

Wyclif's philosophical position led him to stress the authority of the Scriptures, to promote the notion of the absolute right and indeed duty of the state to reform the Church, to elevate the king in all things and to debase the papal Church equally (which he saw as the home of Antichrist). The aim was to return to holy poverty, and if this meant the state disendowing the Church, then that was no bad thing. His message was timely, for in the 1370s the Hundred Years' War that had first looked like a profit-making venture was now a desperate loss, and taxation was the only recourse to solve the finances of an ailing state. John of Gaunt, Duke of Lancaster and uncle to Richard II, found Wyclif's views to have the groundwork of an alternative solution, and until the Peasants' Revolt changed everything in 1381, he supported his protégé against all the

The Anniversary Alms Dish for ARMADA 1588 – 1988

To celebrate maritime history, Garrard, The Crown Jewellers in association with ARMADA at the National Maritime Museum have produced the Anniversary Alms Dish for ARMADA 1588-1988. Inspired by an Elizabethan design, it has been especially made to commemorate the 400th Anniversary of the Great Armada. The Anniversary Alms Dish depicts the events of the day in the form of a finely etched decorative pattern of the Armada story.

* The sterling silver and parcel gilt Anniversary Alms Dishes are a Limited Edition of 1588. These historic Collectors' items are available in 4 sizes.

* Each Limited Edition Commemorative Dish bearing the Anniversary Year London Hallmark, will be numbered and supplied in an individual case. No more pieces will be produced after 31st December 1988.

* The Commemorative Dishes are available in the following sizes and quantities:

  3½ inch diameter dish: £150
  Limited Edition of 900

  5 inch diameter dish: £250
  Limited Edition of 400

  8 inch diameter dish: £650
  Limited Edition of 200

  10 inch diameter dish: £950
  Limited Edition of 88

* The Anniversary Alms Dish is available by mail order or may be viewed and purchased at Garrard in Regent Street and all branches of Mappin & Webb, as well as at the National Maritime Museum in Greenwich.

GARRARD
THE CROWN JEWELLERS

BY APPOINTMENT TO
H M THE QUEEN
GOLDSMITHS & CROWN JEWELLERS
GARRARD & CO LTD
LONDON

BY APPOINTMENT TO
H M QUEEN ELIZABETH THE QUEEN MOTHER
JEWELLERS & SILVERSMITHS
GARRARD & CO LTD
LONDON

112 REGENT STREET · LONDON W1A 2JJ · TEL: 01-734 7020

I wish to order the Limited Edition Anniversary Alms Dish for ARMADA 1588-1988:

Quantity

. . . . 3½" dia. dish at £150 each
. . . . 5" dia. dish at £250 each
. . . . 8" dia. dish at £650 each
. . . . 10" dia. dish at £950 each

Please add £2.50 PPI for each dish
I enclose cheque for £........./or please debit my Sears Card, Barclay/Visa, Access, Diners Club, JCB, American Express (delete as necessary)
My number is:

Expiry Date:

Signature_____
Daytime tel no._____
Name_____
Address_____

Please send the coupon to:
Mr Nicholas Winton
Garrard & Co Ltd
112 Regent Street
London W1A 2JJ

Tel: 01-734 7020

Please allow 21 days for delivery

THE GARRARD QUATERCENTENARY DISH

GARRARD, The Crown Jewellers, have been commissioned to produce a special Elizabethan Dish to celebrate the 400th Anniversary of the Spanish Armada.

The Special Commissions Department at Garrards maintains a long tradition of fine craftsmanship in association with England's maritime history.

The House of Garrard grew from a company founded in the 18th century by the eminent silversmith, George Wickes, and acquired by another, Robert Garrard, 100 years later.

During their long association with silver models, Garrards have produced a number of impressive maritime centre-pieces. The *Cutty Sark* and *HMS Victory* are among many impressive models supplied to naval organizations around the world. More modern pieces include an impressive, large-scale model of *HMS Maritius*, a World War II cruiser. In addition to the models, Garrard have supplied commemorative pieces for some of the great sea battles throughout history. A sterling silver centrepiece of Nelson's Column in Trafalgar Square celebrates Trafalgar.

A personal reminder of another engagement took the form of a silver tray engraved with the signatures of the wardroom officers of *HMS Exeter*. This was presented to Captain Bell in December 1939, after the Battle of the River Plate and the sinking of the *Graf Spee*.

Garrard's association with the Navy continues to this day. At the end of the Falklands' conflict in 1982, Garrard were commissioned to produce a number of pieces celebrating naval and military achievements.

The company still insists on the same high standard using the skills of many exceptional designers and craftsmen. It is fitting, therefore, that Garrard should produce the special quatercentenary dish to celebrate Armada 1588-1988.

efforts of the Church to prosecute this heretic.

For heretic he was, denouncing the visible Church and going further to denounce its most profound support, the doctrine of transubstantiation. The magical power of the mass was enormous, and its denunciation equally astonishing. Few people communicated (and then of course only after confession) more than once a year at Easter, and they took only the bread. The priest officiated behind the rood screen, his back to the people, muttering the words that changed bread and wine really into body and blood of Christ, in secret, and turning to the people to elevate the host for them to worship.

Such was the power of the mass that a number of people had extraordinary visions: one George Carter, a thresher in the service of Sawtrey Abbey, Buckinghamshire, deposed in 1525 that once at the time of consecration when he looked at the host held above the priest's head he saw in it a naked child standing erect and holding out a bleeding heart, round which was a thin coating of pure white bread. When the priest broke the bread, it was of the colour of an amber bead, and when the priest went to wash his hands, he saw six green drops hanging at the priest's two forefingers which he wiped off with a towel.

In the context of such beliefs, the assertion that there was no physical change in the materials of the Eucharist at the speaking of the words of consecration was revolution indeed, and it was at this point that many of Wyclif's academic supporters who had greatly admired his confidence and capacity for scholarly argument left his company and became his enemies. Yet a number remained with him in his retirement at Lutterworth, Leicestershire (and indeed scholars from Prague came too, to learn at the feet of the master, and take back his ideas to Bohemia, where they were largely influential on Huss and his followers).

Among these followers was John Purvey, who was in many ways responsible for the most significant act in the creation of Lollardy. Following Wyclif's insistence on the fundamental truth of the Scriptures, and the necessity for scriptural knowledge as a foundation for all belief, Purvey directed the translation of the Bible into running English prose, and added to it interpretative prefaces and notes. Wyclif's insistence on 'sola Scriptura', only the Bible, was like Martin Luther's later insistence on the aloneness of justification by faith, a veritable opening of Pandora's Box. Both allowed the individual to make up his own mind, to be, in effect, his own priest unto himself. What need of a church in all this? How could something made with man's hand, something so demonstrably sullied by man's corrupt nature, how could this compare with the individual in direct touch with God, fired and powered by the revelations of God's own word?

No wonder that Convocation, the English Church's council, got around to banning Wyclif's Bible formally in 1408 - perhaps they should have acted sooner, but from then on they burnt every copy they could find. As I sit here writing a short article, I feel some of the physical pains of writing, and the notion of writing out the whole of the Bible text is quite overwhelming - there were no printing presses then. To have seen the product of such labour burn must have been horrific, yet in 1850 when Forshall and Madden, the editors of the Wyclif Bible, reported on their researches they noted 150 texts still surviving that they had seen. They had been well hidden during the 130 years in which the ban held sway.

Lollardy was a rational, sceptical faith, more concerned with what it did not believe than with what it did. The Lollards were hard-headed folk who objected to paying the Church for services they did not want and regarded pilgrimages and image worship as being merely silly. Why not worship a man with outstretched hands rather than a wooden crucifix, or if you must respect wood, then look to a living tree in the forest. It is God's handiwork that should make us marvel, not man's. And if we have money to spare, let us spend it on the poor and needy rather than on rich unreliable priests.

Once the Church had got its act together, the opposition was formulated. A new king who had deposed and murdered his predecessor needed all the help he could get, so in 1401 Henry IV gave the Church the act *de heretico comburendo*, of the burning of heretics. His son, Henry V, pious to a degree, eagerly supported the persecution of Lollards, especially after the Lollard revolt of 1414 - if they were against the Church that was one thing, but when they went for the state, then they must be wiped out. A further campaign in the late 1420s and early 1430s convinced the Church that all was well. So much so that, in the mid-century, when Bishop Reginal Pecok began to write against the Lollards, the Church was happy to prosecute him for his cocksure ways, sure in their own minds that they did not need an opponent of a dead sect. As we shall see, they were to be proved wrong.

In Europe at large, the 15th century brought a number of lessons and warnings, only some of which were heeded. The advance of the Turks in the East, with the fall of Constantinople in 1453, marked effectively the end of an era dominated by a crusading ideal that looked constantly eastward. Now the vision was swivelled, first south, where Henry the Navigator of Portugal's protégés and their heirs explored ever deeper the coast of Africa, and west, where in 1492 Christopher Columbus brought the unenviable banner of missionary commitment to what he thought was the East Indies, but what was to become America. The concentration of the process of discovery and colonization in the Iberian peninsula, and the validation of that colonial bid to control three-quarters of the world by the papacy was to have dramatic effects. The bull *Inter Caetera* and the title of *Catholic kings* were to put an onus upon the heirs of Ferdinand and Isabella, the rulers of Spain, that would not be denied. They wanted to win, and had cast their lot, but France stood out against them, with England as a side bet: a century of war was being forged.

Yet in this war-filled time, amid this corruption, a new mood was stirring, one that hoped by a combination of scholarship and gentle mockery to make its point. In 1494, Sebastian Brant began his famous publication:

All lands now know of Holy Writ
And books for cure of souls, to wit;
The Bible, Early Fathers' teaching,
A quantity of holy preaching;
Amazed I see mankind unmoved,
By pious writings unimproved,
With Scripture cast aside outright,
The world lives on in darkest night
And men persist in sin most blind.
On streets or highways you can find
A pack of fools who vaunt their shame
And yet prefer to shun the name
Thus have I thought this was the time
To launch a Ship of Fools in rhyme...

● The murder of Thomas Becket.
CANTERBURY CATHEDRAL.

● King John's tomb.

The mocking spirit of the *Narren schiff* was succeeded by the more intimate laughter of the greatest scholar Europe has ever produced, Erasmus. He, the chief exponent of the ideas of humanism by which respect was given to the most pure text, the most proven form was to produce the most powerful book in the Reformation, a text of the New Testament that went right back behind St Jerome's Vulgate to the original sources, and gave at last to the world the purest voice of the faith yet heard. In England, Thomas Bilney bought Erasmus's Latin New Testament in the year of its publication, 1516, hoping for some pleasure from its elegant Latinity. But having read the first verse of the first Epistle to Timothy: "This one sentence ... did so exhilarate my heart, being before wounded with the guilt of my sins, and being almost in despair, that immediately I felt a marvellous comfort and quietness insomuch that my bruised bones leaped for joy."

Erasmus provided scholarship and purity of text, but as we have said, he also provided mockery of an outrageous kind. In a sort of after-dinner joke manner, he wrote about Pope Julius II ascending to heaven and quarrelling

with St Peter, a humble fisherman and a Jew - scarcely could one speak to such a man: "I have set all the princes of Europe by the ears. I have torn up treaties, kept great armies in the field, I have covered Rome with palaces ... And I have done it all myself too. I owe nothing to my birth, for I don't know who my father was; nothing to learning, for I have none ... nothing to popularity, for I was hated all round..."

When he turned his satirical eye on the pilgrimage to Canterbury (which resident Lollards were already denouncing roundly), Erasmus wrote of seeing endless boxes of old bones to kiss (including an arm with flesh still on it, all bloody), used handkerchieves and other such revolting items, all set in jewels and gold. Finally, on the road back to London, an old man offers them the shoe of St Thomas and Erasmus's English colleague bursts out, "What a devil ... would these Brutes have? If we submit to kiss their Shoes, by the same reason we may be brought in time to kiss their Arses too." The time for gentle mocking laughter lasted but a brief period; the 16th century was to show the extent of man's capacity for destruction and horror. In 1525, in

Germany, they say that 100,000 people died in the Peasants' War. In 1527 came the Sack of Rome: "Burned is the great chapel of St Peter and of St Sixtus; burned is the holy face of St Veronica; ... the heads of the Apostles are stolen ... the Sacrament is thrown in the mud ... reliquaries trampled under foot ... I shudder to contemplate this, for Christians are doing what even the Turks never did." Eight years later, Munster, in Germany, fell, the domain of a Leyden tailor who crowned himself king of a communist, polygamous, anabaptist state. There was danger in the wind, no doubt about that.

Back in England, people became aware of the problem early enough. In 1511, a large-scale prosecution of Lollards revealed just how many there were, and how firm were their beliefs. Alice Rowley, one of the Coventry Lollards, said to her captors: "My belief is better than theirs save that we dare not speak it ... I care not, they cannot hurt me, my Lord knoweth my mind already." In 1521, a further drive was instituted against the Lollards, and some 300 were discovered in the Chilterns, many of them from the same families who had

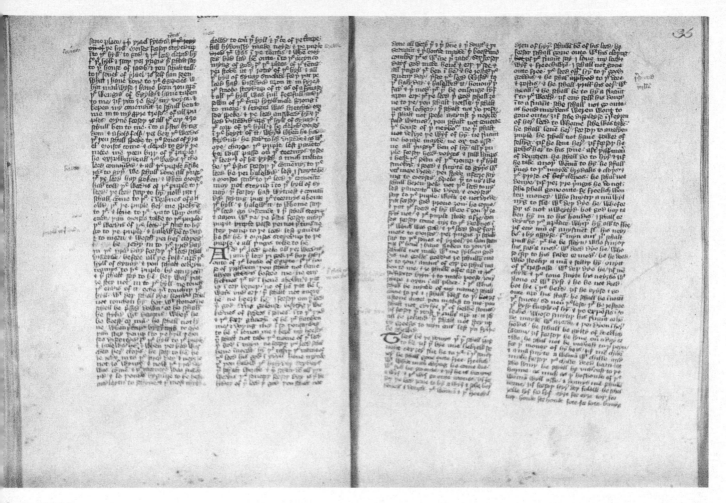

Wyclif Bible.

been prosecuted first by Bishop Chedworth nearly 80 years before. Bishop Longland, who organized the prosecution in 1521, had been born in Henley - how could it be that so many were disaffected, and people had not really noticed?

The tinder was ready to be set fire. All it needed was news from abroad. In London, they were already burning Luther's books, and down there in the Chilterns, in 1530, Richard Field was addressing a Lollard group, describing how he had been "beyond the sea in Alamany (Germany) and there they used not to fast, nor to make such holy days". Soon the messages were to come flooding through.

Yet if one takes one's stance at the fount of all power, by the side of King Henry VIII in the early 1520s, one finds a mind set as far from Reformation as could be, and firmly, passionately opposed to all kinds of revolutionary change. Henry, along with his wife, Catherine of Aragon, whom he had secretly disclaimed all those years before, was much addicted to pilgrimage-going, to observing the old ways. In 1518, indeed, Henry had offered to lead a great

crusade, and had in the same year begun writing an answer to Luther that was to appear in 1521 as the *Assertio Septem Sacramentorum*. The Pope was delighted, and at long last agreed to accord Henry a title such as that given to the Kings of France (Christian Majesties) and Spain (Catholic Majesties): henceforth the King of England was to be graced with the name of *Fidei Defensor*, as sovereigns have done to our own, notwithstanding their headship of the schismatic Church of England.

The King was far above that rising tide of anticlericalism that was to fund the first stage of the Reformation. Recently, scholars have shown that Church courts in this period were not as black as they were painted, yet there can be no doubt that large numbers of Englishmen believed them to be hopelessly corrupt, outdated, and inequitable. They looked back to Hunne's case in 1514, when a man, apparently on trial for refusal to pay the fee of a winding sheet for his child's burial, had been murdered in the Bishop of London's prison. Hunne had used that ancient statute of *praemunire* to attack his persecutors, but they got him in the end, probably during a

bout of "vigorous questioning". An outraged London refused to accept the cover-up, and would not forget the case.

A clear focus for this anticlericalism was the King's own chief minister, Thomas, Cardinal Wolsey, a man of superb skill, with a natural lust for power, an enjoyment of public display of wealth, and an arrogant carelessness of other people's opinions. As Bishop of Winchester, Abbot of St Albans, Archbishop of York, he cheerfully fathered children in whom he took a great interest and concern. As Papal Legate, he saw no conflict with his secular roles, such as the Lord Chancellorship of England. Becket never entered his mind, and he saw no reason to change his ways other than to suit his own good will. When he wanted to set up schools and colleges in his memory, when he wanted to build palaces for himself, he happily saw monasteries dissolved - the process was not new, after all, there were precedents, and it was the fastest way of raising money.

The hatred he inspired in the old nobility and in Protestants and Roman Catholics alike must be set against the good grace of those who saw another side of their wonderful master, people

Cambridge to staff his new Oxford foundation, Cardinal College (now Christ Church), he found to his horror that they were heretics to a man.

They were largely influenced by that great Englishman, William Tyndale, and through him by the King's great enemy, Martin Luther. Tyndale had left England to continue his project of a new translation of the Bible, and to study with Luther, and the two became inextricably mixed. Through Tyndale's biblical commentaries, Luther's ideas were readily mediated to the Bible-hungry English, and with the added power of print, the operation could be on a vastly larger scale than ever the Wyclifite translation had been. John Tyball, on a delegation from Steeple Bumpstead up to London, found Robert Barnes in the Augustinian Friars' and showed their Wyclifite manuscripts, but he "made a twit of it and said, 'A point for them, for they are not regarded toward in new printed Testament in English. For it is of more cleaner English.'" They humbly handed over 3s/2d and went away rejoicing with a Tyndale New Testament.

Tyndale was a new and a better Wyclif himself, for he attracted a number of followers who found it safer to be out of England for the time being, and they rapidly established a system for printing materials (often old Lollard treatises) which some of them could, at great personal risk, take back into England and distribute. George Constantine got as far as Shropshire, which was going some in those days. There was clearly an audience, and as time went on, Tyndale was to believe that the King might be made to figure among that audience: as John of Gaunt once listened to Wyclif's ideas, might not now King Henry VIII consider those of William Tyndale?

There were to be many strands in the cable that was finally to emerge as the English Reformation, and some threads were larger than others: four stand out as we look back. First, there was clearly that home audience of Lollards all ready to receive the message, for in a sense they had it already; there were those leaders of thinking in the English Church and state, men such as Cranmer and Cromwell who were well prepared to take a lead; there were the continental theologians whose message was to give a remarkable stamp of integrity to the

such as Thomas Cromwell; but the hatred outmatched the love: two exiles with William Tyndale, that master of propaganda, wrote back home in a pamphlet of:

The mastiff cur bred in Ipswich town
Gnawing with his teeth a king's crown
The club signifies plainly his tyranny,
Covered over with a Cardinal's hat
Wherein shall be fulfilled the prophecy.
Arise up Jack and put on thy sallet*
For the time is come of bag and wallet,
The temporal chivalry thus thrown
    down,
Whereby priest take heed and beware
    thy crown.

Towards the end of his days in power, Wolsey was getting and spending something like £35,000 a year - no that is not money translated into that of our own times - it is what he received, in real pounds. Too much, too obviously much.

In Cambridge, they were thinking more about holy poverty. Converted by Bilney, a young man of great oratorical power, Hugh Latimer was busy visiting the poor, the sick, and the imprisoned. Others, perhaps more volatile, were attending discussions in the White Horse Tavern, or hearing the wild denunciations of social injustice from the famous Dr Barnes, with his assistant, young Matthew Coverdale. When Wolsey selected the best young scholars of

* (pudding basin helmet)

somewhat insular and self-centred views of the English reformers; there was the man of power himself, the key to change, the man Tyndale wished to address, Henry VIII.

Henry was a complex personality and still escapes our grasp whenever we try to pin him down on paper. Immensely energetic, he was at the same time very lazy and willing to leave things to others; even so he was ever prone to distrust, to "let go" servants who were in fact working very well on his behalf. He was aggressive and cruel, yet utterly convinced that he was persecuted by others (most notably by women, whom he treated abominably). He was intelligent and could well have become learned, yet he saw argument as simply a device to get his own way; that being said, once he had enunciated an argument, while it served his purposes, he believed in it with the fanaticism of a convert. In essence the most conservative and orthodox of men, he viewed change as exciting, chancy, hunt-like; he was himself prone to sudden change, and found it his most powerful tool in government. He longed to emulate Henry V and ride back to victory as King

of France, yet lacked increasingly the money on which to make ends meet at home. As a warlike character, he was terrified of popular revolt. Above all, he wanted two things: his own way and a male heir.

People did talk, and went on telling dangerous stories about Henry's lack of sexual prowess, yet on this he prided himself, and he had living proof he could get a son: Elizabeth Blount had given him Henry Fitzroy. Perhaps he might be legitimated - after all, part of the Tudor claim came through the Beauforts, and they had been legitimated in Parliament. Clearly, Catherine would not give him a son; on December 16, 1526, she celebrated her 41st birthday; her last pregnancy had been eight years before; her only surviving child, a rather strongheaded girl, Mary, was just 10, good enough to make potential marriage alliances, but not old enough to make them real.

Above all, however, Henry had met the solution to his problem - a lady of no great beauty (indeed that vestige of an additional finger marked her for some as clearly a witch, while others simply called her whore) but of great attractive

power, and all the modern ways of the court of France (and not a few modern ideas in religion too). She was Anne Boleyn. Henry was besotted, the more so because she kept him out of her bedroom for a good five years. Henry, with his problems, found the role of beseeching lover, who never had to do more than look hot and bothered and write begging letters, ideal for his circumstances. His love letters (astonishingly preserved for us in the Vatican Library, of all places) betray the attraction and his enjoyment of the role. He drew a heart shape round her initials, mused about kissing her breasts in the future, and promised her all. All, just as soon as he could rid himself of Catherine.

In normal circumstances, this would not have been a great matter (as it came to be called - "The King's Great Matter"). Kings had often enough before set aside barren wives for the sake of the dynasty, and the papacy had been ready to provide the covering dispensation. But on this occasion, Henry was asking the Pope to set aside a papal dispensation that had allowed the marriage with Catherine, an awkward enough matter, but also Catherine was determined to

● Erasmus.

oppose it all, and her nephew, Charles V, King of Spain and Holy Roman Emperor, had the Pope in his grip.

Nevertheless, Henry was determined to have his divorce, and cared not (at the time) for his loss of Wolsey, nor indeed for what his own people and the rest of Europe thought of him. In December, 1529, using that ancient statute, he charged the whole of the English clergy with *praemunire*, and got them to pay a fine of £118,000 and to admit his supreme headship of the Church, "as far as the law of Christ allows". So far so good, and the aid of Parliament at this stage was great. But Henry was beginning to feel the loss of Wolsey, who had died in disgrace, and the need to replace him. He saw a range of possible new servants: at Cambridge, people such as Hugh Latimer and Thomas Cranmer were ready to spring to the support of anyone who was really going to engage in Church reformation, but closer to hand was Wolsey's former secretary, Thomas Cromwell, who could offer Henry a rationale for substantial, beneficial change.

The message Cromwell had for Henry was seductive: complete your power as a sovereign, as English kings have always wanted - make England in reality an empire, governed by one supreme head and king, "furnished by the goodness and sufferance of Almighty God with plenary whole and entire power, pre-eminence, authority, prerogative and jurisdiction". This meant a total abolition of papal rights in England, and it meant that the King would inherit those rights and their concomitant rewards, thus solving a financial problem that grew more serious each day.

The Pope was warned over a long period about what might happen if he failed to cooperate, but in 1533 with Anne Boleyn pregnant, things began to move faster. The new Archbishop (only recently made an archdeacon, so he really was new), Thomas Cranmer, presided over the court that found Henry's marriage to Catherine void, and also presided over the marriage to Anne. The die was cast, and the bills transferring papal power to the Crown plodded their way through Parliament. Surely, that was all that needed doing? Surely, that was all that was done?

Henry, fixed as he was on his project of the marriage, can hardly have noticed effectively what was going on around him, although many of the people he met with daily, and promoted to positions of power and influence, from his barber upwards, were deeply affected by the revolutionary religious changes that were going on on the continent of Europe. So far as *they* were concerned, it meant much more, very much more, than the simple abolition of the Pope's authority.

The extraordinary volatility of opinion coming from the Continent in this period is best summed up for me in the person of John Immanuel Tremelius who began life as a Jew of Ferrara, Italy. He was converted to Roman Catholicism by Reginald Pole, but was later converted further to Protestantism by Peter Martyr.

In Edward VI's reign, he spent some time at Cambridge as reader in Hebrew, and stood godfather to Matthew Parker's son.

The strange heritage of the Church of England is first but by no means foremost Lutheran. Luther was a man who discovered a revolutionary message and had a voice that was uniquely conditioned to his age, one that was heard far and wide; yet he was as conservative and almost as orthodox as Henry VIII, a strange mixture. Luther's message grew from a profound sense of sin, personal and universal (for him the two were the same). Obsessed with his own guilt, he saw around him evidence of man's universal corruption, notably on a visit to Rome in 1510: brothels run by the Pope for profit were the least of it. He could see no way out of the mire, doing good

works, going on pilgrimage, giving alms, praying, obeying the law - none of this would reduce the weight of sin by any measurable point. Even the behaviour of a saint was not sufficient to win salvation, so great was the burden of sin. Increasingly, Luther saw that the Church's behaviour in offering remission for sin that may be purchased, indulgences, was not only a lie, but a vicious insult to his own agonizing concerns, and in October, 1517, he launched his counterattack on the door of the castle church at Wittenberg.

Clearly, indulgences were no good. There was only one thing, a total reliance on Christ's unique sacrifice on our behalf - justification by faith alone. The extraordinary quality of this discovery cannot be overstated, for quite clearly, if each individual person could turn directly to God in his own heart, and accept salvation freely offered, and if that was the only way, then there was no place for the Church at all, mediating between man and God - every man was his own priest.

Luther's message went like wildfire, and in three years had spread all over Europe. Particularly in North Germany, the various princelings turned to accept this new way, and to establish state churches based on the version modelled by Luther's entourage in Saxony. A state church could conveniently take over the revenues, quietly abolishing monasteries, and dealing with its own inner needs (such that later on Philip of Hesse could make the bigamous marriage he wanted - how Henry VIII must have envied his situation). Luther took little account, busy as he was preparing the German Bible, writing hymns of lasting power, and producing a new tract every fortnight. He married his nun in 1525 and gave henceforth a picture of Christian marriage that could be interpreted by the enemy as the most bestial example of rule-breaking carnality. Yet he himself was only for gentle, progressive changes, big though his own steps were. The Peasants' War of 1525 and the extremities of behaviour of some of his followers distressed him greatly. Having fired the starting gun, he wanted a slow race.

Yet the fast advance of Lutheranism in the northern parts of Germany and in Scandinavia, their common forms of

● Cardinal Thomas Wolsey.
NATIONAL PORTRAIT GALLERY, LONDON.

organization, and finally their union in the Schmalkalden League in 1531 made this reformed faith a third force in European politics, an interesting alternative for a small power such as England which previously had merely to choose between Spanish Habsburg and French Valois liaisons.

The Lutheran states united out of fear of Charles V and Roman Catholic revanchism, but they had other enemies. To the south, in Zürich, almost contemporary with Luther the reformed Church established by Huldrych Zwingli was more radical and more aggressive than Luther's version. With a sharp aversion to "papist" ceremonies, a keen commitment to lay participation and a strong aversion to all transubstantiationist doctrine, Zwingli's Zürichers (and after his death in 1531, Büllinger's Zürichers) offered a more up-to-date and "leftish" alternative, which was to attract some of the English emigrés, such as John Hooper, who required something stronger than what Luther had to offer. Clearly, Luther was deadly conservative in his political attitudes and could be more than a touch medieval in his churchmanship. Zwingli and Luther clashed over the mass, with Luther desiring to retain some version of the real presence of the body and blood of Christ to the believing eater, and Zwingli roundly stating that it was a memorial service, no more. The sensible Martin Bucer, leader at Strassburg (but to die in Cambridge and have his bones burnt there under Queen Mary) tried to draw the two contending parties together, putting forth that useful distinction between essential doctrine and adiaphora - that which effectively could be left to the state to decide because it had no dogmatic status, but it was useful to have conformity.

Although he disagreed in many ways with Zwingli, the real heir to radical Protestantism in Switzerland was John Calvin, a Frenchman who published the first edition of his famous manual of belief, the *Institutes* in 1536, the year he went, by chance to Geneva, and at Farel's insistence stayed (with a break between 1538 and 1541) to build there the "holy city". It was a long struggle - Calvin was not to win full control until 1555, but the progress was remarkable, for in building a disciplined

community, firmly keeping to an Old Testament view of right and wrong, fired by that essentially hopeful doctrine of predestination and funded by the beginnings of democracy, Calvin was demonstrating in Geneva that Protestantism worked - good works did flow from faith - come to see them in action. People came in their thousands, many Englishmen in Mary's reign. There they used the educational and printing facilities to prepare to build the cadres and cells at home that would replicate that holy city in many parts of Europe and America. Carrying with them the idea of choosing the elders who would exercise power in the Church

(a revolutionary notion in a society where power was strictly hereditary) and that belief in predestination, they were a force to be reckoned with.

Predestination, the belief that God, being all powerful and all knowing, chose right from before the beginning of the world those who were to be elected to Salvation, and those who were reprobate to damnation might seem to us a gloomy notion. If we think for a moment, however, it will become apparent that few people thought themselves reprobate to damnation - most of Calvin's followers were convinced of their future life. When an Italian, Francis Spera, confessed himself convinced of his own damnation, Calvinist theologians rushed to his bedside, but Spera rejected them, saying that he knew Calvinist theology well enough, he had taught it, he just knew he was damned. Calvin was furious. There was not room for such - it was the enemy, the non-Calvinists who were clearly reprobate. People such as Michael Servetus, who foolishly stopped over on a journey at Geneva and was burned for his pains. Not a happy sign in 1553 when the English were facing up to a burning queen and seeking a home in safety abroad.

Yet there were enemies who were dangerous, and mostly at this time they were called Anabaptists whether they were or not, just as people Senator Joe McCarthy hated were called "Commies" in a later age. There were certainly some anarchistic people about, with wildly flying ideas, many of which spread from theology into social revolution. Basically, the Anabaptists believed that man should enter the Church willingly and knowingly and so they decried infant baptism (and as a part of their doctrine accepted in one form or another the freedom of the will). They believed they should keep all of the Commandments, taking no oaths, not fighting or killing, nor joining civil institutions, the law and its magistracy. Some were clearly Communists (the Hutterites, for example); many of them, because they were forced to move on constantly for their own safety, looked like a modern hippie convoy. When they came to a halt in Münster in 1534 and fought it out there, to the utterance, then the world was deeply shocked.

In England, they learned all about this fast enough. In 1531, William Barlowe wrote *A Dyaloge descrybyng the orygynall grounds of these Lutheran faccyons.* He had been with Tyndale and probably wrote under duress, trying to climb back into the English establishment; what he had to say was convincing and deeply shocking: "There be some which hold opinion that all devils and damned souls shall be saved in the day of doom ... Some affirm lechery to be no sin, and that one may use another man's wife without offence ... Some of them, both men and women, at their congregations for a mystery, show themselves naked, affirming that they be in the state of

● Zwingli   BODLIAN LIBRARY OXFORD

● Luther.   BODLEIAN LIBRARY, OXFORD.

● A page from Tyndale's New Testament of 1525.
BBC HULTON PICTURE LIBRARY.

innocence. Also some hold that no man ought to be punished, or suffer execution for any crime or trespass, be it never so horrible..."

Soon enough in England, people would be able to judge on the actions of a Protestant church for themselves, for Thomas Cromwell was moving fast with his plan to show the King that protestantism was profitable too. In 1535, he disestablished all religious houses with an income of less than £200 a year and in the following four years he got the remainder. Some 800 institutions, many of great antiquity and not a few of great service to religion and the common wealth of their region, most treasuring something of value to the English heritage, in art or scholarship, all without distinction went. The royal income was doubled "at a stroke" by this gigantic act of nationalization, and a fund of land, buildings, and wealth was made available to tie the new noble class to the Tudor dynasty, and effectively to the Reformation itself. Holding monastic lands was halfway to being convinced of the virtues of the changes undertaken in the relations of Church and state in the past few years. The age of the great country house was at hand, and not unnaturally the word abbey became consonant with a smart address.

It was not all done with a clear conscience, and some abbots, some monks, died in defence of their traditions. More and Fisher, two names known throughout Europe and as widely respected, went to the scaffold in the same year as the first monasteries were dissolved. Henry would brook no opposition: the next year the wife he had changed the faith of England to get, but who had only supplied him with yet another daughter (the future Elizabeth I) and had, for some unimaginable reason, taken to expressing her own opinions, against those of her husband, and actually daring to criticize his ways - well, she went too, to the block.

That same year, the North took fire in a great revolt, first in Lincolnshire, then Yorkshire and finally Lancashire, a rising to be known as the Pilgrimage of Grace. It must have been hard enough for those at the time to understand what was going on, though one feels their terror, a mere 10 years after the German Peasants' War. Was it a rising of peasants? Was it backed by the clergy? Was it secretly promoted by the gentry? Were foreign powers involved? Were they after the re-erection of the monas-

BRITANNICA
TWO CENTURIES OF
DEVOTION TO EXCELLENCE

WHEN THREE Scotsmen published the three-volume First Edition of the *Encyclopaedia Britannica* in Edinburgh, 1768-1771, it is unlikely that any of them conceived of the durability of what they had created. From this beginning has grown one of the world's great encyclopaedias, and one that has never been out of print. It is the oldest, continuously published reference work in the English language.

Colin Macfarquhar, a scholarly printer, and Andrew Bell, an engraver, founded the *Britannica*, and they hired a 28-year-old scholar, William Smellie, as their editor. Their First Edition was issued in 100 parts beginning in December 1768, and completed in 1771.

The 10-volume Second Edition appeared between 1777 and 1784, and the 18-volume Third Edition between 1787 and 1797. This edition included articles contributed by people outside the small staff, an idea considered revolutionary at the time.

Many of the authors in subsequent editions were among the most distinguished scholars of their day: Thomas Malthus on population, Sir Walter Scott on chivalry, William Hazlitt on fine arts, Roget on physiology, and James Stuart Mill, the economist, who wrote 12 articles. Through the years, a host of famous names have been contributors to various *Britannica* editions: Albert Einstein, Sigmund Freud, Tomas Masaryk, G K Chesterton, Trotsky, Stanislavski, Swinburne, and George Bernard Shaw.

In 1897, four Americans formed a company in Great Britain with A and C Black to reprint the Ninth Edition, which had been published between 1875 and 1889 in 24 volumes. This edition was offered through advertisements in *The Times* at a 50 per cent discount. This put the *Britannica* in the hands of thousands of families.

The 11th Edition (1910-1911) was the first to be published in Britain (by the Cambridge University Press) and the United States (by *Encyclopaedia Britannica*, Inc). The 11th Edition, of 29 volumes, was praised by critics for its erudition and universality of knowledge.

Early in the 1920s, Julius Rosenwald of Sears Roebuck and Company acquired *Britannica* for Sears after twice rescuing it from financial disaster. With the 14th Edition (1929), a continuous revision programme was begun. Annual printings with substantial changes each year began in 1936.

In 1941, William Benton, Vice-president of the University of Chicago, proposed that Sears donate *Britannica* to the University. Sears agreed, but the university hesitated to assume the financial risks of a commercial publishing operation.

Benton offered to put up his own money and to take administrative responsibility. The University of Chicago accepted the Sears gift, committed the management to Benton, and made an arrangement by which he acquired ownership. During the years of Benton's chairmanship, *Britannica's* business increased 50-fold, and ever since the University has received royalties.

In 1974, the 15th Edition was published after 15 years of effort. The pre-publication costs represented the largest single private investment in publishing history to that time.

Encyclopaedia Britannica is published with the editorial advice of the faculties of the University of Chicago; a committee of people holding academic appointments at the universities of Oxford, Cambridge, London, and Edinburgh; and committees of faculty members from Australian, Canadian, European, and Japanese universities.

teries, the end to all change, or were they more interested in power for the localities, power for the North? Very difficult to tell, now as then, but when Henry by brute force, good luck and telling desperate lies finally solved the crisis everyone breathed sighs of relief. The next year Cromwell took in the remaining possible contenders for the Throne, those of Courtenay and Pole blood, pointing to the fact that Reginald Pole, whom the King, his cousin, had so kindly supported in his studies in Italy and who had so ungratefully written against the divorce, was now plotting some kind of Roman Catholic crusade against England. He was not doing it at all effectively, be it said, but it made a good story in 1538.

Meanwhile, Cromwell and his little band of "young men", some of them scholars who had started off in Pole's household, a veritable "kindergarten" of the Reformation, was rushing through ever more radical changes. In 1536, it was ordained that every English parish church should have and display an English Bible. In 1538, the moves were against elaborate ceremonies, against image worship and pilgrimage, and against prayer to saints. Let us pause in this hectic time to hear of one moment - John Hoker, Minister of Maidstone, writes to Büllinger in Zürich in 1538:

> "There was lately discovered a wooden God of the Kentish folk ... he was able most cunningly to nod with his head, to scowl with his eyes, to wag his beard, to curve his body, to reject and to receive the prayers of pilgrims ... Throughout his channelled body were hidden pipes, in which the master-of-the-mysteries had introduced through little apertures a ductile wire; the passages being, nevertheless, artfully concealed by thin plates. By such contrivances he had demented the people of Kent - aye the whole of England - for several ages, with much gain."

The image was shown off at court. "It is difficult to say whether the King was more pleased on account of the detection of the imposture, or more grieved at heart that the miserable people had been imposed on for so many ages." Hilsey preached a public sermon showing how the puppet worked, and as a grand finale, "the wooden trunk was hurled neck-over-heels among the most crowded of the audience ... he is snatched, torn, broken to pieces bit by

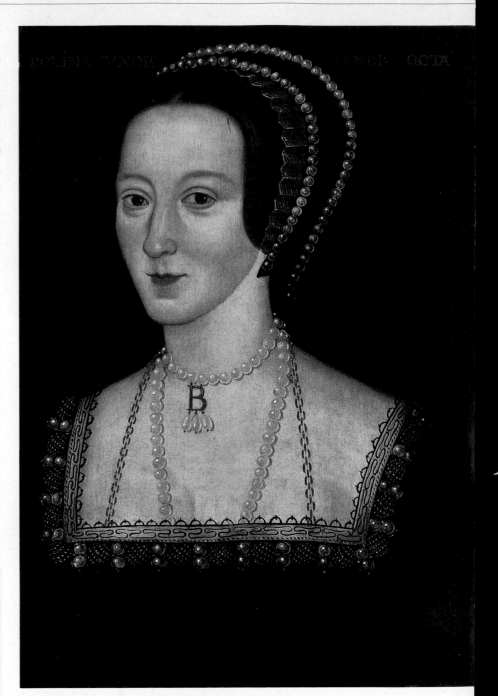

bit, split into a thousand fragments, and at last thrown into the fire; and there was an end of him!"

Not quite the end, however, for in this year of the destruction of the "Rood of Grace of Boxley", the King was beginning to have some second thoughts about all this enthusiasm, and about Cromwell's eager negotiations with the League of Schmalkalden. May be things had gone a bit too far; may be a touch on the brakes was desirable. The occasion came with the trial of John Lambert, who had surprisingly begun his career as a protégé of Catherine of Aragon. He had proved one of the ultra radicals, and had resigned the priesthood and contemplated marriage and life as a grocer. Yet he could not stop himself spreading his views, and even the most extreme Pro-

● Ann Boleyn.
NATIONAL PORTRAIT GALLERY, LONDON.

● OPPOSITE: Thomas Cromwell.
NATIONAL PORTRAIT GALLERY, LONDON.

testant bishops, Cranmer, Latimer, an Shaxton, were hot against him. Pers cuted by those who should have been h friends for his Zwinglian views on th mass, Lambert eventually appealed the King, naively hoping to get a prop hearing. Henry set up a show tria appearing in person in a white suit, ar bullying Lambert unmercifully. Whe Lambert was burnt in November, 153 the fire was deliberately withdrawn fror him and he was spitted on a pike to lifted clear to prolong his agony. Th message could not be more clear.

ARL OF ESSEX.

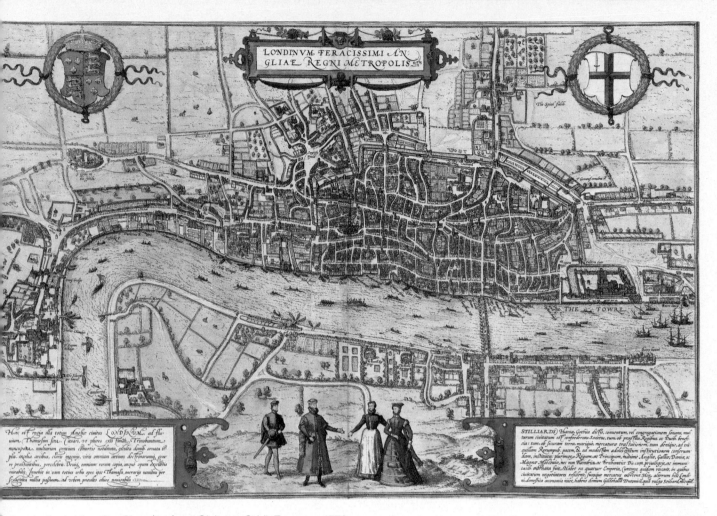

Lambeth and the city of London from *Civitates Orbis Terrarum*, 1572.

The next year, Parliament passed the Six Articles Act, reinstating the full sacramental position of the Roman Catholic Church, excluding only the Pope. This was the position Henry had wanted all along - no change, except to be rid of the Pope. Cromwell kept working on behalf of his changeable master, but in the following year he went too, on a charge of heresy. Apparently, the new Protestant Church of England had declared war on Protestantism.

Well in the firing line was the Archbishop of Canterbury, Thomas Cranmer. He had publicly (and bravely) opposed the Six Articles in the House of Lords, and had, when they were passed into law, been forced to send away his wife, a niece of the leading German Lutheran, Andreas Osiander. Yet he was also the man who had consistently given the King what he wanted, and the man above all others who *believed* in the supremacy. For most people, the supremacy was a convenient constitutional device; for Cranmer it was a reality

that this was the head of the Church, and what he said was what the Church would do. In many ways, Cranmer, remote and thin in personality in comparison with his King, was Henry's best of friends. Late in April, 1543, the friendship was to be sorely tried. The group of courtiers who favoured Henry's move back towards Roman Catholic doctrine wished to crown their successes with Cranmer's death, and gathered extensive evidence to show him to have been, like Cromwell three years before, a heretic. They approached the King and said they would arrest him next day at Council.

That night, the King sent over for Cranmer to come to Whitehall from Lambeth. He told him all of what had happened, and Cranmer meekly thanked him for the forewarning. Henry bluffly replied "O Lord God! What fond simplicity have you; so to permit yourself to be imprisoned, that every enemy of yours may take vantage against you. Do you not think that if they have you once in prison, three or four false knaves will be soon procured to witness against you and to condemn you ... No, not so, my Lord, I have better regard unto you

than to permit your enemies so to overthrow you." He gave him his ring, and the next day he was not admitted to Council for three-quarters of an hour, being kept outside the door with the servants. When they brought him in for that same grand scene they had had before with Cromwell, he quickly disabused them of their aim, and they were soon rushing off to the King to explain how it had not been their intention to harm the Archbishop in any way.

Cranmer it was, then, in the night of January 27, 1547 who held tight the hand of his dying sovereign. He had obeyed him publicly in all matters, yet during this last year he had been led by Ridley to hold the extreme Zwinglian position on the mass. He had, in the name of his sovereign, presided over many prosecutions of others for that selfsame view, had prosecuted fornicating priests, when he himself was married. A confused position, only to be explained in terms of the supremacy - hold hard to that and all will be well...

Dr Fines is a member of the History Department at West Sussex Institute of Higher Education.

OPPOSITE: Thomas Cranmer.

DIVORCES AND EXECUTIONS

HENRY VIII, EMPEROR IN HIS OWN KINGDOM

David Starkey describes how the King's need for a male heir led to a religious reformation in England.

"NO MAN is an Island, entire of itself; every man is a piece of the Continent, a part of the main", wrote John Donne. No country is an island either — and certainly not "this sceptred isle" of England. In the 16th century, England was not even an island geographically, since it shared Britain with the still independent kingdom of Scotland. Hence it was at best, in Pope Sixtus V's phrase, "only half an island". And politically it was not insulated (from the Latin *insula*, "an island") at all. We remember the defeat of the Spanish Armada, and Shakespeare's proud boast, written a decade later, that England was a "precious stone set in the silver sea, ... which serves it ... as a moat defensive to a house". We forget that four times in the previous century (1399, 1469, 1471, and 1485) this "moat defensive" had availed nothing and England had been invaded — as it would be again in 1688. Nor was the traffic in only one direction. For much of the Middle Ages, the kings of England had claimed — and held — large tracts of France, while from 1340 they claimed the French Crown itself. Most surprising of all is the fact that the Tudors themselves, whom we think of as the first (and last) English or rather British dynasty, were the product of foreign intervention. Elizabeth I, the last and perhaps the greatest of the House, might proclaim herself "mere English", and declare, as she mustered her troops to repel the Spaniards in 1588, that she

"thought it foul scorn that Parma or Spain, or any prince of Europe, should dare to invade the borders of my realm". Yet her grandfather and the founder of the dynasty, Henry VII, had not been so nice, and his successful invasion of 1485 had been backed by French men and money.

Indeed, it could not have succeeded without them. Henry, then Earl of Richmond and an exile in the French satellite duchy of Brittany, had carefully cultivated the French Court. He had at least one meeting with the veteran diplomat Philippe de Commynes, and in April 1485 he accompanied the young French King, Charles VIII, on his ceremonial entrée into Rouen, the capital of Normandy. The purpose of the Royal visit was to ask the Norman Estates for a grant of taxation to cover the costs of French assistance to Henry in enforcing his claim to the English Throne. The Estates responded generously and Charles was able to give Henry 40,000 livres. As well, Henry borrowed other sums from the French King and French merchants. With these funds, he raised about 4,000 troops and equipped a flotilla of ships. The troops were made up of the 1,800 French first mustered; another 1,500 newly discharged from the French military base of Pont de l'Arche; perhaps up to 1,000 Scots, and finally a mere 400 English exiles. Three out of four of Henry's followers, therefore, were French, and it was the commander of the

French troops, Philibert de Chandée, whom Henry rewarded most generously after the victory of Bosworth Field by creating him Earl of Bath.

All this represents a striking turnaround. Earlier in the century, it had been the English king, Henry V, who had been able to exploit divisions within the French Royal Family to seize the throne itself in 1420, and triumphant English soldiers who had been showered with French noble titles. Partly the change was a matter of mere personal accident. As part of the settlement with France in the treaty of Troyes of 1420, Henry V had been married to Catherine, daughter of Charles VI of France. And the son of the marriage, who became Henry VI of England, inherited not only his grandfather Charles's kingdom, but his incompetence and eventual madness as well. The effect of Henry's weakness was to split England, just as Charles's had divided France a generation earlier.

But there were also structural changes as well. Charles, son of Charles VI, who had been disinherited by the treaty of Troyes, not only regained his kingdom as Charles VII of France, but also reformed it. He instituted permanent taxation and a standing army. England resolutely refused to take the same path, and the royal finances weakened accordingly. With good luck and good management, it was possible to balance the books in peacetime and even leave a bit over. What was almost impossible vas war. Each campaign needed a huge effort and left behind a mountain of debts: extended war, therefore, was out, as was the maintenance of any sort of permanent military establishment. Extended wars and standing armies, however, were the hallmarks of the new great powers of the Continent: France and the rapidly rising Spain. England simply could not compete on equal terms and fell from the first to the second rank of European states. As it did so, the cockpit of Europe swung south. For much of the later Middle Ages, the struggle between England and France had been crucial; now Italy became the battlefield of Europe, and France and Spain the protagonists.

THE END OF THE HOUSE OF LANCASTER

Of course, in the mid-15th century, the full implications of all this were scarcely to be glimpsed; on the other hand, Henry VI's imbecility quickly reopened the question of the succession. There had been difficulties about this since the revolution of 1399, in which Henry Bolingbroke (the grandfather of Henry VI) overthrew his cousin, Richard II, and seized the Throne as Henry IV. Richard was autocratic, unwarlike, childless, and played fast and loose with the rights of inheritance, which was the essential cement of aristocratic society. His Court was also tinged with the fashionable heresy of Lollardy. Henry, on the other hand, was the most vigorous and capable member of the Royal House. He was a proven soldier, the father of a brood of four fine sons, of unimpeachable orthodoxy, and heir to the richest inheritance after the Crown itself, the duchy of Lancaster. But was he (Richard once out of the way) heir to the Crown? Here the answer was ambiguous. Henry, as eldest son of John of Gaunt, third son of Edward III, was heir in the direct male line. On the other hand, if female succession were allowed, then his cousin, Roger, Earl of March, had a prior claim through his mother, Philippa, daughter of Lionel, Duke of Clarence and Edward III's second son.

At the time, these niceties, like the fact of the usurpation itself, did not matter too much. Men combined an almost religious awe of monarchy with a remarkable pragmatism about the actual wearer of the Crown. Kings did not only rule by divine right, they were themselves miracle-working semi-divinities. Or at least they were when they were

successful. But when "the divinity that doth hedge a king" was breached, then, men argued reasonably enough, it was because the king was not true king anyway — otherwise, of course, God would not have withdrawn His protecting hand. This admirably unsentimental approach left little room for legitimism and strings of pretenders. These instead are primarily phenomena of later centuries. So long, therefore, as the House of Lancaster seemed able to command the God of battles, in putting down rebellion at home or conquering France abroad, its rather murky origins were forgiven, if not forgotten. But once success turned into first stalemate and then defeat under Henry VI, memories revived and old claims were dusted down.

Most important of these were the claims of Richard, Duke of York. He descended from the Royal House on both sides: his grandfather was Edmund, Duke of York, fourth son of Edward III; while his mother, Anne Mortimer, daughter and sole heiress of the Earl of March, carried with her descent from the elder line of Edward III's second son, Lionel of Clarence. Neither claim alone was unimpeachable, but together they were very strong. Richard's position was strengthened still further by the genetic catastrophe that befell the House of Lancaster. Henry IV's five sons seemed to guarantee the succession, but between them they produced only one legitimate child: Henry VI himself. With the death (in mysterious circumstances moreover) of King Henry's last surviving uncle, Humphrey, Duke of Gloucester in 1447, the dynasty hung by the single thread of the King's life. The following year, Richard of York, now unquestionably heir presumptive, assumed the ancient royal surname of "Plantagenet".

Richard's anxieties about his title, which largely shaped his actions in the next fraught decade, showed that things were not so straightforward, however. For though John of Gaunt's issue seemed to be dying out in the legitimate line, the offspring of his mistress, Katharine Swynford, were plentiful. Gaunt had eventually done the right thing by Katharine and married her in 1396, while their children were legitimized the following year and given the surname of Beaufort. The legitimization was confirmed by Henry IV, the Beauforts' half-brother, with the important (though dubiously legal) provision that it was not to extend to "the Royal dignity". Henry VI was far more unreserved in his affection for his

cousins of the half blood: John Beaufort was made Duke of Somerset, and when he died without male issue the title was revived in favour of his brother Edmund in 1448. That, of course, was the year York assumed the name Plantagenet, and it seems clear that the two events were closely connected.

Henry, in fact, can be seen as pursuing a "dynastic policy", which hedged his own thinning line with a fence of Royal cousins. Next to benefit were the Tudors. Catherine of France was still a young and vigorous woman on the death of her husband, Henry V, in 1422. She solaced her widowhood with the charms of Owen Tudor, a personable if impoverished Welsh gentleman of her household. One story says he first caught the Queen Dowager's eye when he fell drunk into her lap at a ball; another that she was smitten with him when she glimpsed him stripped naked for a swim. At all events, the couple were married secretly and had several children. With Catherine's death in 1437 the veil of secrecy was torn aside: Owen was arrested and his sons were taken as the King's wards. But Henry took a liking to them and in 1452 Edmund was made Earl of Richmond and Jasper Earl of Pembroke. Both were titles that had been held by Henry's Royal uncles. Three years later, Edmund, the eldest, was married to Margaret, only child of John Beaufort, first Duke of Somerset. Both semi-Royal lineages — Beaufort and Tudor — were thus united in the offspring of the marriage, Henry, later Henry VII.

Shakespeare makes Henry VI prophesy that his young nephew was "likely in time to bless a regal throne". If so, he showed a foresight sadly lacking in his conduct of affairs. These henceforward went from bad to worse. York determined to secure the place of the King's first councillor, to which he felt entitled by his birth. Henry, with a sort of feeble obstinacy, determined to block him. When in 1454 the King went mad, never fully to recover, the cudgels were taken up by his formidable wife, Queen Margaret of Anjou. She had finally given birth to a son, Edward, Prince of Wales, in 1453, and she saw York as the greatest threat to the boy's inheritance. Her implacable hostility finally drove York to claim the Throne itself in 1459. A compromise was reached, which left Henry as King, but disinherited Edward in favour of York. Over the next two years, fortune swung wildly from one side to the other. In the north, York was defeated and executed by Margaret; in the south, York's son, Edward, Earl of March, and his ally, the Earl of Warwick, seized London and Edward was proclaimed King as Edward IV on March 4, 1461. On the 29th, he confirmed his position by inflicting a crushing defeat on Margaret's forces at the battle of Towton.

YORK AND TUDOR: TRIUMPH AND DISASTER

For the first decade of his reign, however, Edward's hold on power remained insecure. In particular, he alienated his principal backer, the Earl of Warwick. Much against Warwick's will, Edward had married Elizabeth Woodville, a mere baron's daughter and a widow to boot. Providing for her family monopolized the marriage market and left Warwick without suitable matches for his two daughters and co-heiresses. Edward also crossed Warwick on foreign policy: Warwick inclined to France; Edward to Burgundy. The gage was the hand of Edward's sister, Margaret. Warwick negotiated for her to marry the French King's brother-in-law, but Edward vetoed the negotiations and in 1468 Margaret was married to Duke Charles of Burgundy.

Outraged, Warwick executed a complete *volte face*. Hitherto the chief enemy of the House of Lancaster, he now entered into alliance with Queen Margaret of Anjou. The honest broker was Louis XI of France, Margaret's cousin and the inveterate opponent of Edward IV's new brother-in-law, Charles of Burgundy. The unlikely coalition enjoyed striking initial success. Edward was driven into exile in Burgundy and Henry VI, who had been imprisoned in the Tower since 1465, was restored as King. But the coalition quickly broke up. The third member of the triumvirate, Edward's brother, George, Duke of Clarence, proved particularly indigestible and his defection paved the way for Edward's recapture of the Throne in 1471: Warwick was killed at Barnet; Edward, the Lancastrian Prince of Wales, at Tewkesbury; Edmund Beaufort, titular Duke of Somerset and the last male Beaufort, was executed the following day. Three weeks later, the second-time deposed Henry VI conveniently died of "pure displeasure" in the Tower. The House of Lancaster was almost finished.

Almost, but not quite. For the Tudors — Jasper, titular Earl of Pembroke, and his young nephew, Henry,

Earl of Richmond — managed to escape the débâcle. They set sail from Tenby in September 1471, intending to take safe refuge in France. But storms blew them off course and they were forced to land instead in Brittany. Brittany, though a fief of the French Crown, was a near-independent duchy, and its duke, Francis II, was determined to keep it that way. To do so required an elaborate diplomatic game between the two neighbouring great powers of England and France. In this game Henry Tudor was a valuable pawn, and he was protected accordingly for the next 13 years. Edward IV made fairly determined attempts to recover him, by fair means as well as foul. In particular, he promised to restore Henry to his earldom and marry him to a suitable bride, perhaps even his own daughter, the Princess Elizabeth. Henry's mother, the Lady Margaret, appeared to view the proposal kindly. She had married in 1472 as her fourth husband Thomas, Lord Stanley, Edward's Lord Steward and a great man in his Court. Like everyone else, in other words, Margaret thought that Lancaster was finished, and she sensibly wished to provide for her son in the Yorkist scheme of things. She no doubt was sincere; Edward's motives were more doubtful. Henry was unwilling to make the experiment. In 1476 it was nearly thrust on him willy-nilly: he was actually handed over to Edward IV's ambassadors, but feigned illness and escaped into sanctuary. This desperate bid for time worked, as, meanwhile, Duke Francis changed his mind again and resolved to keep his guest-cum-prisoner. Henceforward, however, Henry's movements were more restricted and he was lodged in powerful and isolated *chateaux*.

But seven years later, everything changed. Hitherto, the best that even Henry's mother could hope for was to make her son a satellite to the "sun of York". In 1483, however, the sun was eclipsed and Edward died. His son and heir, Edward V, was aged only 12. In the testing circumstances of a Royal minority, the factious Yorkist Court split asunder. First, most of the establishment united behind Edward's brother, Richard, Duke of Gloucester, to dish Queen Elizabeth and her hated Woodville brood; then the victors fell out as Richard, supported by the Duke of Buckingham, bid for the Throne itself. By June 1483, Richard had removed every obstacle from his path: he had beheaded the Queen's brother and one of her sons by

her first marriage, as well as his erstwhile ally, Lord Hastings, Edward's closest associate and the Lord Chamberlain; while Edward V and his younger brother Richard were his prisoners in the Tower. On July 6, with great magnificence, the usurper was crowned as King Richard III.

Richard had got the Throne, but in so doing he had alienated every powerful interest group in the country. The Woodvilles, though bloodied, were still a force to be reckoned with, as were the knights and gentlemen of Edward IV's household. The latter had been hurt in their honour by Richard's usurpation of their young master; and they were hurt in their pockets by Richard's promotion of his own followers from the North. Even Buckingham, Richard's staunchest backer, began to have his doubts: the new King had given him viceregal authority in Wales, but might not the Duke's own descent from Thomas of Woodstock, the youngest son of Edward III, open the way to higher things still? These divisions within the Yorkist coalition only widened as the rumours of the murder of the "Princes in the Tower" began to circulate. Suddenly, the fortunes of the House of Lancaster, which seemed to have been extinguished forever in 1471, revived.

Three people in particular fanned the dying embers back to life: Lady Margaret Beaufort herself, her servant, Reginald Bray, and John Morton, a Lancastrian cleric who, finally reconciled to Edward IV after the débâcle of 1471, had been made Bishop of Ely. Between them they pulled together the different threads of opposition to Richard III into what should have been a formidable alliance. But their plans were badly bungled: in the autumn of 1483, the Woodvilles and Edward IV's Household knights rose in a series of ill co-ordinated county rebellions that were easily picked off by Richard; while Buckingham, who should have been the strongest link, proved the weakest. Not only was he ambitious, he was a grasping landlord too. The result was that his tenants supported him reluctantly, deserted him quickly, and finally betrayed him to Richard, who promptly executed him.

Henry Tudor's own role was little more distinguished. Duke Francis of Brittany provided him with men and ships, but he set sail late; storms separated the fleet; and, when he finally hove to off Plymouth, he confronted an England where Richard III had decisively restablished his authority. Not even daring to land, he turned tail and eventually made his way back to Brittany. The bright hopes of a few months before had faded. Things were to get worse before they got better. Richard now made a determined attempt to secure Henry's surrender, and he only saved himself by a precipitate flight into France.

But the cloud had a silver lining. Richard might have defeated the rebellions of 1483, but most of the rebel leaders had escaped his clutches. They fled to join Henry and, by their very presence, turned him from a solitary refugee into king-in-exile. Much more important, however, was the breakdown in relations between France and England. The Orléanist opposition to Anne of Beaujeu, the Regent for her young brother, Charles VIII, allied with Brittany and aimed to bring in Richard III and Burundy as well. That was enough to throw the French government wholeheartedly behind Henry Tudor. A second expedition, as French as the last one had been Breton, set sail and landed at Milford Haven. Henry then marched through an England that remained studiously neutral, and on August 22 1485 confronted and killed Richard III at Bosworth Field. The pawn had become King, but only by courtesy of the King of France.

HENRY VII: THE FOUNDER OF THE DYNASTY

Henry never forgot these extraordinary events. To have accompanied him "on our late victorious journey" to Bosworth remained a sure passport to favour. Even more importantly, he remembered the lessons of his own experience. He exercised an eternal vigilance to make sure that no pretender should repeat his own success against him; and he moved quickly to fill the dynastic vacuum. The scheme to marry him to Elizabeth of York, eldest daughter of Edward IV, which had first been floated in the 1470s, was revived after Richard's usurpation. Henry was not in too big a hurry, however, for he was determined that no one should think that he held the Throne in right of his wife. So first he was crowned on October 30) and met Parliament (on November 7); only then was he married, during the Christmas recess on January 18, 1486. Nine months later, almost to the day, a son, Arthur, was born. Over the next decade, the couple had three other children who survived infancy: another son, Henry, and two daughters,

Margaret and Mary. By the standards of some other royal broods, this was a relatively small family, but it was enough to guarantee the succession.

His growing family also provided a useful tool in diplomacy. The importance of foreign policy was the remaining lesson of Henry's apprenticeship. His accession had been a mere episode in the long power struggle of the states bordering the English Channel; for the first decade of his reign the game continued as before as the long simmering crisis of Brittany finally boiled over. Duke Francis died in 1488, leaving as his heir his daughter, Anne. Self-interest, as well as the debt of gratitude for the protection Brittany had given him in exile, compelled Henry to try to defend the duchy against annexation by France. Direct and indirect means were tried, and both failed. An English expeditionary force flopped; the betrothal of Anne to Maximilian, King of the Romans and head of the House of Habsburg, promised better. But Maximilian proved as unreliable in this as in most other roles, and in 1491 Anne, having repudiated Maximilian, married Charles VIII of France, taking her duchy as her dower. Outraged (or pretending to be), Henry invaded France itself the following year, but was bought off by the treaty of Étaples.

Rapprochement with France inevitably alienated Burgundy. After the death of Charles the Bold in 1477 the duchy had been inherited by his daughter, Mary, who had saved her lands from the clutches of Louis XI of France by marrying Maximilian. On Mary's death in 1482, Maximilian had not been allowed to assume the regency for his son Philip. But he remained one of the key figures in the Netherlands; another was the formidable Dowager Duchess Margaret, Edward IV's sister. She remained implacably opposed to the Lancastrian/Tudor victory in England and was prepared to back any Yorkist or pseudo-Yorkist claimant. Her latest protégé was a young man of dubious ancestry, but pleasing appearance and address, called Perkin Warbeck. Thanks to her support, Warbeck was passed off variously as the Earl of Warwick (son of George, Duke of Clarence, the executed brother of Edward IV), or Edward's younger son, Richard, Duke of York. Maximilian, bearing a grudge against Henry over the affair of Brittany, now joined in and gave Warbeck an honoured place at the funeral of his father, the Emperor Frederick III. Henry retaliated by imposing an

embargo on trade with the Netherlands. Since the Netherlands were much the most important outlet for English woollen cloth (its chief export), this was tantamount to Henry's cutting off his nose to spite his face. But the embargo hurt the Netherlands at least as much, and in 1494 an honourable way was found of getting rid of their awkward guest by sending Perkin off to claim his "inheritance" of England.

The expedition was a substantial one, but the attempted landing in Kent was a fiasco. Warbeck, who had not dared to land, abandoned the 200 or 300 of his men who had, and sailed off to try his luck in territories further away from the centre of Henry VII's power. Ireland proved unpromising, so he essayed Scotland instead. The King of Scots was the young James IV, who had succeeded his murdered father James III in 1488. He was impetuous and ambitious and determined to cut a large role on the European stage. Warbeck was an apt instrument to his hands. "King Richard IV", as he now styled himself, was given a pension and the King's cousin as a wife, and together the two invaded England. The invasion was not a success, and, once again, Warbeck was sent on his travels. This time, he finally landed in the West Country and laid siege to Exeter. But his forces were repulsed with heavy losses and he surrendered into Henry's hands. His imposture was exposed; his wife taken off to Court (where she went through three other husbands in quick succession); and he was imprisoned in the Tower. In 1499, perhaps with Henry's connivance, he tried to escape and was executed, along with the real Earl of Warwick.

THE NEW CONSTELLATION OF POWER: ENGLAND, SPAIN AND FRANCE

Pressure for the executions had come from Spain; indeed Spain was the hidden hand behind much of the diplomacy of these years. Spain was the new great power. For centuries, the Iberian peninsula had been divided into rival kingdoms which had warred ceaselessly with each other and with the Moors, who still held the south. In 1469, however, Ferdinand, King of Aragon, had married Isabella, heiress of Castile. Isabella succeeded in 1474, and, after a long civil war, finally established her claims in 1479. Thereafter, the union of the crowns went from strength to strength: Royal power was consolidated inside Castile; in 1492,

Granada, the last stronghold of the Moors, fell, and that same year Columbus sailed to the New World. In all of this it was the passionate crusading spirit of Castile that was dominant. The traditional concerns of Aragon were different. With its capital in the great port and trading city of Barcelona it looked to the Mediterranean and to Italy in particular, where a branch of the Royal House ruled Sicily and Naples.

But other eyes were also turned on Italy. King Charles VIII of France had inherited the alternative Angevin claim to Naples; while Louis, Duke of Orléans, the heir presumptive to the French Throne, was one of the legitimate successors of the Visconti dukes of Milan, whose inheritance had been usurped by the Sforzas. Now that the annexation of Brittany had made him master of the north, Charles VIII's ambitions increasingly turned to making good these claims on the south: in 1493 he styled himself King of Jerusalem (which had also been held by the Angevins) as well as King of Naples; he even dreamed of reviving the Byzantine Empire. In 1495, he turned dreams into reality by invading Italy. The invasion became a promenade: in November, he took Florence; in December, he was in Rome; in February, he conquered Naples. Appalled, most of the other European powers settled their own differences to form a grand coalition against Charles and he was driven out of Italy as quickly as he had come in. Architect of the anti-French coalition was Ferdinand of Aragon, and, for the next 50 years, the struggle between Spain and France for mastery of Italy was to be the dominant theme of European politics.

These developments completed the revolution in European politics that had begun with Henry VI's loss of France in 1450. The English defeat paved the way for France's re-emergence as a great power; this culminated in 1492 with the annexation of Brittany. That same year, as we have seen, Spain had completed its own reconstruction by the conquest of Granada. Secure at home, the two heavyweights then squared up for battle in Italy. England's role in the fight was limited to being either a spectator or a second — or occasionally even an umpire. It was a descent from the days of the great Edwards and Henrys; but it was by no means a retreat into insignificance. England was still strong enough to be a useful ally; it was perhaps even more effective as an enemy.

Although the centre of the European stage had swung to Italy, France and Spain had interests in the north and hence remained vulnerable there. France now occupied the whole of the south coast of the English Channel, apart from Calais. But the exception was important: the King of England still styled himself King of France; he still quartered the lilies of France with the lions of England in his arms; while Calais — so long as it was English — remained a potent symbol of past greatness and a possible bridgehead for reconquest. It was recognition of this that led Charles VIII to be so accommodating to English susceptibilities in the treaty of Étaples, which ended Henry VII's invasion of 1492. Charles wanted to free his hands for Italy, so he was prepared to buy England off with an annual payment of about £5,000. The French called this sum a pension; the English, however, could represent it as a tribute.

But if France played at diplomacy with bullion, Ferdinand of Aragon played with brides. Ferdinand and Isabella had four children who survived fancy: John, the son and heir, and three daughters: Isabella, Joanna, and Catherine. Isabella was already married to the king of Portugal, but the rest were used to cement the anti-French coalition of 1495-6. With Maximilian a double knot was tied: John was married to his daughter, Margaret, while his son, Philip, heir to Burgundy and the Empire, married the Infanta Joanna. On the death of John in 1497 and Isabella in 1498, the alliance between Spain and Burgundy became a fusion of dynasties. Joanna was now heiress to Aragon and Castile, and the issue of her marriage to Philip would inherit Spain, Burgundy, and the Habsburg lands. No ruler of England could ever ignore the Netherlands and the Netherlands were now tied firmly to Spain.

As indeed was England. Henry VII and Ferdinand had quickly spotted that their common hostility to France could be a bond of union and as early as 1489 the Infanta Catherine had been promised to Henry's son and heir, Arthur. The sweeping French victory in Italy lent urgency to the affair: a new marriage treaty was concluded in 1496 and ratified the following year; fresh delays then intervened, but in 1501 the marriage finally took place in St Paul's. Also in 1497, Ferdinand achieved another of his aims. Ever since its narrow escape from conquest by Edward I, Scotland had looked to the "Auld Alliance" with France to preserve its independence from England. France had its own interest in the connection, since the threat of Scottish incursions was one means of keeping English ambitions in France in check. Now Ferdinand, as part of his policy of isolating France, managed to rupture the "Auld Alliance" by acting as honest broker for the marriage of Henry VII's elder daughter, Margaret, to James IV of Scotland. The delays were even longer this time, but in 1503 the marriage was celebrated. The couple had five children, who died within a year or so of birth, and one son who survived, the future James V.

The hazards of marriage and procreation were to affect Henry VII's English descendants even more powerfully. In 1502, less than six months after his marriage to Catherine, Prince Arthur died. His father and mother were grief-stricken, but Queen Elizabeth comforted her husband by reminding him that the dynasty was still secure: he himself, she pointed out, though an only child, had nevertheless entered into his inheritance; moreover "God had left him yet a fair prince [and] two fair princesses". Thereafter, however, Henry helped God as much as possible and the "fair prince" Henry was brought up in almost womanish seclusion: the only access to his apartments lay through the King's bedchamber; while his participation in jousts and other martial exercise was carefully limited.

Marriage too was an experience from which he was to be protected as long as his father lived. After Arthur's death, Ferdinand's first thought was to offer Catherine to Henry, and the betrothal took place in 1503. The prince, who had only been born in 1491, was of course too young for a real marriage, for which moreover a papal dispensation was necessary. Rome delayed and Pope Julius II even affected to doubt his ability to dispense in the case in view of the explicit Biblical prohibition of marriage with the spouse of a deceased brother. These delays were nearly fatal to the marriage, for the death of Queen Isabella in 1504 markedly diminished Ferdinand's power and hence his attractiveness as an ally. Isabella's heir in Castile was Joanna, and her husband, the Archduke Philip, pressed for her to take over the government immediately. Ferdinand strongly demurred. In this rupture between Burgundy and Spain, Henry took the side of Burgundy, and betrothed his younger daughter, Mary, to Charles, son and heir of Philip and Joanna. Ferdinand, supple as ever, reversed the policies of a lifetime and allied himself with France. The casualty of these high manoeuvres was Catherine. In 1505, Henry made a secret but formal protest about the validity of his marriage, which left Catherine stranded in England without friends, money, or, increasingly, hope.

THE YOUNG HENRY VIII: THE MARS AND SERVANT OF VENUS

Such was the position when Henry VII died on April 22, 1509. He had been lucky even in the timing of his death. He had lived just long enough to avoid the problems of the succession of a minor. Precedents for the age of Royal majority varied between 16 and 18; Henry VIII was 17 years and 10 months old, and that was clearly felt to be adequate for him to assume immediate personal rule. On the other hand, had Henry VII lived longer, his highly idiosyncratic style of government might well have provoked open rebellion. His financial exactions were widely perceived to be unjust and extortionate, while his treatment of the nobility in particular was (by contemporary standards) scandalously unfair. His death, however, released the tension harmlessly, even advantageously.

In an obvious bid for popularity, Henry VIII encouraged the reaction against his father's rule. He squared this piece of political calculation with filial piety by claiming that he acted for the good of his father's soul. In keeping with this, Henry VII's great benefactions to his Chapel at Westminster and to King's College Chapel at Cambridge were allowed to stand; otherwise the late King's policies were comprehensively reversed: cooperation with the nobility would replace coercion; instead of wringing the last penny out of the Royal lands, the King would throw himself on the generosity of his subjects by asking for taxes in Parliament; while in return the fountain of Royal patronage, long reduced to a trickle, would flow again. These changes all have a common theme: they were the necessary adjustments in policy to bring about the biggest reversal of all, the replacement of peace by war.

Henry, in short, determined to be the antithesis of his father. Indeed, in appearance and character he *was* utterly different. Henry VII had been wiry and highly strung: Bishop Fisher noted his sensitivity to physical pain, which made the agony of his final illness peculiarly hard to bear. After it was over, his death mask shows a face ravaged into an almost mystical intensity of expression (more prosaically, it has been described as looking like the face of a Welsh miner after a lifetime in the pit). Mysticism was not a quality anyone ever discerned in Henry VIII. He took after his mother's side of the family, and in many ways was more obviously the grandson of Edward IV than the son of Henry VII. He had the same tall, fleshy build; the same broad face and fair skin, and the same easy, winning charm. As he grew older, more of his own father showed in him, in particular the same corrosive suspicion, and the resemblances to his grandfather wore thinner. Edward had been an accomplished roué, well able to back desire with performance. Henry's sexual capacity, despite the legend and the codpiece, was much less impressive: it can hardly have been his wives' fault that six marriages produced only three children who survived infancy; indeed, from the early 1530s the signs are that he was half-impotent. And he was no more successful in the service of Mars than Venus: Edward never lost a battle; Henry never won a real one.

But he looked wonderful in armour and was a natural jouster and that deceived everybody — including himself. His determination to play the soldier was clear very early. A spectator of the jousts of May 1507 already noticed the young prince's promising physique, his enthusiasm for knightly lore, and his eagerness to hear talk of battles and war. His very name recalled England's past greatness under Henry V; even his accession day seemed to presage future conquests, for April 22 was the eve of St George's Day, dedicated to England's warlike saint and the patron of the Order of the Garter. But there was more to it than a boyish desire to play soldiers. Henry already had a settled and truly kingly appetite for glory. "Our King", Lord Mountjoy wrote, "does not desire gold or gems or precious metals, but virtue, glory, immortality." Machiavelli put it more succinctly: Henry was "rich, ferocious and greedy for glory". So war it was, and the target, obviously, was France.

Henry could not have signalled his intentions more quickly. His first reported act after his accession was to swear to invade France "immediately after his coronation". Then, when a French ambassador arrived to propose renewal of the peace treaties, he exploded publicly: "I ask peace of the King of France, who daren't look at me, let alone make war!" But as the ambassador was about to leave in a huff because no place had been reserved for him at the following jousts, the King relented and gave him a cushion. The Royal conflict between bellicosity and courtesy is not the only division revealed by this incident. The ambassador had been sent in response to an *English* proposal for a renewal of the Anglo-French treaties. Henry, no doubt truthfully, disclaimed all knowledge of the letter; instead, it would have been sent by the powerful peace party on the King's Council.

Henry's fire-eating aroused very mixed feelings. One group of his councillors was alive only to the disadvantages. Men such as Bishop Fox, the Lord Privy Seal, knew of the uncertainties of war, of the ruinous expense, of the possibility of the King's death which, since he had no heir, would risk plunging the realm back into civil war. Such men might also have been influenced by the new "Humanist"

doctrines, which despised war and lauded peace. These councillors were mainly ecclesiastics; ranged on the other side, however, were the King's noble councillors. War was the *raison d'être* of noblemen; it was also their chance to recover their fortunes and influence after the setbacks of Henry VII's reign. The leader of this group is usually seen as the Earl of Surrey, but the younger members of his family were more vehement still. Indeed, the war/peace divide reflected the generation gap: youth was for war and its leader was the youngest of all: the King himself.

Alongside the King was the rather less youthful Queen (she had been born in 1485 and so was 23). Henry decided after all to marry Catherine. In public, he claimed to be fulfilling his dying father's wish; his real reasons, however, were more mixed. He wanted a wife; he might even have wanted Catherine; but most of all he wanted her father's support in the forthcoming conflict with France. Catherine's attitude to her marriage was the mirror-image of her husband's: even her love for Henry, she wrote to her father, was chiefly due to the fact that he was so true a son to Ferdinand. Hostility to France might be a source of division at the council board, but it united the Royal marriage bed.

The two were married privately on June 11 in the Franciscan church attached to the Royal palace at Greenwich; three weeks later, on Midsummer's Day, the feast of young lovers and renewal, they were crowned King and Queen at Westminster Abbey. In the month after the coronation, as Henry wrote in a chatty letter to his father-in-law, he had diverted himself with jousts; now he was about to go hawking and hunting, to visit divers parts of his realm and look to public affairs.

The order of priorities is interesting; so is the fact that Henry remained a mere spectator of the jousts, not a participant. That he did so was due to the pressure of the conciliar old guard, fearful for the Royal safety, and fearful too perhaps for the Royal dignity which Henry VII's remoteness had protected so effectively. But by early 1510 Henry could contain himself no longer and took part in his first public jousts. He rode, however, *incognito* and only a severe accident to his companion in arms forced him to reveal himself. The incident was hardly reassuring and there was still much tut-tutting, to the effect that "steel was not so strong, but it might be broken, nor no

horse could be so sure of foot, but that he may fall". It was the generation gap again: the "doubters" were the "ancient fathers"; youth, on the other hand, was all applause. Henry had ears only for the applause and carried on regardless. Catherine in turn clapped with the loudest. Duty required that she preside over the jousts as Queen, but duty was turned to pride and pleasure as her husband confirmed his early promise and emerged as the champion jouster of his Court.

The beginnings of real war were as tortuous as Henry's début in the mock war of the jousts and they were delayed even longer. Henry had to argue every inch of the way. First, he got agreement to limited intervention as Ferdinand's ally. The intervention was a dismal failure and many councillors were inclined to cut England's losses. But in a set-piece debate before the Great Council of nobles, Henry's fiery eloquence carried the day. He reminded them of his "duty to seek fame by military skill" and spoke of "his ambition ... not merely to equal but to excel the glorious deeds of his ancestors". He was given his chance. He was to lead an army royal into France while Catherine remained behind as Regent in England with another army led by the Earl of Surrey. They, it was anticipated, would have their hands full in resisting an invasion of England by James IV of Scotland. He was Henry's brother-in-law, but it was clear that he would put the Auld Alliance with France above the new treaties with England.

Both halves of the Royal team did well. Henry captured Thérouanne and razed it to the ground; he took and garrisoned Tournai; and, treading in the footsteps of Henry V, he comforted his troops, bedraggled in the rain. He even had an Agincourt of a sort when he intercepted a column of French cavalry who were trying to draw him off the siege of Thérouanne. In the ensuing encounter known as the Battle of the Spurs, the French turned tail and fled, leaving Henry with spoil, noble prisoners, and what he craved most of all, the name of victor. Marx observed that events happen twice: the first time as tragedy; the second as farce. Contemporaries took the second "Henry V's" triumphs for real, however, and no one more so than Catherine, who hailed the Battle of the

● OPPOSITE: Henry VIII, by Holbein
c.1536
NATIONAL PORTRAIT GALLERY, LONDON

Spurs as a victory "so great that I think none such hath been seen before". But she soon had one of her own to set beside it. On September 9, Surrey met the Scots army at Flodden in the foothills of the Cheviots, where the invaders were overwhelmed and their King and the flower of the nobility slain.

It exceeded even Catherine's expectations. Shortly before she had promised to send Henry the King of Scots in return for the Duke of Longueville, who had been captured at the Battle of the Spurs and despatched to England for safe keeping. Now instead she sent a piece of James's blood-stained coat. "In this," she wrote, "your Grace shall see how I can keep my promises, sending you for your banners [again captured at the Battle of the Spurs] a King's coat." There was not much doubt about who had won the exchange. Nor was there any doubt about who had won the greater victory. "This battle," Catherine wrote to Henry of Flodden, "hath been to your Grace and all your realm the greatest honour that could be, and more than if ye should win the Crown of France." Behind every great man, we know, there should be a great woman, but Catherine perhaps overplayed the part.

The part was in any case dangerous. Catherine was not only Queen of England, she was Ferdinand's ambassador and best advocate. In the immediate aftermath of the marriage, Ferdinand had assured Catherine by his secretary, Almazan, that "he loves her most of all his children and for her sake considers the King as a son to whom he will communicate all his secrets, and from whom in return he expects equal confidence". Henry as well as Catherine evidently believed the assurances. But Ferdinand, as Machiavelli well knew, was the consummate hypocrite, who "never preaches anything except peace and good faith, and [yet] he is an enemy of both one and the other". Henry and Catherine were soon to learn this bitter lesson. Within six months of Flodden, Ferdinand opened separate negotiations with France, in which Maximilian, Henry's other ally, also joined. Henry resolved to play them at their own game. He in turn approached France and trumped Ferdinand's ace. Not only did England and France make peace, but the treaty was cemented by marrying Henry's sister, Mary, long promised to Charles, the grandson and heir of Ferdinand and Maximilian, to Louis XII of France.

Women, as usual, were the victims of these male power games. One was Henry's pretty little sister, Mary, sacrificed at 18 to a decrepit roué of 52, "who rode out to meet his bride like a gay bridegroom ... licking his lips and gulping his spittle". Another was Catherine herself, caught between her husband and her father. The Spanish ambassador, Carroz, accused her to Ferdinand of "forgetting Spain in order to gain the love of the King and the English, so that she neglects to be useful to her father". Henry, on the other hand, was said to have reviled his wife for Ferdinand's perfidy — so much so, the story continued, that her grief had provoked the miscarriage of the child she was carrying. It was even rumoured that Henry had threatened her with divorce, "because with her he cannot have any issue".

For not only had Catherine become a diplomatic embarrassment, she was also (for the blame was always put on her) a dynastic failure. Back in 1509, Ferdinand had soothed Henry's scruples about marrying his brother's widow by citing the case of his other son-in-law, Emanuel, King of Portugal. Emanuel had married, successively, Catherine's sisters, Isabella and Mary, and "is blessed with a numerous offspring and lives happily". It proved to be cold comfort. Catherine conceived readily enough, but the children failed to survive: they either miscarried; were delivered prematurely; or died within a few weeks — like the infant Prince Henry, whose birth caused so much rejoicing in 1511. In 1516, the cloud seemed to lift and a healthy child was born. But it was only a girl, the Princess Mary. Henry consoled himself with the thought that "if it was a daughter this time, by the grace of God the sons will follow". But they did not. Catherine miscarried again in 1517, and there was another still-birth in 1518. That was to be her final pregnancy. She was now 32, and the grounds for hope diminished with each passing year.

Other hopes bore fruit, however. James I's first years in England almost 100 years later were described as "Christmas" after the shower of gifts that descended on his favourites. The first French war brought similar benefits to Henry's companions in the tilt and the battlefield. Best rewarded was the great family of Howard. The Howards had first come to real prominence under Richard III. He had recognized their claim to the inheritance of the Mowbrays, dukes of Norfolk; in return they gave him their unstinting support. Bosworth was therefore a catastrophe for the family. John, the 1st Howard Duke of Norfolk, was killed and his son, Thomas the Earl of Surrey, was captured and attainted. Surrey then set out to rehabilitate himself by serving Tudor as well as he had done Plantagenet. He succeeded beyond perhaps even his own hopes: no task was too small or too great. Carefully measuring the reward to the achievement, Henry VII first restored him to his earldom and a substantial slice of the family lands; then in 1501 he made him Lord Treasurer. Under a king like Henry VII, who was his own Chancellor of the Exchequer, the appointment was almost a sinecure, but, since it ranked second in the Council after the Chancellorship, it was a prestigious one. Henry VIII took the restoration a stage further by making Surrey Earl Marshal, an office to which he had an hereditary claim. But still the dukedom eluded him. It came as his reward for Flodden.

The creation took place on February 1, 1514. At the same time, Charles Brandon was made Duke of Suffolk. Brandon, the son of Henry VII's standard bearer at Bosworth, was Henry VIII's favourite boon-companion and partner in the jousts. He had accompanied his King to France, so his promotion was a way of asserting that Henry's victory at the Battle of the Spurs stood on an equal footing with Norfolk's at Flodden; it was also designed to counterbalance Norfolk territorially, since otherwise he would have exercised an almost viceregal sway in East Anglia.

Brandon was to go further still. At the time of Louis XII's marriage to Mary it had been prophesied that the King would not last out the winter if he did not moderate his amorous excesses. The prophecy proved accurate and Louis died on New Year's Day 1515. Brandon was sent to escort the widowed Mary back to England and, she feared, to another dynastic marriage. That, after her first experience, was a prospect that appalled her: she would, she bluntly told her brother, "rather be torn in pieces". As well as fear there was love: she had, as she again reminded Henry, "always been of good mind to my lord of Suffolk". The upshot was that, showing for once true Tudor will, she promptly married Brandon and presented Henry with a *fait accompli*. The couple were fortunate that they were dealing with the younger, milder Henry, rather than the monster he became. The King huffed and puffed, but finally contented himself with imposing a severe financial settlement on the pair. Suffolk lay low for a time, but soon took his place alongside Norfolk as one of the leaders of the nobility. The only rival to the two was the Duke of Buckingham. But he was too stiff-necked in his pride of place and Royal lineage to be an effective politician at the Tudor Court. His ineffectiveness only deepened his discontent, and he destroyed himself by meddling half-heartedly in conspiracy. He was executed in 1521.

The challenge to Norfolk and Suffolk, in fact, came from the other end of the social scale: from Wolsey, the butcher's son. He was the greatest beneficiary of the French war. There was irony in this, since Wolsey had first come to prominence as the protégé of Bishop Fox. As such, he had thrown himself with characteristic gusto into Fox's struggle with Surrey, the leader of the war party on the Council. His first surviving letter, dated September 1511, inveighs against the Earl and his son, Edward Howard, "by whose wanton means his Grace spendeth much money and is more disposed to war than peace". At this stage, Wolsey was still reasonably confident that Henry's "appetite" for war could be "suppressed". Six months later, it was clear that it could not be: "the young councillors, by whom the King is ruled, advise this invasion [of France]". Wolsey's way was clear. "He was," as George Cavendish, his gentleman usher and biographer, noted, "the most earnest and readiest among all the Council to advance the King's only will and pleasure without any respect to the case." If Henry wanted war, he should have it, and Wolsey would be the means.

Over the next few years he was indefatigable. He negotiated taxes with Parliament; he raised troops; he scraped together victuals and munitions; he found ships and carts for transport. Above all, he coordinated. The result was that when Henry sailed to France with the largest and best equipped English army since Henry V, the credit largely was his. He accumulated more as he showed himself as competent at diplomacy as the commissariat. Before the invasion, he patched up the shaky alliance with Spain and the Habsburgs; afterwards he engineered the *renversement d'alliances* that led to the treaty with Louis XII. His reward was commensurate. By 1515, he was Cardinal Archbishop of York, Chancellor of England, and indisputably the King's chief coun-

cillor. In his ascent to power he showed himself a consummate politician as well: he moved into close alliance with the Howards without forfeiting the trust of Fox, and he managed Parliament successfully, not only in raising taxes for the war, but also in helping to bridge the deficit afterwards. But as his position became entrenched, he grew arrogant and sometimes careless. The result was tension with great nobles, such as Norfolk and Suffolk, and downright hostility on the part of leading courtiers.

But in 1515, such problems were far off and Wolsey, like his master, seemed on top of the world. "Hitherto," a Venetian resident in London wrote home, "small mention has been made of King Henry; whereas for the future the whole world will talk of him. For gold, silver, and soldiers, not another king in Christendom can be found to compare with him." All the world did talk, and, like Queen Catherine, expected "many more such victories". But they did not come. Partly it was a question of resources. Whatever the Venetian thought about Henry's "incomparable" wealth, England was starting to scrape the barrel: it simply could not afford to continue the expenditure of the last few years. But more important were events abroad. In France, the ageing Louis XII had been succeeded by the young and ambitious Francis I. Within a year of his accession, he had invaded Italy and won the great victory of Marignano against the supposedly invincible Swiss. Henry's skirmish at the Battle of the Spurs suddenly looked very small beer. Exactly a year after Louis XII, his old rival Ferdinand of Aragon died as well. His heir was his grandson, Charles, in whose person the vast inheritances of Burgundy and Spain were now united. From both branches of his family, Charles also inherited a struggle with France, which he was now able to wage with incomparably greater resources. In this struggle of young Titans, Henry was outclassed: the *jeune premier* had become a fading matinée idol, and his kingdom at most a useful makeweight to the two great powers.

Naturally, he did not like it. His first reaction to Francis I's Italian victories had been to try to hire Maximilian and the Swiss to fight against him. It was hardly an heroic posture; yet Henry contrived to invest it with a grand air. "Be assured," he told the Venetian ambassador, "I have now more money and greater force and authority than I myself or my ancestors ever had; so that what I

will of other princes, that I can obtain." In reply, the ambassador acknowledged "his extreme authority with all the princes of Christendom, whom I see all prostrate themselves before him". So saying, the ambassador prostrated himself too, bowing before Henry "down to the very ground". Perhaps the gesture was also useful in hiding a smile at Henry's empty vanity. The "other princes", whom Henry thought to command, did not bother with such polite concealment. Instead, at Noyen, Charles and Francis settled their differences. Charles, desperate to make good his Spanish inheritance, was willing to promise whatever Francis wanted — though performing his promises was to be quite another matter. The result was that France now drew back to England, with whom the Treaty of London was signed in September 1518. France got Tournai, garrisoned by the English since 1513; England got a pension and prestige, since the agreement was tricked out with the trappings of a "treaty of universal peace". Spain, the Empire, and the Pope all acceded, and Europe, presided over by King Henry and his Cardinal Minister, prepared itself for a crusade against the Turks.

It was, of course, all a charade. It was exposed as such by the death of Maximilian in January 1519. Charles, his grandson, was his heir as well and in the course of the year (against stiff French opposition) he added the title of Holy Roman Emperor to his already lengthy Royal style. As an addition to his power, the imperial title was relatively unimportant. But it did mark his status as the leading sovereign of Europe and it was to provide a marvellous vehicle for propaganda as the advancing tide of his authority seemed about to recreate the Roman empire indeed. At first, though, it was more trouble than it was worth, as Spain, which Charles had left too precipitately for Germany, erupted in the revolt of the *Comuneros*. The revolt was eventually crushed. But even before its suppression, Charles had begun the diplomatic manoeuvres to isolate France in preparation for a full-scale attack.

That meant a renewal of the alliance with England. For the next few years, therefore, England found itself courted by France and the Empire. After the isolation of 1516, it was a sweet revenge and Henry and Wolsey made the most of it. Wolsey, in particular, rejoiced in his role as arbiter of Europe. In public, England seemed to incline to France, and Francis and Henry staged the face-to-face meeting known as the Field of Cloth of Gold, which has become a byword for diplomatic ostentation. It was also a byword for duplicity, since immediately before Henry sailed to meet Francis at Calais, he had entertained Charles in England. The two had then entered into an understanding which ended two years later in an alliance and joint invasion of France. The invasion was not a success and Wolsey toyed with yet another change of sides. This seemed especially appealing as Francis had launched another triumphant invasion of Italy. But all these calculations were upturned by the crushing defeat of France at the battle of Pavia. Francis himself was captured and taken prisoner to Spain. Wolsey's first thought was to propose the partition of France between England and the Empire. But Charles showed himself disinclined to do much for so fickle an ally as England had proved to be.

But even worse than fickle, England had been shown as weak. The Parliament of 1523 had been loath to finance the joint invasion of France, and in 1525 the attempt to raise extra-parliamentary taxation (known as the Amicable Grant) to take advantage of Francis I's discomfiture at Pavia had been met with a blank refusal to pay. The government backed down at home, and sought peace with France abroad. These events make a striking contrast to the genuine enthusiasm which had greeted Henry VIII's first French war. Then the King's subjects, inspired by Henry's own evident commitment, had been prepared to dig deep into their pockets. But a decade later, this enthusiasm had been dissipated by the too-clever diplomacy of the intervening years. If the King was not single-minded about his Crown of France (and he had shown himself to be anything but), why should his subjects bestir themselves overmuch either? As the singleness of purpose of foreign policy fragmented, so too did unity at home: Wolsey's ministry was now arousing significant opposition — from the nobility and the inner circles of the Court alike. The Cardinal's attempts to counter the problem by purging the Court of his enemies and packing it with his supporters only delayed the day of reckoning.

Ironically, it was the masterstroke of his diplomacy, the peace with France signed at the Treaty of the More in August 1525, that opened the floodgates. Hitherto, for all its backslidings, the main thrust of English foreign policy had been pro-Spanish/Imperial and anti-French. Now it reversed direction and for the next decade and a half England was generally friendly to France and hostile to the Empire. The consequences were momentous, for it was the understanding with France that paved the way to the Divorce and the Reformation.

DIVORCE AND REFORMATION

On June 18, 1525 took place the largest crop of peerage creations in the reign of Henry VIII. The official reason was to celebrate "the joyful news of the Emperor's victory at Pavia" and the even better tidings from Henry's point of view that Richard de la Pole, titular Earl of Lincoln and the last "Yorkist" claimant to the Throne, had been killed in the battle as well. No less than seven peers were made or promoted: one duke, one marquess, three earls, and two viscounts. The duke was the King's bastard son by Elizabeth Blount, who was given Henry VII's title of Richmond, and all the rest were Royal connections. Two were very close relations: the Marquess of Exeter, Henry Courtenay, was the King's cousin through his mother, Catherine, sister of Elizabeth of York; and Henry Brandon, to whom the de la Pole Earldom of Lincoln was granted, was son of Charles Brandon and Mary Tudor and the King's nephew. The remainder were more remote: the Earl of Rutland descended from Edward IV's sister, Anne; the Earl of Cumberland was a scion of the Beauforts; while Viscount Fitzwalter numbered a Woodville among his ancestors and was married to a Stanley. The last creation, Sir Thomas Boleyn, Viscount Rochford, was connected by affinity rather than blood: his elder daughter, Mary, was the King's discarded mistress; his younger daughter, Anne, was his future mistress and wife to be.

This extraordinary reinforcement of the peerage shows that concern about the succession had reached a crisis. Henry's first thought had been to settle the problem by a suitable match for his only child, the Princess Mary. The chosen husband had been the Emperor Charles: not only was he mighty enough to make good his future wife's claim to the Throne, he was also, as Catherine's nephew, family already. It was to secure the marriage that Henry had allied with Charles in 1521 and flung his depleted resources into war with France. The alliance was not, as we have seen, a success: not only had Henry and Charles very different war aims (the former wanted France, the latter was only interested in Italy); there was also the great disparity in years between Mary and Charles. In 1521, when they were betrothed, she was five and he was 21. If England could prove its worth as an ally, Charles might wait. By 1525, however, England's credibility was exhausted and Charles threw Mary over for another cousin, the richly dowered Isabella of Portugal. "Charles had failed Henry even more disastrously in 1525 than Ferdinand had failed him in 1514." In 1514, it had been Catherine who had borne the brunt of her husband's displeasure with her father; in 1525, she once again had to pay the price for her nephew's betrayal, but this time the price was to be far heavier and included her daughter as well.

The celebrations for her nephew's triumph at Pavia contained the first blow. The elevation of the King's bastard into an acknowledged Royal duke could only be a threat to her daughter as the legitimate heir. Catherine resented it accordingly and was punished by being stripped of three of her most loyal Spanish ladies. The promotions of Exeter and Lincoln were likewise ominous: if not immediate heirs, they were certainly spares; but it was the promotion of Thomas Boleyn that boded worst.

Thomas Boleyn was a competent and successful courtier-administrator, who had first come to real prominence as a member of the Howard circle at the beginning of the reign. He belonged to it through his marriage to Elizabeth, sister of the Earl of Surrey, who was to succeed his father as Duke of Norfolk in 1524. The marriage produced three children: Mary, Anne, and George, who was considerably younger than his two sisters. Mary had accompanied Mary Tudor to France in 1514 as one of her ladies and after her return had become the King's mistress. In 1520, Henry made as honest a woman as possible of her by marrying her to his favourite and intimate attendant, William Carey (who also had a drop or two of Beaufort blood in his veins). Anne was the second child, but she was clearly much brighter than her sister and received a significantly fuller education. It was entirely abroad. She began in the service of Margaret of Austria, Regent of the Netherlands; then she joined her sister in the entourage of Mary Tudor as Queen of France. But, unlike Mary, she stayed on in the service of Mary's successor as Queen, Claude, the gentle, ugly wife of the dashing Francis I. She only returned to England in 1521, on the eve of the war between England and France.

In these years, Anne had learned three things: the French language, and manners, and perhaps even something of the religious heterodoxy that was just becoming fashionable in some Court circles as she left. She arrived back to an England that was eager to appreciate her. For francomania was the rage. Despite recurrent war with France, French influence — in dress, food, and fashions — had never been stronger. The lead was taken by Henry himself and a circle of francophile young men round him, who were known as the King's "minions". Prominent among these was Anne's brother-in-law, William Carey. It was under her sister's wing that Anne made her début at the English Court in 1522, as a performer in a masque entitled the *Château Vert*. Mary played Kindness; Anne, Perseverance. They appear to have been type-cast. In the next few years, Anne's attractions embroiled her in two unsuccessful marriage negotiations: one to her cousin, Thomas Butler, heir to the Earl of Ormonde; the other to Henry Percy, heir to the Earl of Nor-

thumberland. Percy was, and probably remained, hopelessly in love with her, and his frustrated passion ruined his eventual marriage to Mary Talbot and destabilized his whole character. Cearly, Anne could make an effect. Next to be smitten, but how seriously it is hard to be sure, was the courtier-poet, Sir Thomas Wyatt, who was already married, though lovelessly. Finally, Henry himself joined in the pursuit.

At first, his involvement, like Wyatt's, may have been a mere episode in the game of courtly love. A plausible legend has Henry and the courtier-poet staking their claims on Anne during a game of bowls; while in the jousts of Shrovetide 1526 the King appeared in the lists with the device of a "man's heart in a press, with flames about it" and the motto "Declare I dare not". Soon, however, the affair was transformed into something more serious — indeed into the most serious thing in Henry's life. Partly it was Anne's own sexuality, already powerfully evinced in the case of Henry Percy. Even a mind as strong as Wyatt's (and a body as experienced) was fascinated. Henry began like Wyatt and finished like Percy.

It was Anne who wrought this alchemy. The magic word was "no". Hitherto, all the women in Henry's life had surrendered to him unresistingly because it was their duty: for his wife, it was her dynastic duty; for his mistresses, like Mary Boleyn, it was their duty as subjects (and one which plainly they were not very disposed to dispute). But Anne did resist, and in resisting and then surrendering she seemed to choose him out of desire, not duty. To begin with, however, she showed (or feigned to show) only indifference. That merely spurred Henry on to offer to "take you for my only mistress, rejecting from thought and affection all others save yourself, to serve you only". In other words, he was undertaking to make her his *maîtresse en titre*. Most women would have jumped at the chance; Anne went home to her father. But she relented far enough to send Henry a lover's trinket. That was enough: Henry's next letter spoke plainly not only of love, but marriage "as God can bring to pass if it pleaseth him".

Step-by-step with his pursuit of Anne, Henry, just as irrevocably, was rejecting Catherine. In the immediate aftermath of Charles V's betrayal, as he

saw it, he had probably ceased to sleep with her. The couple put on a brave face of amity in public, but in private Henry's long-stilled doubts about the validity of his marriage were surfacing. Three people were accused of planting the fatal seed: the French Bishop of Tarbes, Cardinal Wolsey, and the King's confessor, John Longland, Bishop of Lincoln. The first two can be safely ruled out, but Longland, as his own later agitated exculpations suggest, played some role. The exculpations were no doubt right in insisting that the initiative came from the King himself (who had a convenient conscience which always managed to turn his wishes into moral imperatives). But Longland, as Henry's spiritual father, must finally have given his sanction to the King's scruples.

For Henry, his own conscience was the final court of appeal. That had given its verdict. But for the world, there were other tribunals. Normally, a king who had been as loyal a son of the Church as Henry would have had few problems in persuading Rome to annul his marriage (if he needed reminding of the convenient flexibility of the canon law of matrimony he had to look no further than that accomplished bigamist, his brother-in-law, Charles Brandon). But there were two problems. The first was largely of Henry's own creation. Confident of his theological learning, he insisted that his lawyers take the high ground of declaring that his marriage was invalid because the Pope could not have dispensed in the case. Popes were quite willing to reverse the acts of their predecessors; they thought much harder about denying the powers of their office. But more important was something over which Henry had no control at all, namely the situation in Italy. It was Charles's crushing Italian victories that had led to his break with Henry; it was the continuation of his hegemony that frustrated Henry's determination to dissolve the marriage that still tied him to the ghost of the Spanish alliance and had itself become an empty shell. Pavia made the Pope Charles's puppet; two years later, the Sack of Rome turned him into his prisoner. Charles was not going to let his prisoner sanction his aunt's divorce.

On this rock all attempted solutions foundered. First, Henry went for a quick kill and ordered a secret trial in England. Catherine appealed that to Rome. Then there was a trial before Cardinals Wolsey and Campeggio as delegates of the Papal Court. That was aborted by Campeggio on orders from Rome. The best that could be hoped for was that French pressure in Italy might free the Pope from Imperial clutches. But that hope was extinguished by the "Ladies' Peace" of Cambrai between France and the Empire in August 1529.

The immediate consequence was the fall of Cardinal Wolsey. He had already been badly shaken by Anne Boleyn's rise. His relationship with Henry had been as much personal as political, and Henry signed his letters to him as "Your loving master and friend". But now Henry adressed his letters to Anne as "My mistress and friend". There followed a struggle for the King's affections between the minister and the mistress. Anne had the more powerful cards and she played them ruthlessly. Wolsey remained useful only so long as he could draw on his credit at Rome to procure the divorce. By autumn 1529 his credit in Rome and England was exhausted and his enemies were unleashed. The common lawyers indicted him in King's Bench; the nobility, led by the dukes of Norfolk and Suffolk, attacked him in the House of Lords.

Four days after the Peace of Cambrai was signed, writs were sent out to summon a Parliament. Frustrated in Italy, Henry and his advisers had decided to put pressure on the Church at home. The next three or four years were like a hostage drama. The English Church was subjected to increasingly unpleasant penalties in the hopes of extracting concessions from the Pope over the divorce. First, clerical privileges and fees were attacked; then papal revenues from the English Church were threatened; finally, Henry secured recognition from the clergy of his "supremacy" over the Church. To begin with, this was hedged and limited to merely temporal matters, but the line between that and a Royal usurpation of the papal sovereignty was a fine one. In the face of the Pope's intransigence, that line too was crossed.

Once again, foreign affairs played a crucial role. In October 1532, Francis I and Henry met at Calais and Boulogne. Henry was accompanied by Anne, newly created Marquess of Pembroke in her own right. Francis's Queen and her ladies were conspicuous by their absence, but the King himself had acknowledged the liaison. Fortified by this recognition abroad and confident of Parliament at home, Henry moved at last. In early December, he and Anne, who had long lived as man and wife, finally slept together; by mid-January it was clear that Anne was pregnant and on the 25th they were married. There are signs in all this that Henry thought that the Pope was coming round at last, and certainly Rome was unusually cooperative about the appointment of the new Archbishop of Canterbury. Warham, the old Archbishop and a firm opponent of the divorce, had died the previous year. His successor was a man of a very different stamp: Thomas Cranmer, an eager young don and a Boleyn client. The necessary bulls were issued between February and March and on the 30th he was consecrated. He swore the usual oath of obedience to the Pope, but qualified it by the formal assertion that he was not bound to anything contrary to the law of God or to the King, realm, laws, and prerogatives of England.

The exception was quickly put to use. Parliament had also reconvened in February and the Act in Restraint of Appeals was passed. This declared Canterbury the final court for the English Church, and all further appeal to Rome was cut off. Availing himself of these powers, Cranmer convened his court to try the validity of Henry's first marriage in the deliberately remote priory of Dunstable. Catherine contemptuously refused to appear and was declared contumacious. On May 23, Cranmer duly pronounced her marriage void; five days later, the second marriage to Anne Boleyn was confirmed. Meantime, in confident expectation of the result, preparations for Anne's coronation had been going ahead. It took place, amid unparalleled magnificence, on June 1. Anne wore virginal white and her fine hair hung long and loose down her back. Towards the end of August, as protocol dictated, Anne withdrew among her women for her forthcoming confinement and on September 7 she was successfully delivered. But the child for whom so much had been done and undone was a bitter disappointment. Instead of the longed-for heir, it was only another girl, Elizabeth. The same month, the Pope published the sentence of greater excommunication against Henry, which he had prepared in July. Next year, Henry retaliated by putting the fullest claims to the Supreme Headship of the Church on the statute book: he was and ought to be Supreme Head of the Church of England and his style as such was annexed forever to "the imperial crown of this realm".

So far, we have presented these

great events exclusively in terms of personalities, high politics, and diplomacy. These are certainly the start of the story. But they are not all of it. Anne herself introduces the other dimension, for she was a sincere believer in the "new learning" and imported Bibles and other devotional literature in the vernacular from France. Her agent was her silk merchant, William Locke. This combination of sex and religion was potent. Anne made religion fashionable at Court and was herself an important patron. Many a young scholar, talent-spotted like as not by William Butts, the King's physician, owed his advancement to her. This laid down the seed corn for the next generation. More important at the time was her episcopal patronage: this began with Cranmer and continued with such leading radicals as Latimer and Shaxton. In 1536 she succinctly referred to them as "her bishops". But most important of all was that she could take the new doctrines into the King's chamber and his very bed. But Henry's attitude to the new doctrines (as to his new wife) was always conditional. So long as the new doctrines and their adherents served his own purposes, he was happy to give them their head. But if they created too many problems, at home or abroad, Henry was ready to reverse direction at a moment's notice and throw his best servants to the wolves.

Anne Boleyn herself was an early victim. She was exposed by her failure to give Henry his son; also her strength of character, which had played so large a part in her rise, made her many enemies and ended by alienating Henry himself. Anne was perfect as a mistress; she was less successful as a wife. But so long as Catherine of Aragon dragged out her life, her supplanter was safe. In January 1536, however, Catherine died. The following May, Anne and her closest followers were removed in a bloody faction coup. Her marriage was declared (by Cranmer again) invalid from the beginning and her daughter thereby rendered illegitimate. Anne was replaced by Jane Seymour, who was groomed to be her antithesis. Her motto was "Bound to obey and serve", and serve her essential purpose she did by giving Henry a son at last. The boy, born on the eve of St Edward's Day (October 12, 1537), was christened Edward after England's Royal saint; but 12 days later, on October 24, Jane died. These events convinced not a few that the break with Rome was over. Both the contentious wives were dead,

and Edward was the unquestioned heir.

The lesson seemed to be driven home by the fall of Thomas Cromwell, the King's ardently reforming chief minister of the 1530s, four years later. In 1539, Francis I and Charles V had settled their differences by the Treaty of Toledo and a joint attack on schismatic England seemed a real possibility. Henry responded by military preparations at home and a diplomatic offensive abroad: the fleet was strengthened; troops mustered, and fortresses built. The diplomatic weapon was his own marriage to the German princess, Anne of Cleves, whose brother was a dangerous irritant on the frontiers of Charles's dominions. The marriage was a disaster: Henry found Anne personally repulsive, and he liked being linked to German princelings (who were also heretical) little more. Cromwell was kept alive long enough to undo his own handiwork and then took the route to the block, where he had sent so many others. No other single minister was appointed; instead power passed into the hands of a largely aristocratic Privy Council. Even before these events, Henry had already trimmed to the prevailing winds abroad by reaffirming the essentials of Catholic orthodoxy in the Act of Six Articles. In particular, the full doctrine of transubstantiation, by which the consecrated bread and wine become the very flesh and blood of Christ, was declared to be the faith of the English Church, on pain of burning.

The reversals of 1539-40 were as complete in their way as the political revolution that had followed Henry VIII's accession. And they also presaged a shift from domestic policy to active warfare. The understanding with France — the cornerstone of the Reformation — was repudiated and the Habsburg alliance revived. Henry took a great army to France and captured another town (this time it was Boulogne); while at home one of his generals won a much greater victory against the Scots.

SCOTLAND

The Reformation had complicated further England's already tangled relations with Scotland. James V, who had been "erected" as King in his own right by his mother, Margaret Tudor, in 1524, had proved himself well able to withstand his uncle Henry's blandishments. These had increasingly taken the form of encouraging James to follow in England's footsteps and "reform" his church. James's inclinations lay rather in the opposite

direction, however, and he was greatly strengthened in his determination by the influence of David Beaton, who came to exercise an authority in Scotland that echoed Wolsey's in England. He was at once Cardinal, Papal Legate *a latere*, and Chancellor. His aim was to preserve Roman Catholicism in Scotland, which made him the inveterate enemy of England and the equally warm friend of France. This double commitment produced a mirror image in the Cardinal's opponents: they linked the reformed cause in Scotland with a pro-English policy. This development was big with implications for the future; it also had an immediate impact.

Henry had finally persuaded James to agree to a face-to-face meeting at York in 1541. The Scottish King had agreed during Beaton's absence in France; with his return he broke tryst. In reprisal, Henry ordered the Duke of Norfolk to attack Scotland. He did not repeat his father's triumph of Flodden, however. Instead that was left to the man who was emerging as the Duke's leading rival at Court, Edward Seymour, Earl of Hertford. Hertford was brother to the dead Queen Jane, and uncle of Prince Edward. He intercepted the Scottish counterattack at Solway Moss, and inflicted a defeat even more shattering than Flodden. Then at least the Scots had died fighting; this time they were led away prisoner in droves: two earls, five barons, and 500 lairds headed the list. James had not been present but, highly-strung as he was, he died "of shame" of the news on December 14, 1542. His only heir was a little girl a few days old: Mary Queen of Scots.

In the aftermath of defeat, events seemed to play into Henry's hands. A coup by Beaton failed, and instead the Earl of Arran, the heir presumptive, was appointed Regent. The Earl was pro-English, while the Scottish Parliament that met in March inclined in the same direction. The Bible was made available in the vernacular, and ambassadors were appointed to treat for an English marriage for Mary. On July 1, 1542 they signed the Treaty of Greenwich, by which Mary was to marry Prince Edward. The treaty was ratified in Edinburgh in August; Protestant sentiment ran high and the cause of Catholicism seemed lost in Scotland. But Henry pressed his claims of suzerainty too hard and the old Scots cause of independence from England outweighed the new loyalties to the Reformation. The Catholic party revived, and savage new incursions by Hertford only broadened their support. French military intervention now played a part and the eventual upshot was that in 1548 (the year after Henry's death) Mary was spirited away to France to marry the Dauphin Francis, while her mother, Marie de Guise, acted as Regent in Scotland. Henry's determination to grab what he could have had for the asking seemed to have lost him everything.

THE DEATH OF HENRY VIII: RULE BEYOND THE GRAVE?

These events in Scotland had a significant impact on the final scenes of Henry's reign. As Hertford covered himself in glory, the star of the Howards began to set. Not only had the Duke failed in Scotland, his son, the Earl of Surrey, had blundered in France by — characteristically — exceeding his instructions. He had been recalled under a cloud. His loss had been gain for John Dudley, Viscount Lisle, whose career was made in France in much the same way as Hertford's in Scotland. The two also had more in common than military success and they began to work together politically. Meanwhile, in a final twist of his vertiginous diplomacy, Henry made peace with France in July 1546. The next month, the Admiral of France came to ratify the treaty. He was received at Hampton Court. There, leaning on the Admiral on the one hand, and Cranmer on the other, Henry — gross of body, but nimble of mind — explained that not only had the new allies decided to abolish papal authority in France as well as England, but they were also to change "the mass in both realms into a communion service".

Whether the remark was fully serious or not, it showed which way the wind was blowing. The altered direction of affairs was also noticed by the Imperial ambassador in England. Hitherto, he had been well pleased by the conservative drift in religion. But after the treaty with France and the return of Hertford and Lisle to Court (he observed with regret) the "great persecution of heretics and sacramentalists" had ceased. All eyes, of course, were now on the future. Henry clearly could not live long. He would be succeeded by his son, but his son was only a boy. A regency of some sort would be necessary. The usual expedient of a protectorate in the hands of the King's senior uncle of the Blood Royal was not available, thanks to the thinness of the Tudor line. The choice instead lay between a government dominated by the Duke of Norfolk as the premier peer, or one run by Hertford as the King's maternal uncle. The line-up on the conservative and aristocratic Privy Council would have supported the former, but powerful voices in the King's Privy Chamber (the body of his most private domestic servants) were violently opposed. The Privy Chamber was a hot-bed of religious radicals, for whom Norfolk and all he stood for was anathema. Hertford's own earlier career had not suggested much religious commitment, but clearly he decided that England was worth a communion service. On this basis, an alliance with the Privy Chamber was cemented.

In the next few months the alliance carried all before it. The Privy Chamber controlled three things: access to the King, the stamp of his signature, which at this time was used to authenticate all documents, and his private treasures. All were now put at Hertford's service. First, the Court was closed to conservative voices. Hearing only their enemies, Henry was brought to destroy the Howards on trumped up charges of misappropriating the Royal arms: Surrey was executed; Norfolk only escaped because Henry died first. Then the King's will was tampered with. Henry was, of course, busily engaged in drafting and redrafting his will. But the one that purports to be his is a very fishy document: it is signed only with the stamp, which was applied almost certainly after his death. This expedient was necessary to guarantee Hertford's control of the Council and the Royal patronage; the remainder of the will, in particular the section dealing with the succession, bears every mark of being a product of Henry's own imperious and idiosyncratic mind.

Henry had been empowered to leave the Crown by will by the two Acts of Succession. First in line, of course, was Edward; then, in default of his heirs, came Mary; and finally, in default of Mary's heirs, Elizabeth. Both Henry's daughters had been bastardized when their mothers' marriages were declared null, but Henry ignored such details (as did Elizabeth, who never bothered to declare herself legitimate). For the succession to have wandered so far would have seemed very bad luck in 1547, but Henry looked further beyond his own children. If Elizabeth died without issue, the Crown was to go to the offspring of his younger sister Mary; the line of his elder sister Margaret was, however, ignored. This is because they were foreign-born, and in any case Henry probably assumed that the question was an irrelevance since Mary, Queen of Scots's marriage to Edward would go ahead.

Confident that he had provided for the succession to his kingdom, and confident too in his salvation, Henry died on January 28, 1547, his hand clasped in Cranmer's. As it happened, the line of succession laid down in his will was tested to its limits and beyond. His son died tragically of tuberculosis at the age of 15 and "on the threshold of power". He was a passionate Protestant, and, rather than countenance the succession of his equally passionately Catholic half-sister, Mary, he willed the Throne to Lady Jane Grey, granddaughter of Charles Brandon and Mary Tudor. Mary, however, put herself at the head of the one successful Tudor rebellion and wrested back the Throne that was rightfully hers. By a deep irony she married Philip, son of Charles V, to whom she had been betrothed long ago in the 1520s. So long as it seemed possible that the couple would have children, Mary's attempt to return England to Rome went remarkably smoothly. But once her pregnancy was proved false (and probably the symptom of a fatal illness) her regime disintegrated. She refused to recognize the inevitability of Elizabeth's succession (which would undo everything she held dear) but she did nothing to stop it. With Elizabeth on the Throne, however, unmarried, childless, and vulnerable (as it seemed), the place of heir presumptive assumed a special significance.

The obvious heir was Mary, Queen of Scots — provided, that is, that Henry's will was proved to be invalid and so no obstacle. That was readily done. The Succession Act required that the will be signed with the King's own hand; but Henry's will, as Mary's partisans were able to show with many proofs, had only been signed with the stamp. Elizabeth's Privy Council called for the will and examined it. Clearly not much liking what they saw, they directed that the will "with divers secret writings", be sealed up in a bag, "which bag is not to be opened but by the Council". And there, sensibly unopened, it remained when Mary's son James VI of Scotland succeeded unopposed to the Throne of England in 1603.

Dr Starkey is at the London School of Economics.

THE BOY KING AND BLOODY MARY

Henry VIII was succeeded by his sickly son for only six years. On Edward VI's death, his half-sister, Mary the Catholic, tried to turn back the religious clock. David Loades traces a decade of violence.

WHEN HENRY VIII died in January 1547, he bequeathed a highly unstable sitution to those whom he had chosen to rule during his son's minority. The war with France had been brought to an unsatisfactory conclusion, but that with Scotland continued, to confuse the priorities of the English government. The Crown was heavily in debt. Monastic lands to a capital value of about £800,000 had been sold since 1540, and substantial parliamentary subsidies received, but the wars since 1542 had cost almost £400,000 a year. In 1545, the King's advisers, at their wits' end for money, began to debase the coinage, and although this made a handsome profit the apparent benefits were deceptive. The value of sterling was undermined on the Antwerp Bourse, with the result that Edward VI's Council found it increasingly expensive to renew the King's loans, and impossible to pay them off. The price of English cloth began to decline in real terms, and although this at first had the effect of stimulating production, eventually it created a glut and caused the market to collapse. At the same time, the religious situation was full of uncertainties. After the fall of Thomas Cromwell in 1540, his particular brand of reformation appeared to have been discredited, and traditional orthodoxy reasserted. However, Henry had refused to budge over his commitment to the Royal Supremacy, and reformers of a somewhat more discreet aspect, such as Thomas Cranmer, continued to be influential. During the last few months of Henry's life, an intense power struggle had raged at Court, with the reformers, led by Cranmer and Edward Seymour, Earl of Hertford, competing for access to the ailing monarch against the conservatives led by Stephen Gardiner, Bishop of Winchester, and the Howards, Dukes of Norfolk. Thanks to the support of such key political figures as Sir William Paget, the Principal Secretary, and Sir Anthony Denny, the Chief Gentleman of the Privy Chamber, by December 1546 the reformers had secured complete ascendancy. As the King increasingly lost touch with reality, they manipulated the arrangements for the impending minority. As a result, when he died, his executors hastened to constitute themselves the Council of the new King, and with flagrant disregard for Henry's last expressed intention, raised the Earl of Hertford to the Dukedom of Somerset and appointed him Lord Protector of the realm and Governor of the King's person.

Somerset and Cranmer made no secret of their intention to introduce religious change, and signalled that intention immediately by granting new commissions to the bishops. The highly Erastian implications of this move were challenged at once by Stephen Gardiner, but without success. When the first Parliament of the new reign repealed the Act of Six Articles, which was the statutory basis of the existing orthodoxy, and the repressive censorship legislation of the previous decade, there was an upsurge of radical preaching and publishing, which considerably heightened the atmosphere of tension and uncertainty. Henry had not hesitated to appropriate the property of the Church on the grounds of his own pressing needs, but the Chantries Act of 1547 attacked the whole doctrine of intercessory rites. Unlike the dissolution of the monasteries, the confiscation of these relatively minor endowments removed an important aspect of popular piety, and added another ingredient to the social discontent which had been building up for a decade. The underlying reason for that discontent had nothing to do with the government. For more than a century, the profitability of sheep farming had led to the enclosure of arable land and waste by enterprising farmers great and small. Thanks to the demographic catastrophe of the Black Death, and the failure of population levels to recover, this had caused few problems before the 16th century. However, as the long-delayed recovery began to be noticeable after 1500, enclosure became associated with depopulation, and was seen as a social evil and a threat to the manpower resources of the kingdom. When Protector Somerset began to address the prob-

Vol. VI PL XXII, p. 208.

Tonnage.... 1000.

MEN
Soldiers...........349
Mariners...........301 } 700
Gunners............50

● "Henry Grace a Dieu" (the "Great Harry"), from the Anthony Roll of Shipping.

lem in 1547, he took up the traditional responsibility of the Crown to protect the interests of the Commonwealth against the particular interests of landholders or merchants. His manner of doing so, however, transcended traditional limitations, and created the impression on both sides that he was encouraging the discontented to take direct action. Coming at the same time as the development of his controversial religious policies, the enclosure commissions and their accompanying proclamations exposed Somerset's government to popular revolt and aristocratic opposition.

He might have survived this crisis, which came to a head in the autumn of 1549, if it had not been for his obsessive concern with the Scottish war. Henry had originally attacked Scotland in 1542 as a means of neutralizing his northern neighbour while he pursued more grandiose schemes on the continent. However, victory at Solway Moss in 1543, and the subsequent death of James

V had opened up an attractive prospect of long-term control. James was succeeded by his infant daughter, Mary, and it became the prime object of English policy to secure a marriage between the young Queen of Scots and the six-year-old Edward, Henry's heir. The so-called "rough wooing" which followed had already failed by the time Henry died, but Somerset, who had been the principal military commander in Scotland in 1545 and 1546, remained committed to the policy which it represented. The summer campaigns of 1547 produced another victory in the field, at Pinkie Cleugh. English garrisons were planted all over the Scottish Lowlands, and as far up the east coast as Broughty Crag, but the country was not subdued. The Queen Mother, Mary of Guise, appealed to her fellow countrymen, and in the summer of 1548 a large French army arrived in the north. The young Queen was removed to France, and shortly after betrothed to the Dauphin, the heir to the throne, Francis. Within a few months,

Somerset faced a formal renewal of war on the continent, as Henry II of France sought to recover Boulogne, and the total collapse of the English position in Scotland. In two-and-a-half years, the war had cost more than £350,000, leading to renewed debasement of the coinage, and had achieved nothing. Debasement in turn had intensified the existing inflation, and worsened every kind of social and economic distress. With his military and financial resources overstretched, the Protector was unable to respond swiftly or resolutely to the challenges of 1549, giving an impression of equivocation where none was intended and alienating his natural allies in the Council. In October 1549, he was overthrown by coup, and a further period of instability ensued while his supplanters struggled for control.

In one respect, however, Somerset's preoccupation with the Scottish war was

● OPPOSITE: Edward VI. Artist unknown.
REPRODUCED BY GRACIOUS PERMISSION OF HER MAJESTY THE QUEEN.

positive and constructive. Henry VIII's development of naval administration had been completed only some two years before his death, with the formal recognition of the Council of Marine or Admiralty Board. The Patents issued in April 1546 had confirmed the appointments of seven senior officers, and fixed their fees at generous professional levels. The best rewarded had been Robert Legge, the Treasurer, who had been assigned 100 marks a year, plus expenses, but the others had not been far behind. The navy had become a major department of state, consisting of a standing fleet of some 30 vessels, three large dockyards and numerous storehouses. By 1547, the permanent staff, apart from the senior officers, was made up of master mariners, gunners, shipwrights, and clerks. Ordinary seamen and labourers were taken on and discharged as necessary. By continuing the war in the north, Somerset ensured that this organization was maintained in full working order. Additional shipwrights were appointed in 1548, and in 1550 the post of Surveyor General of Victuals was added to the board. At least one new ship was laid down in 1549, and two others rebuilt. At sea, the navy continued to perform creditably, but failed to prevent the arrival of French forces in 1548, probably because it was unprepared for the scale of that operation. Somerset was not particularly interested in maritime affairs, but because he was so concerned to subdue Scotland he made his own contribution to the development of the navy.

The Earl of Warwick, who eventually emerged victorious from the power struggle of October to December 1549, was a man with very different priorities. Although, like Somerset, he had made his original career as a soldier, as Lord President of the Council his first object was to secure peace. This he achieved by the Treaty of Boulogne in March 1550. Although described as "the most ignominious ... signed by England during the century", this treaty freed the country from almost a decade of fruitless and ruinously expensive conflict, and enabled the Council to concentrate on other matters. Foremost among these was the unresolved religious conflict. When Somerset was overthrown it had been widely assumed that the protestant settlement of 1549, embodied in the Act of Uniformity, would disappear with him. Religious conservatives, such as the Earl of Southampton, had been prominent among the leaders of the coup, and

it was rumoured that the Lady Mary, Henry VIII's daughter and Edward VI's half-sister, would be offered the regency. Warwick, however, had no sympathy with such aspirations. Adroitly exploiting the previous protestant ascendancy, he allied instead with those who believed that the Reformation was still woefully incomplete — radicals such as John Hooper and the Scotsman, John Knox. His political victory signalled a further spell in the wilderness (if not actually in prison) for Gardiner and his Catholic allies. It also initiated a major revision of the 1549 Prayer Book, and a further assault on the remaining property and endowments of the Church. Subsequent events were to show that in following this course Warwick (Duke of Northumberland from 1551) was advancing far beyond the limits of active support. Only a small minority of the political nation welcomed the revised Prayer Book and second Uniformity Act of 1552. The reception of both was deceptively docile, but the radicalism which they represented seriously undermined his political position when the test came on Edward's death in 1553. Meanwhile, Northumberland strove to con-

front the other problems, responsibility for which he had worked so hard to assume. Financial retrenchment inspired a commission of inquiry into the state of the Crown revenues, a series of fruitless attempts to control inflation by "crying down" the debased currency, and drastic reductions in government expenditure. One of the victims of this latter process was Northumberland's own security. The German mercenaries who had performed such valuable service against the domestic risings of 1549 were paid off, and the special companies of men-at-arms raised for the first time in 1550, were disbanded in 1552. Another victim was the new naval establishment. With the end of war, a lower level of activity was to be expected, but the abrupt cessation of ship-building and maintenance which took place threw the whole organization into disarray. Over the next three years offices which fell vacant were left unfilled, services run down, and many ships disposed of by sale or breaking.

Paradoxically, Northumberland, a former Lord Admiral, was more interested in maritime affairs than Somerset had been, but he believed in private as opposed to public enterprise. Sebastian Cabot, Emperor Charles V's Pilot Major, had been tempted into English service in 1548 with a generous pension of £166 13s 4d. In December 1551, he became Governor for life of the newly incorporated Merchant Adventurers' Company, and was actively involved in planning and promoting Sir Hugh Willoughby's search for the North-east Passage in 1553. Cabot's services were much prized by Northumberland, who appreciated how far his knowledge and experience transcended what was otherwise available in England. Charles V made repeated and unsuccessful representations for his return to Spain, and Cabot was granted a "reward" of £200 in June 1550. Supported by the Lord President, Cabot rallied aristocratic as well as mercantile support behind the 1553 voyage, and created in the process an entirely new kind of enterprise, which was to provide the model for many similar operations later in the century. In this entrepreneurial climate it is not surprising that the officers of the Admiralty Board spent most of their time and energy trading on their own account, or that they hired and borrowed the King's ships to do so. Nor was Cabot the only foreigner to contribute to England's rapidly changing attitude to long-distance voyages. Jean Ribault, variously described as

"stranger", "gentleman", and "of Dieppe" (France), had entered Henry VIII's service in 1545 at an annual fee of £75. He was a cartographer and navigator of recognized skill, who subsequently emerged as a determined Protestant, and died in an attempt to establish a French colony in Florida in 1565. His career in England seems to have been somewhat chequered, involving two periods of imprisonment in 1550 and 1551, but in March 1552 Jehan Scheyfve, the Imperial Ambassador, noticed that he was "the right-hand man" of Vice-Admiral Henry Dudley. Northumberland's involvement with these enterprises and the men who promoted them was not altruistic, but it was far-sighted. The cloth trade more or less collapsed in 1551 because inflation had stimulated over-production and the Antwerp market was flooded. It therefore became imperative to find other markets, and while the cautious or conservative might look to Middleberg, Germany, or Bordeaux, France, the more enterprising were already looking to Muscovy and Cathay. To that group the Lord President belonged, and the Council's horizons in maritime matters became permanently widened in consequence.

Politically, this did nothing to help Northumberland in the short term. Discovering in the spring of 1553 that the young King was terminally ill, he was forced into the desperate expedient of attempting to alter the succession to the Crown. Setting aside Mary and Eliz-

abeth as illegitimate, he advanced the claim of his daughter-in-law, Jane Grey. Jane was the daughter of his ally, Henry Grey, Duke of Suffolk, and derived her royal blood from her mother, Frances, the elder daughter of Henry VIII's sister, Mary. She was also a committed Protestant, and Northumberland expected her to command the full support of all reformers, lay and clerical. Events betrayed his expectation. As long as Edward was alive, the Council acquiesced in what was ostensibly his "device" for the succession, but as soon as he was dead the power of Tudor legitimacy, enshrined in Henry's last Succession Act of 1543, reasserted itself. Some Protestants did support Jane, and recent research has indicated that they were rather more numerous than used to be supposed, but most did not. Even radicals such as John Hooper declared for Mary, despite her notorious religious conservatism. In the end, Mary's support proved to be so overwhelming that the issue was never put to the test. Northumberland's apparent command of the Council, the Treasury, and the armed forces, which so impressed the Imperial ambassadors at the beginning of the crisis, was revealed as illusory. Neither at the time nor subsequently did he receive adequate credit for his substantial achievements in office. Even the reforming divines denounced him as a "carnal gospeller", and he died a traitor's death within a few weeks of his fall, losing what scanty credit remained to him by

● Engagement in the Solent, 1545.
The Cowdray engraving.
NATIONAL MARITIME MUSEUM.

abandoning his Protestant professions in a vain attempt to save his life.

Mary, thus suddenly elevated to the Throne at the age of 37, was unmarried and totally inexperienced except in the management of her domestic household. Her health was uncertain, having been undermined by many years of psychological stress which her constitution was ill-adapted to sustain. She had yielded to intense pressure from her father in 1536, and had accepted the Royal Supremacy. This surrender had troubled her conscience ever since, and she brought with her to the Crown a determination to expiate that sin, as well as to restore the traditional rites of the Church, so recently abrogated by her half-brother's Council. The other priority of the new Queen was marriage. Not only did Mary hope desperately for an heir of her body, but she also believed that the government of the realm required an effective king. This did not arise from any doubts about her royal status, or the legitimacy of her position, but rather from a conventional Renaissance education on the role of women in society. Her age made the question one of extreme urgency, and her personal history greatly limited the range of choice. Any potential suitor needed to be of royal blood and unimpeachable Catholic antecedents. The only Englishman who satisfied these conditions was Edward Courtenay, son of Henry Courtenay, Marquess of Exeter, who had been executed in 1538, and grandson of Catherine, the second

daughter of Edward IV. Edward had spent his entire youth and early manhood in the confines of the Tower. Released and created Earl of Devon on Mary's accession, the intoxication of unaccustomed liberty had made him frivolous, petulant, and unstable. Although he enjoyed the support of Stephen Gardiner, now Mary's Lord Chancellor, and other influential councillors, it had become apparent by October 1553 that the Queen had no intention of marrying him. Her cousin, Reginald Pole, although only in deacon's orders and consequently within reach of dispensation, had nevertheless been a Cardinal for almost 20 years, and never seriously considered altering his state. A foreign marriage thus became inevitable, which had the immense advantage of removing any possibility of the kind of factionalism which was to develop in Scotland after Mary Stuart's union with Lord Darnley. There were only two realistic candidates, Dom Luis of Portugal, and Philip, Prince of Spain.

In many ways, Dom Luis was the more suitable. He was Mary's senior by some three years, and although of the royal blood was not the direct heir to a throne. Philip, by contrast, was 26, and the only legitimate son of the Emperor Charles V. Within a few years, he would be the ruler of a great empire. He certainly commanded the necessary resources and experience to support Mary's position, but by the same token represented a threat to English inde-

pendence which was generally and promptly perceived. Nevertheless, Philip was Mary's choice. The main reason for this was that she had long looked to Charles for protection and support, as the head of her mother's kindred, and Charles had made his wishes perfectly clear. A marriage between Philip and Mary would suit his diplomatic plans to perfection. As a ruling queen, a marriage to Mary was the most prestigious in Europe. Strategically, England could be used to complete the Habsburg encirclement of France, and could also provide Philip with the necessary support to maintain his position in the Netherlands when Charles effected his long-planned abdication. Once it became apparent that the Queen had made up her mind her councillors, many of whom had opposed the match, concentrated upon securing the best possible conditions. Charles, having gained his main object, was disposed to be generous over terms, and did not consult his son in the process of negotiation. As a result, the treaty which was signed in January 1554, while according Philip the title "King of England", placed severe restrictions on his power. When he learned of such dishonourable limitations, Philip was extremely annoyed; and the English aristocracy was by no means reassured. In the event, neither of these circumstances impeded the progress of events. Sir Thomas Wyatt's armed demonstration was premature, and although briefly threatening, collapsed after about two weeks. Philip grumbled, dragged his feet over the preparations, and was far from gracious to his intended wife, but eventually swallowed his anger and came to England in July 1554.

The following six months were the zenith of Mary's life and reign. Within a few weeks of her marriage, she believed herself to be pregnant, and it seemed as though the new dynastic union was about to bring the country a stable and Catholic future. By the end of the year, thanks to Philip's positive intervention, Reginald Pole had been admitted as Papal Legate and Parliament had brought the 20-year-long schism with Rome to an end. Popular ballads celebrated the Queen's most fortunate reign, and Catholic pamphleteers deduced the favour of God from the prosperity of her enterprises. Rocks, however, lay beneath the apparently smooth surface of events. To Henry II of France, Mary's marriage had represented a serious diplomatic setback. He had inherited from Francis I a struggle against the Habsburgs which had been going on for almost 30 years. In 1552, thanks to the financial difficulties of England and the rebellion of Duke Maurice of Saxony against the Emperor, he had brought that struggle to the verge of success. Only long-engrained habit and profound obstinacy appeared to be keeping the Emperor in the field by the summer of 1553. Then had come the English marriage negotiation, and the balance of advantage abruptly shifted. Henry had done his best to stir up English opposition; he had threatened and blustered; but he had been unwilling to risk an immediate extension of the war. Realizing by 1554 that Mary's Council was as reluctant as he was to embark on hostilities, he ventured a little further in his efforts to neutralize Philip's influence. English exiles, such as Henry Dudley and Christopher Ashton, were discreetly welcomed at the French Court, and given the resources to harass English and Spanish shipping in the Channel. Attempts were made to infiltrate Calais, and to stir up religious discontent there. Ironically, at a time when he was doing his best to suppress Protestantism within his own frontiers, he was supporting Protestant malcontents in England and in Germany - using any method available to embarrass his enemies. The older generation of English Protestant leaders would have no truck with such political methods of defending the gospel, but by 1555 the situation was changing. Active persecution began in February, and not only did the resistance of rank and file Protestants begin to harden, but a new generation of more radical leaders, such as John Ponet, reassessed the limits of legitimate authority. In March 1555, the pro-Habsburg Pope, Julius III, died and was replaced after a short interlude by the violently anti-Spanish Paul IV. Not only did Philip's influence in the Curia abruptly decline, but relations between the Holy See and the newly reconciled English Church became cool and difficult. In July, Mary's pregnancy was finally acknowledged to have been a delusion, and Philip left England for the Netherlands, having made very little impression on his wife's government or its policies.

In the autumn of 1555, the harvest failed, and in November Mary lost the ablest of her advisers through the death of Stephen Gardiner. The parliamentary session of October to December was unusually troubled, and it was subsequently discovered that French agents were again busy, encouraging resistance to taxation, and endeavouring to prepare the way for an exile invasion designed to set Elizabeth on the Throne. Philip's intentions were unclear. At first it had been thought that his absence would last no more than a few weeks, but the longer he was away, the more he became immersed in other tasks, and the more distasteful the thought of return became. He began to press for an English coronation, a matter which had hardly been mentioned while he was in the country, and suspicions of his motivation grew and multiplied. Nevertheless, in January 1556, the Truce of Vaucelles between France and Spain removed the immediate spectre of war. The financial records show the Council making steady progress with the reduction of the Queen's debts, and Reginald Pole, the Legate and Archbishop of Canterbury, laid down in Synod and by visitation a disciplinary programme designed to restore the Church to order and prosperity. Pole was very much in charge of ecclesiastical policy, and the merits of his approach to his brief are vigorously debated. After so many years of rapid change and uncertainty, an emphasis on discipline was inevitable; also, given the nature of the Catholic Church, an emphasis on the sacraments and on the training of clergy. On the other hand, the failure of Mary's pregnancy in the summer of 1555 meant that a secure, long-term future could not be assumed, and persecution was conspicuously failing either to break or to silence the Protestant opposition. Furthermore, Philip's prominent role in the reconciliation with Rome had presented them with an opportunity to associate Catholicism once again with foreign political interference and domination. In fact, the restored Catholic Church in England appears to have been remarkably insular, and to have drawn hardly at all on the resources of the counter-reformation. Nevertheless, as Mary's reign advanced the Protestants succeeded in presenting themselves as the "patriotic party" in a manner which they had never achieved in power. In the event, Pole's deliberate and administrative approach to reconstruction failed because it ran out of time, but his refusal

to adopt more urgent and evangelical methods meant that there was little sign of lay Catholic zeal when the next test came in the Parliament of 1559.

For a number of reasons, the confidence and momentum of Mary's government was beginning to flag by 1556. The Queen's failure to bear a child was the underlying reason, but Philip's dwindling interest in England, and his failure to maintain any kind of affinity among the English aristocracy, was an important contributory factor. Despite official encouragement and some individual zeal, the expected monastic revival never materialized, and Philip's deteriorating relations with the Papacy, resulting in war in September 1556, placed the English in an extremely difficult position. Henry II soon found cause to come to the assistance of his ecclesiastical ally, the Pope, and the Truce of Vaucelles broke down. England was not at first involved in these hostilities, but Philip found the neutrality of a country whose royal title he bore an intolerable affront to his honour. Besides, he was hard pressed, and England's limited military and financial resources would have been extremely useful. He therefore began to apply pressure on Mary and her Council. The Queen herself, despite his neglect of her needs and interests over the previous 18 months, responded willingly. Her Council, however, with the exception of Lord Paget who had always been Philip's main English supporter, resisted stubbornly. They were still holding out in March 1557 when the King at length decided that he would have to deal with them personally, and returned to England specifically for that purpose. Neither Philip nor his advisers had any opinion of English military skill, but the country was by his standard ridiculously under-taxed, and strategically crucial for operations in the southern Netherlands. It also possessed an efficient navy.

Despite the Duke of Northumberland's retrenchment, the Admiralty Board had still been in existence when he arrived in England, with some 10 or 12 ships of various sizes in commission. At least two of the seven principal offices had been vacant, the maintenance programme was four years behindhand, and no new ships were building, but the structure had been intact. Exactly when and how Philip intervened to improve this situation is not clear, but it was during his residence in England that the first steps were taken. The Gillingham dockyard was reactivated in the summer of

● Cardinal Reginald Pole.
NATIONAL PORTRAIT GALLERY, LONDON.

1555, and several of the more dilapidated ships brought in for repair during the autumn. Towards the end of the year, after Philip's departure, the building programme recommenced with the laying down of two medium-sized warships — subsequently called the *Philip and Mary* and the *Mary Rose*. Shortly after, in January 1556, the Council issued a series of orders relating to the state of the navy. The Lord Admiral was instructed to make a careful survey of the state of his command. He was to muster the men, and to make returns of equipment and victuals. Thereafter, regular musters were to be held, the system of provisioning overhauled, and requisitions prepared for "cables, hawsers, pitch, tar, and other necessities". Consideration was also to be given to the "wise placing of the ships for ready service". Philip's instructions that the Queen's ships should be available at short notice were clearly being implemented, but the preparations were general and not specific in their purpose. Early in 1556, he had no urgent need of naval reinforcement, but Henry II's continued support for the piratical activities of the English exiles, and the extent of their depredations, provided ample justification for such a course of action. In July 1556, the Queen's ships caught up with one of these pirate fleets in the Channel and destroyed it, capturing most of the officers. The overhaul of naval administration was completed almost a year after its inception, in January 1557, when the pressures for war were again becoming strong. It was then directed that an "ordinary" of £14,000 a year was to be paid to the Treasurer of the Navy in six-monthly instalments, thus giving the Admiralty Board a budget for the first time. This sum was to cover building and rebuilding; repairing, caulking, and trimming; the provision of tackle, equipment, and apparel; and a reserve fund from which wages and provisions were to be found for up to one month in emergency. It was not expected to provide for the greatly enhanced costs of war. The oversight of this new system was placed in the hands of the Lord Treasurer "with the advice of the Lord Admiral", thus bringing the navy for the first time under the direct control of one of the principal offices of state.

The reluctance of the English Council early in 1557 to become embroiled in Philip's war did not arise from a lack of reasonable preparedness. The harvest of 1556 had been the worst of the century, and malnutrition had been followed by an influenza epidemic of lethal proportions. War taxation and the recruitment of a large army out of such depleted resources could not be undertaken lightly. The Queen Mother of Scotland, Mary of Guise, held the Regency of that country with French support, and would certainly attack the north of England if open war broke out in the south. Moreover, the marriage treaty of 1554 had specifically rejected English participation in the war "which now is" between the Emperor and the French King. The Emperor had abdicated by 1557, but the war had been interrupted only by the Truce of Vaucelles, and was undoubtedly the same conflict as that which had been going on three years earlier. Nevertheless, no 16th century council could

hold out indefinitely against its monarch's clearly expressed wishes. Also, in April 1557, Henry II appeared to offer a deliberate provocation. A group of English exiles, led by Thomas Stafford, landed at Scarborough from two French ships ostensibly on their way to Scotland, seized the castle and proclaimed Stafford "Protector of the Realm". They were swiftly overpowered, and Henry vociferously denied any knowledge of their enterprise. He was not believed, even by those who wanted to believe him, because he had made many such denials in the past, even when the evidence clearly convicted him. Reluctantly, the English Council at last agreed to provide men and money for Philip's war, although they were still endeavouring to minimize the commitment when Mary's herald formally called upon Henry (somewhat to his surprise) in June. The full story behind the Scarborough raid may never be unravelled, but the fact

that the French ships were commanded by Jean Ribault, with his long history of service in England and long-standing connections with Lord Paget, creates the suspicion that Paget may have contrived this otherwise hare-brained enterprise specifically to further the cause he had in hand. If so, his coup succeeded brilliantly.

By the autumn of 1557, the Pope had negotiated a separate peace, but his hostility to the Habsburgs and all those connected with them was undiminished. Prominent among the recipients of that hostility was Reginald Pole, the Cardinal of England. Twenty years earlier, Pole and the then Cardinal Caraffa had belonged to different parties in the complex politics of Catholic reform. Pole's party, known as the *spirituali*, had then been in the ascendancy, favouring a negotiated settlement with the Lutherans. Their programme had failed, and in the opening sessions of the Council of Trent they had been decisively defeated by their less compromising opponents. To Caraffa, who had restarted the Roman Inquisition out of his own resources, the *spirituali* had all been tainted with heresy, and as Pope Paul IV he had not changed his mind. In April 1557, he withdrew Pole's Legatine commission, and summoned him to return to Rome to stand trial. Left to himself, Pole would have obeyed, because obedience to the Holy See had become the cornerstone of his theology, but Mary refused to let him go. She also refused to accept his designated successor, William Peto, and relations between England and the Papacy became so bad that a renewal of the schism was widely expected. That did

not happen, and Pole continued to run the English Church as Archbishop of Canterbury, but in many respects he was a broken man. By the end of 1557, it was hard for even the most committed Catholic to argue the justice of his cause from the evidence of divine approval. Philip had gone back to the Netherlands, the influenza epidemic raged unabated, and Sir Edward Carne, Mary's ambassador in Rome, was reporting insuperable difficulties in promoting the Queen's affairs. Only the weather had relented, producing an excellent harvest and removing the threat of famine which had haunted the country for the past two years.

The war had so far cost less than had originally been feared, and had achieved rather more. Although the Council, the merchant community, and probably the population at large, had been averse to hostilities, there were those to whom war was a golden opportunity. The earls of Pembroke, Rutland, Shrewsbury, and Westmorland received important and remunerative commands; Thomas Percy was restored to the Earldom of Northumberland to defend the north; and numerous gentlemen enlisted under Pembroke to serve in the expeditionary force despatched to Philip's assistance in July. Such service also created chances for those who had fallen foul of the régime to rehabilitate themselves. Henry, Robert, and Ambrose Dudley, the surviving sons of the Duke of Northumberland, were among those to receive commissions in the army, and Peter Killigrew in the navy. Pembroke's small force acquitted itself well at the siege of St Quentin, and Philip met all the

costs of the expedition. The Scottish attack, threatened in the autumn, did not materialize, a fact which indicated weakening French control in that kingdom. Then in January 1558, disaster struck. Despite his desperate financial plight, Henry II was determined to redeem the defeat at St Quentin, and recalled the Duke of Guise from Italy to the northern front. In a brilliantly conceived and executed campaign lasting only eight days, Guise overran the Pale and captured the supposedly impregnable fortress of Calais, which had been held by England since 1346. With the advantage of hindsight, it can be seen that this was a fortunate development for England - removing the heavy cost of the garrison, and forcing the country to turn away from obsolete continental ambitions towards a wider world - but it did not look that way to contemporaries. The first reaction in England was one of disbelief, rapidly followed by a determination to redeem the catastrophe. However, when the emergency summonses went out, very little happened. The musters near Dover were far too slow in assembling, and inadequate in quantity and quality. The bitter truth was that England was unable to mount a counterstroke, and took refuge instead in recrimination. The Council blamed the defeated commander, Lord Wentworth, and accused him of treason. Popular opinion blamed Philip (quite unfairly) for not coming to the rescue and it was darkly hinted that he was not sorry to see the English lose control of a place of such strategic import-ance. Philip and his advisers blamed the English Council for poor intelligence work in the first instance and for supine incompetence in failing to counter-attack. The truth was complex, and beyond the scope of this brief discussion. What mattered at the time were the reac-tions.

Such enthusiasm as had existed for the war evaporated, and military defeat was added to the Queen's childlessness and the influenza epidemics as evidence of divine judgment. English land forces played no further part in the war, and Philip's relations with the English Coun-cil deteriorated sharply. He had already suspended most of the payments to his English pensioners and servants, and his envoy in England, the Count of Feria, sent back a stream of damaging and dis-couraging reports. The Protestants were much encouraged, attributing Mary's many misfortunes to the idolatry which she had insisted upon restoring. Catholic controversialists, such as Miles Hug-garde, were loyal but dismayed, seeking rather lamely to blame the country's troubles on the ingratitude of her sub-jects rather than on the Queen. Philip

found his low opinion of the English con-firmed. The Pope celebrated a *Te Deum* for the discomfiture of the Habsburgs, and seems to have believed that the semi-heretical islanders had got no more than they deserved. Mary's own notor-ious words about Calais being written on her heart, if they were ever uttered, ref-lected her sense of dishonour, and her bewilderment about the hidden pur-poses of God, rather than a political judgment on the situation.

In fact, the loss of Calais changed very little. The Parliament which met soon afterwards responded half-heart-edly to the demand for subsidies, but eventually voted £168,000; not much by Philip's standards, but as much as could reasonably have been expected. Acts were also passed to improve the effi-ciency of the musters, and the poor response from the counties probably owed more to the continuing influenza than to any politically motivated foot-dragging. Naval activity, being less dependent on manpower, continued briskly. Two more new ships were laid down, and two others rebuilt. Between 1555 and 1558, some 2800 tons were added to the fleet, more than in the

equivalent period before the Armada. Despite having been caught completely unawares in January, the English navy was a competent fighting force, and took part with credit in two actions later in the year. In June, it supported Count Egmont's successful defence at Grave-lines, and in July joined with the Flemish fleet in an attack on Brest which was eventually unsuccessful. At this junc-ture, the navy was costing some £15,000 a month, and apart from the defence of the Scottish border was by far the most expensive aspect of the war. Philip understood this priority perfectly well, and the carefully compiled lists of Eng-lish ships from this date which survive in his archive at Simancas, testify to that understanding. By the end of Mary's reign, England was well on the way to becoming a maritime power. The char-tering of the Muscovy Company in 1555, with its powerful blend of court and city membership, was an important step in that direction. Efforts to trade to Guinea and the New World were deliberately frustrated by Philip in the interests of his Flemish subjects and Portuguese allies. This caused justifiable annoyance in London, but the compensation which he

REFURBISHMENT OF THE QUEEN'S HOUSE, GREENWICH

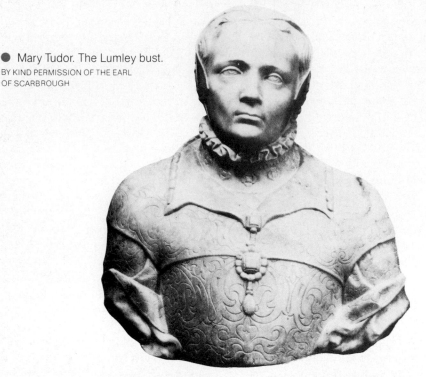

● Mary Tudor. The Lumley bust.
BY KIND PERMISSION OF THE EARL
OF SCARBROUGH

● OPPOSITE: Mary, from a Book of Hours
attributed to Levina Teerlinc.
BY PERMISSION OF THE ADMINISTRATOR, WESTMINSTER
CATHEDRAL.

gave was of great value. In 1558, Stephen Borough was allowed to visit the Casa de Contratacion in Seville, and to study its secrets. On his return, he published a translation of the *Arte de Navegar*, and his influence on English navigational education in the early part of Elizabeth's reign was immense.

Peace negotiations between France and Spain commenced in May 1558. Philip and Henry were bankrupt, and each had one major victory to salve his pride. England took part in these discussions, but its participation had mainly nuisance value. The English commissioners were under strict instructions not to accept the permanent loss of Calais. Philip acknowledged the justice of their stand, but the French would not budge and he urgently needed peace. From about June onwards, Mary's health began to deteriorate, and Philip was clearly reluctant to put her under severe diplomatic pressure. By October, her condition was alarming, and her Council tried to persuade Philip to visit her. He did not come; not so much out of callous indifference, as was alleged, as out of anxiety not to become embroiled in the question of the English succession. The King himself had long since accepted Elizabeth's claim, but Mary only did so at the last moment and with great reluctance. Had Philip been present in England when his wife died, her importunities and his own sense of honour might have drawn him into a civil conflict which he could certainly not afford. In the event, Mary's death on November 11, 1558 must have

come as a considerable relief to him. Not only had she attempted to make emotional demands to which he could not respond, but she had expected him to act as King of England without any power-base in the country. She was prepared to be as obstinate over Calais as over her marriage, and she had given him no heir. Philip was 32 in 1558, and had only one son, Don Carlos, by his first marriage. Soon he would have faced an impossible dilemma over Mary; the more so because his return to Spain in 1559 could not have been delayed except at the jeopardy of his control over that kingdom. To be free to marry again, and to have England as a semi-dependent ally rather than a recalcitrant partner had immense advantages.

Elizabeth at first also attempted to hold out for Calais, reluctant to lose face at the outset of her reign; but her position in reality was always more flexible. When peace was signed at Cateau Cambrésis in March 1559, she accepted a meaningless formula for its future restoration, and gained in return the inclusion of Scotland in the peace. Philip had never declared war on Scotland, despite its dependence on France, but Elizabeth was extremely anxious to extract a recognition of her Crown from the Scots and the French. This she did, although the young Mary Stuart, recently married to the Dauphin, never accepted it.

In the 16th century, 1559 was a watershed year. In England, it saw the final establishment of a Protestant church, and in Europe at large the end of a protracted series of Habsburg-Valois

wars going back to the French invasion of Italy in 1494. Philip returned to Spain to run his empire from Valladolid, and later the Escorial. In France, the unexpected death of Henry II during a tournament to celebrate the peace destroyed the fragile factional stability of that country, and set it on course to protracted civil wars. As a result of all these things, the political map of Europe was to be significantly different in the second half of the century. Instead of France facing the Empire of Charles V, there arose a shifting network of alliances endeavouring to control the overwhelming power of Spain. In that network the Netherlanders, the French Huguenots, and the Ottoman Turks all played an important part. But we are mainly concerned with the role of England because, thanks to her navy, England was for a few years Spain's most dangerous and effective adversary, despite the discrepancy in their resources. That navy Elizabeth inherited from Henry VIII and from Mary, just as she inherited a spirit of maritime enterprise from Edward VI. At the very outset of her reign, Elizabeth's advisers drew up a series of policy documents continuing the naval establishment and the ordinary financial support of £14,000 a year. At the same time a standing fleet of 24 ships was planned, to be available at 14 days' warning if not already at sea. This continued to be the basis of the peacetime navy down to the outbreak of war in 1585. It was the most sophisticated and flexible naval establishment in Europe; one which could be mobilized and expanded to a war footing in about two months, and capable of making an almost instant response to any challenge at sea. If Philip had possessed a similar organization, the preparations for the Armada might have been very different. Whether he failed to appreciate this aspect of English naval strength when it was close at hand, or whether he found it impossible to apply in the different conditions of Spain, is not known. What is clear is that the outcome of the Armada conflict was prefigured in the years when Philip was also King of England.

*Professor Loades is Professor of
History at the University College of
North Wales at Bangor*

THE NOBILITY OF ENGLAND AND SPAIN

By Cecil Humphery-Smith

THE WARS of the Roses were over. There was peace at home. The blood of the old nobility had been drained away in the French wars and the internecine conflicts, though much still flowed through that of the new order. Farmers, artisans, armament and provision suppliers had profited from war. New rich people came forward, a few descended from long-forgotten junior limbs of old families, but many from remoter origins, from immigrant refugee stock, freebooters, mercenaries, and from those who had once been proud to be distinguished as yeomen. The tabard had long ceased to display heraldic identifications at the jousts and on the battlefield. It remained a funeral garment for the display of heraldic achievements and pretentions to pedigree. In stained glass, on monuments, and in brasses the nobility and the gentry of the Tudor age showed forth their status and lineage in heraldic tinctures (colours).

The new people were anxious to establish themselves with the security of antiquity. This was no better achieved than in the vastness of quarterings in arms which could show, however remote, lineages from heiresses of ancient houses in stone, glass, and fabrics. The use of badges was commonplace and their number among all ranks multiplied. Even the crest became detached from armorial displays to be used like a badge as a popular ornamental form in vague allusion to the family, appearing on church monuments and in most incongruous places - in ceiling panels, doors, gateposts, and horse trappings. Pennons were still in use on the battlefield, but these too might be seen displaying crests and badges rather than the full arms.

The crest had come into popularity

barely a century and a half earlier as an adjunct to the panoply of those who could afford the sport of tournaments, a means for young men to show off to the ladies in the truly chivalric age. Many families bore no crest in their arms at all until Tudor times when, it might appear, they were shamed into following a mode. Some to this day will claim that their lack of a crest portrays the antiquity and respectability of their stock and their refusal to be persuaded by Tudor heralds to follow the foolish fashion.

Heralds had had a raw deal for centuries, wandering in loose attachment to the courts of Crown and nobility, carrying with them their increasing libraries of books, records, and ancient collections of rolls of arms and pedigrees, for the most part in precious manuscripts. They had been formed into a chartered society and given a permanent home at Coldharbour by the Thames in 1484. Their great benefactor, King Richard III, was not able to patronize their work for long and with the advent of Henry VII they were homeless once more. Henry VII and Henry VIII could not afford to maintain heralds in a permanent office and relied on their finding lodgings near Court. Once again, the completeness and integrity of their records were endangered. But Henry VIII conjured up an idea that was to provide them with a worthwhile activity and a means of livelihood.

Recalling Henry V's precept that only those who had borne arms with him at Agincourt in 1415, who could prove ancient usage, or who had received letters patent granting arms were to be deemed gentle, the heralds of Henry VIII's Court were sent out into the shires. With the help of the sheriffs, their visitations were announced and the gentry came forth to substantiate their claims to

the right to be credited with the title gentlemen and to the use of armori insignia. The nobility reported the cases to Garter, the Principal of the Kin of Arms. Family trees were presented local antiquaries and genealogists wor ing closely with the visiting heralds a pursuivants. Evidence was examin and the pedigrees recorded with t descriptions of the armorial bearing often including notes from churches a monuments. The age of the antiqua and local historian was begun with the perambulations.

The heralds made copies and fair li rary editions of their notes which we later to be deemed the authentic recor of the proven rights of use of titles a arms.

Those whose evidence was insuf cient were respited for proof. Those wl could not prove the right were public disclaimed and many were offere grants of new arms. Those without cres were offered grants of confirmation wi crests. The heralds' records grew, b they had to wait until the middle of tl century before they once more had home in which to collect them togeth in some order. In 1555, Philip and Ma granted a new charter to the corporatio of the College of Heralds and a ne home near the steps of St Paul's. Apa from temporary absences during tl Civil War in the 1640s and the Fire London in 1666, this has been the hor of the College of Arms ever since, house of great dignity and charact which, while it has been somewhat mu ilated in the past, has recently be admirably restored. There is much ne for financial support to pay for this re toration.

Until Queen Mary's charter, the he alds had had to rely on their granting ar

● Charles, Lord Howard of Effingham, Admiral of the Fleet, commander of the *Ark Royal*.

● Francis Drake, commander of the *Revenge*.

● Sir William Wynter was with Howard on the *Ark Royal*.

● Sir Martin Frobisher was on the *Victory* with Lord Henry Seymour.

● Sir Henry Palmer commanded the *Rainbow*.

● The Fenners William and Thomas commanded the *Aid* and the *Nonpareil*, respectively.

● Lord Henry Seymour.

● Sir John Hawkins.

● Lord Edmund Sheffield.

visitation fees for an income. Now they were given reasonable salaries, which have not been increased by any other monarch and were in fact reduced by William IV. Visiting the counties to record arms and descents in each generation became a lucrative form of subsistence and occupied them between the decreasing number of ceremonial occasions.

Tudor heralds delighted in pedi-grees, long ones heraldically decorated and terminating in splendid armorial displays of quarterings. Tudor heralds delighted in marshalling funerals with pomp and ceremony and took their *droits* (emoluments) from whatever remained from the processional display. Cadency differencing to distinguish branches of the same house was introduced in a fussy manner. They advised on the increasing use of coat armory to adver-tise status and lineage and kept profit-able leagues with artisans and craftsmen throughout the country, frequently dis-puting and protesting against their privi-leged positions and the perquisites asso-ciated with them.

Newly devised arms of this age were mostly splendidly designed to dem-onstrate the newness of the armiger. Somehow the heralds, perhaps craftily guided by the principal kings of arms,

● The Spanish fleet was under the command of the Duque de Medina Sidonia, Don Alonso Perez de Guzman el Bueno, leader of the Portuguese squadron.

● Don Diego Flores de Valdez, chief of staff to the Commander-in-Chief.

● Don Diego Tellez Henriquez, Tobermory galleon commander, of the Order of Santiago.

● Don Hugo de Moncada, commander of the galleasses from Naples — killed in action.

● Don Diego Medramo, like many, was a Knight of Santiago. He had command of four of the Portuguese galleons.

● Don Antonio Hurtado de Mendoza, a noble prince of many titles, was responsible for 22 brigs and tenders.

● Don Miguel de Oquendo, commander of the Guipuzcoa squadron out of San Sebastian.

● Don Juan Martinez de Recalde sailed out of Bilbao with the Vizcaya squadron. He was second-in-command.

● The Basque Don Martin de Bertendona commanded the squadron from the Levant.

were able to create new arms which bore much of the simplicity and skilful recognizability which was essential in medieval heraldry, yet they portrayed something which says this is not mediaeval, this is a Tudor coat. The heralds did not themselves particularly stem themselves from the old families, nor does it appear that they necessarily despised the new gentry, but there is evidence that there was much secret lampooning in the

designing of arms for these people. Heralds have always been a race apart and competent heraldic designers can say much in the elements of tinctures and charges in a new coat. While medieval arms are characterized by their sheer simplicity, seldom more than two tinctures or charges and with frequent modulations upon similar themes, Tudor heralds introduced new and extra charges and colours.

As heraldry became elaborate so it was less associated with warfare and the feudal host. The demand for armorial bearings now grew for social and economic reasons. Town guilds and municipal authorities grew and schools, colleges, and other corporate societies were founded. The Reformation placed Church lands at the disposal of the Crown and nobility, and profits were made. Merchants and lawyers moved to e country. All these needed armorial nsignia and the heralds took care of their ants, especially for the corporations d towns.

Reflecting feudal and familial relationships, Tudor heraldry expanded. uarterings were multiplied to display ccessful marriages and pride of pedi- ee. Heralds and their kings did indeed aintain a simplicity of design for the ost part, but repetition of themes ems to identify the designer or the ign of a king of arms rather than the lationships of the recipients of new ants.

There is little doubt that the commanders of the opposing fleets in the nglish Channel and the North Sea in 88 would have worn the regalia of ighthood and chains of office deco- ted with Royal and personal badges. e galleas *Girona* of the Naples Squad- n of the Spanish Armada sank off cada Point in northern Antrim on ctober 26, 1588 more than seven onths after it had left the port of Genoa Italy under its captain, Fabricio Spin- a. Nearly 1,300 men were lost and the lgian nautical archaeologist, Robert enuit, discovered the ship's remark- le treasure in 1967, including the cap-

tain's gold cross as a Knight of Malta.

By this period, heraldic art and usage had deteriorated, though the ships' commanders would have worn deeply cut armorial insignia on their rings and seals. It is likely that troops wore livery. Surely, the captains' banners were flowing in the breeze from the sterns of their ships. Had the English had any armament with which to pursue the Spanish, the matter might have been ended when Drake cut them off up the coast of Gravelines. Then we might have seen some shredded banners from the action. When the cressets had been lit and the beacons were flaring across the Downs from Stonor and Ditchling, Crowborough and Birling, when bells restricted to a single knoll through five years of waiting peeled out again, Drake awaited the turn of the wind and tide, when he could more readily identify the heraldic display that flew from the massing ships and could find his place among them to propel his line ahead against the curious Spanish crescent.

The heraldry of the Spanish contrasted markedly with that of the English. Quarterings and impalements divided their coats of arms to display their direct ancestry. Bordures told more

of the history of their families and the angelic prayer to the Blessed Virgin of their religious affections.

The English coats were mostly simple. William Borough, commanding one of the few English galleys, had a simple wavy bend between two fleurs-de-lys to compare with Mendoza's 10 hearts and saltire of chains. Sir John Hawkins, guiding Lord Edmund Sheffield aboard the *Victory*, had a coat barely 20 years old which must have been displayed somewhere aboard the ship. Compared with the gold patonce cross of Ambrose Warde flying from the mast of the *Spy* out of Folkestone, it was a complex Tudor concoction. Even with the Flodden augmentation on his bend, Lord Howard's banner was easier to identify than Medina Sidonia's. Yet, it was not far into the Tudor age before the new gentry houses were emulating the gross Spanish displays of ancestry not with four, but with 14 or more quarterings to a shield. A socially insecure people turns to supposed ancestry for the support of antiquity and displays the symbols that boast of long brave roots.

Cecil Humphery-Smith is Principal of the Institute of Heraldic and Genealogical Studies at Canterbury.

ELIZABETH AND HER DAZZLING COURT

Bastardized by her father, threatened with death by her sister, courted by the most powerful men of Europe, Elizabeth was one of the greatest monarchs. Peter Roberts describes this mercurial woman

IN ELIZABETHAN England, the Royal Court was the centre of political gravity and also of civility and sophistication. In its cultivation of magnificence as an attribute of power, it was a truly Renaissance court: as William Harrison claimed in his *Description of England* (1577), it was "in these days one of the most renowned and magnificent courts that are to be found in Europe". Its ritual dazzled foreign as well as English observers, as it was designed to do. With its aura of power and privilege, it was a cynosure to all those with an eye to the main chance, the talented and the merely ambitious. As the creation of a single and singular woman, it also came to enjoy a not always savoury reputation for faction, intrigue, and romantic liaisons of various kinds, not least of which was the elaborate wooing of the Queen by her chosen courtiers, favourites, and suitors for her hand in marriage.

The Court was an institution and a community. Its nucleus was the Royal Household, the suite of apartments which were reconstructed wherever the monarch lived, as she moved from one palace to another, or to the country houses of her great subjects. "Below stairs", the board of green cloth, with its staff of salaried professionals and high-born officials, supervised the provisioning of the household. The other department was known as the *domus regie magnificencie*, consisting of the royal bed-chamber and the reception rooms for public appearances and meetings. The Lord Chamberlain was in charge of the privy chamber, with its gentlemen, ushers, and ladies-in-waiting; as official master of ceremonies, he controlled access to the Queen and arranged audiences with her. Elizabeth was attended only by her gentlewomen in the privacy of her bedroom, while the guards of honour and the corps of gentlemen pensioners served in the outer chamber. All these royal servants in attendance "above stairs" were carefully chosen from gentry and noble families from different parts of the country; some of them had formed part of her household as Princess, and others were members of courtier families who had served her father, Henry VIII, and brother, Edward VI, in similar capacities. Their responsibilities need not be confined to the round of domestic duties as body servants and guardians of the royal person. After the Queen's death, Lord Hunsdon, captain of the gentlemen pensioners, informed James I that they had formed a nursery of talents trained for royal service in peace and war, as ambassadors, councillors, and commanders.

As the central body of administration, the Privy Council has its separate institutional history, but in its political role it is best regarded as an integral part of the Court. Discussions of affairs of state were in theory confined to the council board, and leading councillors resented any breach of this convention. However, they had to reckon with the Queen's idiosyncratic style of ruling: she did not usually preside at their meetings and preferred to consult them individually for advice about the making of policy. Moreover, the politics of the Court involved those who were not members of the Privy Council. The favourites exercised political influence before they were promoted to the Council, a distinction which one of them, Sir Walter Raleigh, never achieved. When a majority on the Council urged unpalatable action on her, she would either ignore their advice or rule through an inner ring.

A quorum of councillors was always in attendance on the Queen, who was, therefore, surrounded by councillors and courtiers. Men of ability who enjoyed her confidence could serve in both capacities. She retained most of her sister's councillors, but placed her confidence only in those who had faithfully served her as Princess and in the Protestant establishment who supported the parliamentary settlement of the Church in 1559. Power did not always go with office and rank. The most important courtier for most of the reign, the Queen's favourite, Robert Dudley, created Earl of Leicester in 1564, was a councillor but never aspired to a great office of state as an expression of authority.

● The "Armada" portrait, attributed to George Gower, c.1588.

ity. He was Master of the Horse and, for a brief time, Lord Steward, both of them places attached to the household. His adversary, Thomas Howard, Duke of Norfolk, expected deference as the premier peer of the realm, but did not aspire to cut a great figure at Court. Two lesser favourites, Thomas Heneage and Christopher Hatton, graduated in the Royal service from the Privy Chamber to the Privy Council. Hatton had come to the attention of the Queen through his performance in a masque (he had danced his way into favour, his enemies said), but he excelled himself as a spokesman for the Crown in the House of Commons and, though he was not a trained lawyer, he was made Lord Chancellor in 1587. As captain of the guard, Raleigh was no mere functionary, but Elizabeth did not trust his judgment sufficiently to make him a Privy Councillor. Sir Philip Sidney, who is reputed the Elizabethan courtier *par excellence*, received no

important promotion in the household; Elizabeth made him her cup-bearer and, reluctantly, joint master of the ordnance with his uncle, the Earl of Warwick, but then Sidney was more a protégé of Leicester than a favourite of the Queen.

Most of her ministers had served their apprenticeship in office in the reigns of her father and brother. The Marquess of Winchester, appointed Lord Treasurer in 1550, had served her sister, Mary, and was continued in office until his death in 1572. He said he was made of the willow, not the oak, and was therefore able to bend to the prevailing winds of religious change with each successive regime. Others like her confidant, William Cecil (created Lord Burghley in 1571), had kept a decent retirement during the Catholic restoration of Mary's reign. Cecil became her principal secretary, a post still technically attached to the Royal Household, but since Thomas Cromwell's time the lynchpin of govern-

ment. He and Sir Nicholas Bacon, her keeper of the privy seal, were the leaders of a Protestant establishment, bound by common ties forged in Cambridge and consolidated by intermarriage.

Elizabeth's own kindred — her Boleyn cousins — formed a special circle of privilege. The Earl of Leicester, according to Robert Naunton, regarded them as "of the Tribe of Dan ... they were not to be contested with". Sir Francis Knollys, who was married to the Queen's cousin, Catherine Carey, was one of the Earl's puritan allies and became his father-in-law, but the other Royal cousins, Henry Carey, Lord Hunsdon, the Lord Chamberlain, and Thomas Sackville, Lord Buckhurst, who succeeded Burghley as Lord Treasurer in 1599, kept aloof from any alignments in the Council. Royal Family connections, however, were no guarantee of a place in the sun. After the execution of the Duke of Norfolk in 1571, the Howards, compromised by their recusancy and their association with the cause of Mary, Queen of Scots, remained under a cloud for a generation: only the Protestant Lord Howard of Effingham, Lord Admiral at the time of the Armada, remained at the centre of affairs.

Robert Naunton, who in the reign of Charles I wrote a series of character sketches of Elizabeth's foremost courtiers, distinguished between those of the *militia* and the *togati*. About the earls of Leicester and Essex, her chief favourites among the "nobility of the sword", Naunton had little good to say, and he dismissed Christopher Hatton as "a mere vegetable of the court", but he commended her civil servants "of the robe" without exception. There were personal reasons for these predilections and prejudices: he was himself a career administrator who had enjoyed the patronage of the Cecils and he was married to the granddaughter of Hatton's enemy, Sir John Perrot. But the distinction he makes between the courtiers is valid enough, and he does not deny that even the adventurers were exceptional men. The Queen chose her servants well; she liked to have handsome and accomplished men around her, but even her favourites were no mere ornaments, and she entrusted them with responsibility only after they had proved their worth. Naunton's verdict was that she "ruled much by faction and parties, which herself both made, upheld, and weakened, as her own great judgment advised". The balance was not always steady in her hands, but she left them in no doubt that, as the Court was her creation, so the courtiers were her creatures.

Courtly love was elevated by Elizabeth into a power game which enabled her to dominate in a man's world so long as the players observed the rules. She encouraged her courtiers to compete for favour in an elaborate love-play that is reflected in the poetry of Raleigh and the high-flown love letters of Hatton. Leicester was able to master his jealousy at the emergence of a new favourite, such as Hatton and Sir Thomas Heneage, and work in harmony with each of them. Elizabeth accorded her favourites affectionate nicknames: Leicester was her "eyes", Hatton her "lids" (or "mutton") and each subscribed his letters to her with hieroglyphs denoting these sobriquets. Raleigh she dubbed "Water", a pun he capitalized on in his poetic conceit, "The Ocean's love to Cynthia", the moon goddess: just as the moon controlled the

tides, so the Queen exercised an irresistable magnetism on her courtiers. A more common metaphor was that of the "Sun Queen". "When she smiled, it was pure sunshine that everyone did choose to bask in if they could", wrote her godson, Sir John Harington; but when the storm-clouds of her temper hid these rays, woe betide the unfortunate creature who crossed her. An all too common cause of offence was the seduction of her "maids of honour", the vestal virgins at the temple of Eliza. Most of the leading courtiers — Leicester, Oxford, Essex, Pembroke, Raleigh — fell into disgrace on this score. Hatton was the only consistently successful courtier in Elizabethan terms, for he never married and did not compromise his devotion to his royal mistress. A number of such scandals caused William Harrison to the second edition (1587) of his *Description of England* to add the comment that the courtiers' morals detracted from their reputation for learning.

The Queen's women were her companions, and as such were strategically placed to gain limited access to the Queen, or patronage for a well-connected suitor. Blanche Parry, who had attended on Elizabeth since she was a child, composed a doggerel epitaph for her own monument in a Herefordshire church:

I lived always as handmaid to a Queen
In chamber chief my time did overpass ...
Preferring still the causes of each
    wight [person]
As far as I durst move her grace's ear
For to reward deserts by course of
    right.

But as Rowland Vaughan, Blanche's nephew, wrote in the next reign, though the gentlewomen might prove useful contacts for their friends at court, "none of these [near and dear ladies] durst intermeddle so far in matters of commonwealth". Those who tried to interfere in the royal matrimonial plans were given short shrift. Elizabeth had many close companions among her ladies-in-waiting, but none seems to have wielded any political influence. Their role as intimate servants of the sovereign did not lend itself to the play of factions as had happened in the masculine Privy Chamber of her father and brother.

Elizabeth jealously guarded her Court as a unique setting for majesty and focus of allegiance in the state, and she would not be outshone by any other

woman. Her suspicions of Mary, Queen of Scots as a rival queen who, with her own feminine wiles and vanity, could exert a comparable or even greater magnetism continued during Mary's captivity in England. Even so, she was concerned that Mary as an anointed queen should live in some dignity in the country houses where she was confined; and so she allowed her a small household and private chambers in which the Stuart cloth of state hung above a throne. However, when Elizabeth heard that her cousin, Lettice, had joined her husband Leicester in the Netherlands in 1586, and that (as the Court gossips reported) "there should be a court of ladies as should far pass Her Majesty's Court here", the shock waves of her anger crossed the Channel to stop the Countess in her tracks.

Elizabeth was a difficult mistress to serve. In the early years of the reign, Cecil was more than once reduced to despair by her chronic lack of resolution and her emotional attachment to Dudley, but she had too high a regard for Cecil's ability and integrity to release him from her service at those moments of crisis when he came near to resigning. On assuming office, he had sworn to give Elizabeth disinterested advice, and his tact and finesse were of a different order from those of the courtier. There were other plain-speakers among her councillors, men without the Cecillian touch who could not wrap up their advice in flattery. Thomas Smith, a Cambridge civil lawyer, served as ambassador to France and second secretary: his diplomacy failed him in his dealings with Elizabeth's wiles and irresolution. Another loyal councillor not gifted with a silver tongue was Sir Francis Knollys. He urged a more severe treatment of Mary, Queen of Scots from the time of her arrival in England in 1568; he was exasperated by Elizabeth's inconsistencies and was forever fearful that she might succumb to the flatterers around her who were not committed to the reformed faith.

Imperious and unpredictable as she was, Elizabeth was not an ungrateful mistress. Unlike her father, she was not given to casting to the wolves those subjects who displeased her: even the convicted rebels and traitors, most notoriously Norfolk and Essex, were consigned to their fate only with reluctance and much heart-searching. There were few dismissals from office in this reign. The one exception among her bureau-

rats who was arbitrarily treated was William Davison, Sir Francis Walsingham's associate as secretary and former ambassador to the Netherlands, who was made a scapegoat in 1587 for the Queen's refusal to accept moral responsibility for despatching the signed death warrant for the execution of Mary Stuart. Even Davison did not forfeit his salary as secretary, though he was heavily fined and imprisoned, and after his release, Essex failed to have him reinstated in office. Edmund Grindal, Archbishop of Canterbury, was suspended from his duties in 1578 for challenging royal authority in the matter of the "prophesyings", the assemblies in which laymen were instructed in the Scriptures. Grindal's defiance offended her religious conservatism as well as her prerogative as Supreme Governor of the Church, but his sequestration scandalised moderate Protestants as well as Puritans. She was no great respecter of bishops and she disapproved of married clergy. Grindal's successor, John Whitgift, remained a bachelor; she called him her "little black husband" because he implemented the kind of clerical discipline she approved of, and he was the only Primate she elevated to the Privy Council.

Another casualty among the favoured few who held high office was the Welsh magnate, Sir John Perrot, a Falstaff-like figure who was the Queen's putative half-brother (as Henry VIII's natural son, or so Naunton claimed) and a privy councillor from 1589. He was arraigned for treason for allegedly communicating with the Spaniards while serving as Lord Deputy of Ireland (1584-8). These charges were probably trumped up by his enemies in Dublin and based on false witness and forged documents. But, more importantly, his stock had fallen at Court, for he had spoken disparagingly of the Queen, and this could not be lightly treated, and he had seduced Christopher Hatton's illegitimate daughter. He died in the Tower of London before the sentence for treason could be carried out or (as seemed more likely, according to William Camden) suspended by a royal pardon.

The courtiers were by definition those who were sworn to the Queen's service and who were entitled to lod-

gings at court either *ex officio* or by grace and favour. For the rest of the aristocracy and gentry, seasonal attendance at Court was essential for favour or advancement. Whereas in an earlier period ambitious men could attach themselves to the household of provincial nobles, this became a less certain pathway with the increasing dependence of the aristocracy on the Tudor Monarchy. By a discreet dispensation of patronage, Elizabeth managed to domesticate her great subjects at Court. Not only the great, but their aspiring clients; for an ambitious man of modest means who wished to advance in the world, it was more important to cut a figure at Court than in the House of Commons. Gabriel Harvey, Cambridge scholar and man of letters, who sought employment as Leicester's secretary, believed "the prince's court" to be "the only mart of preferment and honour: a gulf of gain". Rewards for services rendered were not to be had without the asking. When Sir Ralph Sadler made suit for the lucrative post of Chancellor of the Duchy of Lancaster in 1568, William Cecil advised him to make his presence felt at Court: "as fishes are gotten with baits, so are offices caught with seeking". The great majority recognized the need as well as the duty to attend on the Queen at least once a year, and from this obligation (as well as the calls of litigation at the Westminster law courts and attendance in Parliament) there evolved in this reign and the next the London season for high society, the growth of more sumptuous town houses in the West End and, to some extent, of the London playhouses. Courtiers and suitors for patronage paid their respects to Elizabeth with casual presents, mostly of jewellery or items of clothing, and regularly with New Year gifts, when she reciprocated with items of silver graded according to rank. Lists of these exchanges survive for certain years as a reliable index of those currently in favour. Her parsimony is notorious and yet she knew when it was politic to be generous. Grants of money and leases of Crown land were made but sparingly, and in large quantities only to the highly favoured, such as Leicester, who as a younger son of an attainted duke required an endowment to maintain his state. Through an extended network of patronage, as much as through the institutions of law and government, the Court exercised its sway over the country. With the nobility and gentry tied by leading strings to the Queen, clientage

came to be focused on the Court as well. So long as the resources lasted, the system contributed to social harmony and political stability. But Elizabeth was dealing with a wasting asset as the Spanish war continued to consume the Royal treasure. When the supply began to dry up in the 1590s, competition for patronage turned sour and factional conflicts threatened to engulf the monarchy itself.

The cumulative effect of the system of patronage was to consolidate the position of the Protestant establishment, to the general exclusion of Catholic subjects, who were not to be weaned away from their faith by the blandishments of Royal bounty. The importance attached to sound religion in appointments to strategic offices of state is shown in the criteria applied in the selection of the Chancellor of the Duchy of Lancaster, to which the reliable Protestant Ralph Sadler was nominated in 1568. The Privy Council insisted that "it is very meet that the place be bestowed upon such an one as is indeed religious and very well settled in Her Majesty's favour and obedience; for more requisite is it to be careful to govern well the subjects than to husband well the revenues of that country" Judicious appointments thus served the purposes of political stability, by fostering not necessarily efficiency but loyal service.

The revolt of the northern earls in 1569 was caused partly by their alienation from the Court, by the hostility within the Privy Council of the conservative Duke of Norfolk and, at an early stage, Leicester towards Cecil, and support among certain English Catholics for the claims of Mary, Queen of Scots to be recognized as heir apparent to the English Throne. In the aftermath of the revolt, the forfeited estates of the rebels were systematically redistributed to the loyal supporters of the Crown. All this was conducted as a deliberate act of policy. Ten years later, Cecil spelled out for his mistress the advantages of calculated generosity: "... gratify your nobility and the principal persons of your realm, to bind them fast to you ... whereby you shall have all men of value in the realm to depend only upon yourself". To a large extent, Cecil already operated this policy as Master of the Court of Wards, which sold to the highest bidder among suitable candidates the wardship and marriage of the offsprings of orphaned tenants-in-chief of the Crown during their minority. The Court of Wards, therefore, acted as an agent of Royal control over the aristocracy as well as one of patronage.

Catholic propaganda accused the Queen and the Protestant establishment of systematically destroying the "old nobility" established before the Reformation, while some modern historians have argued that the whole estate of the aristocracy was seriously undermined by Elizabeth's failure to replenish and endow on a large enough scale. If there is any truth in this last charge, it may reflect her own sterility and awareness of her inability to perpetuate the Tudor dynasty however much she enjoyed the exercise of power. Certainly, almost all the courtiers were in debt to the Crown, for all their privileged access to patronage, and she did not delegate authority or dispose of honours lightly. She was sparing of titles, created few new peers, and resented her great subjects receiving honours from foreign states. When the Catholic soldier, Thomas Arundell, was made a count of the Holy Roman Empire in 1596 for service in the campaign against the Turks, Elizabeth was far from impressed. According to Camden, she said: "I would not have my sheep branded with another man's mark". She kept even Robert Dudley waiting before she elevated him to the peerage and a seat on the Privy Council. Yet when she almost died of smallpox in 1562 she urged the council to make Dudley Protector of the realm until Parliament could be summoned to settle the succession. The danger passed, but it was a revealing moment, and she never did nominate her successor in any formal document. However attached she was to Leicester, she never succumbed to his charms completely, despite the slanderous gossip about them, and she would not gratify all his ambitions. Having declined the offer of the sovereignty of the Netherlands by the Estates, she was outraged when Leicester, as leader of the English expeditionary force, accepted the title of governor of the rebel states without her permission, and she hectored him into relinquishing it. Their close relationship survived this crisis and many another disgrace, including his marriage. There is no doubt that she loved her "sweet Robin". After an early infatuation and teasing scenes of indiscretion in front of the Spanish ambassador, she kept her affections under control. Her intimate keepsakes tell their own story: the miniature portrait of him she wore on a pendant at her neck, and "his last letter", so treasured after his death.

It would be a mistake to regard Elizabeth's Court as a permanent institution, fixed immutably in the mould in which it was cast at her accession. It was rather something makeshift which suited her personality and reflected her unmarried state. Contemporaries never lost sight of the possibility that, if she married, the character of the Court would be transformed — and with it, some of them feared, that of the regime itself — with the establishment of a separate household for a consort. Most of her councillors thought she should marry and beget an heir to secure the succession to the Throne. A series of foreign suitors was considered in turn, but unfortunately most of them were Catholic princes who might compromise the religious settlement in England. Though these overtures caused division in her council, and sometimes discord between the Queen and both Council and Parliament, they served the purposes of English diplomacy as well as gratified the Royal vanity. Until she reached middle age and it lost its credibility, the prospect of her hand in marriage was used as a bargaining counter in negotiations aimed at a foreign alliance that would prevent the isolation of England by the Catholic powers. It was not always a cynical stratagem, and her coy declarations that she would remain a spinster and was rather married to her people should not be taken at face value. There were moments during the prolonged wooing of the Duke of Anjou (formerly the Duke of Alençon) in the late 1570s when she seemed to have been genuinely interested. They were an incongruous pair — he was more than 20 years her junior — but despite his unprepossessing appearance he made a good impression on Elizabeth when they finally met in 1579, and she had been courted by his proxy, Simier, since the previous December. She had now reached her climacteric and must have been aware that this was her last chance of marriage. Leicester, who claimed to know her mind better than anyone, was sufficiently alarmed to oppose the marriage treaty openly. To neutralize his influence, Simier disclosed to Elizabeth the news that the Earl had been secretly married to Lettice Knollys since the autumn of 1578. Elizabeth was shocked by the deceit and Leicester was out in the cold.

The negotiations for a match with Anjou may have been prolonged in revenge for his unfaithfulness, as she saw it, but Elizabeth convinced every-

one, including perhaps herself, that sh was in earnest. She certainly raised th hopes of a group of pro-French Catholi gentlemen about the Court who wer intriguing with Simier and the Frenc ambassador in favour of the marriage These included Lord Henry Paget an his brother, Charles, the Queen's kins men, Charles Arundell and Lord Henr Howard, the younger brother of the exe cuted Duke of Norfolk, who wrote a trac in support of Anjou's claims. For a time the Earl of Oxford, who had a brief flirta tion with the Romish religion, was c their number. With the exception of Lor Oxford, this coterie had long since bee excluded from the Elizabethan magic ci cle, but with the Queen married to Anjo they could expect an entrée and a mea sure of toleration for their co-religior ists. As in the crisis of 1569, the amb tions of disaffected, high-born Catholic impinged on Court politics and diplom acy, and a palace revolution seemed i prospect with Leicester's disgrace. Th Catholic faction on the fringe of th Court (none of them seemed to have hel household office, except possibly Arur dell, who is known to have taken th oath of service in some capacity) cam within an ace of success, but it was gamble which turned on Elizabeth commitment to the marriage. Th moment passed with the cooling of he ardour; Leicester was forgiven and reha bilitated as her close companion, and th negotiations for a French allianc lingered on until 1582, when Anjou, afte a second visit to England, departed wit assurances of financial support for hi campaign in support of the Dutch rebel against Philip II of Spain. The card of dynastic marriage had been played fo the last time, and with its failure th Catholic coterie lost all hope of a place i the sun. Once restored to favour, Leices ter set out on a vindictive campaign t hunt the Catholics from the Court. Som of them, including Charles Paget an Charles Arundell, fled into exile in Pari where they dabbled in conspirac against the Queen, and were implicate in the Throckmorton plot of 1583. The former associates who had stayed a home were also discredited. Lord Henr Howard was the only one not driven int exile or discovered in treason. H wriggled out of all the traps laid by S Francis Walsingham, the principal secre tary and spy-master, to compromise th supporters of Mary, Queen of Scot Howard survived his enemy, Leiceste but was not received back at Court unt

With branches both north and south of the border we're an even easier source of riches than the Spanish Main.

These days you don't have to mount a major expedition to lay hands on a few doubloons. The Royal Bank of Scotland has branches all over the country (North and South of the border) so your money can always be readily accessible, along with a wide range of other banking services and facilities.

✳ The Royal Bank of Scotland

London Regional Office, Regent's House, 42 Islington High St., London N1 8XL.

● Elizabeth. Miniature by Nicholas Hilliard.

the last years of the reign. From 1580, there was a stricter enforcement of the anti-Catholic laws in which Elizabeth reluctantly acquiesced as the dangers to her position were pointed out to her by the Privy Council. Those who refused to conform to the religious settlement were heavily penalized for their recusancy. With the growing threat of a French invasion to be launched by the Guises in the cause of their kinswoman, Mary, Queen of Scots, and associated attempts on the Queen's life by desperate English Catholics, the Protestant councillors closed ranks against the common enemy. The rivalry between Burghley

and Leicester, once characterized by historians as the classical form of Tudor Court faction, arose out of mutual suspicion about their relative influence with the Queen. Once the tensions caused by the matrimonial politics of the 1570s had relaxed, the minister and the favourite achieved a working relationship, a *modus vivendi*, as the Queen's "surrogate husbands" (as Professor Wallace McCaffrey calls them). The death of Anjou followed by the assassination of William of Orange in the summer of 1584 persuaded Burghley and finally Elizabeth herself of the need for direct English intervention in the Netherlands, a virtual declaration

of war against Spain. In 1585, she reluctantly appointed Leicester as commander of the expeditionary force, a role for which he had been actively preparing himself for a decade or more.

Leicester was thus able to pose as the champion of embattled Calvinism on the Continent as well as the patron of puritans at home. His Catholic enemies accused him of building up a puritan party and a network of clients in England that sought to undermine Royal authority in Church and state. But though his protection of puritanism was not to the Queen's liking, this was black propaganda that convinced no one except the atholics themselves. There were feuds among the Protestant courtiers and ouncillors, but Court factions, as the recursors of political parties, did not make their appearance in this reign. here was a broad spectrum of religious ommitment among the Protestant stablishment, but its members understood that the preservation of the religious settlement and their own ascendancy depended on Elizabeth's survival. n advising her, they differed on means, ot ends. Although there were differences between even a moderate Protestant, such as Burghley and Archbishop Whitgift, who imposed a tighter uniformity in the Church from 1586, these were not disruptive of the basic nity of the Privy Council. One eccentric ouncillor, Sir James Croft, who may ave been a crypto-Catholic, received a panish pension and leaked secrets to he Spanish Ambassador, Mendoza, but e was an isolated and ineffectual figure, etained by Elizabeth in recognition of is early loyalty to her in the difficult ears of her sister's reign.

Late in 1584, the Privy Council evised the notorious Bond of Association as a league to protect the Queen's fe and to avenge her death should she all victim to an assassin. Those who igned the Bond pledged themselves to revent the accession of any claimant to he Throne who would profit from the urder of Elizabeth. The targets were learly Mary, Queen of Scots and her on, James VI, and the aim was to discourage Stuart support for any plots against lizabeth. It amounted to a kind of lynch aw adopted as state policy, a product of he paranoia of the age. As an act of oyalist partisanship sponsored by the Privy Council, it was an attempt to flush ut and compromise the crypto-Catholics and sympathizers of Mary. Elizabeth istanced herself from this measure of ealpolitik and refused to allow it to be nacted by Parliament in 1585 except in a milder form, shorn of its most dangerous mplications for the Stuarts. Even so, the ssociation can be seen as a political xpression of the knight errantry of the Court, as Elizabethan Protestant chivlry in arms, when devoted champions f the Virgin Queen swore to wreak engeance on her enemies. It was in this pisode, perhaps, that the Arthurian cult t Elizabeth's Court came nearest to the morality of Camelot.

There were quarrels and conflicts of nterest in the hothouse atmosphere of he Court, but no subversive factions.

Leading councillors had their network of clients reaching out from the Court to their spheres of influence in the provinces. Dudley's enemies interpreted his clientage in a sinister light as forming a "Leicester's Commonwealth", but this in part reflected the resentment of the Catholic "outs" at their exclusion from the privileges of the Court. He did build up a following in his Barony of Denbigh, which he used in the Queen's service as part of his contingent in the Netherlands campaign. Burghley, on the other hand, was more concerned with consolidating the fortunes of his family than with establishing a body of dependants who looked to him as sole patron. Long absence from court prompted courtiers to suspect that their rivals were stealing a march on them, but this was the price to be paid for military adventure. When Leicester and his followers in the Netherlands expressed disquiet that their interests were neglected, Burghley was stung to reply to the charge that he was turning England into a *regnum cecilianum* — the reverse of a "Leicestrian Commonwealth". In fact, in Leicester's absence, two counterweights to his influence were promoted to the Privy Council, Richard Sackville, Lord Buckhurst, and Archbishop Whitgift, but there was no suggestion that these appointments represented Burghley's advice being accepted against the Queen's better judgment.

Elizabeth managed to control the rivalries at her Court — it was part of her policy of "divide and rule" — until the last years of the reign. When the tensions between the Earl of Essex and Robert Cecil turned into dangerous in-fighting at Court, it was partly because the former would not abide by the rules of the game by which Elizabeth sought to be evenhanded in the distribution of office and patronage. Essex tried to engross the favour of the Queen, who would not allow her judgment to be affected by her emotional attachment to him, but his accusations that the Cecils monopolized place and privilege were not without foundation. Essex was popular in the country as Leicester had never been, and Elizabeth resented this popularity, which she felt detracted from the allegiance which subjects owed to the Throne. Her worst fears were realized in 1601 when Essex made a reckless bid for power, which led to his trial and execution for treason. His rebellion should be seen as a resurgence of the subversive power politics of the "overmighty sub-

jects" of the previous century, rather than a foreshadowing of the "Court and Country" conflicts of the next. His disgruntled "country" following espoused no cause greater than their own material interests; neither Catholics nor puritans looked to him for positive leadership. Until the *débacle*, which signalled the ageing Queen's faltering touch on the mechanism of patronage and favour, the interests of all sections of the Protestant political nation had been contained within the Court.

The recruitment of members of the Royal Household, men and women from landed families up and down the country, had established a relationship of symbiosis between the Court and most of the shires of England and Wales. The Queen also took the Court into the countryside when she went on her progresses in the summer months, though these were confined to the Home Counties. This annual round of the royal palaces and the country seats of the aristocracy and gentry, when she battened on free hospitality, was undertaken as a means of consolidating her hold on her people's imagination and loyalty. Another reason for this constant movement in the summer months was her aversion to smells. One story relates how the Welsh soldier, Sir Roger Williams, presented himself before her with a petition. "Tush, Williams, thy boots stink!" to which he quipped: "Nay, Your Majesty, 'tis not my boots but my suit which stinks." In 1596, her godson, Sir John Harington, published his work on the water-closet, *The Metamorphosis of Ajax*, a punning title that Elizabeth found distasteful. But until Harington installed his invention in Richmond Palace at the end of the reign, the primitive sanitary conditions of the age rendered even the best equipped palace in need of complete ventilation after a short period of residence by a large retinue.

One Spanish envoy who accompanied her on one of these journeys described the spontaneous applause which she relished, remarking on "how beloved she was by all her subjects and how highly she esteemed this ... She would order her carriage sometimes to be taken where the crowd seemed thickest, and stood up and thanked the people". Francis Bacon later reported on her courage, for she did not curtain these public appearances even after the attempts to assassinate her. With her natural acting ability, she created the role of Queen Regnant in England as it had not been performed by her sister, Mary. She continued indefatigably with these progresses until her last years, and enjoyed the elaborate receptions and pageants mounted for her in great houses, cathedral cities, incorporated towns, and the universities of Oxford and Cambridge. Many reluctant hosts dreaded her arrival with a large entourage that had to be accommodated and fed at great expense, but the courtiers at least welcomed the opportunity to impress her with their hospitality. When Sir Christopher Hatton built his new house of Holdenby in Northamptonshire, reputed to be the finest in England, it was in imitation of Burghley's "prodigy house" of Theobalds, and dedicated to Elizabeth. Hatton declared that he would not visit the finished house until "that holy saint" deigned to inspect his "shrine" to her. After Burghley had stayed there in 1579, he wrote a thank you letter to Hatton, expressing approval and commenting: "God send us both long to enjoy Her, for whom we both meant to exceed our purses in these" architectural extravagances. In the 1590s, Hatton's Northamptonshire neighbour, the Catholic, Sir Thomas Tresham, constructed on his estate at Rushton a triangular lodge dedicated to the Trinity, as if in lapidary comment on the Protestant Queen-worship. He maintained his family's lavish tradition of hospitality, but the Queen did not visit Rushton. Whereas the courtier houses strained the finances of their builders, Tresham built cheaply with locally quarried stone. It was rather recusancy fines which took their toll of the fortunes of the Treshams and other Catholic families, as their estrangement from the Court cut them off from mainstream aristocratic life.

Not all the grandiose new houses reflected court influences. The most splendid creations of all, Sir John Thynne's Longleat and the Hardwick and Chatsworth of Bess, Countess of Shrewsbury, glorified not Elizabeth's but their own emerging aristocratic dynasties. These prodigy houses were visible signs of eminence in their own countryside, achieved from shrewd investment in land rather than the fruits of office or patronage acquired by paying

● The "Procession" picture of Queen Elizabeth under a canopy supported by her courtiers. Attributed to Robert Peake, c.1601.
PRIVATE COLLECTION.

assiduous court to Elizabeth. Their architectural styles were a characteristic blend of the Gothic and the Classical, which did mirror in their way the intertwined neo-medieval and Renaissance motifs fashionable in the pageantry and literature of the Elizabethan Court. If in an indirect way the Queen can be said to have inspired notable examples of what is called Elizabethan architecture, she did not commission new works herself. She did not need to build anew, since Henry VIII had created or appropriated residences for the dynasty on such a vast scale. It is perhaps significant of her attitude to dynastic monuments that the most ambitious item of "the Queen's Works" was the temporary banqueting hall put up for Anjou's visit in 1581-2, the last of three such structures of wood and canvas improvised in the reign to entertain embassies from France.

This visit was also the occasion for a special tournament in Anjou's honour. The tournament as an enactment of the cult of chivalry was regularly performed to glorify the Virgin Queen at the anniversaries of her accession. Accession Day, November 17, came to be celebrated by the Court as a national holiday,

another red-letter day to supplant the Roman calendar of saints. William Camden, the first historian to write about the reign, relates that this observance dated from 1570, possibly as a feast of thanksgiving for deliverance from the danger of the northern revolt of 1569. The defeat of the Armada was marked by a double celebration, as the Accession Day Tilt was followed two days later, on November 19, by another to commemorate St Elizabeth's Day. Like the annual ceremony of the Garter on the Feast of St George, these celebrations symbolized national unity. They were also opportunities for courtiers to exercise their martial prowess; and in ritualized feats of arms potentially dangerous rivalries might be sublimated. The contestants canalized their energies by cutting a figure before the Queen, who received their pledges of devoted service. Philip Sidney, Lord Essex, and Robert Carey used the occasion of an appearance at the tilt to recover favour after disgrace (Sidney protesting in 1580 against the proposed match with Anjou, the other two for marrying without royal permission) through a symbolic display of contrition. Raleigh was the only prominent court-

ier-knight who did not engage in the tilt. His gallantry was of a different order: as a man of the sea, he did not aspire to knight-errantry like the nobility of the sword. Like so many others, he fell from grace for compromising one of Elizabeth's women, Bess Throckmorton, whom he secretly married. He was not entirely forgiven, and was received back at Court on probation. His poetry now failed him as a means to recover favour, and he gave vent instead to cynical disillusionment, which chimed in with his agnosticism:

> Say to the Court it glows
> And shines like rotten wood,
> Say to the Church it shows
> What's good, and doth no good.
> If Church and Court reply,
> Then give them both the lie.

Only part of the expense of the tournaments was defrayed from the Royal coffers, as the participants spent vast sums on their accoutrements. After the tilt of 1590 a witness reported: "These sports were great and done in costly sort, to Her Majesty's liking, and their great cost." Her reputation for magnificence rests on

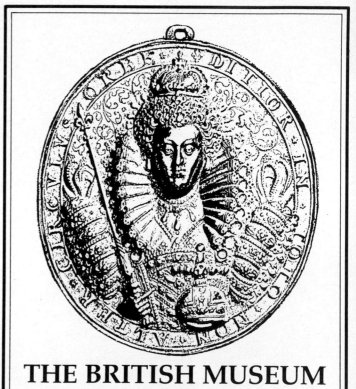

Robert Dudley, Earl of Leicester. Miniature by Nicholas Hilliard.

her lavish provision for a proper setting for her own majesty. But even in elaborate ceremonial and ritual, she contrived at splendour with economy.

A Spanish visitor to England remarked on the mystique of Tudor monarchy: "in pompous ceremonies a secret of government doth much consist". Elizabeth had an instinctive understanding of the political importance of spectacle, and the revival of chivalry at her Court served a larger purpose than recreation. In this manifestation of the Court as theatre, the Queen's Champion, Sir Henry Lee, was impresario and choreographer. The pageantry of the tilts and "entertainments" he devised for fes-

tivities held in the London palaces and at the royal manor of Woodstock (1575) and his own house of Ditchley (1592), like the literary conceits of Sidney's *The Shepherd's Calendar* and Edmund Spenser's *The Faerie Queene*, contributed not only to the cult of the Virgin Queen but to English Protestant mythology. Their constant motif was that Elizabeth's rule, characterized by good government, justice, and pure religion, presaged the return of the golden age.

Elizabeth was the only Tudor to possess charm (the young Henry VIII had *brio*, but hardly charm), and she managed to make her femininity and even her maidenhood into powerful

assets where, in a weaker character, they might have been the undoing of the dynasty. As she reached middle age, the role of the most eligible spinster in Christendom had perforce to be abandoned, and it was in these years that the cult of the Virgin Queen was fostered to vindicate her status as Queen Regnant without a consort. To what extent she contributed to this image-making is not clear, but it must have afforded her either psychological compensation for the sacrifice of fulfilment in marriage or else an enhanced satisfaction in the enjoyment of power as sole ruler. Her position was a vulnerable one — she was the target of common gossip and vicious propaganda

— so it was important for her image-makers to assert her maidenly innocence as part of the rhetoric of power. Poets, painters, and publicists drew on all the resources of classical mythology to create the cult of the Virgin Queen, a goddess-like being, for ever unattainable to those who wooed her. As an embodiment of the virtues she was cast in many *personae*. As a character in the prologue to Thomas Dekker's comedy, *Old Fortunatus*, performed at Court at Christmas 1599, put it:

> Some call her Pandora, some Gloriana, some Cynthia, some Belphaebe: all by several names to express several loves. Yet all those names make but one celestial body ...

In the crisis of the 1580s, the posture answered a national mood of defensive defiance, for England too was represented as unassailable and indomitable. Thus Elizabeth had become, literally, a legend in her own lifetime, until in her declining years the cult waned at Court, as she outlived her contemporaries, who were its chief acolytes. The ageing woman behind the mask of royalty received from the younger generation of courtiers a respect that fell far short of worship.

At the beginning of her reign, Elizabeth had been careful to take the title of Supreme Governor of the reformed church she had restored, rather than the more controversial one of Supreme Head assumed by her father, Henry VIII. She moved cautiously to avoid stirring conventional prejudices against a female ruler. By the middle of the reign, all such scruples had been laid aside and a process of deification was well under way. Where Protestants on her accession had hailed her as a Deborah sent to redeem the true faith, by the 1580s she was identified in paint, print, and pageantry with the goddesses of classical mythology. When the puritan Lord North bullied the Bishop of Ely into complying with the royal command to surrender his London house to him as part of a compulsory exchange of lands, the Bishop was reminded that "she is our god in earth: if there is perfection in flesh and blood, undoubtedly it is in Her Majesty". Not all the puritans were happy with this extravagant worship, and the preacher, Robert Wright, got into trouble for objecting to it as idolatry. Catholics, writing from the safety of exile, denounced the supplanting of the cult of

the Virgin Mary by that of the Virgin Queen. Alexander Nowell, Dean of St Paul's, was criticized by his more fastidious fellow clergy for flattering Elizabeth in his Court sermons. His defence was that he had "no other way to instruct the Queen what she should be but by commending her". In his sermon at the opening of Parliament in 1563, he ventured, among other things, to "censure excess of apparel", one of the social abuses of the day, but not a tactful subject to bring up in the presence of the gorgeously costumed Elizabeth. His insinuating rhetoric rebounded on him two years later when he deigned to attack the cross in the Royal Chapel; Elizabeth interrupted the sermon and saw him off with a flea in his ear. Later in the reign, Bishop Aylmer of London committed a similar indiscretion in preaching in the Royal Chapel "on the vanity of decking the body too finely". The Queen tartly remarked to her gentlewomen that if the bishop continued on that theme "she would fit him for heaven, but he should walk thither without a staff, and leave his mantle behind him". She would not be patronized by her clergy, from whom advice on the image of majesty was not more welcome than on the limits of her prerogative.

The role of Elizabeth as the Virgin Queen was projected in the formal portraits which have fixed her image in popular memory, but which to begin with were accessible only to the privileged few. It was only when some of them were reproduced as prints and appeared as illustrations to books that they made any impact on the larger, literate public. The image which reached all classes of society was that replicated in simplified versions on medals and coins of the realm. The earlier portraits were commissioned partly as gifts for fellow sovereigns, or to impress princely suitors, but the later, more ornately emblematic paintings were executed to commemorate great events, such as the triumphalist Armada portrait by George Gower. These were prominently displayed in the galleries of the palaces and great houses. In 1600, The German Protestant Count Waldstein was given a guided tour of the palaces. At Hampton Court, he viewed the Painted Chamber (demolished by Christopher Wren at the end of the following century to make room for his additions) on the ceiling of which he noted a painting of Elizabeth in apotheosis. Another German visitor in the 1570s seems to have had an entrée into the privy chamber, for he has left a

drawing of the Queen giving audience to Dutch envoys, the only depiction of the inner sanctum of the Court that we have for this reign.

This link with Protestant countries, and the refugees from Catholic persecution, had a cultural impact on England which is reflected in some of the allegorical paintings of Elizabeth. In one of them, dated 1569, she appears in the company of three goddesses, Minerva, Venus, and Juno, representing wisdom, love, and marriage, who appear to defer to the Queen's greater claims to at least the first two of these virtues. The work has been tentatively attributed on stylistic grounds to Joris Hoefnagel, one of the emigrants who fled to England to escape Alva's persecuting regime in the Netherlands. If this is true, and the portrait was commissioned by members of the Dutch community in London as a thank-offering, it follows (as Sir Roy Strong has argued) that the series of allegorical paintings of Elizabeth began with a tribute from Protestant exiles.

From 1579, a new symbolic content is discernible in the Royal portraits, an increasing identification of Elizabeth with England's destiny. The series of "sieve" portraits (ascribed to George Gower and Cornelius Ketel, 1579-83), stressing the Queen's chastity, are thought by some art historians to make propaganda points, both bolstering the argument against the match with Anjou and elaborating "the imperial theme". The magus Dr John Dee was the first writer ever to define the phrase "British Empire" in terms of sea power; he and fellow publicists, like Richard Hakluyt, urged on the Queen her country's claim to territory in the New World in defiance of Spanish imperialism. She certainly listened to Dee's affirmation of the British ancestry of the Tudor dynasty and his claim that America had been discovered by Madoc ab Owain Gwynedd, Prince of Wales. The sponsor of the iconography which reflected this campaign is thought to have been Christopher Hatton, patron to Dee and Ketel and a proponent of imperialist schemes. A new dimension was thus added to the cult of the Virgin Queen in which she was depicted as an empress who would fulfil dreams of empire for the English.

The Privy Council's efforts to disseminate a standard likeness of the Queen and to have debased copies destroyed were not uniformly successful. George Gower, who was attached to the Royal Household as Serjeant Painter from 1581 to 1596, the Herald William Segar, and the goldsmith and miniaturist, Nicholas Hilliard, were responsible for developing a "household style" which repeated a similar face-pattern, thought to have been based on one established by Federigo Zuccaro. This lasted until the end of the reign and flattered Elizabeth with a "mask of youth" which could also be reproduced without distortion by skilled copyists. The exquisite miniatures of Hilliard and Isaac Oliver were intimate objects which could be worn as costume jewellery. Hilliard's full-length portraits of the Queen were less successful than those painted "in little", and the absence of shadow on the face - a technique of the miniaturist - make his compositions more icon-like than the others. For Hilliard, Royal service brought more prestige than reward: despite the commissions he received for miniatures of Elizabeth and the courtiers and for designing a new Great Seal, he continually complained of great poverty. In his *Treatise on the Art of Limning* (about 1601) he lamented the low estimation in which artists were held in England and the inadequacy of Royal patronage compared to what they could obtain in foreign courts.

The Elizabethan Court has been seen by some cultural historians as the reception centre of the Renaissance in England. This is only partly true, and the continental humanism which impinged upon the English strain in the milieu of the Court did not travel directly from Italy. The Reformation had led to the increasing isolation of England. A contemporary phrase was "an Englishman Italianate is the Devil incarnate", and the Protestant English attitude to things Italian was tinged with suspicion and ambivalence. From the foundation of the dynasty, Tudor Court culture and the organization of the Royal Household had owed more to Burgundian and French models. Elizabeth and many of her courtiers spoke Italian fluently and Leicester sponsored translations into English of Italian books on such courtly subjects as equestrianism. The Italian mannerist painter, Federigo Zuccaro, visited England in the summer of 1575, probably at Leicester's invitation, and drew sketches for full-length portraits of the Queen and the Earl (the paintings themselves, if they were ever finished, have not survived). There were very few direct contacts between the two countries in this reign. Only spies and Catholic exiles made the journey to

Rome, and no prominent Englishman made the Grand Tour after Sir Philip Sidney in 1572 and the Earl of Oxford, who left without the Queen's permission, in the following year.

Nicholas Hilliard has left an account of a sitting Elizabeth gave him about 1572 for one of his miniature portraits. Her only recorded statement of any aesthetic curiosity was singularly ill-informed about Italian *chioroscuro*, for she was under the impression that "the Italians, who had the name to be the cunningest and to draw best, shadowed not". There is little evidence of any connoisseurship on her part or indeed on that of any of her courtiers. Leicester, Burghley, and others had large collections of pictures in their houses, including portraits of contemporary popes and Catholic grandees, but these seem to have been chosen for their subject matter rather than their quality or the reputation of the artists. In 1571, Burghley received an offer from Nicholas Houel, the Parisian apothecary who acted as art dealer to Catherine de Medici, Regent of France, to supply Elizabeth with a collection of paintings and prints, including work by Albrecht Durer. The offer was not taken up, and for whatever reason Houel's expectation that the Queen of England would be a collector of the fine arts was disappointed. England was not

● Frontispiece to *General and Rare Memorials pertayning to the Perfect Arte of Navigation* by John Dee, 1577.

to have a Royal gallery of paintings on the grand scale until Charles I bought the Gonzaga collection from the bankrupt Duke of Mantua.

The cult of the Virgin Queen in all its forms involved Elizabeth as inspirer rather than active patron of artistic endeavour. She received many dedications — of poetry, musical compositions, and books — passively, and not always with appreciation when over-solicitous suitors for the royal bounty ventured into print without securing prior permission. Apart perhaps from the portraits, there is little evidence of royal initiative taken in commissioning original works of art or of learning. The records of the Revels Account show how much was dispensed in official rewards to actors and musicians on festive occasions; and the few instances of state pensions being granted - sparingly and belated - to Edmund Spenser and Nicholas Hilliard. Elizabeth's aestheticism is as elusive of definition as her religion, and is perhaps revealed best in the dresses she wore - which were not always as ornate or as colourful as those worn in her portraits - and in the conservative yet restrained liturgy she preferred to observe in the Royal Chapel. If anything, we know more about her learning, musical skill, and gift for languages, which she liked to boast about. As a "blue-stocking" and one of the best educated women of the century, she enjoyed the company of cultivated men, though she was not particularly generous to scholars. For the most part, she was content to devolve the responsibility for what might be called "cultural patronage" to others, those courtiers in her confidence.

Burghley and Leicester were chancellors respectively of the universities of Cambridge and Oxford, where, as the Queen's representatives, they extended their sponsorship to scholars and clergy who were reconciled to the religious settlement. In this way, the pattern of Court patronage in the world of learning as well as politics was determined by the Queen's choice of men to serve her in complementary capacities. The London households of Leicester and Burghley were not so much rival centres of patronage as subsidiary courts which complemented without overshadowing the Royal Court. Cecil House in Strand during his Mastership of the Court of Wards formed an informal academy, with resident tutors for those scions of the aristocracy who were in his own charge. (Though not always with successful results as far as their education in the state religion and the royal service was concerned: a number of his wards turned out to be dissolute, Catholic, or rebellious — as witness the earls of Oxford, Essex and Southampton.) Likewise, Leicester House in London was frequented by men of letters — not just the puritan publicists who dedicated their books to the Earl, but Edmund Spenser and Gabriel Harvey, who were university men rather than "Court poets". In 1582, the grammarian, Richard Mulcaster, dedicated his *Elementarie* to Leicester, as "a very mean sacrifice for so great a saint", for "there is no one to compare with him about the Queen either for the encouraging of students to the attainment of learning, or for helping the learned to advancement of living".

Court culture as idealized by Castiglione in *The Courtier* (translated into English by Sir Thomas Hoby in 1561) and as practised by Elizabeth's courtiers, fostered the noble amateur and despised the professional. Court poets like Sidney thought it beneath their dignity to publish their verses; they circulated them in manuscript among friends before they could be persuaded to commit them to print. It was no part of the function of literary patronage to encourage a class of professional writers. When writers, like George Gascoigne and Edmund Spenser, dedicated their works to Elizabeth, they expected not honours in recognition of their achievement as men of letters, but employment under the Crown. In both cases, it was Leicester and not the Queen who offered a livelihood, however short-lived. After the Earl's death in 1588, Spenser was bereft of a patron: the publication of *The Faerie Queene* (1590), the epic which has immortalized the Elizabethan Court in its idealized form, did not bring the expected reward. The poet blamed this neglect on Burghley, and in the poem *The Ruins of Time* tactlessly condemned the Cecilian monopoly of patronage which would not countenance a career open to the talents. The elder Cecil,

> ... broad spreading like an aged tree Lets none shoot up that nigh him planted be.

Despite this outburst, he did receive an annual pension of £50 in 1591. But the most active literary patronage extended even by Leicester was to prose works of an edifying or practical character. The creative arts of the so-called Elizabethan Renaissance were a by-product of the Court, and there was nothing of a formal design about its growth as a centre for learning and "high culture", a meeting place for patrons. The Huguenot politician, Hubert Languet, was less impressed than most visitors by what he witnessed at the English Court in 1579, finding its habits "unmanly" and its courtesy "affected". Languet's contact was Philip Sidney, whom he had introduced to a number of European scholars, and between them Sidney and Leicester maintained links with the intellectual leaders of what might be called the "Calvinist International". Sidney was the true Maecenas of those Elizabethan poets, who were also Protestant humanists, and yet his circle is associated less with the environs of the Court than with hospitality at the family home, Penshurst, and at Wilton House, the home of his sister, Mary, Countess of Pembroke.

The patronage extended by the Court to the drama in this reign was actuated as much by the need to entertain and pay tribute to the Queen as by the prestige it conferred on the patron. The company of players formed by great lords protected them against the rigours of the laws against vagabonds, travelling minstrels, and players of interludes. The Earl of Leicester's Men, the first of such companies, was founded in 1559 and in 1573 they petitioned the Earl to be allowed to wear his livery as household servants. They did not thereby become salaried servants of their lord — they survived on their box-office takings — but they enjoyed his protection against the puritans, Leicester's other clients, who attacked plays and acting as sinful, and the City of London authorities, who objected to the playhouses as meeting places for the criminal underworld. These early theatres were also a health hazard, and were closed down in times of plague. What saved them from complete closure, which is what London magistrates and the puritans clamoured for, were the "Royal command performances" held in the palaces during the winter months, especially the 12 days of Christmas. In exchange for this service, the patrons procured licences from the Crown to enable their companies to travel around the countryside in the summer.

In 1583, a Royal company — the Queen's Men — was formed of the best available actors, who thereby, as Grooms of the Chamber, became members of the Royal Household, though they did not have a monopoly of performances at Court. The most famous company of all, to which Shakespeare belonged, was the Lord Chamberlain's Men. Shortly after the accession of James I, this company was re-formed as the King's Men, and Shakespeare and his fellow actors became liveried Royal servants and, in a sense, minor courtiers. The plays of Shakespeare, Marlowe, and the other great dramatists were, of course, the most original of the age, but they were not the most fashionable or successful of those performed at Court, where plays in the classical mode and masques continued to appeal to Royal and aristocratic tastes. The great flowering of English Renaissance drama was incidental to the literary concerns and aestheticism of royalty and courtiers.

If Shakespeare's genius was celebrated by contemporary writers, such as Francis Meres and Ben Jonson, there is no record of a comparable appreciation

● OPPOSITE: Robert Devereux, Earl of Essex, by William Segar.
NATIONAL GALLERY OF IRELAND.

of a professional on the part of the courtly dilettanti. In that hierarchical age, there is little sign that the select audience of the Court was anything but diverted by what was intended as ephemeral entertainment. There is a story that relates how Elizabeth was so fascinated by the character of Falstaff in the Shakespeare History plays that she prevailed on the dramatist to write a sequel showing Falstaff in love, hence *The Merry Wives of Windsor*. It is a pretty tale, but most likely apocryphal. In his History plays, Shakespeare did contribute to the propagation of the Tudor myth, with its claim that the dynasty had replaced the chaos of the "Wars of the Roses" with social harmony and political stability. But he did not address the cult of Elizabeth herself, except in an oblique way on one occasion, in a posthumous tribute. At the end of *King Henry the Eighth*, of which Shakespeare is believed to be joint author, Archbishop Cranmer christens the infant Elizabeth and utters a prophecy:

This Royal infant — heaven still move
   about her —
Though in her cradle, yet now
   promises
Upon this land a thousand thousand
   blessings,
Which time shall bring to ripeness ...
A pattern to all princes living with
   her ...
In her days every man shall eat in
   safety
Under his own vine what he plants,
   and
Sing the merry songs of peace to all
   his neighbours ...
Nor shall this peace sleep with her;
   but as when
The bird of wonder dies, the maiden
   phoenix,
Her ashes new create another heir
As great in admiration as herself.

The heir was, of course, James I, Shakespeare's Royal patron. Though Renaissance courts provide the setting for many contemporary plays, including Shakespeare's, the world of the Elizabethan Court is captured only in the literature of idealized chivalry which it inspired — particularly the epic poetry of Sidney and Spenser — and which is replete with its own arcane symbolism.

Dr Roberts is lecturer in History at the University of Kent

124,000 CANNON BALLS

Sir Francis Drake's physique was rather like the ships he sailed in, stout and strong, and at York's Friargate Museum your guide for our 1988 Exhibition, The Armada and After, has been chosen for his close resemblance to the man Queen Elizabeth I once called a pirate.

The Exhibition will be situated in Friargate's history gallery and visitors will enter through the moving hull of Drake's ship, the Revenge, to the accompaniment of seagulls, gun fire, and the aromas of the sea. Artefacts of the period and costumes will be on display, and a full-sized figure of Drake, sculptured by a top London artist, will be seen accepting Queen Elizabeth I's welcome on his triumphant return to England.

Queen Elizabeth I in her stunning "Armada dress", which cost £2,000 to reproduce, is watched over by her parents, Henry VIII and Anne Boleyn. Mary, Queen of Scots, whose execution incited anger in the King of Spain, can also be seen.

Friargate, York's award winning Museum's original approach to all their Exhibitions makes a visit a must in 1988 to pay your respects to one of Britain's greatest heroes, Drake.

About 124,000 cannon balls were fired by the Spanish Fleet during the engagement. This and many other absorbing details are free and available from Mrs Wendy Skelton, The Friargate Museum, York. (0904) 658775

ARMADA 1588 – TILBURY FORT 1988

HISTORY. WHERE IT HAPPENED

This year English Heritage also celebrates the Armada Invasion at Tilbury Fort, Essex. The very site where Queen Elizabeth I rallied her troops at the time of the conflict. We'll take you back 400 years in one of our exciting living exhibitions – exhibitions that bring alive the sights, smells and sounds of distant times.

Other English Heritage exhibitions bring different times and events to life – at Berwick Barracks in Northumberland see the award-winning 'By Beat of Drum' exhibition on life in the British Infantry 1660-1880. At Dover Castle, Kent, 'All the Queen's Men' re-creates distant battles and past glory of The Queen's Regiment.

These are only a few of the many special events, festivals and exhibitions being held at English Heritage properties throughout England this year.

Meet the Romans at Corbridge Roman Fort, Northumberland. In Yorkshire watch the Normans invade Scarborough Castle again and at our Celebration of Yorkshire Abbeys discover medieval fairs, Punch and Judy shows, morality plays and music at beautiful monastic sites like Rievaulx and Whitby Abbeys.

With over 350 historic properties in our care, English Heritage give you more than a taste of history; we help you relive the past – where it happened.

For more information see your local Tourist Information Centre or for details on special events, exhibitions and membership contact Coral Sealey, Special Events Unit, English Heritage, 15/17 Great Marlborough Street, London W1A 1AF. Telephone: 01-734 6010.

English ⊞ Heritage

THE GUIDE TO THE EXHIBITION

Sponsored by Pearson plc

PATRON: HER MAJESTY THE QUEEN

Stephen Deuchar, of the National Maritime Museum, takes us through the Armada Exhibition.

THE EXHIBITION WILL BE AT THE NATIONAL MARITIME MUSEUM, GREENWICH, FROM 20 APRIL TO 4 SEPTEMBER 1988 AND AT THE ULSTER MUSEUM, BOTANIC GARDENS, BELFAST, FROM 12 OCTOBER 1988 TO 8 JANUARY 1989

THE NATIONAL Maritime Museum's Armada Exhibition, which opened in Greenwich in spring 1988 and transfers to Ulster in the autumn, is the world's only comprehensive visual celebration of the quatercentenary. The Exhibition aims to entertain and inform — to draw out the excitement of the Armada story and at the same time to promote a greater understanding of its background, cause, course, and effect. The year 1588 is viewed in the context of the 16th century as a whole, and the Anglo-Spanish confrontation is presented in relation to wider movements in contemporary European history.

The story is told by the exhibits — a spectacular array of more than 500 original artefacts lent by 80 museums and individuals from a dozen countries. The objects stand not just as an impressive physical record of what happened in 1588, how it happened, who was involved and why. Some of them also provide clues to how modern-day perceptions of the Armada story have been fashioned: for the conventional, but simplistic, view that has endured in England — representing the event as a triumph of bravery over insolence, of skill over audacity, of right over wrong — derives in part from the imagery produced during the anti-Spanish propaganda campaign that began in 1588 and intensified thereafter. In drawing out the full significance of Armada artefacts, and in presenting them objectively in their full and proper context, the Exhibition shows that the reality is more complex, but more appealing, than the myths with which we have become so familiar.

The Exhibition is divided into 16 sections, which are summarized in this Guide together with a small selection of illustrations of the exhibits themselves. The information given here is drawn from the Exhibition's official catalogue, published by Penguin Books and

available at the Exhibition for £10.95. The catalogue has been written by 32 experts from the Museum and elsewhere, and contains more than 400 illustrations, many in colour. As well as including detailed information on the objects on display, based on the latest research, there is a substantial introduction by Mía Rodríguez-Salgado (lecturer in International History at the London School of Economics and the Exhibition's historian) which explores Philip II's motives and preparations for the launch of the Armada.

The National Maritime Museum, Greenwich

The NMM opened in 1937 at Greenwich, birthplace of Queen Elizabeth I. It contains the world's most comprehensive collection of maritime art and artefacts, and its buildings are considerable historic interest. At its heart lies the Queen's House, a Royal palace designed by Inigo Jones in the early 17th century. The main Museum galleries are situated in the West Wing (right), and the Armada Exhibition occupies the entire East Wing (left).

Section 1: ENGLAND AND SPAIN BEFORE THE WAR

Throughout much of the 16th century, England and Spain were allies, not enemies. The Spanish Catherine of Aragon married Henry VIII in 1509, and their daughter, Mary, was twice betrothed to the Emperor Charles V, Philip's father, before marrying his heir, Philip of Spain, as Queen of England. Though the prolonged Anglo-Spanish alliance was often tense (notably during Henry VIII's divorce from Catherine and consequent confrontation with Rome) it was sustained largely by both countries' enmity towards France. The Exhibition's opening section focuses on the period of Philip's marriage to Mary (1554-58). Although one of Philip's companions during his sporadic visits to England at this time noted "the English like us Spaniards as much as they like the devil — and they treat us accordingly", the King and his advisers were aware of the value of his dynastic link with the English Monarchy. After Mary's death he even made a proposal of marriage to her successor, Elizabeth I. Influence over England was, he believed, not only the key to successful defence against France and supremacy in the Netherlands, but the means through which he might effect the country's return to the Catholic fold.

Cat. no. 1.1

Allegory of the Tudor Succession, attributed to Lucas de Heere (1534-84),

c.1572. Oil on panel (1295x1803mm). *Trustees of the Sudeley Collection, Sudeley Castle*

This didactic painting eulogizes Elizabeth I and criticizes her sister's earlier marriage with Philip II. On the left, Mary and Philip draw in Mars (the god of War), a reference to the war with Henry II of France which, through Philip, involved England. On the right, meanwhile, Elizabeth is linked with the figures of Peace and Plenty. Mary thereby implicitly disappoints her father, Henry VIII, while Elizabeth by contrast is represented as his worthy successor.

Cat. no. 1.3

Mary I of England and Philip II of Spain, by an English copyist, 17th century. Oil on canvas (990x762mm). *National Maritime Museum*

A 17th century copy of the 16th century panel painting at Woburn Abbey, this image (unlike no. 1.1) records the union

between England and Spain without criticism. The inscription celebrates Philip and Mary's combined domains in 1558, though the composition itself probably dates from 1554, the year of their marriage.

Cat. no. 1.18

Bust of Philip II (1527-98), attributed to Leone Leoni (1509-90), c.1554. Bronze (889mm height). *Her Majesty The Queen*

This important sculpture, inscribed *PHI. REX. ANGL*, was produced at the time of the sitter's marriage to Mary Tudor. It is evidently a pair to cat. no. 6.2, a bust of the Duke of Alba, also lent to the Exhibition by Her Majesty The Queen.

Section 2: POLITICAL AND RELIGIOUS DIVISIONS IN EUROPE

England's relationship with Spain was but a small piece in the wider jigsaw of 16th century European politics. Economic, strategic, and religious rivalries created a complex web of ever-shifting alliances and international tensions. Many causes were pursued, as they have always been, in the name of religion. Catholic and Protestant spheres of influence were fairly evenly matched, but there was little conspicuous political unity within either camp. Each was torn by its own internal divisions and competing ambitions. The papacy, for example, offered moral

support to the objectives of the Catholic Philip II, but privately feared his increasing power, especially in Italy. Lutheran and Calvinist regions, meanwhile, tended to mistrust each other — and both were suspicious of Anglicanism. Part of France sought friendship with Protestant England, and part with Catholic Spain. It was from a background of circumstances such as these — the focus of the Exhibition's second section — that the steady deterioration of Anglo-Spanish relations developed.

Cat. no. 2.1

Pope Sixtus V (1521-90), by an unidentified Venetian artist, c.1588-90. Oil on canvas (1608x1090mm). *The Vatican Museums*

This is the best-known contemporary painting of Sixtus V. He was the successor to Gregory XIII and an international politician of great aptitude, confidence, and guile, determined to extend the scope of Catholic control into the Muslim and Protestant worlds. He urged Philip II to act against England, but avoided paying for the cost of the expedition, promising him instead a million *scudi* should it succeed.

Cat. no. 2.6

The St Bartholomew's Eve Massacre, 1572, by François Dubois (1529-84), c.1575-80. Oil on panel (940x1540mm). *Musée Cantonal des Beaux-Arts, Lausanne*

About 3,000 Huguenots were

91

massacred by a Catholic mob in Paris on the night of August 23-24, 1572 in one of the bloodiest episodes in the French Wars of Religion, graphically recorded here by a Huguenot painter who fled to Geneva in its wake. The murder of the Huguenot leader, Coligny, is depicted in the centre; the figure in black in the left background, overlooking a pile of bodies, represents Catherine de Médici.

Cat. no. 2.24

Catherine de Médici (1519-89), from the studio of François Clouet (c.1510-72), c.1560. Oil on panel (239x191mm).
Musée Carnavalet, Paris

The sitter was the wife of Henry II of France, and later the adviser and Regent to her sons, Francis II, Charles IX, and Henry III. Ruthless and politically adept, she remained Catholic throughout the French Wars, but tried to

▼

promote compromise between the competing factions. The picture's striking marquetry frame is early-17th century Flemish.

Cat. no. 2.32

The Battle of Lepanto, October 7, 1571, by H Letter, c.1572. Oil on canvas (1265x2338mm).
National Maritime Museum

This famous sea battle followed the papacy's formation of a Holy League of Christian allies to check Ottoman expansion in the Mediterranean. The Turkish fleet lost 180 vessels and more

▼

than 25,000 men at the hands of the Christian fleet under Don John of Austria. The painting features the clash between the squadron of the Genoese Gianandrea Doria and an enemy squadron under the King of Algiers. The Spanish role in the Christian victory was fundamental.

Cat. no. 2.35

Votive model of the "Real" galley of Lepanto, late-16th century. Wood (1140x660mm).
Museu Marítim de Barcelona

The large crucifix carried at Lepanto by

▲ the *Real* of Don John is preserved in Barcelona cathedral. This *ex-voto* (or thank offering) ship model was placed beside it, and is presumed to be a loose representation of the *Real* herself. Though inaccurate in many points of detail, the model gives a good idea of the form of 16th century galleys.

Cat. no. 2.48

The execution of Mary, Queen of Scots, by a Netherlandish artist, c.1613. Watercolour (219x264mm).
Scottish National Portrait Gallery

The Catholic Mary, Queen of Scots' claim to the English Throne was

▲
Cat. no. 2.18
Crucifix from the *Girona*. Bronze (81mm length).
Ulster Museum, Belfast

This small and simple bronze cross, retrieved from the wreck of an Armada ship, is typical of the kind carried to war by individual soldiers and sailors. Like several campaigns in 16th century Europe, the action against England was perceived by many of its participants as a kind of crusade.

...erminated by her execution for treason on February 18, 1587. The event cleared the way for Philip's own claim to the Throne, though his plans to invade were already well advanced when it occurred. Mary is portrayed clutching a crucifix, while outside her garments are burned to prevent their use as relics.

Section 3: THE COURT OF ELIZABETH I

This part of the Exhibition provides a summary visual survey of the English Court at the time of the Armada. At its centre is a large tableau, designed by Martyn Bainbridge, giving a composite interior and exterior view of Greenwich Palace — Elizabeth's birthplace and one of the most favoured of the group of

Royal palaces frequented by the Court. By contrast with its counterpart in Spain (Section 4), the English Court was culturally insular if rich in pageantry. England's physical isolation from the rest of Europe and the unmarried Elizabeth's dynastic independence from continental family networks promoted the growth of a distinctive form of courtly culture: it celebrated the Queen as the personification of glory, adored by her courtiers, and her England as a golden age of domestic harmony and potential international might. Myth-making, as ever, was at its most intense when Crown and country were under greatest threat, and as tensions with Spain rose so too did the cultivation of Elizabeth's status as national heroine and rightful "empresse of the world".

Cat. no. 3.3
William Cecil, 1st Baron Burghley (1520-98), by an unidentified English painter, c.1580. Oil on canvas (1310x1130mm).
Curators of the Bodleian Library, Oxford

Burghley was Lord High Treasurer and Elizabeth's chief minister from 1572, closely involved with international

affairs in general and the Armada preparations in particular. The mule on which he rides symbolizes constancy, loyalty, fortitude, and nobility.

Cat. no. 3.5
Elizabeth greeting Dutch emissaries, by an unidentified Netherlandish or German artist, c.1585. Gouache (244x375mm).
Staatliche Kunstsammlungen, Kassel

A rare view of an Elizabethan Court interior hosting not a pageant but a state meeting. The emissaries are identified by the inscription as Vestlan

and Walbrun; Walsingham, Leicester, Howard, and Mary, Queen of Scots are also present. Mary's inclusion suggests that the picture was a commentary on her influence on English negotiations regarding Spain and the Netherlands.

Cat. no. 3.18
A lead-glazed earthenware candle-sconce, late-16th century (395x272mm).
Trustees of the British Museum

This is one of a number of objects in the Exhibition's third section representative of the range of craftsmanship in Elizabethan England.

Cat. no. 3.22

Elizabeth I: the "Sieve" portrait, attributed to Cornelius Ketel (1548-1616), c.1580-3. Oil on canvas (1245x915mm).

Pinacoteca Nazionale, Siena

The sieve is a symbol of chastity — the basis, it is suggested, of Elizabeth's godliness and mystique through which she is morally equipped to build a world empire. The picture may have been commissioned by Sir Christopher Hatton, an exponent of the Queen's right to imperial power; he is portrayed in the centre of the group in the right background.

Section 4: THE COURT OF PHILIP II

At the heart of the fourth gallery lies the Exhibition's second tableau: it features a complete scale model of Philip II's palace of San Lorenzo el Real de El Escorial and accurately reconstructs the King's private study. The Escorial was conceived in the late 1550s and built between 1563-84. Dedicated to St Lawrence, its formal purpose was to thank God for His guidance at the start of Philip's reign and to elicit divine favour in the future. It was a palace, monastery, school, seminary, and family mausoleum all in one. As the home of Philip's Court — and some of the machinery of government too — its size and awesome splendour contrasted with the humbler milieux of the Elizabethan Court in England. The building and the lifestyle of the Spanish Court closely reflected the King's own tastes: on one hand, it was lavishly furnished, and provided the setting for his great collection of paintings, books, and relics; on the other hand, austerity, restraint, and moderation in behaviour were encouraged among the courtiers who resided there. It was from the Escorial that the final invasion plan of the Armada was approved by the King.

Cat. no. 4.4

Don Fernando (1571-8), by Alonso Sánchez Coello (1531/2-88). Oil on canvas (1199x998mm), 1577.

Patrimonio Nacional. Monasterio de las Descalzas Reales

Don Fernando was the eldest son of Philip II and Anne of Austria and one of many Royal children about the Spanish Court. He died shortly after the picture was painted. Sánchez Coello was a favourite of Philip II and painted several other members of the household (e g cat. nos. 4.2 and 4.3).

Cat. no. 4.7

Philip II (1527-98), attributed to Sofonisba Anguisciola (c.1530-1626) c.1580. Oil on canvas (880x720mm). *Museo del Prado, Madrid*

The austerely dressed King is portray holding a rosary, aptly bearing out th virtues of restraint and devotion encouraged at his Court. The artist w one of six painter sisters from Crem

94

Cat. no. 4.12

The Escorial under construction, attributed to Juan de Herrera (c.1530-97). Pen and wash drawing (508x775mm).
The Marquess of Salisbury

Juan de Herrera was principal architect of the Escorial after 1567. The building's main facade is shown in the foreground; the completed monastery is on the left; the college and seminary are depicted in progress on the right. The drawing was acquired by Elizabeth I's chief minister, Lord Burghley.

Cat. no. 4.18

Writer's set belonging to Philip II. Bronze, wood, and velvet (140x350x100).
Patrimonio Nacional. Real Monasterio de El Escorial

This exhibit, one of a group lent to the Exhibition from the Escorial, is normally kept today in Philip II's study. The *escribanía* is decorated with engravings of Philip's arms and the gridiron — the symbol of St Lawrence, on which he was roasted to death.

Section 5: THE SPANISH EMPIRE

The extent of Spain's world territorial possessions was the backbone of Philip II's international power and also the source of his greatest potential weakness. As well as his kingdoms in the Iberian peninsula (including Portugal after 1580), he held land elsewhere in Europe, in Africa, and above all in the New World. Such a diverse range of territory was all but impossible to control and administer effectively from Spain alone. The economic advantages of trade opportunities were outweighed by the sheer insufficiency of the Crown's income to meet the costs of running and maintaining so large an empire. France and the Ottomans provided the most consistent strategic threat to Philip's possessions. Meanwhile, the piratical campaigns against New World shipping undertaken by Englishmen such as Drake — acting sometimes with and sometimes without the backing of Elizabeth — were by the 1580s beginning to represent a real economic problem rather than a mere irritant. Moreover, they compromised Philip's reputation and authority, and helped to convince him of the need to invade England.

Cat. no. 5.1

World chart by Sebastião Lopes (fl.1558-96), c.1585. Four coloured MS sheets (2180x1145mm overall); scale c.1:1,850,000.
Bibliothèque Nationale, Paris

This shows the extent of Philip's empire after the conquest of Portugal in 1580. Among several recently-acquired Spanish territories are the Phillipines (1565), named after the King. The 15 flying crescents denote Arab power, a source of great concern to Spain.

Cat. no. 5.19

Plan of the attack on Cadiz, April 29, 1587 by William Borough (1537-98). Pen and watercolour (460x360mm).
Public Record Office, London

Sir Francis Drake's assaults on Spanish interests and territory worldwide began in earnest in the 1570s. His raid on Cadiz in 1587 remains his best-remembered single action: it led to the sinking or capture of more than 20 Spanish ships and helped to postpone the sailing of the Armada until 1588. This map, prepared by Drake's vice-admiral, William Borough, defended its maker against charges of cowardice by suggesting that the *Lion*, under Borough's command (marked at *b*, *f*, and *J*), was in the thick of the fighting.

Section 6: WAR AND REBELLION IN THE NETHERLANDS

The Netherlands proved to be the most troublesome of all Philip's possessions abroad, and their revolt against Spanish control became the forum for the most direct confrontation between England and Spain in the years leading up to 1588. The Protestant faction in the Netherlands and the long-established Dutch nobility each had their own reasons for resenting Spanish control: the former were affronted by Philip's dogmatic Catholicism and insistence on imposing it on their homeland, the latter by a foreign overlord's threat to their traditional social and economic privileges. Outbreaks of violence led Philip to send in an army of 10,000 men under the Duke of Alba in 1566. Alba's severe suppression of dissent brought new waves of unrest which in turn encouraged France and England to exploit Spain's difficulty in controlling their unstable neighbour. Elizabeth's discreet support to the rebel cause gave way in 1585 to open aid in the form of the Earl of Leicester and an English army — a provocative act against Spain which Philip could tolerate no longer. Though Leicester returned home in January 1588, Philip's campaign against England was finalized. The Armada was preparing to sail.

Cat. no. 6.1

An allegory of the tyranny of the Duke of Alba, by a Netherlandish artist, late-16th century. Oil on panel (1200x1920mm).
Stedelijk Museum Het Prinsenhof, Delft

Alba was sent by Philip II to restore order in the Netherlands. His harsh rule was bitterly unpopular, and this painting took its part in the propaganda campaign organized by the rebels. Alba, enthroned on the left, is crowned by the Devil. The chained kneeling figures represent the Seventeen

▼

Provinces, with members of the nobility passively looking on. In the background are scenes of torture and hanging.

Cat. no. 6.4

William of Nassau, Prince of Orange (1533-84), attributed to Adriaen Thomasz. Key (1544-c.1589), c.1579. Oil on panel (480x340mm).
Royal Cabinet of Paintings, Mauritshuis, The Hague

William of Orange became the best known opponent to the Spanish presence in the Netherlands. His essentially moderate stance may have alienated him from the more extreme Calvinist rebels, but the Estates of Holland invited him to become their governor in 1572, in place of Philip II. Although he was to be the leading figure of what in 1579 became the United Provinces, he never attempted to make himself their sovereign ruler.

▼

▲

Cat. no. 6.13

The Prince of Orange milking the cow of the Netherlands, by an English or Dutch artist, c.1583-4. Oil on panel (520x670mm).
Rijksmuseum, Amsterdam

This allegorical picture is evidence of Protestant opposition to religious compromise in the Netherlands and warns against attempts to exploit or control the rebel provinces.
The cow of Flanders is given essential sustenance by Elizabeth (left), but is milked by William of Orange (lower centre) and antagonized by the Duc d'Anjou (right).
Philip II, meanwhile, unwisely attempts to control the cow by riding it.

Section 7: RIVAL ARMIES

The principal objective of the Armada was to safeguard the passage of the Duke of Parma's 17,000 troops from the Netherlands to England. In addition, it carried its own supporting army of some 20,000 soldiers. Once the invasion force had landed, it would be up to Parma and the commander of the Armada, the Duke of Medina Sidonia, to decide what role the fleet would play henceforth. The English were uncertain precisely where along the coast the Spanish would attempt to land. Several thousand men were brought to London to protect the Queen; and 17,000 infantry were massed at Tilbury under the Earl of Leicester to guard against an attack up the Thames. The southern maritime counties of England, meanwhile, mobilized a militia nominally 29,500 strong, and county forces further north also made preparations. At its peak, the defence forces may have reached almost 76,000, greatly outnumbering their opponents, although many of the English troops were ill-trained and poorly armed. It is impossible to know what would have happened had the invasion succeeded, but it is clear that the Spanish planned to lay siege to many towns, and most were patently ill-equipped to withstand this kind of assault. The seventh section of the Exhibition surveys in some detail the potential clash between the armies of England and Spain.

▲
Cat. no. 7.5
Parade helmet of Alessandro Farnese, Duke of Parma (1545-92). Steel damascened and embossed with gold and silver (300x240mm). *Kunsthistorisches Museum, Vienna*

This is from the suit of parade armour reputedly given to Parma by Philip II. Armour of this kind was intended for public display rather than use in battle. The helmet is of the burgonet type, and its decoration embodies a mixture of Classical and Christian symbolism.

Cat. no. 7.6
Parade shield of Alessandro Farnese, Duke of Parma (1545-92). Steel damascened and embossed with gold and silver (650x500mm). *Kunsthistorisches Museum, Vienna*

Like cat. no. 7.5, this shield was formerly part of the armour collection of Archduke Ferdinand II of Tyrol (1529-95), purchased by him from the Duke of Parma. The central panel shows Alexander the Great receiving the keys of Babylon, thereby linking Parma (Alessandro) with the theme of military conquest.

Cat. no. 7.24
Spanish priming flask, late-16th century. Iron and leather (130x90mm). *Museo Archeólogico Nacional, Madrid*

▼

This flask of the Armada period held the fine gunpowder used for priming firearms. It is one of a group of Spanish military artefacts lent to the Exhibition by the Archeological Museum in Madrid.

Cat. no. 7.42
Armour for the tilt of Robert Dudley, Earl of Leicester, made for him by John Kelte (fl.1552-76) in the Royal Workshop at Greenwich, c.1575. Steel (1778mm height). *Trustees of the Royal Armouries, London*

Probably made for the entertainment given by Leicester for Elizabeth I at Kenilworth in 1575. The badge of the Order of the Garter, flanked by Leicester's initials, lies at the centre of the upper part of the breastplate. Leicester served as commander of the English army in the Netherlands and during the Armada campaign: by 1588 he was in poor health, however, and he died before the victory celebrations were over.

▼

Section 8: RIVAL FLEETS

This part of the Exhibition compares the form and capabilities of the English and Spanish fleets. Among the exhibits are three specially commissioned 1:96 scale models — of a Spanish galleon (no. 8.1), an English galleon (no. 8.3), and an English pinnace (no. 8.4) — based on the Maritime Museum's latest research into 16th century ship design. The models are displayed among a wealth of original contemporary material, providing a narrative of the fleets' preparations to confront one another. The David and Goliath myth is dispelled: the total number of English ships mobilized in 1588 was 226 (34 royal ships and 192 privately owned) compared to the 151 of the Armada (27 belonging to the Crown and the remainder drafted into Royal service, requisitioned, or hired). The English ships were generally smaller, however, but on balance the fleets were very evenly matched.

▲
Cat. no. 8.2
Spanish votive ship model, 16th century. Wood and iron (1115x420x350mm).
Museo Naval, Madrid

Votive ship models were used to seek divine favour for a forthcoming voyage, or to give thanks for one safely completed. This model represents a multi-purpose *nao* of the type that sailed on Spanish trade routes worldwide and also participated in armadas (Royal fleets).

Cat. no. 8.5
Page from *Fragments of Ancient English Shipwrightry*. Photograph of MS by Matthew Baker (c.1530-1613) and others, in Pepys Library.
By permission of the Masters and Fellows of Magdalene College, Cambridge

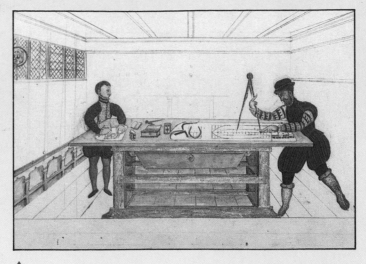

▲
Baker's manuscript is exhibited in photographic form. It is the earliest known English shipbuilding treatise. Baker was a Royal master shipwright; his drawings of ships are the clearest and most accurate extant representations of Elizabethan warships.

Cat. no. 8.29
***Fanal* (lantern) used from c.1570 on *La Galera Capitana* of the Marquis**
▼

of Santa Cruz. Wood, glass, and brass (1870x700x700mm).
La Marquesa de Santa Cruz

The purpose of ships' lanterns of this kind was largely to denote the high rank of their owners, but they were also used for station keeping at night. In peacetime, Santa Cruz kept this lantern, an exceptional piece of craftsmanship, in his chapel beside examples he had captured from enemy commanders.

Section 9: ORDNANCE

The Armada was an invasion force as well as a navy, and it brought with it a great range of heavy weapons for use on land and at sea. In all, when the Armada first left Lisbon it carried 2,431 pieces of artillery. Originally, this was thought to outweigh the armament aboard the English ships: in fact, the total Spanish armament weighed about one-third less than that of the fleet it sought to overcome. The old belief that the battle was essentially a contest between short Spanish "cannon" guns firing heavy shot a small distance, and long English "culverin" types firing light shot at longer range, can also be disproven. More decisive may have been the differences between English and Spanish gun carriage design: the English favoured four-wheeled carriages which were more manoeuvrable than their counterparts in the Armada and allowed faster reloading. Even so, the rate of gunfire during the battle would have been slow the era of massed and rapid broadside gunfire lay in the future. Care was taken in aiming single guns (though they stood little chance of hitting anything beyond about 200 yards) and firing them separately.

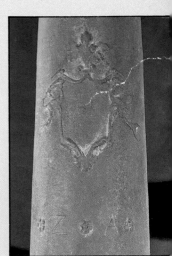

▲
Cat. no. 9.3
Long Venetian sacre from the wreck of the *Trinidad Valencera*, late-16th century. Bronze (3430mm long; 95mm calibre).
Ulster Museum, Belfast

This sacre was made by Zouanne

Alberghetti: his initials may be seen in relief towards the end of the chase. The gun must have been part of the ship's "civilian" armament when it was impounded in Sicily by Philip II's officials in January 1587.

Cat. no. 9.5

Swivel gun from the *San Juan de Sicilia*, 1563. Bronze (1372mm long; 50mm calibre).
The Museum, Charterhouse

This gun from an Armada ship was recovered from Tobermory Bay in 1905. It fired an iron shot of about 10 oz, and would have been deployed on the open deck of the ship.

Section 10: LIFE ON BOARD

The third tableau of the Exhibition is located in this section: it is a one-quarter of full size representation of an Armada ship at sea, viewed as if from the waist of an accompanying vessel. Elsewhere in Section 10, a great range of objects retrieved from the wrecks of Spanish ships — many of them the personal effects of those on board — is displayed. The *Trinidad Valencera* and the *Girona* were just two of the 20 or more Armada vessels which went down off the coast of Ireland on their way home; material excavated from their wrecks now belongs to the Ulster Museum. The selection of this material included in the Exhibition provides a fascinating record of life on board an Armada ship. Among the exhibits are bowls, plates, shoes, the neck of a stringed musical instrument, part of a birdcage, and even a brazil nut. Other finds included the skeleton of a rat, evidence of the

unhealthy living conditions endured by those who took part in the campaign.

Cat. no. 10.19

Chinese bowl from the *Trinidad Valencera*, possibly of the Wan Li

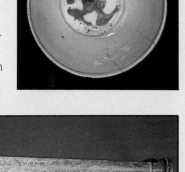

Dynasty. Porcelain (152mm diameter).
Ulster Museum, Belfast

The Spanish empire had contacts with China through Portuguese traders — presumably the means by which this bowl came into the possession of someone aboard the *Trinidad Valencera*, a converted Venetian merchant ship.

Cat. no. 10.24

Boatswain's pipe or call from the *Girona*. Silver (70mm long).
Ulster Museum, Belfast

One of the duties of the boatswain was to stay by the pilot to transmit orders to the crew by means of his whistle. This exhibit was retrieved from the wreck of the *Girona*, a galleass of the Naples squadron which sank off Lacada Point, Co. Antrim.

Cat. no. 10.47

Ear- and tooth-pick. Gold (47mm long).
Ulster Museum, Belfast

This retrieval from an Armada wreck is a luxury item which presumably belonged to a gentleman of relatively high standing. It takes the form of a dolphin: the flattened tail is the ear-pick, and the projection from the head is the tooth-pick.

Section 11: MEDICINE

Illness and disease were rife among the English and Spanish fleets. Typhus struck the seamen awaiting the Armada

at Plymouth during June 1588, and the epidemic revived more seriously — especially in the ships of Lord Howard's squadron — after the battle. There had been no hospital ships in the English fleet, and there were few adequate medical facilities ashore: many sick and dying men were discharged without pay onto the streets. Aboard the Spanish fleet there were severe medical problems too. Outbreaks of disease before the Armada sailed were contained, but, during the long and hot journey north to England on overcrowded and dirty ships, food and water became badly contaminated. Careful preparations for medical treatment had been made, but after the storms off La Coruña most of the hospital facilities were placed on one ship, the hulk *San Pedro el Mayor*, and were of little use when the fleet was later scattered by the fighting and the poor weather. The influence of disease and inadequate medicine on naval strategy should not be underestimated: both sides must have wished the battle to be concluded as swiftly as possible.

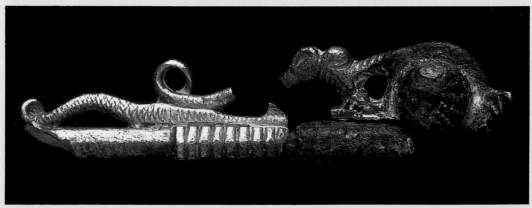

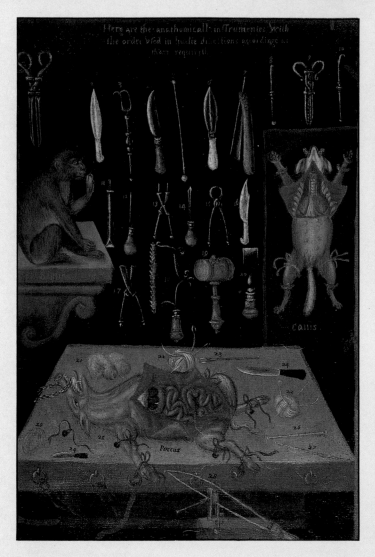

▲
Cat. no. 11.3
Anatomical Tables, by John Banester
(1540-1610), 1581. Oil on paper
(305x210mm).
Glasgow University Library

Banester was the chief surgeon on the
East Indies voyage of 1582-3. His
writings offer valuable information about
Elizabethan surgical knowledge and
practice. This Table depicts vivisection,
but also shows instruments commonly
used by Tudor surgeons, including the
saw, mallet, and chisel.

Section 12:
NAVIGATION

In the 16th century, the Spanish and
Portuguese were acknowledged leaders
in the skills of oceanic navigation. Even
so, it was expected that little of this
wealth of experience would need to be

tapped during the relatively
straightforward coasting voyage
northwards from Spain and then along
the English Channel. Furthermore,
some of Medina Sidonia's pilots were
already familiar with the route to the
Baltic through the Channel, and
instruments no more complex than a
simple compass and sounding lead
would have been strictly necessary for
each ship. Few of the pilots, however,
would have left their more sophisticated
navigational instruments behind, and in
the event they were put to full use
when the Armada was unexpectedly
forced to head for home round Scotland
and the Atlantic Ocean. Only those
ships in urgent need of repair or
reprovisioning ventured near the Irish
coast — with catastrophic results. More
than two-thirds of the Spanish fleet
returned safely to their home ports
despite the exceptionally bad weather
— some indication of the navigational
skills of their pilots and the
effectiveness of their equipment.

▲
Cat. no. 12.3
The Mariners Mirrour, by Lucas
Jansz Waghenaer (1533-1606) with a
frontispiece by Theodor de Bry. Printed
book published in London, 1588.
National Maritime Museum

In 1585, Lord Howard ordered that the
important *Spieghel der Zeevaerdt* by
Waghenaer should be published in
English. The *Spieghel* brought together
charts, sailing directions, coastal views,
and navigational tables, previously
available only separately. Publication in
England, with re-engraved plates, was
finally achieved in 1588 shortly after the
Armada campaign.

Cat. no. 12.9
Universal planispheric astrolabe,
1588. Brass- gilt (250mm diameter).
National Maritime Museum

Ordinary planispheric astrolabes could
be used to solve problems of
time-finding and position-fixing, but had

▲
to carry different plates for use in
varying latitudes. The universal
astrolabe was developed to overcome
this shortcoming. This example was
made in Augsburg in 1588.

Cat. no. 12.11
Sundial, by Christopher Schissler
(1531-1608), 1582. Brass-gilt
(76x76mm).
National Maritime Museum

This is an adjustable horizontal dial, o
of many remaining examples of the

100

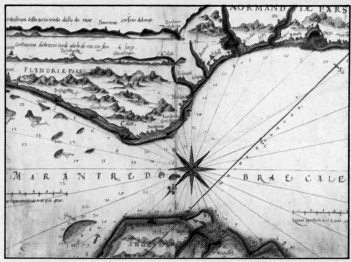

▲

work of Schissler, who was among Europe's leading instrument makers.

Cat. no. 12.22
English sandglass, 17th century. Wood and glass (365mm height).
▼

National Maritime Museum

Ships' sandglasses were used for measuring time at sea, and helped to keep a check on a vessel's progress. This glass measured the passage of one hour.

Cat. no. 12.23
Chart of Dover Strait, by Luis Teixeira (fl.1564- c.1613), c.1587. Watercolour on vellum (518x406mm).
National Maritime Museum

This is thought to be a copy from Waghenaer's *Spieghel der Zeervaert* (see no. 12.3), made in Lisbon by Teixeira for the Armada. It shows Nieuport and Dunkirk, where Parma and his troops intended to embark, and East Kent where they hoped to land.

Admiral, Charles Howard, stood in overall command with Lord Henry Seymour (stationed in the Downs) and Sir Francis Drake as vice-admirals. After the battle off the Isle of Wight, additional commanders were appointed: Howard divided the fleet into four squadrons, led by himself, Drake, Sir John Hawkins and Sir Martin Frobisher. Strategy on both sides was determined at Councils of War, often a forum for argument as well as agreement.

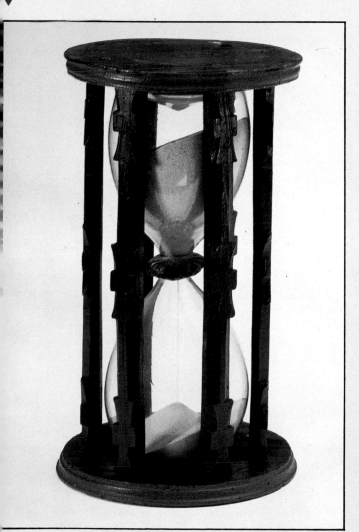

Section 13:
COMMANDERS

Although Philip II himself stood at the head of the Spanish command structure, ultimately responsible for the Armada's preparations and strategy, by 1588 the Duke of Parma and the Marquis of Santa Cruz had been appointed joint commanders-in-chief of the expedition. Santa Cruz's death in February 1588 led to his replacement by the able and experienced Duke of Medina Sidonia as Captain General of the Fleet and Army of the Ocean Sea. Medina Sidonia, matched in rank and personal wealth only by Parma, was well suited for the role. Juan Martínez Recalde was placed second in command, and was also Captain General of the Andalusian squadron. The Armada's eight other squadrons had their own commanders too. On the English side, meanwhile, the Lord

▲
· Cat. no. 13.1
The "Burgundy Cross" equestrian armour of Philip II, by Wolfgang Groschedel of Landshut (d.1562), 1551.
Patrimonio Nacional. Real Armería de Madrid

Philip II's place at the head of the Armada's command structure is marked in Section 13 by this field armour for man and horse, made for the King by a German armourer who had once worked for Henry VIII at Greenwich. It is one of an important group of loans from the Royal Armoury in Madrid.

Cat. no. 13.2

Don Alvaro de Bazán, 1st Marquis of Santa Cruz (1526-88), by an unidentified Spanish artist, c.1585-90. Oil on canvas (1246x900mm). *La Marquesa de Santa Cruz*

Don Alvaro de Bazán enjoyed a distinguished naval career, and played a crucial part in the victory at Lepanto (see no. 2.32). He was largely responsible for preparing the Armada, and his death in February 1588 was a temporary setback to Spanish plans. He is depicted here in full armour, holding a commander's baton.

Cat. no. 13.8

Cross of a Knight of the Hospital of St John of Jerusalem, from the wreck of the *Girona*. Gold and enamel (60mm long). *Ulster Museum, Belfast*

A number of personal possessions of senior officers aboard the *Girona* and the *Trinidad Valencera* are included in the Commanders section of the

Exhibition. This cross is decorated with motifs which, it has been suggested, were symbols of the family of Fabricio Spinola, the *Girona's* captain.

Cat. no. 13.15

Ring from the *Girona*. Gold (21mm diameter). *Ulster Museum, Belfast*

One of the most poignant of all recoveries from the Armada wrecks,

this ring depicts a hand holding out a heart. It is inscribed *No tengo mas que darte* (I have nothing more to give you) and may have been a farewell gift from a woman to her departing lover.

Cat. no. 13.19

Charles Howard, Lord Effingham and Earl of Nottingham (1536-1624), by Daniel Mytens (1590-1648), c.1620. Oil on canvas

(2515x1447mm). *National Maritime Museum*

Mytens' portrait of the Lord Admiral of the English Fleet was originally in the Royal Collection, and was painted at the end of Howard's long career as an admiral and a naval administrator. He is portrayed wearing Garter Robes; beyond is a representation of his flagship in action - perhaps during the Armada campaign, in which his judicious leadership played an important part in the English victory.

Cat. no. 13.21

Sir Francis Drake (?1540-96), possibly by Marcus Gheeraerts the Younger (1561-1635), dated 1594. Oil on panel (1168x915mm). *National Maritime Museum*

Such is his status as the best-known of all Elizabethan seamen, a mistaken belief persists that Drake led the English fleet against the Armada and was singlehandedly responsible for the victory. In fact, his great contemporary fame rested largely on his historic voyage of circumnavigation (1577-80), and on his raids against Spanish territories and shipping in the 1580s which both prompted and then delayed the sailing of the Armada. He captained the *Revenge* during the 1588 campaign itself (see Section 14). He was to suffer a court martial and five years of disgrace after his leadership of the ill-organized Portugal expedition of 1589, in which several thousand English sailors and soldiers died.

Cat. no. 13.27
Sir Martin Frobisher (c.1537-94), by Cornelius Ketel (1548-1616), 1577. Oil

on Canvas (2100x990mm).
The Bodleian Library, Oxford

Frobisher was captain of the *Triumph* during the Armada campaign. He was knighted by the Lord Admiral on board the flagship after being appointed to command one of the fleet's four squadrons engaged with the Armada in the Channel. He is portrayed in Ketel's striking portrait holding a wheel-lock pistol.

Section 14: THE BATTLE AT SEA

This section of the Exhibition gives a day-by-day visual account of the final encounter between the English fleet and the Spanish Armada. The story is told chiefly by the 10 contemporary charts prepared by Robert Adams (nos. 14.2-14.11), by the 10 pictorial interpretations of them (nos. 14.12-14.21) engraved by John Pine after a set of tapestries designed by Hendrick Vroom in the 1590s, and by 10 graphic charts prepared for the Exhibition by the National Maritime Museum. A group of additional exhibits relating to particular aspects of the battle's progress is displayed alongside this main sequence. Pictorial and written evidence allows us to trace the course of the battle as follows:

The Armada first set out from Lisbon on **May 30**, but bad weather enforced a delay at La Coruña for regrouping and repairs. The fleet finally set forth again on **July 22**. On the same day, an English squadron which had set out from Plymouth hoping to intercept the Armada before it arrived, was forced by unfavourable winds to turn home. Ninety English ships, with Howard in command and Drake as his vice-admiral, regrouped at Plymouth to lie in wait for the now inevitable arrival of the invasion force. Meanwhile, Lord Henry Seymour, Howard's other vice-admiral, was stationed in the Downs with his own squadron, guarding the south-east coast from the expected arrival of Parma's forces from the Netherlands.

On the afternoon of **July 29**, the Armada was finally sighted off the Lizard, and by evening the tides allowed the English captains to begin warping their ships out of Plymouth ready to engage the enemy. By Saturday **July 30**, with beacons flaring on the English coast, the Armada was put into battle order, with Medina Sidonia in the *San Martin* commanding the main body of the fleet. The first confrontation came on **July 31**, an inconclusive four-hour skirmish off Plymouth during which it became apparent that the defence force would not attempt boarding actions (at which the Spanish were experienced and skilled), but simply aimed to hamper the Armada's advance up the Channel. The first Spanish casualties were self-inflicted — a collision between Pedro de Valdés' *Rosario* and a sister ship, and an explosion aboard the *San Salvador* — but the Armada pressed steadily on. Drake was ordered to track its progress through the night, with the rest of the fleet following his stern lantern, but he was tempted by the possibility of capturing the stricken *Rosario* and went off in search of it — leaving the following English ships in confusion. Howard in the *Ark Royal* was able to restore some order by taking up the main chase himself, though much of **August 1** was spent waiting for the English fleet to re-form. Drake himself appeared by evening, having taken the *Rosario* (and its Royal money chest) that morning: Valdés surrendered without a shot being fired, and his ship was brought into Dartmouth. The crippled *San Salvador* was also captured.

On **August 2**, the Armada, now grouped in a crescent formation and lying to the north of the English near Portland Bill, turned to make a direct attack on the enemy, with an unsuccessful attempt by the *Regazona* to board the *Ark Royal* marking the start of the action. The *Ark* itself later tried an assault on the *San Martin*, her rival flagship, but never attempted the boarding action which Medina Sidonia must have wished for. The rate of fire was high, and there was a heavy expenditure of shot by both sides.

Wednesday **August 3**, with the fleets now off the Isle of Wight, was

103

marked by an English attack on the straggling *Gran Grifón* which dissolved when the Spanish rearguard came to her rescue. In response to the organizational discipline displayed by the Armada, Howard decided at this point to divide the English fleet into four squadrons (under himself, Drake, Frobisher, and Hawkins) with the aim of improving its manageability. On **August 4**, Hawkins' new squadron led an attack on further stragglers from the main body of the Armada; the *Ark Royal* and the *Golden Lion* became embroiled in a fierce — if once more inconclusive — action with three galleasses; and Frobisher's squadron made a renewed assault on the *San Martin* before his own ship, the *Triumph*, was chased off by two Spanish galleons.

August 5 saw little progress for either fleet. Medina Sidonia's main preoccupation that day was to get a message to Parma, requesting the assistance of 40 or 50 small craft to distract and engage the enemy — thereby allowing, it was hoped, the larger Armada vessels to move in and board the English ships at last. On **August 6** the Armada headed towards Calais, and despite a south-west wind, rain, and poor visibility, anchored there by 7 pm to await Parma's arrival. The English, meanwhile, anchored off Calais Cliffs, were joined now by Seymour's squadron which had been guarding south-east England — a measure of Lord Howard's respect for the Armada's strength. In fact, his risk was less than he knew, for Parma was far from ready to attempt invasion. Nor did he know that a number of Dutch ships led by Justin of Nassau had just left Flushing with the intention of preventing Parma's boats from even reaching the open sea.

Early on the morning of **August 7** an English council of war aboard the *Ark Royal* decided to make a fireship attack on the anchored Spanish fleet — a manoeuvre by which a number of ships loaded with combustibles would be set alight and directed towards the enemy before being abandoned by their crews. Sir William Winter, captain of the *Vanguard*, seems to have suggested the use of fireships, and the council approved the plan. Eight privately owned ships were readied and

dispatched that night, and, in the confusion of darkness, at least six of them got close enough to their targets to prompt the Armada to cut cables and head rapidly out of harbour. Unfavourable winds, as the Spanish pilots were only too well aware, were now likely to prevent a return to Calais, and the Armada was drawn north, inexorably away from its would-be liaison with Parma.

In the morning light of **August 8**, with the Armada still regrouping after the night's tribulations, it was clear that the advantage now lay with the English fleet, and they pressed into battle off Gravelines in an ever-freshening north-west then west-north-west wind. The battle lasted from about 9 am until early evening, the longest and bloodiest of the campaign. Reports of the fighting are sketchy and confused, but a central encounter was certainly that between the flagship *San Martin* and the *Revenge*, *Triumph*, and *Victory*. Spanish casualties were high. The *San Mateo* and *San Felipe*, for example, were badly damaged, and were taken by the Dutch as they were driven helplessly towards the shore. The English claimed to have sunk three further ships and forced others onto the shoals and into Dutch hands.

During the night and into the morning of **August 9**, the wind drove many more Armada ships ever closer to the sandbanks. Disaster seemed imminent, averted only by a wind change to west-south-west which pushed the fleet away from the shore at last. Though Medina Sidonia would have liked to attempt a return to Calais, he realized that neither the weather nor the waiting English fleet (ready for battle if hampered by the same hazards of wind and shallow waters) would allow it. The decision to head for home, northwards round Scotland and Ireland, was the only realistic option.

Cat. no. 14.1
The English and Spanish ships engaged, by an unidentified English artist, c.1590. Oil on panel (1118x1435mm).
National Maritime Museum

If the action depicted here was meant to represent any one part of the battle, it must be the battle of Gravelines, the only stage at which large numbers of opposing ships were engaged in sustained conflict. More importantly, the picture embodies the post-battle English view of the campaign as a whole: the central foreground galleass, flying the papal banner, is represented as a "ship of fools" carrying a jester as well as a number of zealous monks. The galleass is flanked by two English ships, probably intended for the *Revenge* and the *Ark Royal*.

Cat. no. 14.2
The Spanish fleet off the coast of Cornwall, July 29, by Augustine Ryther (fl.1576-95) after Robert Adams (1540-96), no. 1 of a set of 10 engravings (381x508mm each), 1590.
National Maritime Museum

The Armada charts accompanied a brief history of the campaign written by the Florentine Petruccio Ubaldini, based on Howard's own record of the battle — in other words the "official" story. This, the first plate, shows the Armada sighting the Lizard, with the *Golden Hind* heading for Plymouth with a warning to the English fleet.

Cat. no. 14.7
Engagement of the fleets between Portland Bill and the Isle of Wight, August 2-3, by Augustine Ryther (fl.1576-95) after Robert Adams (1540-96), no. 6 of a set of 10 engravings (381x508mm each), 1590.
National Maritime Museum

This plate shows the continuation of the battle off Portland Bill, and takes the story on to the point when the English

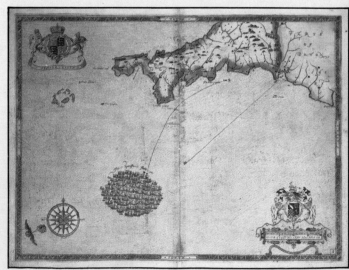

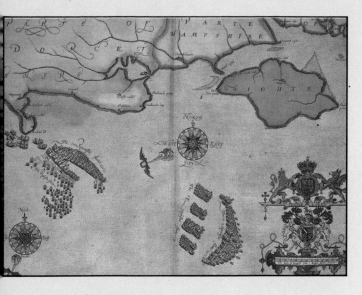

fleet was re-formed into four squadrons. In the Narrow Seas, Seymour's squadron is shown leaving the Downs to join Howard's force off Calais Cliffs.

Cat. no. 14.12

The Spanish fleet off the coast of Cornwall, July 29, by John Pine (1690-1756) after the tapestry of Hendrick Vroom (1566-1640), no. 1 of a set of 10 engravings (380x660mm each), 1739.

National Maritime Museum

Lord Howard commissioned a set of tapestries depicting the Armada campaign from the Netherlandish weaver Francis Spierincx. Spierincx hired Vroom to make the designs, which he did on the basis of the Adams charts (see nos. 14.2 and 14.7). The 10 tapestries were installed in the House of Lords during the 17th century, and

they were copied in Pine's set of engravings published in 1739. The tapestries were destroyed by fire in 1834, leaving the engravings as the only detailed record of their content.

Cat. no. 14.17

Engagement of the English and Spanish fleets between Portland Bill and the Isle of Wight, August 2-3, by John Pine (1690-1756) after the tapestry of Hendrick Vroom (1566-1640), no. 6 of a set of 10 engravings (380x660mm each), 1739.

National Maritime Museum

Like no. 14.12 this engraving provides a pictorial interpretation of its corresponding chart by Robert Adams (see nos. 14.2 and 14.7). Though Pine was supposedly working directly from Vroom's tapestries, some of his ships include 18th century features.

Cat. no. 14.28

The seventh day of the battle of the Armada, by Hendrick Vroom (1566-1640), c.1600. Oil on canvas (914x1528mm).

Tiroler Landesmuseum Ferdinandeum, Innsbruck

Vroom presents a composite summary of incidents that marked the "seventh day". The fireships are seen in the middle distance, with the Spanish ships making their escape northwards. The engagement of Spanish and English

ships in the foreground seems to represent the Battle of Gravelines; the *Ark Royal* lies astern of the *San Martin* which is on the left.

Cat. no. 14.29

The Armada in the Strait of Dover, by an unidentified Flemish artist,

c.1600-10. Gouache on vellum (133x318).

National Maritime Museum

A miniature painting combining various images of the campaign: in the right distance appear the beacons on the English coast, defended by an army bearing Elizabeth's standard. The fireship episode appears in the centre, and to the left two small Dutch craft attack a Spanish ship.

Section 15: "THE TERRIBLE JOURNEY"

Despite a crippling shortage of victuals and ammunition aboard many English ships, as the Armada headed northwards Howard decided to make chase as far as the Firth of Forth. For the demoralized Spanish the outlook was grim. Temperatures dropped, food and water ran out, and weather worsened as they set about their circuitous homeward route of some 750 leagues through unknown and dangerous waters. On September 3, Medina Sidonia filed a report for Philip

II, noting that since August 21 there had been four nights of gales and 17 more ships were missing. As the Armada, now widely dispersed, headed around Scotland and the west coast of Ireland, matters went from bad to worse. Battered ships which sought refuge and fresh water along the coastline were greeted with hostility by local communities often under direct orders to "apprehend and execute" any Spaniard encountered. Thousands died through shipwreck as the storms multiplied, and many of those who made it to the shore were massacred on sight or imprisoned, interrogated and put to death. Nearly two-thirds of the original force of Armada ships did return safely to home ports, but in all some 11,000 Spanish lives had been lost.

Cat. no. 15.1
Chart showing the track of the Armada, by Augustine Ryther after Robert Adams, 1590. Engraving (795x545mm).
National Maritime Museum

The English fleet gave up the chase at the Firth of Forth, though two ships remained in the Armada's shadow as far as the Orkneys. Medina Sidonia led a safe course, but damage through battle

▼

and storms meant that many ships of his fleet were unable to follow, foundering on the coasts of Scotland and Ireland in mid-September. The chart is from *Expeditionis Hispanorum in Angliam vera descriptio*.

Cat. no. 15.3
Map of Donegal Bay, by John Baxter and Baptista Boazio (fl.1583-1606), c.1603. Pen and watercolour (550x420mm).
National Maritime Museum

At least 20 Armada ships perished off the coast of Ireland, a source of immediate interest to mapmakers and

▼

historians. This map from the very early 17th century shows the sites of three unidentified Armada wrecks. Efforts have been made ever since to pinpoint as many wrecks as possible, and excavation projects have been in progress in Irish waters since the 1960s (see Section 10). If there is an Armada exhibition in 2088, it may well include material from Spanish ships that as yet lie undiscovered.

Cat. no. 15.7
Sir Richard Bingham (1528-99), by an unidentified English artist, 1564. Oil

▲
on panel (584x495mm).
National Portrait Gallery, London

This is the earliest known portrait of Bingham, who was Governor of Connaught at the time of the Armada. Along with the Lord Deputy, Fitzwilliam he was responsible for much of the slaughter of survivors from Spanish ships who reached the Irish coast. His actions were harsh even by the standards of the time, and he remaine a controversial figure.

▲
Cat. no. 15.16
The Chatham Chest, 1625. Wrough iron (1060x630x590mm).
National Maritime Museum

As a result of privations suffered by English seamen in the wake of the Armada campaign — for illness and disability were the legacy of victory fo many English sailors — a benevolent fund was established in 1590. All seamen were henceforth required to contribute sixpence a month from the wages to be placed in the "Chest at Chatham". In an attempt to prevent misuse of funds, five officers held separate keys to the chest, the reason for its complex lock mechanism.

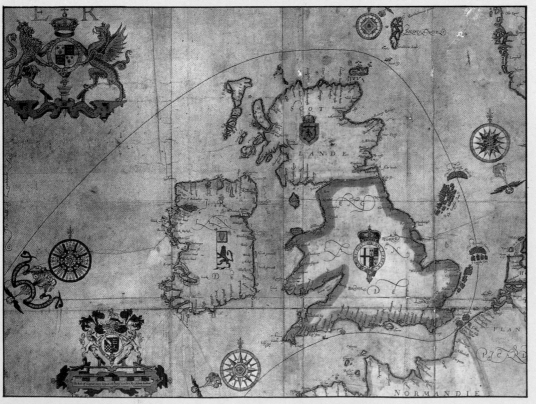

Section 16: AFTER THE ARMADA

Once Elizabeth was sure that the Armada wasn't coming back — for there were some fears that Medina Sidonia would renew the attack after rounding the coast of Ireland — she ordered the English fleet to sail into the Atlantic to intercept the Spanish treasure fleets coming from the New World. In view of the battle damage to ships and men, this was an impractical brief, and instead plans were put in hand for a 'counter-Armada' the following year, combining an attack on the Iberian mainland with an interception of Spanish trade routes. Sir Francis Drake and Sir John Norris were given charge of the expedition, which sailed in April 1589.

It began with an attack on La Coruña (instead of the scheduled assault on surviving Armada ships at Santander and San Sebastian) and then proceeded to Lisbon, where a number of local ships were burned or captured. Plans of advancing an army into the peninsula were abandoned through lack of either proper supplies or the expected local support, so the fleet made instead for the Azores in a vain search for prizes. 'They went to places more for profit than for service', noted Elizabeth, surveying the campaign afterwards. Poor preparations, dubious strategy and muddled leadership had cost at least 10,000 lives: Drake was formally ostracized for five years. The state of war between England and Spain continued into the 1590s; there were several hundred privateering expeditions against Spanish shipping,

and a number of further attempts by Spain to invade English and Irish soil. Both nations were distracted throughout by their involvement in both France and the Netherlands, however, and after Philip's and Elizabeth's deaths in 1598 and 1603 respectively their successors were happy enough to conclude peace in 1604.

The Armada of 1588, seen in the context of the expeditions mounted by both England and Spain against each other in the surrounding years, was an event of less military, political, and moral significance than Protestant propagandists of the late-sixteenth and seventeenth centuries proclaimed. Nonetheless its effect on morale in England and the Netherlands was certainly marked, for it heightened the conviction of Protestants that God was on their side and appeared to endorse

the righteousness of their religious and political opposition to the Catholic world.

Cat. no. 16.1
Elizabeth I: the Armada portrait by an unidentified English artist, c. 1590. Oil on panel (1130x1280mm).
W. Tyrwhitt-Drake Esq

This portrait appears to have been owned originally by Sir Francis Drake. In between representations of the Armada battle and the demise of Spanish ships in the storms, sits the Queen, architect of the successful campaign, resting her hand on a globe to suggest her new international might.

▼

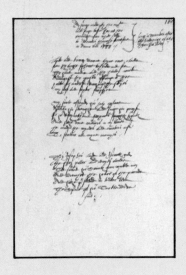

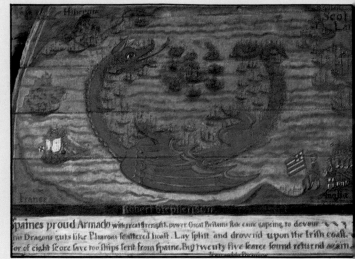

Vroom (1566-1640), 1598. Wool and silk tapestry (3187x3350mm).
N.C. Worms, Esq

One of the continuing encounters at sea between English and Spanish ships occurred off the Azores in August 1591, in which the *Revenge* (captained by Drake against the Armada but in this action by Sir Richard Grenville) surrendered to the enemy after a vigorous fight. The great cost of tapestries such as this indicates that its patron must have been of high rank — possibly Lord Admiral Howard of Effingham, who witnessed the episode.

▲

Cat. no. 16.3
Poem on the Armada victory, said to have been composed by Elizabeth I, 1588. MS (294x198mm).
National Maritime Museum

After the Armada a great thanksgiving ceremony was held in St Paul's Cathedral, and this poem was probably sung before the Queen. Protestants were eager to emphasise divine intervention, and the 'songe' notes 'he made the wynds and waters rise/to scatter all myne enemyes'.

Cat. no. 16.23
The last fight of the *Revenge*, August 1591 designed by Hendrick

▼

Cat. no. 16.27
The Heneage Jewel, c. 1600, containing a miniature portrait of

▼

Elizabeth I by Nicholas Hilliard (1547-1619), 1580. Enamelled gold, set with diamonds and rubies (71x52x11mm).
Victoria & Albert Museum, London

This locket, traditionally known as the Armada Jewel, was said to have been given by Elizabeth on the defeat of the Armada to her Vice Chamberlain of the Royal Household and Privy Councellor, Sir Thomas Heneage (1556-95). The jewel nonetheless seems to be of a slightly later date, and the inscription of *Ano 1580* on the miniature is not contemporary.

Cat. no. 16.30
An allegory of the defeat of the Spanish Armada as St George and the Dragon by Robert Stephenson, c. 1610. Oil on panel (1525x2045mm).
Lent privately

▲

The famous crescent-shape of the Armada is represented as a dragon, over which England (bottom right) triumphs under the flag of St George. This re-working of the popular legend, and the implicit suggestion that the victory was one of good over evil, was symptomatic of the way in which the event was commonly perceived in the seventeenth century. Armada myths persist to this day.

Cat. no. 16.35
The Somerset House Conference, by Juan Pantoja de la Cruz (1551-1608) 1604. Oil on canvas (2045x2700mm).
National Maritime Museum

The peace negotiations between England and Spain, initiated by James and Philip III, took place at Somerset House on the Strand from May to

▼

August 1604. The English delegation is portrayed on the right, the Spanish on the left. There is another version of the picture in the National Portrait Gallery, London.

▲
Cat. no. 16.36
The 1604 peace treaty between England and Spain, ratified by Philip III, 15 June 1605. Illuminated MS (350x460mm).
Public Record Office, London

This was the formal ratification of the Anglo-Spanish peace treaty. It is decorated with the arms of Spain and a miniature portrait of Philip III. A similar ratification, complete with a portrait of James I, was sent from England to Spain. The treaty brought to an end nearly twenty years of war between the two countries, though the issues it addressed — trade, religious toleration, and the Netherlands — were little affected in practical terms by its conclusion.

GETTING TO GREENWICH

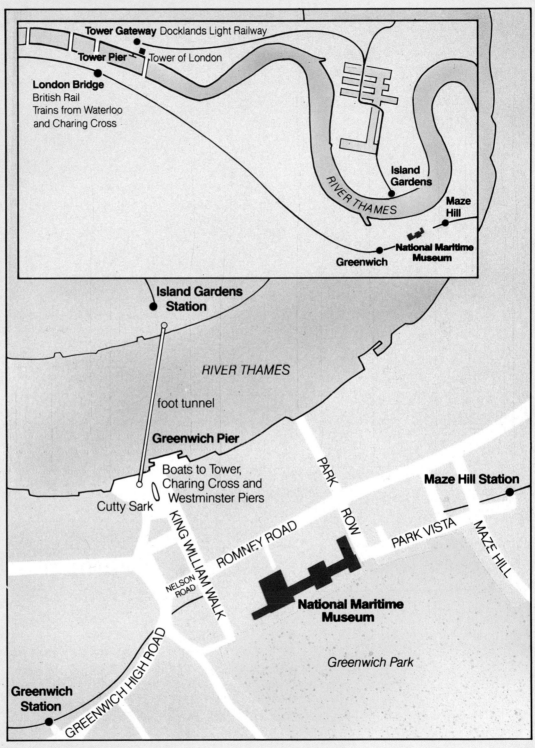

HISTORICAL ASSOCIATION
PLYMOUTH ARMADA 400 MAIN EVENTS

July 2
ARMADA – PLYMOUTH PHILHARMONIC CHOIR
The premiere of this work by Derek Bourgeois will be performed in Plymouth Guildhall by the Plymouth Philharmonic Choir, accompanied by the Bournemouth Sinfonietta.

July 3
IT'S AN ARMADA KNOCKOUT
Crazy Elizabethan games organized by the Junior Chamber of Commerce on Plymouth's famous Hoe Promenade. A day for all the family.

July 3
ARMADA COMMEMORATIVE SERVICE
A service at St Andrews Church, to be televised nationwide, commemorating the events of July 1588 attended by civic and service representatives.

July 3
ARMADA TEA DANCE
Dancing to the Bournemouth Salon Trio in an Elizabethan Street Atmosphere in the Armada Centre Mall.

July 5-9
COMBINED SERVICES WEEK
A spectacular show on the Hoe Promenade by the Royal Navy, Army, Royal Marines, and Royal Air Force.

July 10
ARMADA OPEN BOULES TOURNAMENT
Sixty-four costumed teams from far and wide will compete on the Hoe Promenade in the Devon Open Boules Championships.

July 10
COSTUMED PICNIC
Feast on strawberries and mead in an Elizabethan atmosphere in the historic grounds of Drake's home, Buckland Abbey.

July 10
KINGS SINGERS CONCERT
Plymouth Guildhall will be the setting for the World Premiere of the Kings Singers' new work.

July 13-23
"DRAKE"
A musical staged by the Theatre Royal in association with the National Youth Music Theatre involving local talented children.

July 16
ARMADA CUP RACE
The yachting world's modern Armada races this year from San Sebastian in Spain to Plymouth for the Armada Cup.

July 16
ELIZABETHAN FASHION PARADE
A rare opportunity to compare today's fashion with the elaborate costumes of the Armada Period.

July 19
RE-ENACTMENT OF DRAKE'S FAMOUS GAME OF BOWLS
One of the most famous events in our history will take place once again on Plymouth Hoe.

July 19
MODERN DAY ARMADA
A fleet of every type of vessel from ships of the Royal Navy to bath tubs will set sail in Plymouth Sound.

July 19-21
ARMADA FLOWER FESTIVAL
An exhibition in St Andrew's Church depicting Drake's life and travels and our links with Spain.

July 23
ARMADA COSTUME BALL
A glittering evening of Elizabethan elegance when costumed revellers will dance the night away at the Royal Naval College, Manadon.

July 23
PHILATELIC EXHIBITION
Exhibition and stamp fair in Plymouth Guildhall, staged by Plymouth Philatelic Society.

July 24
ARMADA HISTORIC BANQUET
An Elizabethan feast with period entertainment set in historic Buckland Abbey, Drake's former home.

July 28
GRAND FINALE
A dramatic re-enactment of the battle in Plymouth Sound with fireworks, music, and spectacular effects of all kinds.

For further information contact
Jean Imm or Nuala Kelly,
Tel. (0752) 674301,
Telex 45350,
Fax 674303.

HISTORICAL ASSOCIATION
BRANCH LECTURES

9 January **The Armada Campaign Re-examined**
Contact: Miss L J Greenhill, 5 Ashburnham Close, Chichester, PO19 3NB

19 January **The Spanish Armada: a colossus stuffed with clouts**
Contact: R K Field, West Midlands College of HE, Gorway, Walsall, WS1 3BD

2 February **The Spanish Armada**
Contact: A J Bristow, 11 Durrington Gardens, The Causeway, Worthing, BN12 6BU

10 February **The Armada of 1588**
Contact: P Kenyon, 19 Ridgley Drive, Ponteland, Newcastle upon Tyne, NE20 9BJ

10 February **The Spanish Armada**
Contact: Miss C M Bartlett, 12 Arnold Crescent, Iselworth, Middx, TW7 7NT

18 February **The Spanish Armada**
Contact: C A Linfield, Platt's House, The School, Wellingborough, NN8 2BX

22 February **The Elizabethan Navy at the Time of the Armada**
Contact: M Bower, Church Cottage, Oxenton, Cheltenham, GL52 4SE

2 March **The Spanish Armada**
Contact: Mrs E Bremner, 18 Park Road, Redhill, RH1 1BT

8 March **The Spanish Armada of 1588**
Contact: C W Clark, 143 Sussex Way, Cockfosters

9 March **The Armada Campaign Re-examined**
Contact: Mrs E Sparey, 44 Clifton, York.

10 March **The Elizabethan Navy**
Contact: Tom Holder, 4 Woodlands Close, Chandler's Ford, Hants, SO5 1AT

11 March **Elizabethan Foreign Policy and the Armada**
Contact: A J Till, 1 Chestnut Close, Hanwood, Shrewsbury, SY5 8BR

16 March **The Elizabethan Navy**
Contact: R T Bettridge, Buckinghamshire RO, County Offices, Walton Street, Aylesbury

18 March **The Spanish Armada: 400th Anniversary**
Contact: R J Romans, 37 Bridge View, Wadebridge, Cornwall

24 March **Philip II's Spain: Golden Age or Black Legend?**
Contact: Mrs W W Hanna, Shirley Cottage, Beechen Cliff, Bath

22 April **The Elizabethan Navy and the Armada Campaign**
Contact: H Patterson, 49 Norman Road, Tunbridge Wells

19 May **1588: A Close Run Thing**
Contact: Mrs E Dulwich, 15 Whiterow Park, Trowbridge, Wiltshire

● *Interested in History?*

What a fascinating story of enterprise and conflict, conviction and prejudice, the Spanish Armada makes! But there is a great deal more to History than just the Armada and 16th-century Europe. The Historical Association will introduce you to all periods of the past and bring you into contact with other people of similar historical interests. Visits, tours, lectures, conferences, a free quarterly magazine (*The Historian*), and a wide selection of publications and the journals (*History* and *Teaching History*) at half price, are just some of the benefits of membership. Details of how to get the Association's many publications will be sent to you when you join. Why not begin by purchasing *The Spanish Armada* by Simon Adams, (lecturer in Modern History, Strathclyde University) at the members' price of £1.60?

We are offering FREE membership until October 1988 if you join for October 1988 – September 1989 from this advertisement. In addition, you will be given this 1988-89 subscription at the 1987-88 rate and we will also send you a FREE leather bookmark embossed with the Association's logo in gold (while stocks last).

- ✂ -

Membership Application Form October 1988 – September 1989

Please enrol me as a member immediately (free of charge until October 1988) and send me a FREE bookmark and details of current activities and Journals.

I enclose my cheque for the special subscription rate of *£14.50*, made payable to *The Historical Association*

Please send me a copy of *The Spanish Armada* at £1.60 to those joining (or £3.20 to non-members) and to speed delivery I enclose A SEPARATE CHEQUE to the value of £ ....

NAME _____ TITLE _____

ADDRESS _____

_____

_____

SIGNATURE _____ DATE _____

Return this form to: The Historical Association, 59a Kennington Park Road, London SE11 4JH. *Telephone: 01-735 3901.*

PLYMOUTH ARMADA CONFERENCE

15-17 July 1988

The Historical Association, in conjunction with the College of St Mark and St John, Plymouth, presents The Spanish Armada 1588-1988, a residential weekend in Plymouth from Friday, 15 to Sunday, 17 July 1988. Armada specialists will present current thinking on different aspects of this dramatic episode in our country's history. The conference is to be held at the College of St Mark and St John where there is excellent residential accommodation in single study bedrooms with wash basins in a hall set in pleasant campus grounds just outside the city.

Registration is on Friday from 4.30 pm onwards. In the evening there will be a Civic Reception hosted by the Mayor of Plymouth, followed by Joyce Youings (Exeter) lecturing in the Guildhall on *Devon and the Armada*. On Saturday the lectures continue with D M Loades (Bangor) on *Elizabethan Foreign Policy and the Armada Context*, Glanmor Williams (Swansea) on *Philip II's Spain: Golden Age or Black Legend*, and Margarita Russell (National Maritime Museum) on *The Armada in Art*. On Sunday we will hear Ian Friel (National Maritime Museum) speak on *The Elizabethan Navy* and Anthony Ryan (Liverpool) on *Drake and the Armada*.

On Saturday afternoon participants can either visit Cotehele House, near Saltash, built 1485-1627, or attend a teacher session looking at coursework, assessment and the use of documents with special emphasis on the Tudors and Stuarts. Mr T Ridd, Chief Examiner JMB, will be among the speakers. The conference ends on Sunday afternoon with a privilege visit to Buckland Abbey, the home of Sir Francis Drake. Participants will return to Plymouth by about 4.00 pm.

The *residential* fee for the conference is £85 to members, £95 to non-members. It includes all meals, coffee and tea from Friday evening to Sunday afternoon, accommodation, all transport and admission charges. *Non-resident* fees are £50 to members, £60 to non-members, which includes lunches, coffee, tea, transport and coach visits. You can reserve your place with a deposit of £10, residential or non-residential. All fees, including the deposit, include a *non-returnable* booking charge of £5. British Rail conference discount fares are available and details will be sent to participants nearer the date. Transport on Friday afternoon from Plymouth Railway Station to the College and on Sunday afternoon from College to the Station can be arranged on request. The Association is also organising a short tour of both sides of the Tamar immediately following the weekend from 17-23 July, again based at the College. If you would like to see a detailed programme of the conference, or would like more information about the tour, please write to Adrian Ailes at The Historical Association, 59a Kennington Park Road, London SE11 4JH or phone 01-735 3901.

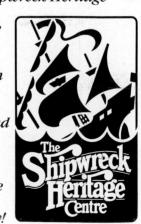

FIRE OVER ENGLAND

At the trial lighting of an Armada beacon at Fobbing, Thurrock, Essex, pikemen and women of the London Trayned Band, Mrs. Ann Geaney, Leader of Thurrock Borough Council, dressed as an Elizabethan Alderman, Bruno Peek, National Organiser of "Fire Over England", local Fobbing citizens and members of NACRO.

On July 19, 1588, the first galleons of the Spanish Armada were sighted off the Lizard in Cornwall, sailing eastwards towards the Thames and London.

That evening the first warning beacons were lit, in a chain of hundreds of high points all over England.

The beacon system of England, unique in the world, dating back to the early 14th century, had by the reign of Henry VIII become an effective and highly organised network, to warn of danger to the kingdom. Particularly prolific around the coast, the beacons played a key part in mustering local militias and directing them to suspected landing sites of hostile armies.

Watched by 'wyse and vigilent' locals, working in shifts, the beacons remained active until the time of the Civil War, but with the growth of standing armies, became less relevant and fell into disuse.

In 1588, however, they had been invaluable to warn of the approaching Armada and probable land invasion by the Spaniards.

On July 19 this year, to mark the 400th anniversary of the Armada, a chain of more than 150 beacons will be lit in Fire over England.

Many of the beacons will be on or near the original sites; specially built braziers, based on Elizabethan designs, will remain as lasting tourist attractions and reminders of a crucial episode in English history. In some areas, 'beacon trails' will be evolved to attract visitors in future years.

Fire over England is the brain child of Bruno Peek, already a veteran of beacon chains in recent years to launch Maritime England, Operation Seafire and Old Father Time, an English celebration of New Year's Eve, which was broadcast two years running by BBC television.

As National Organiser of Fire over England, he reports that a large number of organisations and groups have agreed to sponsor beacons on July 19, including local authorities, public and private companies, the National Trust, English Heritage, Sea Cadets, Lions Clubs, the Round Table, the Royal Navy, the Royal Observer Corps and the Army.

The first three beacons to be lit, appropriately on the Lizard, will be sponsored by British Telecom International — whose nearby Goonhilly Satellite Earth Station is one of the most sophisticated communication centres in the world — in co-operation with the National Trust and the local council. All three braziers will remain as permanent memorials to the event.

Among the many other permanent braziers around England will be three at Thurrock, a borough rich in associations with Queen Elizabeth I and the invasion threat of the Armada. There a series of commemorative events will start with the opening of English Heritage's Armada 1588 exhibition at Tilbury Fort at the end of March and climax with the Great Armada Pageant on August 6 and 7.

The Great Armada Pageant promises to be one of the biggest ever staged in England to mark a single historical event.

On August 6 Queen Elizabeth I (to be played by a well-known actress yet to be named) will travel from Tower Pier to Tilbury aboard the Tudor barge or shollop built for the film, 'A Man for all Seasons', under the experienced eyes of the Queen's Bargemaster, Edwin Hunt, who will be consultant waterman for the voyage.

For two days more than a thousand men and women, all in Tudor dress, will re-enact the stirring events which took place in Thurrock four hundred years ago. There will be jousting, funfairs and sideshows, ox roasts, falconry, ale tents, tumblers, jesters, jugglers, fire-eaters and fireworks. The Pageant is expected to attract to Thurrock over a hundred thousand visitors from home and abroad.

Robert Stannage

For further details of Fire over England and the Great Armada Pageant, please contact: Bruno Peek, Armada 88 National Working Party, Civic Offices, New Road, Grays, Thurrock, Essex RM17 6SL.

MARY, QUEEN OF SCOTS

THE GREATEST THREAT TO THE TUDOR THRONE

Elizabeth I kept her cousin and heir a prisoner in England. Gordon Batho tells why the Queen of England took 19 years to send Mary to her death

THE BEGINNING

"IT CAME with a lass, it will pass with a lass." James V of Scotland is traditionally reputed to have uttered these words when he was told that his wife, Marie de Guise, had given birth to a daughter at Linlithgow Castle on December 8, 1542. Following as it did the deaths of two infant sons in the previous year, the advent of the person known to history as Mary, Queen of Scots, was a grievous disappointment to her father. The Scottish Throne had come to his family, the Stewarts, by the marriage of his ancestor, Walter, to Marjorie, daughter of Robert the Bruce, and James had every reason to believe that no woman could rule his troubled people successfully. He himself lay dying in Falkland Palace, a building of his own creation, just over 20 miles away from his family, exhausted by the trials and tribulations of life at 30, from the combined effects of inherited physical weakness, of a licentious personal life, and of mental anguish at the rout of his army as much by Scots defection as by the English at Solway Moss in the November of 1542.

During his reign — he had succeeded at 17 months in 1513 and assumed power at 16 years of age — Scotland enjoyed an importance in European politics quite out of proportion to its intrinsic value, as rival powers sought its support. James favoured the auld alliance with France; he made a Francophile, his ex-tutor, Gavin Dunbar, Archbishop of Glasgow, his Chancellor in 1528 and he pursued the offer of a French princess in marriage mooted in the Treaty of Rouen between France and the then governor of the kingdom, his cousin, John Stewart, Duke of Albany, as long before as 1517. James' marriage to Madeleine, daughter of Francis I of France, ended tragically in her death at 16 in July 1537, but by marrying Marie de Guise shortly afterwards he at least acquired two substantial dowries, no small consideration for a financially stricken sovereign. He had already manipulated the Pope into making unprecedented grants of tax levies on the Church (normally not subject to tax) as well as providing ecclesiastic dignities for his six illegitimate sons. The excommunication of Henry VIII in 1538 made

the English King anxious to secure the Scottish alliance, but when his nobles prevented James from travelling to York to negotiate with Henry in 1541, out of a concern for the safety of his person, war followed with England. Two centuries of no fewer than seven Stewart minorities had increased noble power in Scotland, and James' own aggressive acquisitiveness had alienated many of the better off from him so that his reign ended disastrously with a country divided against itself economically, politically, religiously, and socially. "The poor man's King", as he was called, bequeathed a poor country to his daughter.

Soon after James' death, the pro-English party gained the ascendancy in Scotland, led by James Hamilton, Earl of Arran, heir presumptive to the Crown since Albany had died in 1536. The power of the Anglophiles was strengthened by the return from exile in England of the unpopular but influential Archibald Douglas, Earl of Angus. To cement the English alliance, marriage was proposed between Henry's heir and only legitimate son, Edward, and Mary,

● Mary as a child.
MUSÉE CONDÉ, CHANTILLY.

...ater Queen of Scots. But within days of the ratification of the treaties of Greenwich, as the settlement was known, Arran was reconciled with the Catholic Church and the pro-French party led by Cardinal Beaton. The day after, September 9, 1543, Mary, Queen of Scots, was crowned in Stirling Castle's chapel, as Sir Ralph Sadler commented "with such solemnity as they do use in this country, which is not very costly".

Arran's *Volte-face* effectively determined Mary, Queen of Scots' upbringing as a Catholic, and the conclusion of the Franco-Scottish treaty of Haddington in July 1548 made her the nominated bride of the Dauphin, Francis, the heir to the French Throne. Mary went to France where she was warmly welcomed by her Guise relatives. As her grandmother, Antoinette, Duchess of Guise, remarked at the time somewhat breathlessly:

> She is brune, with a clear complexion and I think she will be a beautiful girl, for her complexion is fine and clear, the skin white, the lower part of the face very pretty, the eyes are small and rather deep set, the face rather long, she is graceful and not shy, on the whole we may be well contented with her.

The words were prophetic; Mary imbibed the culture of the French court, of which there was none finer in contemporary society, freely and enthusiastically. She charmed her hosts exceptionally as she matured from girlhood to young womanhood, cosseted materially and educated carefully by them and above all prepared spiritually for her role as a Catholic consort by her uncle, the Cardinal of Lorraine, a man who combined the advocacy of the authorization of the Bible in the vernacular with a ruthless persecution of Protestants. But Francis II, always weak, survived his father, King Henry II, by only 17 months and Mary was a widow by December 1560. If she was not classically beautiful or given to deep classical scholarship, and she was neither, she possessed at 18 in 1560 undoubted charisma, a quick wit, and the power to win affectionate loyalty, and by her punctilious religious observance she appeared to be a devout and certainly a conventionally correct adherent of the Catholic faith. When she left France to return to Scotland in August 1561, her friend, the poet Ronsard, expressed what was probably the common view uncommonly well:

> Like a beautiful meadow stripped of all
>   its flowers,
> Like a painting of its colours all deprived,
> Like a heaven void of all its myriad stars,
> Like a dry sea, a ship without a sail,
> A leafless woodland, cavern without
>   gloom,
> A royal palace with no royal pomp,
> A ring having no priceless pearl inset—
> So shall France grieve at this her
>   heavy loss,
> Her ornaments, and all her Royalty,
> Who was her colour, beauty, and her
>   flower.

The Scotland to which Mary returned had been ruled by her mother from the time of Arran's fall after Edward VI's death in 1553 had rendered the pro-English party's position untenable until Marie de Guise's own death in June 1560. Fortunately, Marie was a conciliator, for the French were unpopular in Scotland. Indeed, religious toleration was a necessity, since only force far beyond Marie's government's power could have exacted compliance with the conventional faith; in any event, with Catholic Mary Tudor on the English Throne, Protestants did not constitute a political threat in Scotland, even if they had the eloquence of a John Knox. Knox, of course, wrote about Mary I of England and Marie in his *First Blast of the Trum-*

pet against the Monstrous Regiment of Women (Geneva, 1558):

> To promote a woman to bear rule, superiority, dominion or empire above any realm, nation or city, is repugnant to nature, contumely to God, a thing most contrarious to his revealed will and approved ordinance, and finally it is the subversion of good order, of all equity and justice.

The death of Mary Tudor in November 1558 and the consequent assumption of the style and arms of sovereigns of England by Francis and Mary brought about a change in political attitudes in Scotland. The reformers could now hope for English aid and began to take militant initiatives literally as well as metaphorically. Knox returned to Scotland in May 1559 and preached at Perth a sermon which heralded the start of a half-hearted civil war between the armed, and usually amateur, supporters of the religious dissidents and Marie's professional soldiers, mostly Frenchmen recruited with French money. The only hope for the insurgents was comparable assistance from England, but the Treaty of Berwick with England in February 1560 did not mention religion; it provided only for English protection of the Scots' "old freedom and liberties". Marie's death allowed the withdrawal of English and French forces from Scotland by the Treaty of Edinburgh. The Scots, left to manage their own affairs, renounced the claim to the English Throne for Francis and Mary and showed no desire for a political revolution. Instead, they called a parliament which proved inclined to only modest religious reformation. The death of Francis II in December, however, again altered the situation as it made possible a return of Mary, Queen of Scots, to her own country, a development which looked most improbable before this, and the reformers, fearing that a Queen Regnant who in their eyes was essentially a Frenchwoman might rally Catholic adherents against them, hastened to establish a systematic organization for the Church in Scotland by what came to be called the "Book of Discipline". Scotland awaited Mary with feelings as mixed and even clouded as the weather which greeted her departure from France; she arrived at Leith on August 19, 1561, no doubt as apprehensive for the future as any of her subjects.

THE PERIOD OF POWER

Sir Nicholas Throckmorton, the English Ambassador in Paris, wrote at the time of Mary's mourning for her husband that little account had been taken of her when she was "under band of marriage and subjection to her husband", but that he found her to have "both a great wisdom for her years, modesty, and also of great judgment in the wise handling herself and her matters". Moreover (in contrast to Elizabeth I, he might have written had he not been too good a diplomat to do so) she was "content to be ruled by good counsel and wise men". She professed herself a confirmed Catholic to him, but to have a pragmatic view of a state religion: "I have been brought up in this religion; and who aught would credit me in anything if I should show myself higher in this case."

It was not inevitable that Mary should return to Scotland after the death of Francis. Her marriage contract specifically provided for her as a widow with an honourable estate in France, and numerous overtures of marriage, including one from the Spanish heir, Don Carlos, were made to her in early 1561. She decided, as now she was inclined to do for herself, to return; it was the first

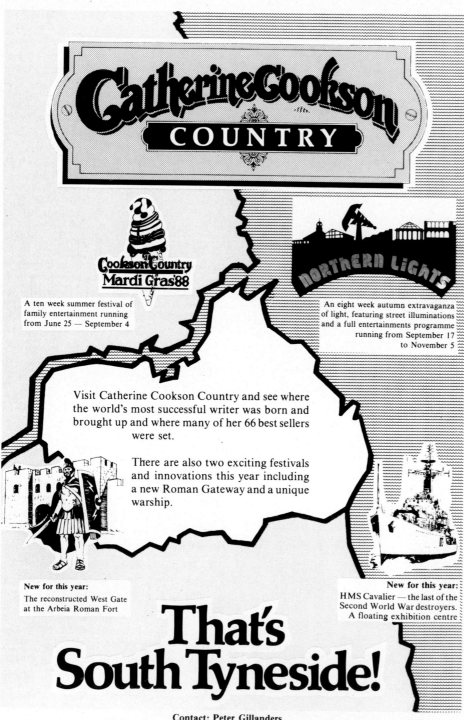

important decision of her own. As the late Professor S T Bindoff wrote, to Mary, Scotland was nothing more, however, than an interlude between the France of her unquestionably fond memories and the England of her dreams. She was nothing if not ambitious and that she wanted Elizabeth's Throne there is no doubt. Meanwhile, she was able to continue to enjoy the pastimes she had learned to love in France, pastimes which so appealed to her restless, active nature — running at the ring, shooting at the butts, hawking, hunting, playing golf and music, dancing, dicing, and gambling at cards, and for more contemplative moments reading a little Livy with her tutor, George Buchanan, or doing the needlework which her mother-in-law, Catherine de Medici, had taught her which was to be a lifelong pursuit.

In the early years after her return, she had considerable success as a personal ruler. At first, she sought to conciliate the reformers, following a policy of moderation advocated by her half-brother, James Stewart, Earl of Moray, and by the Secretary of State, William Maitland of Lethington, whereby the reformed Church was recognized, but Mary had Mass said for herself and her Household. The Crown took revenues from the Church and made appointments to bishoprics, abbotships, and similar benefices, while an Act of 1563 gave the clergy of the reformed Church the right to enjoy the manses and glebes attached to parish churches. On the other hand, she did little to encourage Catholicism and, for example, failed to send representatives to the last session of the Council of Trent — called by the Pope to counter the Reformation — even though there were two Scottish bishops already on the Continent — Beaton of Glasgow and Chisholm of Dunblane. Perhaps it was as William Cecil, Lord Burghley, observed in 1562: Mary was "no more devout towards Rome than for the contentation of her uncles". Of course, whatever Mary did was not enough by way of concession to the Protestant cause to content John Knox who thundered on from his pulpit in St Giles, Edinburgh, in increasing isolation from fellow reformers as well as from Catholic sympathisers. Knox's outpourings must not blind us to Mary's real achievement in bringing about a unity among the Scottish nobility which, in the words of the Historiographer Royal, Professor Gordon Donaldson, "had hardly been

● Miniature by François Clouet of Mary as Queen of France, c. 1560.

paralleled since the days of her grandfather James IV" and in gaining widespread popularity among ordinary people to whom she showed herself frequently. For instance, she went on major progresses to the north of Scotland as far as Inverness in 1562, to the south-west via Dumbarton and Glenluce as far as Dumfries in 1563, and to the south-east as far as Hermitage Castle, Jedburgh, and Berwick in 1566.

Always the eye was to the future, to England and to a marriage which would help Mary to realise her dream. Within a fortnight of her return to Scotland from France, Maitland raised the issue of the succession with Elizabeth; this marked

the beginning of what was to prove a long and fruitless campaign. The negotiations for marriage were many in the early years of Mary's reign in Scotland, but the Spanish marriage was ruled out at the end of 1563 by Don Carlos' development of insanity. In the event, she settled in 1565 for the hand of her cousin, the 19-year-old Henry Stewart, Lord Darnley, heir to the Earl of Lennox. The marriage had many apparent advantages; Henry's claim by blood to the English Throne was only marginally less

117

OPPOSITE: Mary in "white mourning"
(en deuil blanc) for the Dauphin, Francis II.
SCOTTISH NATIONAL PORTRAIT GALLERY.

strong than Mary's as he was the grand-child of Henry VIII's sister, Margaret Tudor, by her second marriage, where Mary was her grandchild by her first marriage, and he had been brought up in England. His claim to the Scottish Throne was, after Mary's, second only to the Hamiltons', if that, for they shared a common ancestor in James II's daughter, Mary. In religion, although his mother in particular had sought to make him a candidate for the English Throne who would be acceptable to the Catholics and although he married Mary by the Roman rite, Darnley was himself said to be indifferent, but outwardly to have shown himself a Protestant. In person, he was (unlike most Scots) tall and lithe, and probably appealed sexually to Mary who was herself unusually tall. On the other hand, the marriage annoyed Elizabeth of England because of the dynastic implications — the Lennox family was unpopular in Scotland with more than their rivals the Hamiltons; Moray was outraged at his displacement as Mary's closest adviser by a boy of 19; and, worst of all, Henry Stewart's personality was catastrophically inadequate to the position of King Consort. As Stefan Zweig has written, "Mary's disappointment in Darnley was political as well as the disappointment of a loving woman".

Not only did Elizabeth treat the marriage with Darnley as an act of open hostility, but Mary had to raise an army against rebel lords led by Moray in the "Chaseabout Raid" as a consequence. Mary declared in December 1565 that she would not adhere to toleration of Protestantism when she had "no assurance of anything that may countervail the same" and, as most Scottish nobles defected, she came to rely increasingly on men of lower birth and, above all, on her Italian secretary, David Riccio. Darnley, whom the Cardinal of Lorraine shrewdly termed an agreeable nincompoop, felt excluded from affairs of state and conspired with the rebel lords to seize the Crown matrimonial, to support Protestantism, and to murder Riccio. Mary handled matters nothing short of triumphantly after Riccio's traumatic death in her quarters in Holyrood House, Edinburgh, in March 1566, pardoning those involved in the Chaseabout Raid troubles, but not the murderers and thus neatly divided the opposition.

The child of Mary and her now estranged husband Darnley, James, was born in Edinburgh Castle on June 19, 1566. His birth undermined rather than strengthened Mary's position. Rumours arose immediately that James was not her child, though there was not, and is not, a shred of evidence to lend credence to James being a changeling. It was clear at once that James' birth could lead to a disputed succession, it made possible the accession of a line of Catholic monarchs in Scotland, and it gave Darnley the hope that he might rule if James succeeded as a minor. In her dilemma, Mary may well have turned to a man of proven loyalty to the Crown, a trusted follower of Marie de Guise who had intercepted English funds sent to the rebel Scottish lords in 1559, and the brother-in-law to Mary's favourite half-brother, Lord John Stewart — he was James Hepburn, Earl of Bothwell. The family were Hereditary High Admirals of Scotland and James, like his father before him, was Lieutenant of the Borders and a considerable landowner in south-east Scotland. Buchanan, now Mary's enemy, invented most of the scandals which he relates of the period and evidence of an affair between Mary and Bothwell in Darnley's lifetime does not exist. Yet it must be conceded that when in February 1567 Darnley died in suspicious circumstances at Kirk o'Field just outside Edinburgh, found with his valet virtually naked, but with no external indication of any injury the morning after an explosion in the night at the house in which he was sleeping, the common people of the capital pointed the finger of scorn first at Bothwell and soon afterwards at Mary. Within two months, a period Mary spent in total physical and mental collapse, placards in Edinburgh proclaimed that Bothwell had murdered the husband of the woman he intended to marry and that he was seeking a divorce.

What finally condemned Mary in contemporary eyes was her marriage to Bothwell on May 15 at Holyrood, a marriage conducted by the Protestant Bishop of Orkney by the reformed rite. The marriage took place after the necessary preliminaries of a trial of the groom for murder, the verdict of acquittal which was unquestionably rigged, and a divorce for the groom's previous wife on the grounds of his adultery with a maid. Mary wrote on the wedding day to the Pope to declare herself his "most devoted daughter", but the Pope ruled on July 2 that the marriage admitted of no defence

and Shakespeare is believed to have modelled Gertrude's marriage to Claudius in Hamlet on it. Within a month of the ceremony, Mary and Bothwell had to confront rebel forces at Carberry with a hastily assembled group of Bothwell's dependants and a few adherents of Mary's. Bothwell fled the country, to die in exile in 1578; Mary was taken to Lochleven and obliged to abdicate in favour of her son and to name Moray as Regent on July 24, 1567. Her reign had lasted just under six years; at 24 years of age she had lost her power for good.

As Dr A L Rowse has observed: "In politics power is what is important, and Mary lost much of her importance when she lost her Throne." But her spirit remained strong. She escaped from Lochleven on May 2, 1568 with the help of young William Douglas, a tribute to her persuasiveness. What is more significant is the signal tribute which followed to the loyalty which she still enjoyed among the Scots. Within six days, a bond was signed at Hamilton by nine earls (out of 19), nine bishops (out of 13), 17 lords, and more than 100 others. Within 11 days, she was able to muster between 5,000 and 6,000 men to fight for her cause at Langside. She had significant support from the Hamiltons and the Hepburns, the Balfours and the Melvilles, and from the people of the southwest who recalled her progress among them five years earlier. Despite all this and the numerical advantage over the enemy forces, she lost the encounter. And she lost her nerve. Had she waited to be better organized and to enlist support from the north, she would still have constituted a viable political figure in Scotland and she could well have routed the forces of Moray. Or she could have gone to France. She had land and money there after all as a Queen Dowager. She was a Catholic sovereign fleeing from Protestant insurgents; as such, she had every hope of support from her Guise relatives and from the French Royal Family. Instead, she resolved to flee, to cast herself upon the mercy of her cousin, Elizabeth, and that decision rendered the success of her party, which was by no means defeated or despondent after Langside, virtually impossible. It was the most serious error of political judgment of her entire career.

THE FUGITIVE

"I have endured injuries, calumnies, imprisonments, famine, cold, heat, flight

119

● Mary, 1578.
SCOTTISH NATIONAL PORTRAIT GALLERY.

not knowing whither, 92 miles across the country without stopping or alighting, and then I have had to sleep upon the ground and drink sour milk, and eat oatmeal without bread, and have been three nights like the owls", Mary wrote to her Guise uncle in June 1568, and to Elizabeth she complained "my condition is pitiable, not to say for a queen, but even for a simple gentlewoman. I have no other dress but that in which I escaped from the field". She left Scotland for good, her head shorn of the radiant red hair as a precaution against recognition, in disguise and accompanied by only a handful of followers, on the afternoon of Sunday May 16 about 3 o'clock and sailed in a small fishing boat from Dundrennan on the Solway coast, reaching Workington in Cumberland at 7pm.

She was received so courteously by Richard Lowther, the deputy governor of Carlisle, where she was taken two days later, that she wrote to the Earl of Cassillis that she expected to be back in Scotland with a French, if not an English, force by mid-August. Her judgment was clearly poor. Elizabeth's statesman, Cecil, was too mindful of Mary's claim to the English Throne and of her potential as a leader of English Catholics to view her coming lightly. It was decided to temporize, to test the reactions of the Scots to the possibility of her return to Scotland, to investigate the accusations made against her by her people. On her part, Mary decided at once to campaign for an audience with Elizabeth and wrote her more than 20 letters in the next few months and even a poem with a last verse which embodies a prophetic fear of the destiny awaiting her:

Ah! I have seen a ship freed from control
On the high seas, outside a friendly port,
And what was peaceful change to woe
   and pain:
Ev'n so am I, a lonely trembling soul,
Fearing - not you, but to be made the
   sport
Of Fate, that bursts the closest,
   strongest chain!

All of course to no avail. On July 13, Mary was moved from Carlisle to Bolton Castle, over 50 miles away in a remote part of the North Riding of Yorkshire and there on July 28 she consented to an inquiry into her conduct in relation to Darnley's death. Moray was demanding from Elizabeth's government that Mary should not be returned to Scotland if she was found guilty of implication in Darnley's murder and it seems likely that Cecil agreed to this privately.

As Cecil put it: "We find neither her continuance here good, nor her departing hence quiet for us." Even if she were acquitted, he intended to make any restitution to Scotland conditional if at all possible — conditional on the acceptance of Protestantism in Scotland and on her renouncing her claim to the English succession. In the summer of 1568, it did not seem impossible that Mary would accept Anglicanism. Sir Francis Knollys, himself a Puritan, reported from Carlisle on July 8:

> Surely the Queen doth seem, outwardly, not only to favour this form, but also the chief articles, of the religion of the gospel, namely justification by faith only; and she heareth the faults of papistry revealed by preaching or otherwise, with contented ears and with gentle and weak replies.

As late as the first weeks of 1569, she was reported to have heard the English service with a book of the Psalms in English in her hand. But the English government's hope of a resolution of the problem which she constituted to them by an inquiry was to be dashed. The investigation by the English commissioners into the cases made by Mary and by Moray opened at York on October 4. The English delegation was led by the Duke of Norfolk, Moray appeared in person, Mary's commissioners were headed by her loyal supporter John Lesley, Bishop of Ross. Although it was now that Moray produced the Casket Letters, that is to say eight letters from Mary to Bothwell allegedly implicating her in Darnley's death together with some verse and contracts for their marriage, on the whole Mary's defence impressed; it was argued that Bothwell had been acquitted of Darnley's murder before the marriage, that she had surrendered at Carberry on promise of her Throne if she abandoned Bothwell, that she had abdicated under duress and that not a tenth of Scottish nobility had taken part in James' coronation.

There was some danger that the York Conference might end with amicable agreement among the Scots so Elizabeth transferred the proceedings on November 25 to Westminster where matters took a much more formal turn. Mary was denied the right to appear in person, but Moray was received by Elizabeth and the outcome, announced on January 10, 1569, was a finding that nothing had been proved to Moray's dishonour or against Mary. As long before as November 21, Cecil had urged that the decision should be: "The Queen of Scots to remain deprived of her crown and the state (of Scotland) continue as it is." Moray took the Casket Letters back with him to Scotland, together with a loan of £5,000 from the English government, and within a few years the letters were irretrievably lost so that all that historians have upon which to make a judgment are contemporary copies of some of them and contemporary published records of others. The judgment of the validity of the Casket Letters has consequently to be as inconclusive as the result of the inquiry into the accusations against Mary, and their authenticity is as dubious as the validity of the proceedings at York and Westminster. The Earl of Sussex, one of the English commissioners, had written from York on October 22: "I think surely no end can be made good for England except the person of the Scots Queen be detained, by one means or another, in England." So it was to be; Mary's flight had ended in detention.

THE CAPTIVITY

Elizabeth's choice of guardian to her prisoner of state was brilliant. George Talbot, sixth Earl of Shrewsbury, who assumed the care of Mary on January 20, 1569, was supremely fitted for the task. He owned, or held from the Crown, a string of defensible properties in the Midlands, safely distant from the coast and ideally suitable as places in which to hold Mary — Tutbury in Staffordshire, Bolsover and Wingfield in Derbyshire, Rufford, Welbeck and Worksop in Nottinghamshire, and Sheffield Castle in Yorkshire. His family badge was the Talbot dog and his character matched it; as a contemporary poet, Thomas Howell, had it:

> The Talbot true that is
> and still hath so remaynde
> Lost never nobleness
> by sprinckle of spot distaynde
> On such a fixed fayth
> Thus trustie Talbot stayeth.

Moreover, he had recently been married to Bess of Hardwick, a formidable woman in whom Elizabeth may well have detected some of her own characteristics. The third daughter of an obscure Derbyshire squire, Elizabeth Hardwick had been married three times before and each widowhood had bolstered her position — to Robert Barlow of Barlow, Derbyshire, whose estates provided useful mineral resources; to Sir William Cavendish, Treasurer of the King's Chamber to Edward VI; and to Sir William St Loe, Captain of the Guard and Butler of the Royal Household to Elizabeth. Edmund Lodge characterized her, writing in the 18th century but from a deep knowledge of manuscript sources, as "a woman of masculine understanding and conduct; proud, furious, selfish and unfeeling. She was a builder, a buyer and seller of estates, a moneylender, a farmer, a merchant of leads, coals and timber." Above all, her husband, George Talbot, was one of the richest of Elizabethan noblemen and could afford to keep Mary, Queen of Scots, in an appropriate style. The settlement proposed to the Earl by his three sons in 1586 was presumably a conservative estimate of his landed income at the time and, leaving among other properties Sheffield and nearby Handsworth in his hands, amounted to a fixed income of £10,070 a year, a very substantial sum indeed.

Now began a period of nearly 15 years' imprisonment for George Talbot, for he could not leave the lady who was his "charge" in more senses than one. At first, he had no choice because of the outbreak of the Northern Rebellion, but to remove with her from one house to the next to provide for her maximum security — to Walton Hall outside Chesterfield, to Wingfield, to Derby, to Tutbury, to Coventry, and to Chatsworth, his wife's house bought with Cavendish money and now being furnished with her St Loe legacy. Always, Mary complained of her conditions.

> I am in a walled enclosure on the top of a hill exposed to all the winds and inclemencies of heaven. Within the said enclosure ... there is a very old hunting lodge, built of timber and plaster, cracked in all parts, the plaster adhering nowhere to the woodwork and broken in numberless places...

So she wrote of Tutbury where Nicholas White, an emissary from Cecil, visited her in February 1569 and asked how she liked the change of air. She replied that she would not have moved for the air,

THE TOWER THISTLE HOTEL

There cannot be a visitor to London these days who hasn't noticed an increased interest in the East End of London or heard about the redevelopment of London's Docklands.

They may even have seen it for themselves from the Dockland Light Railway or perhaps they will have flown into the country's newest airport — London City Airport at The Royal Docks.

Situated on the north bank of the River Thames overlooking Tower Bridge, The Tower Thistle Hotel is uniquely positioned in this exciting area of London. Its location is ideal for the sightseer with local attractions such as The Tower of London and St Katharines Dock. It is also convenient for those with business in the City or as a point of call for those making trips to and from docklands and the east.

Aware of the need to keep ahead of the many changes taking place around it, the hotel has invested £6 million over the last few years in a major refurbishment programme.

Most of its 826 bedrooms have been improved with the last two floors due for completion in 1988. This has included the creation of three floors of Executive bedrooms which cater to the needs of business travellers — particularly the Express Checkout facility located on each Executive floor.

Regular visitors to The Tower Thistle Hotel however would notice the greatest change in the transformation of its public areas — notably the lobby which has been recreated in sophisticated designs of glass and marble including an indoor waterfall which flows over aqueduct-style arches into the pool.

The hotel has three restaurants which are all open to non-residents. For a fixed price The Carvery which overlooks St Katharines Dock, offers a three-course meal including as much as you can eat from the selection of succulent roast joints.

The Picnic Basket Coffee Shop meanwhile, is open from 7.30 am to midnight and serves a wide range of dishes — anything from Pepper Pot soup to a Sirloin Sizzler. Alcoholic beverages are served throughout the day with selected dishes.

The recently refurbished Princes Room Restaurant has one of the best views in London overlooking Tower Bridge and the River Thames. This breathtaking view is complemented by its wide ranging International A la Carte Menu. This includes a fixed price Menu d'Affaires at lunchtime, a Menu de Santee for the health conscious and a six-course Menu de Soiree Galante to accompany dinner dances on Friday and Saturday evenings.

Whether the visitor to this area is looking for a quick snack or wants something more substantial, The Tower Thistle Hotel is the ideal choice for dining. Not only does it offer excellent cuisine but it also provides the perfect setting with magnificent views.

---

but she was glad to be nearer Elizabeth. White earnestly advised Cecil that few should be allowed to see her:

> For beside that she is a goodly personage — and yet in truth not comparable to our sovereign — she hath withal an alluring grace, a pretty Scottish accent, and a searching wit, clouded with wildness. Fame might move some to relieve her, and glory joined to gain might stir others to adventure much for her sake.

It was November 1570 before Shrewsbury could bring Mary to his castle at Sheffield, set in a park eight miles in circumference which in 1637 boasted 1,000 deer and many fine oaks. With the exception of 14 recorded short visits, five to Buxton for the waters, seven to Chatsworth, and two to Worksop, a favourite house of Talbot's, Mary was to be for nearly 14 years, longer than anywhere else in her life, within the bounds of Sheffield Park.

She spent these years occupying the best rooms in the castle, visiting the Manor described in 1637 as "fairly built with stone and timber, with an inward and an outward courtyard" where Cardinal Wolsey had stayed on his last journey in 1530, or being kept so securely that, as Shrewsbury's son, Gilbert, explained to Secretary of State, Dr Thomas Wilson, in May 1573, "unless she could transform herself to a flea or a mouse, it was impossible that she should escape" in the Turret House which Shrewsbury built specially to house her in the grounds of the Manor.

As Shrewsbury was moved to write to Lord Burghley in 1580:

> I do not know what account is made of my charges sustained in the keeping of this woman, but assuredly the very charge of victual of my whole household, with the entertainment I do give to my household servants, is not defrayed with the allowance I have had from her Majesty; besides the which I dare be bold to say the wine, spice and fuel that is spent in my house yearly being valued cometh not under one thousand pounds by the year. Also the loss of plate, the buying of pewter, and all manner of household stuff, which by them is exceedingly spoiled, and wilfully wasted, standeth me in one thousand pounds by

Fast connections to the past.

Every mile along the all-new Docklands Light Railway has poignant reminders of a largely unchronicled past.

Docklands and the East End of London, at the centre of England's once mighty maritime power, were uncompromising places where factories, ships and the

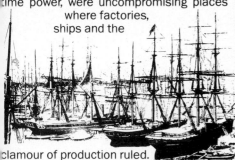

clamour of production ruled.

In this atmosphere the mixture of cockneys and seamen from around the world produced a unique area with a special character of its own.

Much of this past remains untouched alongside the new, insistent, development, and can offer a perceptive traveller many diverse and unusual visits.

Whether these are leisurely or brisk, Docklands Light Railway provides the right kind of service – plenty of stops, frequent trains and a comfortable service.

The Famous Petticoat Lane Market

The railway runs over a mixture of old and new tracks and old tramways, so travellers now get a new perspective of Docklands.

Interesting places are always close at hand; near Tower Gateway there is the first Baptist church in England, and famous Petticoat Lane; a 10th century Saxon stone rood, and the 'Grapes' pub described by Dickens are near Limehouse and Westferry.

An early illustration of St Mary Spital – England's First Baptist Church 1612.

The 'Grapes' Pub

A number of historic ships are moored in West India Docks; and near Island Gardens there's the Island History Trust with its 2,000 photographs, and the site where the Great Eastern was launched.

And there are many, many others.

Historic Shipping moored in West India Docks.

A Photograph from the Island History Trust Collection.

North London Railway, Bow.

And don't forget to visit the Docklands Light Railway shop at Island Gardens station where a variety of momentos are on sale.

The station is just across the river from Greenwich – only a short walk through the river tunnel.

Docklands

The ideal way to make your visits both pleasurable and economical is to get a 'Docklander' ticket which gives you unlimited travel on the railway for a full day for only £1.80.

In itself, the railway – the first of its kind in Britain – offers a new travel experience with spectacular views over the docks.

To check travel times and ticket availability please ring **01-222 1234**

The Tower of London

Tower of London

Docklander £1.80 ADULT 65p CHILD

Map stations
- **Tower Gateway**
- **Shadwell**
- **Limehouse**
- **Westferry**
- **West India Quay**
- **Heron Quays**
- **South Quay**
- **Poplar**
- **All Saints**
- **Canary Wharf** (opening later)
- **Crossharbour**
- **Mudchute**
- **Island Gardens**
- **Stratford**
- **Bow Church**
- **Devons Road**

River Thames

DLR Shop

Foot Tunnel

Greenwich National Maritime Museum

Greenwich

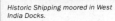

● Linlithgow Palace.
NATIONAL LIBRARY OF SCOTLAND.

the year. Moreover, the annuities I have given to my servants, to the end to be more faithfully served by them, and to prevent any corruption that by want they might be provoked unto, cometh to above £400 by the year, yet do I not reckon the charges to all those soldiers I keep, over that which her Majesty doth allow ... I do leave out an infinite number of other hidden charges which I am driven unto by keeping this woman, for (fear of) troubling you over long.

Elizabeth had promised £500 and £52 a week, but the allowance was irregularly paid. In 1582, we know that Mary and her entourage of about 40 people occupied 12 chambers in the castle, all richly furnished with tapestries, Turkey carpets, embroidered bed hangings, crimson and velvet cushions, and chairs covered with purple velvet and embroidered with cloth of gold and other luxurious materials, and that the Queen had a

choice of 16 dishes at the main meal of the day.

It was a comfortable captivity, but it was captivity and Mary's health declined as a direct consequence. She was never robust, but she was very much an active, outdoor kind of person. The restrictions of movement which she suffered, the inevitable limitations to her riding even within Sheffield Park, affected her severely over the years. As early as March 1569, Shrewsbury wrote of her "grief of the spleen", pains which, he was advised, resulted from "windy matter ascending to the head" and Mary's health was a constant source of concern. The pain in her side at times reduced her to near collapse throughout the 1570s. From time to time, pains in her right arm prevented her from writing. She fell badly from her horse in 1580, damaging her spine. She had dangerous, influenza-like illnesses in 1581 and 1582 and became permanently lame around this time. In recent years, medical historians have diagnosed Mary as suffering from porphyria, the hereditary disease of the

British Royal Family, and the effects of the physical strain which Mary suffered may be seen in the drawn features of the miniature of her executed by Nicholas Hilliard, the portraitist, in 1578 and of the portraits based on that miniature.

Sick she might be, but she never gave up hope of release by one means or another. There were the secret negotiations in 1569 to marry the Duke of Norfolk; though she could not have played more than a minimal part, she was, as Queen Elizabeth commented when the project became public knowledge, "the daughter of debate that eke discord doth sow". She disapproved of the Northern Rising of the Earls of Northumberland and Westmoreland as unlikely to do her cause any good, and she was unenthusiastic about a conspiracy by Sir Thomas Gerard (whose son, John, achieved fame as a Jesuit) and others to rescue her from Chatsworth in the summer of 1570. The Ridolfi Plot of 1571, with the object of placing Mary on the Throne in place of Elizabeth, was less than wholeheartedly supported by her; it resulted in Norfolk's execution and in Mary's being branded as a traitor in the common view of people in England, especially as it came so quickly after the papal bull *Regnans in Excelsis* of February 1570, which formally excommunicated Elizabeth and absolved Catholics from their loyalty to her. The St Bartholomew's Day Massacre of Protestants in France in August 1572 was clearly unconnected with Mary, but it was led by her Guise relatives and reinforced the English view of her as a foreign traitor. Her intrigues were, of course, monitored by the English government and, had it not been for a personal intervention by Elizabeth, the Commons would have passed a bill of attainder on her in the summer of 1572; as it was, they contented themselves with formally depriving her of any claim to the English Throne and with declaring that, should she be involved in further plotting, she would be subject to trial by peers of the English realm.

Not surprisingly, security became a source of concern for the English Privy Council and there were frequent exchanges of letters between Shrewsbury and Cecil on the subject. To take only one 12-month period in 1574-75, two discontented chaplains, Corker and Haworth, had accused the Earl of partiality towards his prisoner and George Talbot replied indignantly on April 16, 1574:

> How can it be imagined that I should be disposed to favour this Queen for her claim to succeed the Queen's Majesty? My dealing towards her hath shewn the contrary: I know her to be a stranger, a Papist, and my enemy.

In mid-October, Shrewsbury's Countess, Bess of Hardwick, and Darnley's mother connived at a marriage between Elizabeth Cavendish and Darnley's younger brother, Charles Stewart, Earl of Lennox, at Shrewsbury's house at Rufford, a marriage which had dynastic implications and aroused Queen Elizabeth's wrath. Additionally, to this point Bess of Hardwick had found her husband's prisoner a useful source of guidance in cultural matters and in particular in the working of embroidery pieces with which to decorate her houses; now she saw Mary as a potential threat to the furthering of her Cavendish sons and of Arabella Stewart, the child born to Elizabeth and Charles in the summer of 1575. Lady Lennox and Lady Shrewsbury were both imprisoned in the spring of 1575 for their part in arrang-

ing the marriage, but no sooner was she released than Bess of Hardwick found that further suspicions were aroused against her husband. As Shrewsbury explained to Burghley on March 3, 1574-75:

> The mislike her Majesty hath of my son Gilbert's wife, brought to bed in my house, as cause of women and strangers repair thither, makes me heartily sorry; nevertheless, the midwife excepted, none such have, or do at any time, come within her sight; and at the first, to avoid such resort, I myself with two of my children christened the child.

The Privy Council stopped short of denying Mary access to messengers from Scotland and France, though no doubt steps were taken to render such access as harmless as possible, but Shrewsbury reasonably told Burghley in the same letter that this was a practice which had its inherent dangers:

> Be you assured, my Lord, this Lady will not stay to put in practice, or make inquiry by all means she can devise, and ask me no leave, so long as such access of her people is permitted unto her.

Intrigue occurred not only within Mary's immediate circle, but also in continental Europe. Pope Pius V's successor, Gregory XIII, was keen that Philip II of Spain, the greatest European King, should take up "the Enterprise of England" as a latter-day crusade. Philip for his part feared that if he attacked England, even in favour of a Queen Dowager of France, France might counter-attack and that for certain it would mean further trouble with his already rebellious subjects in the Netherlands. The result in the 1570s was an uneasy peace, especially during the period 1576-79 when Philip's half-brother, Don John of Austria, the hero of the Lepanto victory against the Turks in 1571, was governor of the Netherlands and expected to attack England once he had settled the Netherlands. Fortunately for Elizabeth, he never quite succeeded in settling the Netherlands and died of the plague before he could invade England. Things took a turn for the worse from 1580, however, from the Protestant point of view. For to the Catholic missionaries to England who had been coming from the seminary at Douai in France were now

added Jesuit priests, a much more disciplined and determined set of men. Worse, the papal patronage of the Jesuit mission was accompanied by the revelation of a Catholic-inspired enterprise against Ireland, and later of a letter from the Cardinal Secretary Como to the Papal Nuncio Sega at Madrid in response to an inquiry from two English noblemen about whether they would be committing sin if they killed Elizabeth?

> ... whosoever sends her out of the world with the pious intention of doing God service, not only does not sin but gains merit.

Pius had made assassination lawful; Gregory encouraged it. In practice, there occurred two attempts on the life of William of Orange, the leader of the Protestants in the Netherlands, and the second, on July 10, 1584, was successful.

In 1580, too, things had changed in Scotland in ways that encouraged hopes that a base might be found there for the "Enterprise against England" and for Mary's restoration. Regent Morton's influence, which had been pro-English and fiercely Protestant, now gave way to that of Esme Stewart, a first cousin of Darnley, who arrived from France in September 1579. Mary proposed in 1581 through the Duke de Guise that she should be joint sovereign with James and this "scheme of association" was renewed several times in the next few years. By 1582, an ambitious project was mooted by which Esme Stewart was, with the help of forces from continental Europe, to secure first Scotland and then England for the Catholic cause. The counter-coup, known as the Ruthven Raid of August 1582, however, dislodged Stewart from power, and extreme Protestantism prevailed until James escaped from the raiders in June 1583. As James' position in Scotland became more secure, his enthusiasm for the "enterprise" waned. After June 1584, the Protestant Henry of Navarre was heir to the French Throne and Guise energy was directed at preventing his acceptance as King. Consequently, Spain rather than France became heavily involved in the "Enterprise against England", now encouraged by Mary as her agent, Francis Throckmorton, revealed under torture when he was arrested in November 1583.

It was not just that Mary became more politically active in the Catholic cause; as the years of captivity wore on,

he gradually came to be a more conscientious Catholic than she had been. As a girl and young woman, it would seem that she had conformed rather than believed, and this accounts for her willingness to flout her faith by marrying Bothwell by Protestant rites, for example. In captivity, deprived by circumstance and by the advance of middle age of active pursuits, she came to have an increasing preoccupation with religion and her household observed regular hours for readings and prayer. She herself wrote poems and essays which reflected the deepening of her depression and the flourishing of her faith. For example, in 1579 she wrote in a Book of Hours:

Was ever known a fate more sad than
mine?
    Ah! better death for me than life, I
ween!
For me there is no sorrow's anodyne:
    T'wards me all change their nature
and their mien.

In 1580, she wrote an Essay on Adversity in which she reviewed a series of biblical, Roman, and medieval examples of rulers who had suffered adversity as she had done. Throughout her imprisonment, she had confessors in her household on one pretext or another and in October 1575 she had asked Pope Gregory for episcopal powers for her chaplain and for him to have the right to absolve her after hearing confession. By the early 1580s, as another poem demonstrates, she had reached a Christian resignation and was evidently in her heart as well as by her mouth and actions a committed Catholic:

Give me, dear Lord, the true humility
And strengthen my too feeble halting
    faith;
Let but Thy Spirit shed his light on me—
Checking my fever with His purer
    breath.

In September 1584, Mary's guardianship was transferred to Sir Ralph Sadler and in January 1585, she was moved to Tutbury, which she detested, in the care of the Puritan bigot, Sir Amyas Paulet. She was deprived of air by strict orders that she should be kept in close confinement,

deprived of communication with the outside world and with her agents abroad especially, and was deprived of the comfort of her religion as when Paulet had destroyed a packet of rosaries and religious pictures sent to her. To add to her misery, in March 1585, her son, King James, in Council declared that the "Association desired by his mother should neither be granted nor spoken of hereafter" and negotiations followed which resulted in a binding treaty between England and Scotland in July 1586. On Christmas Eve 1585, she was moved to Chartley Hall, but she became ill and took to her bed for a month. Finally, in September 1586, she was removed to Fotheringhay in Northamptonshire. By then, her fate was sealed. From January 1586, she was allowed secret correspondence again and when she wrote approvingly in reply to a letter from Anthony Babington disclosing a plot by a group of English Catholics to assassinate Elizabeth as an accompaniment to an invitation from abroad, her letter was intercepted. Babington and his fellow conspirators were arrested, tried, and executed in September 1586; Mary was tried in October at Fotheringhay and found guilty when the court reconvened at Westminster of "compassing and imagining since June 1st matters tending to the death and destruction of the Queen of England". The two Houses of Parliament petitioned Elizabeth to execute Mary, but Elizabeth, conscious of the significance of putting to death an anointed sovereign, prevaricated. An approach was made to her gaoler, Paulet, to do away with her quietly, but he responded in early February:

God forbid that I should make so foul a
shipwreck of my conscience, or leave so
great blot to my posterity, as to shed
blood without law and warrant.

By now, Elizabeth had reluctantly signed the death warrant and Secretary Davison had handed it to Robert Beale, the Clerk of the Privy Council, for transmission to Fotheringhay.

Mary died on February 8, 1587; ironically, the Earl of Shrewsbury, so long her considerate guardian, presided over the occasion. In her last letter to her brother-in-law, Henry III of France, she wrote that "the Catholic faith and the assertion of my God-given right to the English Crown are the two issues on which I am condemned" and she faced death calmly and with great dignity. As

Lord Buckhurst, Elizabeth's cousin, wrote to the Queen four days later, "every hour of her life did endanger your death" and when Parliament assembled it declared the land purged, the wrath of God pacified, and her Majesty's days prolonged in peace to "the comfort of us and our posterity". Henry III expressed the Catholic reaction when he wrote to James VI:

The Queen of England has offended all
the sovereign princes and kings in the
world, subjecting a sovereign Queen
to that from which God has by special
privileges exempted Kings who cannot
be judged except by him.

In France, there followed demonstrations which virtually canonized Mary as a martyr for her faith, in Scotland people felt humiliated and angered, in Spain the preparations for the Spanish Armada were given a new impetus, the Catholic League and Philip II were alike moved by her death as by a Catholic rallying-cry. But her son, James VI, made only token protest and the Anglo-Scottish alliance remained unaffected. Mary's execution was more important in retrospect than even her Catholic contemporaries saw it to be. Years before, she had stitched into one of her embroideries "En ma fin git mon commencement"; it was her mother's motto but it epitomized the real significance of Mary's death superbly. It marked the beginning, not the end, of her imperishable fame.

Further reading

D J Breeze, A Queen's Progress, HMSO Edinburgh, 1987

British Medical Association, Porphyria — a Royal Malady, 1968

Alastair Cherry, Princes, Poets and Patrons: The Stuarts and Scotland, HMSO, Edinburgh, 1987

Gordon Donaldson, Mary Queen of Scots, Hodder and Stoughton, 1974

Antonia Fraser, Mary Queen of Scots, Weidenfeld & Nicolson, 1969

J D Leader, Mary Queen of Scots in Captivity, Sheffield, 1880

Roy Strong and Julia Trevelyan Oman, Mary Queen of Scots, Secker and Warburg, 1972

Margaret Swain, The Needlework of Mary Queen of Scots, Van Nostrand, 1973

Stefan Zweig, The Queen of Scots, Cassell, first published 1935, 1987

See also G R Batho, A Calendar of the Shrewsbury and Talbot Papers, Vol II: Talbot Papers in the College of Arms (now at Lambeth Palace), HMSO, 1971

*Professor Batho is Professor of
History at the University of
Durham.*

THE MOST POWERFUL MONARCH IN CHRISTENDOM

Philip II of Spain was determined to strengthen Catholicism and threw his weight behind the dreaded Inquisition. But his ethic was based on honour, writes Glanmor Williams

*I*N THE YEAR 1558, the Emperor Charles V, feeling the crushing burden of having ruled over his vast, diverse, and ramshackle domains for 40 years, summoned his son and heir, the 31-year-old Prince Philip, from Spain to the Netherlands so that the young man might acquaint himself with some of his future subjects and be given practical guidance by his father on how to cope with the multifarious problems facing a great ruler. Four years earlier, Charles had arranged a second marriage for his young widower-son with Queen Mary of England, herself half-Spanish by birth, as the daughter of Catherine of Aragon and Henry VIII, and, to fit him for the alliance, had given him the kingdom of Naples. Thereby, the old Emperor had envisaged an arrangement which would compensate him for his losses in Germany, enable his son and daughter-in-law to rule over a compact empire consisting of Spain, the Netherlands, and England, and bring additional pressure on encircled France, ancient and irreconcilable enemy of the Habsburgs. In October 1555, Charles abdicated as ruler of the Netherlands and in January 1556 as King of Spain. By November 1558, his earlier plans had gone adrift when England was lost as a result of Mary's death and in 1559 Philip returned to Spain. He had now truly entered into his inheritance. For nearly 40 years, until his death in 1598, he would rule Spain and never again leave the Iberian peninsula. Over much of that period, he was the only adult and experienced male ruler of a major state in Western Europe. Rarely has it been given to any sovereign to stamp the impress of his personality so emphatically on the lives of his subjects.

Charles had reluctantly been obliged to realize that his empire, too large and incoherent for one man to rule successfully, must be divided. Nevertheless, although it was not his son, but his brother, Ferdinand, who succeeded him as Holy Roman Emperor, the empire which Philip was called upon to govern was one of the most extensive known to history, with possessions spread over four continents. In Europe, the kingdoms of Spain, the Balearic Islands, the kingdom of the Two Sicilies and Naples, the duchy of Milan, and the Netherlands and Franche-Comté came under his sway. He occupied bases on the North African coast and in the Canaries. Across the Atlantic, he ruled over the huge domains of the Spanish New World, to which his reign would see number of extensions. In the distant Pacific Ocean, his subjects conquered the Philippines from the 1560s onwards. To all this was added in 1580 the kingdom of Portugal, the acquisition of which fulfilled a centuries-old aspiration to bring the whole Iberian peninsula under one ruler. Furthermore, it brought into his possession the Atlantic ports of Portugal, its impressive maritime resources, and its world trading empire. "The King of Spain is the most potent monarch of Christendom," marvelled a contemporary Englishman, Owen Feltham, "who in his own hands holds the mines of the wars' sinews - money - and hath now got a command so wide that out of his Dominions the sun can neither rise nor set." The second half of the 16th century in European history was assuredly the "Age of Spanish Preponderance".

To assume his awesome responsibility, Philip had been meticulously prepared throughout his childhood and youth. Charles V had carefully super-

Philippus II Catholicus Hispaniarum Rex.
Et Indiarum Noüiq Orbis Monarcha
Potentissimus

Ant. Moro Pinxit   I. Suyderhoef Sculpxit
P. Soutman Effigiauit et Excud   Cum Priuil. S. C. M.

● Mining of precious metals in the New World. From *Americae pars Quinta*, pub. 1595. Theodore de Bry. Engraving.
NATIONAL MARITIME MUSEUM.

NIGRITÆ IN SCRUTANDIS VENIS METALLICIS
ab Hifpanis in Infulas ablegantur.

Tritis & penè abfumptis continuo labore Hifpaniolæ Infulæ incolis, Hifpani aliunde mancipia conquirere cœperunt, quorum miniſterio in perfodiendis montibus, venſque metallicis perfcrutandis uterentur. Itaque redemptis fua pecunia, & accitis ex Guinea Quartæ Africæ partis Provincia mancipiis Æthiopibus five Nigritis, illorum porrò opera ufi funt, donec temporis fucceffu quicquid in ea Infula metallicarum venarum ineffet, exhaurirent. Nam ut Lufitani eam Africæ partem, quam ipfi Guineam (incolæ Genni aut Genna appellant) fibi fubjectam reddiderant, fingulis annis aliquot incolarum centurias exteris nationibus divendebant, quæ mancipiorum vicem fupplerent.

A 2   Nigritæ

vised his son's upbringing, education, and marriages; had left a series of lengthy and detailed instructions for his guidance; and had associated him for some years with his own rule. Moreover, Charles was conscious that, although he had spent 24 years out of his 40 as King of Spain outside that country, it had increasingly become his main power-base; so he had insisted that Philip be brought up as a prince of Spain in a manner thoroughly befitting one who was to become ruler of the country. From his father, Philip inherited three central tenets: that France was the principal enemy of the Habsburg dynasty; that the Roman Church must be safeguarded against heresy and subversion; and that Europe must be resolutely protected against the menace of Islam. He was intensely devoted to Charles's memory and reputation, and longed to be able to emulate his feats, but was always somewhat fearful of his own inadequacy in comparison with his father's heroic prestige and achievement. Philip's mother, the Empress Isabel, with whom he spent most of his earliest years, also influenced him considerably. Herself half-Portuguese, she inculcated into her son the ambition of uniting the Iberian kingdoms and instilled him with a profound attachment to religion and the desirability of appropriately reserved, dignified, even chilly, behaviour on the part of royalty. The tutors appointed to direct his studies and deportment left a further permanent mark on his subsequent development. Among them were Juan Martínez de Siliceo, a cleric who later became Philip's confessor; Honorato Juan, who taught him mathematics and architecture; and Juan Gines de Sepulveda, his instructor in geography and history. Most influential of all was Don Juan de Zúñiga, who brought him up to behave with all the grace, formality, restraint, and self-control expected of a Spanish grandee.

The interests he acquired in his youth remained with him all his life. He was always an avid and discerning collector of books, manuscripts, and maps who, by the time of his death, had brought together the largest private library in Western Europe, consisting of 14,000 volumes. He supported scholarship within the great universities and printing presses of his realm, including

the publication in 1568-72 of the celebrated *Poliglota Regia*, the edition of the Bible in Hebrew, Aramaic, Greek, and Latin. An enthusiastic connoisseur of architecture, painting, drawing, and the fine arts, he was a patron of Titian, the architect Herrera, and other notable artists. Passionately fond of music, he warmly encouraged Vitoria, the greatest Spanish composer of the age, and other musicians. He also revealed a keen interest in the sciences, including mathematics, botany, and zoology, and took great delight in planting his gardens with trees and flowers and in collecting animals in zoos. Hunting was a passion with him and, although not much given to exercise, he would exert himself to pursue game even into his old age. One of the signal weaknesses of his education, however, particularly for one destined to rule over such a mixture of peoples speaking many different tongues and to

conduct extensive diplomacy, was the failure to give him serious instruction in any language but his own. Throughout his life, he remained a poor linguist, always ill at ease with the spoken word and in conversation.

Philip was of rather less than average height, but carried himself so "straight and upright as he loseth no inch in height". He was clean, neat, and fastidious; and soberly elegant and dignified in appearance. Despite his characteristic Habsburg lower lip and jutting jaw, he was a good-looking man. When he was young, his hair and beard were fair, and this, together with his blue eyes, made him look more like a Netherlander than a Spaniard. Later in life, his hair went white, his face became more puffed and pallid, and his eyes red-rimmed and strained as a result of hours of reading. Careful, frugal, and regular though he was in his routine, his health was never

● Drake as "Terrible Draco". Willem and Magdalena van de Passe. Engraving.
NATIONAL MARITIME MUSEUM.

the legislation against the Moriscoes and the conversion of his subjects in the Indies to Christianity. His profound concern for religion found expression in the Escorial, that most typical and enduring memorial of the man and his reign. Part-monastery, part-mausoleum, and part-palace, it took him 20 years to build and was the very image in stone of his own religious aspirations and those of the Counter-Reformation in Spain. Could he have had his own way, Philip would have wished to have all the millions of his subjects untainted by heresy or unbelief and united in their devotion to the faith.

He carried over his religious convictions into his approach to the task of kingship. He regarded himself as being entrusted by God with the most sacred and solemn responsibility for the welfare of all his subjects. To God, he believed, he would in due course be answerable for all his actions in relation to them. Nothing would be too trivial or inconsequential for him not to be held accountable. From this sprang his passionate determination to do justice to all those entrusted to his care. "Justice is his favourite interest," wrote a Venetian ambassador of him in 1563, "and in so far as its administration concerns him, he does his duty well." That did not prevent him, however, from acting in a furtive and savagely arbitrary manner on rare occasions to rid himself of those he deemed enemies dangerous to the state, as when he disposed of Baron Montigny of the Netherlands in 1570, or connived at the murder of Don John's secretary, Juan Escobedo, in 1578, or authorized the assassination of William the Silent in 1584.

For more than one reason, Philip viewed his sovereign power as a prerogative not to be shared with other men. His father, whose precepts he held in such awe, had counselled him not to depend on others, especially powerful nobles. Philip hardly needed any warning against the appetite of his aristocrats for place and power, nor against the equal eagerness of men of lesser rank in acquiring riches and influence for themselves - even if that did not enable him to prevent the existence of a great deal of the corruption and cupidity in court circles that seemed inseparable from 16th

strong and he suffered much in later years from asthma, stone, and arthritis. Death eventually came to him as a blessed relief after months of the most painful suffering, stoically borne.

There was nothing which Philip owed to his Spanish upbringing of greater consequence than his devotion to the Catholic religion. The whole ethos of the Hispanic kingdoms was dominated by their concept of the *Reconquista*, the organizing principle of their history, as the triumph of God's true faith, through the human agency of the Spanish kings and their peoples, over infidel, unbeliever, and heretic. After the final defeat of the Moors by the fall of Granada in 1492, it seemed to the Spaniards that their manifest destiny as the champions of God and the Holy Church had been transferred to the wider theatre of the New World. The kingdom of Castile, in particular, had come to identify its well-

being and prosperity with the continued maintenance of its people's special role as the instruments of God's purpose. It was in this spirit that Philip's parents and tutors indoctrinated him with the centrality of the Catholic religion, for its own sake and as the cement which held his diverse subjects together and confirmed his authority over them. He was himself, without question, a deeply religious individual, the sincerity of whose beliefs were recognized by such important figures as St Theresa and Ignatius Loyola, the founder of the Jesuits. He fulfilled his religious duties punctiliously and conscientiously, attaching great store by the advice and instruction of his confessors. Holding heretics, infidels, and Jews in the utmost abhorrence, he threw all the weight of his influence and authority behind the Spanish Inquisition, was himself present at more than one *auto-da-fé*, and energetically backed century government. Moreover, Philip's cautious and reticent nature tended to make him uncomfortable with many of those around him. He imposed rigid restraint on his own outward emotions, even receiving the news of a victory such as Lepanto over the Turks, or the defeat of the Armada with apparent imperturbability; and kept his opinions to himself to the point of dissimulating his true feelings. He was especially uneasy in his relations with bold, masterful, extrovert men; even with such illustrious servants as the imperious Duke of Alva, the dashing Don John, or the brilliant Alexander Farnese. He never entirely trusted anyone, and an observant Venetian ambassador was of the opinion in 1574 that the King "suffers from the same malady as his father; that is, suspicion". Mistrustful of all, he liked, as far as he could, to play off one party among his nobility against another, as he did for years the rival factions which lined up behind the Duke of Alva on one side and the Prince of Eboli on the other.

But no one could have faulted Philip for lack of commitment or dedication to his *métier* of kingship, however grindingly laborious or demanding it might be. "Being a king is none other than a form of slavery which carries with it a crown," he told his son and heir a year before he died; that was no empty phrase, but summarized for him the experience of a lifetime. He insisted on being fully informed about everything and everybody. As a result, he was overwhelmed by mountains of paper and thousands of memoranda of every kind, "the correspondence of ambassadors, the reports of viceroys and governors, of customs and treasury and municipal officials ... petitions and memorials and findings of judicial meetings, the accounts of dockyards and mints and mines, and of the royal household". From all corners of his far-flung territories, they poured in an endless stream - an almost incredible 400 in one day alone - to such an extent that the French historian, Henri Hauser, dubbed him "le roi paperassier". He devoted himself to infinite, wearisome hours of painstakingly reading documents and annotating them in his crabbed and spidery handwriting. He toiled and moiled with an heroic indefatigability; slaving over them not only in his study but also on board ship, in his coach, and even in the course of picnics. In that largely illiterate age, others were amazed at his dogged perseverance in reading. His own grand almoner, Luis Manrique, thought it unnatural and unseemly that a king should devote so much of his time "sitting forever over your papers, from your desire ... to seclude yourself from the world, and from a want of confidence in your ministers ... Hence such interminable delays as fill the soul of every suitor with despair ... God did not send your Majesty and all the other kings, his viceroys on earth, to waste their time in reading or writing, nor yet in meditation and despair." But Philip found it more congenial to deal with the written than the spoken word. Besides, it gave his hesitant, characteristically irresolute Habsburg mind more time to mull over perplexing decisions and intricate issues. His cardinal defects as an administrator were that he was unbearably reluctant to distinguish between the significant and the trivial, matters of high policy and routine administration, and that he found it almost impossible to delegate responsibility to others. Hence the daunting slowness and delays which characterized his regime, leading one contemporary observer to gibe with weary cynicism, "If death came from Spain, I should live to be a very great age". In fairness to Philip nevertheless, it should be remembered that other contemporary rulers were no less hesitant and unwilling to commit

THE CAMPAIGN OF
The Spanish Armada
PETER KEMP

Published to celebrate the 400th anniversary of this decisive battle, *The Campaign of the Spanish Armada* is a fascinating account of the ill-fated campaign which led to the defeat of Philip II of Spain and his plans to expand the Catholic empire.

The Papal involvement, the naval tactics, so crucial in the heavy open seas of the English Channel, and the effect of the Campaign upon naval power are all examined by this distinguished naval historian in a way which is both compelling and informative.

Complimented by illustrations of contemporary paintings, artefacts and charts, *The Campaign of the Spanish Armada* gives the definitive account of this important turning point in European history.

240 × 210mm 176pp 88 illustrations, including 39 in colour
0 7148 2503 4 £17.95 Published: 10 March 1988

ΦPhaidon
THE · ART · OF · FINE · BOOKS

themselves than he: Elizabeth of England's vacillations were the despair of her Privy Council.

There was, though, another more relaxed and affectionate side to Philip's character. He was an unusually devoted son, a good husband, and an exceptionally affectionate father. The letters that he wrote from Portugal during his stay there in 1580-2 to his two daughters, Isabella and Catherine, for whom he cherished a warm and genuine affection, show a mixture of sensitive concern for their activities and a delightful sense of humour. Not that in general Philip enjoyed a particularly happy family or domestic life. Married four times, he outlived all his wives, but had a deep and sincere affection for the third and fourth of them, Elizabeth of Valois (1559-68) and Anne of Austria (1570-80). Four of his children died in infancy or at a very tender age, and Philip had the melancholy duty of entombing no fewer than 17 members of his near family at the Escorial by 1584. His eldest son, Don Carlos, occasioned him acute anxiety and grief. A diseased fruit not untypical of the inbred Spanish royal stock, Don Carlos was a psychopath who caused his father and all about him growing alarm until, in the end, Philip had no choice but to lock him up in a secure place, where he ultimately seems to have starved himself to death in 1568.

Among his Castilian subjects, their King was tremendously well liked and respected. They envisaged him as the incarnation of their most admired national qualities. He was a sworn and staunch upholder of the faith and all it represented in their existence. He was utterly devoted to his country and the well- being of its subjects; the champion of justice among all its citizens. Pious, regal, dignified, and disciplined, he was also frugal, simple, and unostentatious in his dress and way of life. Perhaps, too, beneath all the inevitable pomp and splendour of his role as king, they sensed the human qualities of the man. He was for them Felipe el Prudente: Philip the Wise; slow-moving, possibly, but wary, watchful, and discreet; incapable of any rash, foolish, or unjust act.

Circumspection Philip certainly needed in grappling with the vast and varied problems of government with which his empire presented him. From Ferdinand and Isabella and Charles, he had inherited a rejuvenated royal authority, armed with the typical conciliar and secretarial instruments of 16th century government, a redoubtable military machine, and an immensely influential church which had undergone a thoroughgoing but conservative reform. The solution of those earlier monarchs to the question of governing disparate and widely-scattered states had been the application on a wider scale of the Aragonese or federal solution to the issue of sovereignty, ie the sovereign became ruler of a federation in which each of the member kingdoms and territories maintained its own identity and its own laws and customs. The emphasis was on the monarch being king in each part and not ruler over them all. In fact, the huge agglomeration of lands and peoples ruled over by Charles and Philip had only two features in common - the person of their ruler and their religion. But even the faith, the main substitute for political unity in the Habsburg domains, had since 1517 been in jeopardy from the assaults of heretics. Charles had fought tirelessly but unavailingly to maintain the Church inviolate within his empire. In the Netherlands, his son would be faced with equally obstinate resistance from Protestants. He would also have to cope with the remains of Moorish religion and culture in Spain and the paganism of the natives in the Indies.

Seeking a measure of more centralized authority would be a daunting operation. It was the kingdom of Castile which offered him the rosiest prospects. Here, the combination of effective monarchical authority, a capable bureaucracy, and national pride and consciousness allied to the royal interest enabled Philip for most of his reign to raise far larger sums in taxation and make heavier demands for manpower than anywhere else in his domains. In the Indies, too, despite their remoteness, Philip's government was able skilfully to blend effective regional government with the maximum degree of centralization possible in such distant, dispersed possessions. The viceroys enjoyed enormous powers, but found themselves closely bound to the relevant council at Court. Elsewhere, Philip encountered strong opposition to many of his measures. The inhabitants of the kingdom of Aragon clung unyieldingly to their *fueros*, their own individual customs and liberties; the Italian possessions were understandably reluctant to contribute any help to projects not directly involving the defence of the Mediterranean against the power of Islam; and in the Netherlands there was strong resentment against any attempt on Philip's part to hispanicize his government and bitter resistance to his religious policy on the part of the Calvinists.

One of the most insuperable obstacles in the way of more effectual government was the slowness of communications over so enormous and widespread an empire in a century when the fastest mode of land transport was a good horse, and sea communications depended on the vagaries of wind and weather. "Space was enemy number one," said Fernand Braudel. Within the Iberian peninsula, it took a fast courier from Lisbon or Seville four days to reach Madrid (which Philip made his capital in 1561). Despatches from Brussels took 10 days and those from Milan a fortnight to get there. Still more time-consuming and uncertain were communications across the Atlantic, which might at best take a month and at worst three or four. Messages to the remote outposts of the Portuguese empire or to the Philippines took even longer. Not infrequently by the time that news from the more distant parts reached Madrid, the whole position on the spot might have changed. And, of course, so dispersed and heterogeneous an empire, brought together by

marriage and accident rather than military design or economic necessity, was not only beset by internal difficulties, but was also surrounded by many external enemies, some dangerous and powerful, others weak and nervous, but all surveying Philip's inheritance enviously and eagerly awaiting the opportunity to take advantage of any weakness, real or suspected.

Defending his territories required Philip ceaselessly to deploy all the resources of war and diplomacy open to him. The Spanish armies, organized into the famous *tercios*, were the most renowned in Europe. Seasoned and battle-hardened troops, since the era of the "Great Captain", Gonsalvo de Córdoba, early in the 16th century, they had been regarded as the best fighting units in Western Europe, and throughout the century were considered to be invincible when fighting on anything like equal terms. The hard core remained Spanish, though the majority of the troops were recruited from among Germans, Italians, and Walloons. The *tercios* consisted of 12 companies of about 250 men each and were rigorously trained and disciplined, and formidably armed with pikes and arquebuses. Philip's naval units were distinctly less impressive than his land troops early in his reign, despite the lengthy and glorious Iberian maritime tradition. During his first few years, he had to exert himself very strenuously to build and equip galleys to counter the threat from the Ottomans and the Barbary pirates. Later in his reign, he was forced to make an equally great effort to create an ocean-going navy to match the fleets of his rivals. It was greatly to his credit that he succeeded as well as he did. Even so, he did not like committing himself to the expense and hazards of warfare. "He fears warfare as the burnt child does the fire," was the patronizing comment of the English Jesuit, Parsons, who, perhaps it should be noted, had never had to bear the onerous responsibility of raising troops and money or submit them to the uncertain arbitrament of war. For the outcome of every battle, Philip warned his son-in-law in 1586, was always in the hands of God not men; and even the most devout of rulers could never be sure that he had not offended God by his sins, as Philip believed he discovered when the Armada was defeated. Philip, like his contemporaries, Elizabeth I and Catherine de Medici of France, preferred to gain his ends by diplomacy whenever he could. To this

end, he maintained resident ambassadors, emissaries, and representatives at most of the leading European courts. After the fashion of contemporary diplomacy, these men advised their master, pressed his cause, lied and deceived on his behalf when necessary, tried to counteract the diplomatic exertions of rivals, and spied diligently on all that was going on, especially in those circles hostile to the regime. A leading Spanish ambassador in London, Bernardino Mendoza, much to his indignation, was dismissed from England for being embroiled in the Throckmorton Plot of 1584 against Elizabeth; he declared with patrician disdain, "he was born not to disturb kingdoms but to conquer them". Like all the high posts in military and naval commands, viceroyalties and senior diplomatic responsibilities were reserved for leading members of the Spanish nobility. Excluded from the domestic government of Spain, their energies and ambitions were diverted to find satisfaction in war and diplomacy, though some of these missions could be ruinously expensive for those who undertook them.

The government of his empire, and especially the campaigns which Philip was obliged to undertake to defend its omnifarious interests, called for an inexhaustible supply of money. In the field of finance, Philip was forced to confess his own inadequacy. "I do not understand a word of it," he admitted, having read a financial memorandum, and, on another occasion, "I have never been able to get this business of loans and interest into my head". Throughout his reign, he was bedevilled by the problem of money. Though some of his territories, such as the Netherlands and his Italian possessions, were among the richer parts of Europe, they were extremely unwilling to contribute to the general expenditure. Moreover, from 1566 onwards, the Netherlands proved to be a bottomless pit into which endless sums had to be poured. Philip was therefore obliged to depend on three main sources for revenue: Castile, the Church, and the silver of the Indies. The non-noble population of Castile was by the end of his reign hopelessly overtaxed, the nobility being exempted from such payments, and was strained beyond breaking-point by the galloping inflation of prices. The Church provided Philip with about 20 per cent of his income; and silver from the New World accounted for about 11 per cent at the beginning of his reign and 20 per cent

● Drake's attack on San Domingo, 1586. Theodore de Bry. Engraving.
NATIONAL MARITIME MUSEUM.

by 1598. Without the credit with which the silver provided him, his empire might not have survived.

Never at any point did Philip succeed in meeting all the financial demands made on him. As early as 1545, he had felt compelled to write to his father to protest that the common people who had to pay the taxes were "reduced to such utter misery that many of them walk naked". Not that this dire warning restrained Charles from further ruinous expenditure and Philip inherited from him an irreparably damaged and imbalanced financial situation. He took over from Charles debts amounting to some 20 million ducats and as early as January 1557 had to declare himself bankrupt. Having, like Charles, no state bank to turn to, he had no option but to depend on the goodwill of Genoese bankers to raise money for his wars. His income in 1560 was 3.1 million ducats and by 1598 it had risen by more than 300 per cent to 9.7 million. But his debts had risen more than 400 per cent to 85 million ducats and he had twice gone bankrupt again in the meantime - in 1575 and 1596. The

Armada alone had cost him 10 million ducats. The strain on Castile had been appalling: crippled by taxation and inflation, beset in the 1590s by economic decline, bad harvests, famine, plague, and devastating mortality and depopulation, this once-proud heart of the empire was by 1600 utterly depressed and exhausted.

Despite all the embarrassments, financial and political, it caused him, Philip strove unceasingly for more than 40 years to maintain his realms inviolable against all the hostile forces which menaced them. For much of that time, the dominant principle was that of "sturdy defensiveness", inherited from Charles V; his campaigns were fought principally to ward off the threats posed by his enemies. Such was his attitude towards the Turkish Ottoman Empire and its allies, his most dangerous adversary for the first 20 years of his reign. Philip found himself confronted by an empire ruled by Sultan Suleiman the Magnificent (1520-66), greatest of all the sultans and the most awe-inspiring and experienced ruler in Europe, who was

pressing inexorably on the central and western Mediterranean. What made the peril all the more alarming was the existence in Spain of a potential "fifth column" in the shape of its large Morisco population. The rising of the Moriscoes in 1568-70, even though the Ottomans neglected the opportunity to support them, was put down only with the utmost difficulty. Its suppression resulted in serious economic loss to Spain, but Philip was reported to have shrugged it off, "valuing religion more than money". Shortly afterwards came the crushing naval defeat imposed on the Ottomans at Lepanto in 1571; but they were able to mount a surprisingly speedy recovery and not until the 1580s did they really disengage. Spain's enemies in Western Europe were fully aware of the Ottoman pressure on Madrid and only too willing to seek the possibility of exploiting Philip's "war on two fronts". When, for instance, Elizabeth I sent Wil-

● The Earl of Leicester as Governor of the Low Countries, c.1585. C. van Sichem. Line engraving.
NATIONAL MARITIME MUSEUM.

years in defiance of the Pope; refused to allow the decrees of the Council of Trent to be promulgated in his territories until he was assured that his prerogatives were not to be infringed; and did not conceal his suspicions of the Jesuits on account of their allegiance to the Pope. But he wished to see the Catholic Church triumphant not only in Spain but in all his other domains and in Europe generally. Already, in 1558, by the Treaty of Cateau-Cambrésis, he and Henry II of France had had no choice but to make peace, not only because of their financial exhaustion, but also on account of their consternation at the spread of heresy.

Did that mean, then, that Philip, as unquestionably the most powerful and committed Catholic ruler, was the undeviating and unhesitating champion of the Catholic religion? One of his most frequently quoted sayings suggests that he was: "You can assure his Holiness that rather than suffer the slightest prejudice to religion and the service of God I will lose all my states and a hundred lives if I had them because I do not wish nor ever intend to be lord over heretics." It would be dangerous, however, to take such a statement completely at face value in an age when Catholic rulers were prone to justify or disguise their political intentions by reference to the need to eliminate heresy. Philip's apparently wholehearted declaration of support for the Roman Church and its pontiff was intended for the Pope's consumption at the very moment when he was refusing to do what the Pope wanted him to do - go to the Netherlands in person. The truth was that Philip was not only a devoted Catholic; he was also the ruler of a great state and there were occasions when the interests of church and state did not, to outward appearances coincide. Not that Philip ever saw it that way; he regarded the interests of Spain and those of the Catholic Church as identical. But if one had to give way to the other, it was the Church which must yield to the state and not *vice versa*. Popes tended to have no illusions about this. "The King of Spain as a temporal sovereign is anxious above all to safeguard and increase his dominions", commented Gregory XIII with undeceived percipience in 1589; "the preservation of the Catholic religion, which is the principal aim of the Pope, is only a pretext for

liam Harbone as her first ambassador to the Sultan in Constantinople (now Istanbul), he proved an assiduous advocate of the notion that Englishmen and Turks were united in detesting the "idolatries" of Spain and strongly urged the Sultan to send a fleet to attack Spain in the Mediterranean so as to divert Philip from his preparations to attack England.

In Western Europe, what Philip had to fear most was the growth of heresy. His upbringing and education, his private convictions, and all his instincts and experience as a ruler combined to implant in him an absolute hatred and dread of heresy as subversive of everything he valued. He was a "king who saw in unity beneath his own personal direction the sole hope of salvation in an embattled and heresy-ridden world," wrote J H Elliott. Within Spain, the Church was indispensable to him as the fount of faith and loyalty, the sole instrument of political and intellectual control common to all his kingdoms, a crucial source of income, and a gold-mine of clerical patronage. He exercised tighter control over the Church than did any other ruler, including Protestants, and he intended to keep it that way. To ensure that, he was prepared to keep his suspect primate, Archbishop Carranza of Toledo, in gaol for several his Majesty, whose principal aim is the security and aggrandizement of his domains." Yet Philip could reproach the Pope that he, too, had his less than altruistic diplomatic interests: "If the Netherlands were ruled by someone else, the Pope would have performed miracles to prevent them being lost to the Church; but because they are my states I believe he is prepared to see them lost because they will be lost to me." The popes were in a genuine dilemma. They had no wish to be over-submissive to Philip's desires, nor to see him exercise such autocratic domination over the Spanish Church, still less to see him masterminding elections of popes. At the same time, they also knew that there was no other secular power on which they could place so much reliance. Besides, the lines of demarcation in Europe, political and religious, were increasingly tending to coincide, and Philip's own interests and those of the Pope were often close enough to make him appear as the chief military and political arm of the Counter-Reformation.

Philip's main political rival in Western Europe was France. Earlier in the century, diplomacy and war had been dominated by the enmity between Valois and Habsburg. Cateau-Cambrésis had marked a turning-point in the sense that Spanish ascendancy in Italy could no longer be subject to any challenge by France and that neither power could any longer hope to control the British Isles. Each country had to recognize that it could not afford the expense of a "hot war" with the other; but that did not preclude them from waging "cold war". Philip's worst fears initially were that the French, through Mary, Queen of Scots, might benefit most from a change of regime in England, or that the French might intervene in the Netherlands to take advantage of disaffection there. Spanish fears of French support for the Netherlands rebels on the part of Coligny and the Huguenots were later reinforced by the Duke of Anjou's acceptance of the title of "Defender of the Liberties of the Low Countries". But, conversely, Philip had ample scope for meddling in the internal affairs of France as the result of the religious civil wars there. Above all, he was determined not to allow any Protestant ascendancy and exerted himself to the uttermost to prevent the Huguenot Henry of Navarre from occupying the French Throne, even after he had become a Catholic. To forestall Henry, he was prepared to go to the extent of diverting Alexander of Parma from his reconquest of the Netherlands.

Mention of the Netherlands is a reminder that it was the provinces of the Low Countries, more than any other part of Philip's empire, which proved to be its Achilles' Heel. His early policies of trying to centralize secular and ecclesiastical government, to control trade and taxation in the Spanish interest, and of refusing liberty of conscience to the growing numbers of Protestants, had led to an outbreak of revolt. From 1566 onwards Philip was never free of trouble in the Netherlands and had to devote an increasing proportion of his resources in efforts to suppress opposition. A succession of governors - Alva, Requesens, and Don John - were all unsuccessful in dealing with rebellion. Only after the arrival of Alexander Farnese, later Duke of Parma, in 1578 did the situation begin to improve. An outstanding general and a gifted diplomat, Farnese had by 1585 recovered most of the southern provinces for Spain. But even he was not allowed to complete his task undis-

PVGNATIO ANTVERPIÆ

EXPVGNATIO TYRI

ANTVERPIÆ

EXPVGNATIO TYRI

Pictor Alexandro Magno dat fulmen Apelles,
Progeniem credi dum studet esse Iouis.
Nomine Alexandro tu par, re maior es haec te,
Farnesi, fulmen, verius arma decent.

Ille sibi imbelles Persas, Indosque subegit,
Belgas tu, et Celtas, Martia corda, Deo.
Tollet ad astriferum belli te fulmen Olympum,
Relligio Parmæ tegmine tuta tuae.

● A drawing of musket and pike drill. Jacques de Gheyn II.
NATIONAL MARITIME MUSEUM.

● OPPOSITE: Alexander Farnese, Duke of Parma, as Philip's Governor in the Netherlands.
NATIONAL MARITIME MUSEUM.

tracted. On orders from Philip, and against his better judgment, he was obliged to divert his troops from their primary purpose, first in 1587-8 for the unsuccessful project to invade England, and in 1590 and 1592 to intervene in France in support of Philip's determination to thwart Henry of Navarre.

The Netherlands having been for so long an incurable running sore for Philip, we are tempted to ask just why he refused to cut his losses and negotiate an end to the conflict sooner. But Philip seemed obsessed with the need to retain his hold over the Low Countries. No 16th century ruler was prepared to allow a rebellion by his subjects to succeed if he could avoid it. Moreover, Philip was a Habsburg, of all the ruling houses of Europe the one with the strongest consciousness of its dynastic rights. In his political testament of 1548, Charles V had adjured Philip never to abandon his claim to the duchy of Burgundy, "our country". This was reinforced by a kind of 16th century "domino theory": the conviction that if rebels in the Netherlands successfully asserted their rights, then other parts of the empire, especially in Italy, might follow suit. Such considerations were strengthened by the belief that fighting in Flanders was preferable to warfare in Spain, which might be the alternative if the French were not attracted to the north. Again, the strategic importance of the Netherlands as a base from which to exert pressure on France, northwest Germany, and England was undoubted. But it seems likely that the most compelling reason of all was Philip's detestation of rebels and, *a fortiori*, heretical rebels. At several critical points - in 1566-7, 1575, 1577, and 1589 - Philip simply could not bring himself to recognize the right of heretics to liberty of conscience. In this he was not markedly different from other contemporary rulers. As he himself wrote to the King of Denmark: "For if it is clear that other sovereigns do not allow their subjects to have a religion other than the one they themselves profess, for reasons of state as well as for religious motives, why should this be denied to me?"

Elizabeth of England might well

have agreed privately with Philip on that issue, however much she dissented from him on others. Relations between the two had always been somewhat strained and uneasy. Philip disliked Elizabeth's heretical religion intensely; but as long as his enemies, the French, seemed likely to be the main beneficiaries if Elizabeth were removed from her Throne in favour of Mary, Queen of Scots, Philip protected her against action by the papacy. In the course of the Anglo-Spanish crisis of 1568-9 and the Ridolfi Plot, 1570-1, nevertheless, he was sorely tempted to take a hand in getting rid of her. As long as religion was the main source of friction, he was unlikely to go to war, but once strategic considerations entered into the dispute, he was much more prepared to proceed to extremes. From 1580 onwards, Philip entered upon a new and aggressive phase of policy. In that year, he acquired the kingdom of Portugal, its overseas empire, and its ocean-going fleet. In the 1580s, considerably increased supplies of silver arrived in Seville from the Indies; between 1590 and 1600 they were four times as large as in the 1560s. Both these developments underlined the intensifying rivalry at sea between Spain on the one side, and the English, Dutch, and French on the other. In 1583, having defeated French naval forces at Terceira in the Azores, Spain's leading naval commander, the Marquis of Santa Cruz, advocated a major enterprise against England. In the mean time, Farnese's campaign was making spectacular progress in the southern Netherlands and in 1585 its greatest city, Antwerp, fell to his troops.

Elizabeth I, feeling increasingly pressed by Philip's much enhanced resources and military successes, reluctantly committed herself to much more drastic acts of hostility. By the Treaty of Nonsuch, 1585, she agreed to intervene militarily with English troops in the Netherlands, having hitherto contented herself with affording moral, diplomatic, and financial assistance. In 1585-6, Sir Francis Drake was unleashed to launch attacks on the coast of Spain and in the Indies. Such brazen defiance was wearing Philip's seemingly inexhaustible patience dangerously near to snapping-point. The crucial question being forced to the forefront of his mind was: "Would a direct assault on England be the best way of defending his vital interests in both the Netherlands and the Indies?"

As late as August 1585 he had still been firmly in favour of postponing any assault on England until after Farnese had completed his conquest of Holland and Zealand. Within a few months, by the end of 1585, he seems to have undergone a change of heart. His diplomats were encouraged to enlist papal support and to enter into a treaty with the Catholic Guise family to ensure French neutrality in the event of a Spanish attack on England. In 1586, it appeared as if his long-standing uncertainty in relation to Mary, Queen of Scots was likely to be removed when she disinherited her son, James, in favour of Philip. After her execution in February 1587, the contriving Spanish ambassador in Paris, the Anglophobe, Mendoza, could write to his sovereign in triumphant expectation: "It would seem to be God's obvious design to bestow upon your Majesty the crowns of these two kingdoms" (Scotland and England). The normally hesitant and slow-paced Philip seems to have been transformed into an ardent and impetuous crusader, burning to see action and convinced that an attack on England was God's work and of the most pressing strategic consequence. Ironically enough, he now found that Pope Sixtus V nursed serious doubts about the sincerity of his motives and was convinced that the whole venture sprang from his secular ambitions. Had Sixtus seen a despatch from Philip's secretary, Idiaquez, sent to the Spanish commander, Medina Sidonia, on February 22, 1587, it might only have served further to underline his misgivings: "The intervention of the English in Holland and Zealand, together with their infestation of the Indies and the Ocean, is of such a nature that defensive methods are not enough to cover everything, but forces us to apply the fire in their homeland and so fiercely that they will have to rush back and retire from elsewhere ... For the objective of this Armada is no less the security of the Indies than the recovery of the Netherlands." There have always been two diametrically opposed views of Philip II, the man and ruler, from his own day onwards. In his lifetime, his enemies - William the Silent and Antonio Pérez most notably - sketched a damningly accusatory portrait of him as a secretive, ruthless, and unscrupulous king; bigoted, obscurantist, and capable of acts of revolting cruelty. In the subsequent national history of a number of European countries, he figured as a threatening ogre bent on thwarting their aspirations to freedom and independence in religion and politics; the Goliath to their David. Inevitably, perhaps, he has usually been cast by the Dutch and the English in the despicable role of national enemy, and hardly less so by the French and the Italians. Furthermore, the ideals and ambitions he cherished as the ostensible champion of the Church and the Counter-Reformation, the upholder of absolutist and dynastic authority and imperialist rule, made him peculiarly unsympathetic and objectionable to those reared in the tradition of the Enlightenment, or the Liberal and Protestant climate of the last century. No historian found him more repugnant than the learned American, J L Motley, whose judgments lived long and sharply etched in the minds of later writers. Motley's condemnation of Philip's record was total and unrelieved: "As for the royal criminal called Philip II, his life is his arraignment ... The horrible monotony of his career stupefies the mind until it is ready to accept the principle of evil as the fundamental law of the world ... His reign was a thorough and disgraceful failure ... If there be such a thing as historical evidence, then Philip is convicted before the tribunal of impartial posterity of every crime charged to his indictment."

Yet, as we have seen, during his lifetime, Philip was as widely loved and respected in Spain as Elizabeth I was in England. As early as 1621 his compatriots were looking back on his reign as a "golden age", part of the *siglo d'oro* of Spanish history - in religion and culture as well as politics. More recent Spanish historiography has also been inclined to point up Philip's virtues as an individual and monarch. Antonio Ballesteros y Beretta upheld his reputation thus: "Philip II incarnated and represented the Catholic spirit of the Spanish people; and the defence of Catholicism became the most important motive for his actions ... Philip always acted as a Spaniard: with dignity. His deeds were impregnated with an *hidalgo* ethic based on honour, the precious knightly legacy of the Middle Ages, which has been and is the theme of Spanish history. What a contrast to the predatory nations, without morals or scruples, whose basis for expansion has been piracy, depredation, and iniquitous despoliation!"

Neither of these one-sided depictions of Philip, it need hardly be said, can be accepted in its entirety. Being mortal, he had his strengths and his weaknesses like other men. As a ruler, there were achievements and failures to be entered

● An English fleet commanded by the Earl of Leicester arrives at Flushing in 1585.
REPRODUCED BY COURTESY OF THE MARQUESS OF SALISBURY.

on his record. Certainly, there was much to be placed on the credit side. He united the Iberian peninsula, maintained reasonably good government in Spain, preserved its splendid army, and revived its navy. He kept his empire intact in the Americas, added to it the overseas possessions of Portugal, and conquered the Philippines. Even in Europe, his policy was far from being wholly a failure. By his exertions he ensured that the southern provinces of the Netherlands remained Catholic and Spanish; he helped to prevent the Huguenots from establishing a Protestant regime in France, and to induce Henry of Navarre to become a Catholic. On the other hand, he was unable to save Spain from economic exhaustion, lost most of his bases in north Africa, forfeited the northern Netherlands, was heavily defeated in the Armada campaign and elsewhere on the high seas, and failed to keep Henry IV (of Navarre) off the Throne of France.

There were, perhaps, two cardinal predicaments that neither Philip nor any other ruler in his position could have overcome. The one was his Habsburg inheritance in the Netherlands. It more than anything else drained away his resources as if into an insatiable maw. If he was ever to settle the issue by negotiation, he could do so only on the basis of recognizing the liberties of the provinces and conceding liberty of conscience. He would never seriously consider either possibility. If, on the other hand, he chose to determine the outcome by military force, he must refuse to be diverted. But he ordered Parma away from his main task - once in relation to the Armada and twice to France. Yet, at the end of the day, the Netherlands were not a Spanish interest, but a Habsburg concern; Spanish vital interests lay in the Atlantic and the Mediterranean not in Northern Europe. As long as retention of the Netherlands remained an obsession with Philip, however, Spanish blood and treasure poured out there in a fatal flow that was never staunched. The other problem was the empire he inherited and extended. That vast accumulation was largely the result of chance and fortunate marriages. It had been acquired too quickly and too fortuitously to be properly assimilated and defended. Yet the very size of it frightened other European kingdoms into making the most determined efforts to resist and plunder it. Philip, indeed, kept it intact, but in doing so put his European possessions under ruinous pressure. Even Atlas eventually cracked under the strain.

Professor Williams is Professor of History at University College of Swansea, University of Wales.

141

THE ENGLISH FLEET

No one in England had ever seen, let alone fought,
a fleet the size of the Armada. Nicholas Rodger describes
the English strategy and how they succeeded
almost to their own surprise

*T*HE GREAT campaign of 1588 was, for everyone involved, and especially the English, a leap in the dark. The English navy had never had to face a threat of this sort. Earlier in the century there had been naval fighting against France, including raids and small campaigns on both sides of the Channel, but nothing like a full-scale invasion had been contemplated. No fleet the size and power of the Armada had ever been seen outside the Mediterranean, no comparable invasion of an entire kingdom had been attempted in modern times in northern waters. How to oppose the Spanish fleet if it came were questions to which in 1588 no English seaman or strategist had a clear answer.

It was however obvious to all informed observers that a serious Spanish invasion attempt faced formidable obstacles. The logistics of assembling, feeding and equipping the necessary forces were certain to tax even the richest 16th-century state. The perils of wind and weather, the uncertainties of navigation on any coast in an age with no reliable charts, were bound to make any sea expedition in any circumstances a hazardous one. It was far from clear how or where the Spaniards could land even if unopposed, even less clear how many troops would be needed, with what guns

and equipment, when they were ashore. England was thinly populated, very weakly defended with modern fortifications and experienced soldiers, and was believed to contain a substantial population of Catholics disloyal to Queen Elizabeth's government, but it remained a much larger country than even Spain, the most formidable military power of the age, had ever attempted to invade.

The English, however, could never rely on wind and accident to defeat a nation which had so often overcome more formidable obstacles than these. They had to find methods of defeating the threatened invasion, or at least of deterring it, and nobody was sure how to do it. In the first place there was disagreement between those who believed outright war inevitable and outright victory possible, and those (including the Queen and her chief minister Lord Burghley) who looked for a diplomatic compromise, and were by no means sure that the Enterprise of England would ever materialize. If it did, there was no single opinion about how to oppose it. Naval strategy was barely conceived, let alone born, and the only existing body of professional knowledge which seemed to offer any guidance was military. Here the obvious analogy was with an army blocking a ford or bridge by massing

along the river-bank, and the first thought of Elizabeth's government (as well as the first assumption of Philip's) was that the main body of the fleet under the Lord Admiral, Lord Howard of Effingham, should on this principle patrol the Straits of Dover opposite the Duke of Parma's army. Here the finest army in Europe was massed nearest to its enemy; surely this must be the crucial point?

The majority of the experienced sea officers, on the other hand, wanted the fleet stationed as far to the westward as possible, which in practice meant at Plymouth. With the prevailing westerly winds, they would there be able to intercept an invasion fleet from Spain before it could reach the south coast, and still be perfectly placed to attack it anywhere further up channel if necessary. This view, of which Drake was the leading exponent, was shared by most of the senior commanders, adopted by Howard the commander-in-chief, and eventually accepted by the government to the extent of sending the bulk of the fleet to Plymouth, leaving only a smaller, though still powerful squadron in the Downs.

● OPPOSITE: Portrait of Sir John Hawkins, 1532-95. English School, 16th century.
NATIONAL MARITIME MUSEUM.

ÆTATIS SVÆ

● Oil painting of the Armada, by an unknown artist.
BY PERMISSION OF THE WORSHIPFUL SOCIETY OF APOTHECARIES.

For the English the central problem was what to do whenever, and wherever, the two fleets met. No one in England had ever seen, let alone fought, a fleet the size of the Armada, and moreover none of them had ever served in a fleet the size of their own. Many of them had been raiding in the Caribbean or trading in the Mediterranean with little squadrons of five or even ten ships, and in 1587 Drake, greatly daring, had taken 17 to attack Cadiz and harry the coast of the Algarve, but how to handle a force which eventually totalled 130 sail, was a completely new and baffling problem. Moreover the Spaniards knew much more about defending large formations of ships than the English knew about attacking them. Spain had been running convoys from the Caribbean since 1526; since 1543 they had been armed and escorted. By 1588 they had long experience of the organization and defence of large squadrons. The French, the Algerines and latterly the Dutch had tried and failed to break into these formations, but the English, latecomers to oceanic warfare, had wisely confined themselves to weaker and smaller targets. No one in the English fleet in 1588 had any clear idea how to defeat the Spanish Armada.

Nevertheless the English had certain advantages not obvious at first sight, and perhaps not fully realized either by themselves or the Spaniards. Putting large ships to sea, let alone commissioning and sustaining entire fleets, was in the 16th century and for long afterwards the most complex, costly and demanding task which any nation ever undertook. It demanded resources technical, administrative and financial which even the wealthiest states were barely beginning to develop. Spain, which was the richest European state by far, had until the conquest of Portugal in 1582 no permanent naval force (apart from galleys) in the service of the crown, and still in 1588 had virtually no naval administration, no logistical system and no dockyards. Though the Spanish armies enjoyed what was for the day very advanced and sophisticated support, Spanish ships were commissioned and employed *ad hoc,* and the administration even of so great an enterprise as the Armada was improvised. The annual revenues of Philip II in 1588 were about 10,000,000 ducats or nearly £3,000,000; Queen Elizabeth's at the same date were about £300,000, though unrepeatable wartime taxation swelled them to £400,000 or somewhat more. With little more than a tenth of the resources of Spain, England was attempting to compete in a business which required immense expenditure sustained over long periods.

The remarkable thing is that it was precisely in this area of administration, support and supply that the English navy had a decisive advantage. In the first place Queen Elizabeth *had* a navy; a permanent force of fighting ships in her own service. Though not very large by the standards of Mediterranean galley fleets, it was by some way the largest standing navy in northern waters, and it was supported by an administrative system which was, for its day, notably efficient and flexible. The Navy Board, the committee of senior officials who dealt with the maintenance, supply and manning of the fleet, had been established by Henry VIII, but to a considerable extent the English naval system of 1588 was that which had been expanded and perfected during Queen Mary's short reign, and at the instance of her consort, King Philip I of England. Not least of the ironies of 1588 is that Philip was defeated by a fleet which he himself had done much to establish. It was he who made available to his English subjects, still very backward in navigation, the expertise and resources of the *Casa de Contratacion* in Seville which licensed and controlled Spain's overseas trade. It was during his reign, in 1557, that for the first time the English fleet received a permanent "ordinary", or budget, with which a continuous naval system could be maintained year after year.

The officials who were responsible were the members of the Navy Board, who were in 1588 John Hawkins the Treasurer of the Navy, Sir William Winter the Surveyor of the Queen's Ships and Master of the Ordnance for the Navy, William Borough the Clerk of the

Ships, and William Holstock the Controller. All of them were seamen and administrators of long experience: Hawkins was the leading merchant and shipowner of Plymouth, and had been Treasurer for ten years. From 1585 he had undertaken the whole "ordinary" maintenance of the Queen's ships by contract for an annual fee of £5,714. Winter was a veteran sea officer who had served continuously for over 40 years, and Holstock had served afloat and ashore since Henry VIII's time. Borough was a famous explorer and navigator. Under their charge were the dockyards at Deptford, Chatham and Portsmouth, of which Chatham, where the ships were laid up when out of commission, was rapidly growing to be the most important. James Quarles, one of the officers of the Queen's household, had the thankless responsibility of victualling the Navy.

The members of the Navy Board were collectively and individually responsible for the administration of the Navy, but its higher direction was the province of the Lord Admiral of England, Charles, Lord Howard of Effingham. His was one of the medieval great offices of state, an office of honour and profit, but not necessarily of active employment. To hold it one had to be a great nobleman, preferably one like Howard with family connections with the office, but it was not essential to have seagoing experience. Queen Elizabeth had among her subjects many experienced captains and sea commanders, but the Lord Admiral could never have been counted as one of them. In a sense the fact that he took his place as commander of the fleet in 1588 is a tribute to the survival of essentially medieval ideas of authority. To the modern mind it has often seemed extraordinary that Drake, the most famous admiral of his day, the terror and despair of Catholic Europe, should not have been given the command. In fact there were excellent reasons why not. Though Drake had more experience of commanding a large squadron than most

of his famous contemporaries, he still had little more than Howard. Moreover, in an age of quarrelsome and touchy captains, he was one of the least tolerant of all. Chivalrous and polite to his enemies, he could be suspicious and overbearing to his immediate subordinates. On his last expedition, in 1587, he had tried to repeat the precedent of his voyage round the world and hang his second-in-command. It was hardly the conduct which would endear him to a collection of proud, temperamental and undisciplined individuals, several of whom were his personal enemies. What was needed was a man of equable temperament and unequalled rank, apt to take advice and able to give orders without offence, a man who could harness and employ the undoubted talents of his captains, not replace them; an Eisenhower rather than a Montgomery. Howard fitted this requirement exactly, and he deserves full credit not only for the successes of 1588, but for the fact that they were not frustrated, as so many Elizabe-

145

ARMADA 400

The Royal Navy – Tradition into technology

In 1588, as now, the most famous and formidable British capital ship of the age was the *Ark Royal*. Queen Elizabeth 1's English Navy took over the *Ark Rale* from its owner Sir Walter Raleigh, the international adventurer, and gave her the new name as recognition of her new patronage.

The original *Ark Royal* had 55 guns and could only fire broadsides or out of her stern. That made her more than a match for the Spanish galleons. Her modern counterpart is armed with Sea Dart medium-range surface-to-air missiles and the Phalanx rapid-firing gun system.

While many of the first *Ark Royal's* complement of 430 men were untrained, the 1980s version can boast 964 highly trained, professional seamen and naval aviators in her crew. They operate the most up-to-date technology in weapons, radar, sonar and ship's engineering. They each specialise in one area of activity, making them all essential parts of the ship's team.

While the motive power for the earlier *Ark Royal* came solely from the vagaries of the wind, today's vessel is driven by Rolls-Royce Olympus gasturbine engines, the same as those which power the supersonic airliner Concorde. And, although she can't achieve supersonic speeds, she can accelerate from 0-30 knots in only three minutes.

The original *Ark Royal* had only two ways of fighting the enemy. She could fire her guns at them or board the rival vessel and engage her forces in hand-to-hand combat. Today's Missilemen are still expected to achieve the highest standards in gunnery, but they have a number of complementary methods of fighting at their disposal in addition. There are the anti-submarine warfare (ASW) helicopters, which are assisted by the Sea King Airborne Early Warning (AEW) helicopters. These aircraft can operate up to a hundred miles away from the Carrier, leaving the vessel extremely well protected against attack.

Should the fighting take place in the air as well as in the sea, the current *Ark Royal* has at her disposal arguably the finest fighting plane in existence — the Sea Harrier. This maritime fighter/reconnaisance/strike Short-Take-Off Vertical-Landing (STOVL) aircraft has a very impressive performance. It can carry a range of weapons and can achieve speeds of 650 knots plus. Again, Rolls-Royce engines provide the power, in this case a vectored-thrust Pegasus engine.

Life in all Her Majesty's Ships is as exciting, responsible and rewarding as it is on the *Ark Royal*. For details of a career in any of the widely varied branches of the Royal Navy, call in at your local Royal Navy and Royal Marines Careers Information Office. We'll advise you on how to join today's senior service.

ROYAL NAVY

● Engravings by Claes Jansz Visscher: TOP: The *Ark Royal*, the Lord Admiral's flagship. CENTRE: The *White Bear*, commanded by Lord Sheffield. BELOW: The *Tiger*, commanded by John Bostocke.
NATIONAL MARITIME MUSEUM.

than naval and military operations were, by indiscipline, quarrels and treachery.

Queen Elizabeth inherited from her half-sister a fleet of about 40 sail, and soon after her accession it was laid down as a policy that 24 ships were always to be kept ready for sea at 14 days' notice. This was a remarkable, for the 16th century quite unique policy, and it was one of the keys to the English success in 1588. Queen Elizabeth could not hope to keep so large a fleet in being for so long as Spain did, but what she had she could mobilize at very short notice. Lacking any equivalent administration, the Spaniards were in effect obliged to keep the Armada on a war footing throughout the whole period of nearly two years during which it was being assembled. Long before it ever sailed, it was suffering severely from disease and depleted stores; the inevitable consequence in that age of keeping a large body of men confined on board ship for any length of time. When it did sail, it was in poor repair and lacked many things essential for a long voyage.

This was in spite of expenditure of 700,000 ducats (£192,500) a month during the preparations, in spite of the crippling of Spain's overseas trade and the suspension of the vital silver fleet to provide shipping for the enterprise. Yet throughout almost all the two years during which the Armada was being made ready, most of the Queen's ships lay at their moorings in the Medway. In the whole year of 1587 Elizabeth spent only £44,000 on her fleet, of which all but £7,000 went to pay for the squadron she did put to sea. Having made no extraordinary preparations during the autumn of 1587, she was able in December, when threatening intelligence was received, to put a large fleet to sea at a fortnight's notice, and then as swiftly to pay most of it off when the threat receded until the spring. Queen Elizabeth was obliged to adopt this policy because of her penury; the impossibility of raising large loans or deficit finance in the modern style left her no alternative. Philip's wealth allowed him to keep a great fleet in being for two years; Elizabeth's poverty permitted her to match that fleet for only a

147

few months. They had to be the right few months, so she could not afford to risk mobilization unless the threat was immediate, but she could not have afforded to risk delaying mobilization if it had not been possible to put her ships to sea very quickly. Because of the efficiency of the Navy Board, the dockyards, and the victualling organization she was able to do so. England's very weak resources were deployed to maximum effect, at exactly the right time and place; Spain's vastly greater resources were dissipated in trying to improvise the great fleet without an adequate logistical base.

What is more, Spain's lack of a standing navy left her at a serious disadvantage in the quality of her ships. Only the Portuguese galleons and the four Neapolitan galleasses (hybrid galley-galleons) could be described as regular warships, and most of the larger ships of the Armada were decisively inferior to the English ships, especially the newer English ships, in two vital respects: speed and armament. The English had come relatively late to modern ship-building, as they had to most aspects of ocean voyaging, but in the 1570s the Queen's master shipwrights had developed a type of warship which was the equal, if not the superior, of anything afloat. Naval terminology was then in a very undeveloped state and there was no single term for these new ships; they were often referred to as "the middling sort", because they were in tonnage terms smaller than the big old high-castled types which were still being built into the 1560s, or as "race-built", in reference to their relatively low superstructure, especially forward. With lower forecastles they were faster and more weatherly than their predecessors, and they carried a much heavier armament. It was galleons of this type which led the English fleet in 1588, and formed its greatest strength. Moreover many of the smaller English ships, down to the little pinnaces of no more than 50 or 100 tons which were the smallest men-of-war capable of cruising independently, were built along similar lines and enjoyed similar advantages of speed.

Because even the best Spanish ships were generally slower and less weath-

erly than the English, they could not hope to force an engagement on their own terms, nor avoid one on the enemy's. Moreover, as they knew quite well, the English terms were likely to be an artillery battle out of boarding range, and the Spanish ships carried many fewer guns, especially heavy guns and those of long range, than the English. If it came to a pitched battle, they were bound to be at a severe disadvantage unless they could grapple and board the English ships. Furthermore much of the Spanish fleet consisted of ill-armed or quite unarmed transports, even slower and clumsier than their escorts, whereas the English ships were all, if not pure warships, then at least vessels designed,

armed and accustomed to fight. They were also in much better condition than the Spanish ships. For some years prior to 1588 the Queen's ships had been maintained on an annual contract awarded to John Hawkins, the Treasurer of the Navy, and because of the controversies raised by his disappointed rivals the actual state of repair of these ships was very thoroughly reported on. It is striking the unanimity, indeed the obvious pride and confidence, with

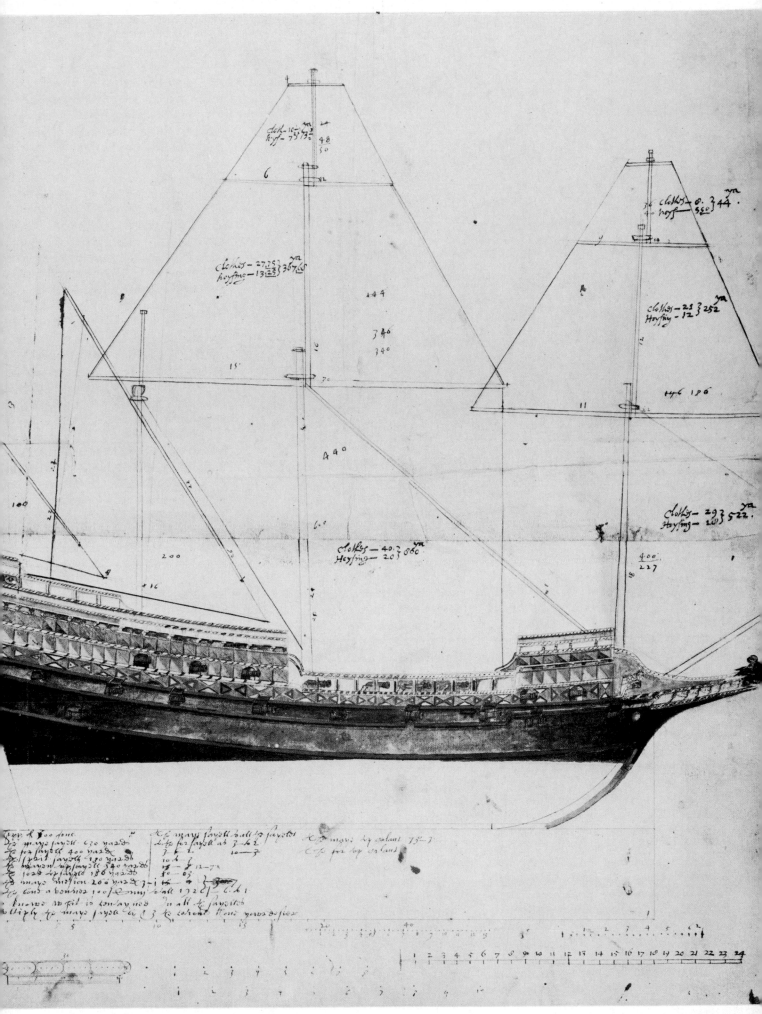

● OPPOSITE: Sir Richard Hawkins (1562-1622), Commander of the *Swallow*.
NATIONAL MARITIME MUSEUM.

● Drake, by Sir Nicholas Hilliard. Miniature.
NATIONAL PORTRAIT GALLERY, LONDON.

men, and the increasing proportion of them accustomed to deep-sea trades, represented a reserve of national strength which money could not have bought, least of all at short notice.

So the English fleet which mobilized in the spring of 1588 was by no means weaker than the Spanish Armada. In simple numbers each side had about 130 ships, of which about 60 on each side could be reckoned as fighting ships of some force, but the English ships were in almost every case faster, better armed and in better condition. Captains and admirals were confident in their ships and in themselves, but they did not know when, or indeed if the Armada would sail, and they were not clear how best to employ their own forces. Everyone wanted a battle; the problem was how and where could one best be brought on. Even after it had been persuaded to station the main body of the fleet at Plymouth, the government tended to think in military terms of dividing the force, or finding some position from which it could simultaneously guard against threats from every direction. Drake and other sea commanders, on the other hand, and eventually Howard whom he won to his point of view, proposed to sail with the whole fleet, or at least a strong squadron, to the coast of Spain, there to attack and overwhelm the Armada while it was still in harbour, repeating on a larger scale Drake's success at Cadiz of the previous year. Elizabeth and her advisers, not without a good deal of wavering, were won over, and during the spring the fleet made several attempts to sail for Spain, only to be driven back by contrary winds. Finally Howard sailed from Plymouth on 7 July for a final attempt. On 9 July they were almost in sight of the Spanish coasts when a south-westerly gale and shortage of provisions drove them back.

The English fleet returned to Plymouth on 12 July, and at once began refitting and revictualling for sea, determined to take the first opportunity to return to the coasts of Spain. They were still hard at work when on the afternoon of 19 July (Old Style; 29 July according to Spanish reckoning) the pinnace Golden Hind, one of the screen of small vessels which had been ordered to patrol to the westward, came running into Plymouth Sound with the momentous news that

which the captains and admirals of the English fleet praised the condition of their ships. "I have been aboard every ship that goeth out with me," Lord Howard wrote, "and in every place where any may creep, and I do thank God that they be in the estate they be in; and there is never a one of them that knows what a leak means."

A further advantage enjoyed by the English was in the number and quality of their seamen. Again this was a very recent gain; even 20 years before, Spain would probably have been superior in men with deep-sea experience, and she still had no lack of experienced masters and pilots. Spanish Atlantic trade, however, was the monopoly of a single port, and to make up the ships and men of the Armada it was necessary to scour the coasts of Catholic Europe. English maritime strength was much more broadly based. Though London contributed the bulk of the biggest and best-armed ships to add to the Queen's own, and undoubtedly predominated in numbers of sea-

men, there were dozens of ports great and small which could and did contribute ships and men to the fight — far more in fact than could be made use of when the English lacked powder and shot for all the ships they had. In 1577 there were 26 English ports owning ships of 100 tons or more, including such places as Chepstow, Walderswick and Aldborough. In 1582 in East Anglia alone there were ships of this size owned not only in Harwich, Yarmouth and Ipswich, but in Cley and Wiveton, Blakeney and Wells-next-the-Sea. So besides the big ships (not much smaller than the Queen's new galleons) like the *Galleon Leicester* and the *Merchant Royal*, the *Edward Bonaventure* and the *Roebuck*, which were contributed by the aristocracy and the London merchants, we find large numbers of substantial vessels like the *Edward* of Maldon or the *Crescent* of Dartmouth, and pinnaces like the *Rat* of Cowes or the *Katherine* of Weymouth. The smallest of all in the English fleet appears to have been the *Pippin*, of 20 tons and eight men. How much she contributed is hard to say, but the great numbers of English ports, ships and sea-

UNDIS·ARUNDO·VIRES·REPARAT
COEDENS·Q·FOVETUR·
FUNDITUS·AT·RUPES·EN
SCOPULOSA·RUIT

If BP had been around 400 years ago we could have mined the gold for the Golden Hind, helped put out the fire that singed the King's beard, provided solar powered buoys to guide the fleet and got them on the move again when the wind dropped.

ARMADA
1588~1988

● George Clifford, 3rd Earl of Cumberland (1558-1605), commander of the *Bonaventure*, by Sir Nicholas Hilliard.
NATIONAL MARITIME MUSEUM.

night the whole English fleet succeeded in working to windward of the Armada; Howard with the main body to seaward, a smaller squadron (probably the last to get out of Plymouth) beating up between the Spaniards and the shore. By morning the Spaniards had lost the great advantage which chance had initially given them, the weather gage. Now the English were to windward, with their faster and more weatherly ships, and the Spaniards had lost for good the chance to force close action.

This morning was the first time the two fleets saw each other properly, and it was the first time that each discovered about the other an unpleasant and unexpected fact. For the Spaniards, or at least for most of them, it must have been alarming and astonishing to find with what ease the English ships had escaped from the trap and recovered the weather gage, and to see with their own eyes how slender were Spanish chances of catching even such small forces as the inshore squadron, which seems at daybreak to have been within gunshot of the Spanish van and all but trapped against the land, but which beat away to windward to rejoin Howard with no apparent difficulty. For the English the morning showed them for the first time the formidable strength of Spanish military discipline at sea. The Armada then took up, and must long have practised, a precise defensive formation, with the heaviest fighting ships disposed ahead and on either quarter, and the main body of transports gathered in the centre. It was impossible for the English to mount an effective attack on the Armada as a whole without breaking up this formation, and to do this they had to scatter either or both of the "wings", the fighting squadrons which now took up position on the quarters of the Spanish fleet. The conception and execution of such a scheme shows the Spanish military genius at its height, and represents a feat of seamanship and discipline which had never been attempted at sea before, and has scarcely ever been achieved again. To form this huge and disparate fleet of ships into a precise formation, and to preserve it in the face of repeated attacks, was an extraordinary achievement. Certainly the English, who as yet had no practice in fleet manoeuvres and very

she had sighted the Spanish fleet off the Scillies. The situation was alarming and dangerous. With a fair wind the Spaniards could in principle have run straight into the Sound and caught the English in just such a trap as Drake had designed for them. It was probably the best, indeed the only chance the Spaniards ever had to force a boarding action in which the English ships, for all their speed and firepower, would be overwhelmed by Spanish soldiery. But to take it they would have had to act with great speed and boldness, risking their whole fleet in a narrow and dangerous inlet from which many of them could scarcely have escaped without a change of wind, and they would have had to disobey King Philip's most explicit orders. It does not appear that they seriously contemplated doing so, at least without more information than they had of the strength and whereabouts of the English fleet, and if they had done it would not have availed, for the English had escaped before the trap could have been sprung. As soon as the ebb began to run, after dark on the same evening that the news was brought, the English ships began to warp out of the Cattewater and down the Sound, towing behind their boats and pinnaces into the teeth of the wind. By morning the bulk of the English fleet was beating out of the Sound, and in the early afternoon Howard sighted the Spaniards, still far off to windward. That

● Fireship attack. Netherlandish School, 16th century.

little idea of how to do them, could not have achieved anything of the kind. No English fleet of merchantmen and war-ships in company attempted to sail in precise formation in the face of the enemy before the 18th century, and nothing as exact as the Spanish order seems to have been attained before the 20th century brought steamships and signalling to make it possible. For How-ard and his admirals the sight of Spanish discipline at sea must have been a very unpleasant shock. They faced a com-pletely new and unexpected problem, for if the Spanish formation was not broken there could be no hope of victory. For the next week they were to make repeated, gallant and futile attempts to do so.

On that first morning each side went into action with the gestures of the tradi-tions of chivalry: Medina Sidonia hoisted his sacred banner to the main-top, and Howard sent his pinnace the *Disdain* to bear his challenge to the Span-ish admiral, like a herald sent forth from a medieval army. Then he led the Eng-lish ships to attack the northern, shore-ward wing of the Spanish fleet. At the same time another group of ships led by Drake, Hawkins and Frobisher attacked the other wing. On both flanks the Span-iards attempted to lure the English to close action, and on the seaward Marti-nez de Recalde, the commander of that squadron allowed himself to be cut off from his colleagues in the hope of pro-voking a boarding action, but the English refused to be drawn. They subjected the Spanish ships to the heaviest fire possi-ble from a safe range, but always kept just out of reach. When the Spaniards attempted to attack, the English ships kept their distance with derisory ease.

So the first day ended, unsatisfac-tory to both sides. The Spaniards had suffered the frustration of being attacked with little prospect of retaliation. More-over it was becoming clear that their intelligence had been wrong, and the squadron which had come out of Ply-mouth was the main body of the English fleet and not a detachment. Expecting to meet the principal English force ahead and to leeward, Medina Sidonia had put his best fighting ships ahead of the con-voy rather than in the two wings astern which were bearing the English attack. For the English affairs seemed much

worse. A regular attack with the whole fleet had apparently achieved nothing. The Spanish formation was unbroken, and, as Howard wrote, "We durst not put in among them, their fleet being so strong". Moreover the English ships, which had put to sea with at most 30 rounds of ammunition a gun, had by then expended much of it, and urgent appeals for powder and shot were dis-patched ashore. So great a cannonade had never been seen before; to find it ineffective was deeply depressing.

After this day's fighting the Spani-ards suffered by accident their only seri-ous losses. The *Nuestra Senora del Rosario*, flagship of the Andalusian Squadron, lost her bowsprit in a colli-sion, and the *San Salvador*, vice-flagship of the Guipuzcoan Squadron, was badly damaged by a powder explosion. Soon afterwards the *Rosario's* foremast went overboard, and having failed in an attempt to tow her, Medina Sidonia was obliged to leave her in the darkness.

Meanwhile in the English fleet Howard had disposed his ships for the night, ordering them to keep station on the stern lantern of Drake's flagship the *Revenge*. Sometime during the night the

fleet lost sight of that lantern, and in the morning the Lord Admiral found himself close astern of the Spaniards but without almost all his own fleet. Sir Francis, meanwhile, had taken possession of the *Rosario,* and neither he nor the rest of the fleet rejoined Howard until the afternoon. Howard was too magnanimous a commander for recriminations at a moment when unity was so important, and Drake's admirers have laboured subsequently to explain his night's work in a favourable light, but it is hard to avoid the suspicion that the instincts of a lifetime of piracy had overcome him. The

character of a respectable admiral sat lightly on almost all the great Elizabethan seamen, perhaps most lightly of all on Drake. It looks very much as though he put out his stern lantern in order to take the rich prize which suddenly offered itself. The result was to put the Lord Admiral in imminent danger, and at best to lose the chance of effective action at the very moment when the Spaniards, had they been contemplating a landing, might have hauled up for Torbay. But naval strategy scarcely existed, all the English commanders had been brought up to regard a rich prize as the

highest object of warfare at sea, and it seems that no one blamed Drake. At least the English had gained their first success, and gained it, against all probability, without a fight, for Pedro de Valdes made little attempt to repair his ship and none at all to defend her. Later that day the English gained their second prize, the abandoned and waterlogged wreck of the *San Salvador.* Otherwise there was no fighting, and the Spaniards employed the day in reorganizing their formation, shifting many of the best galleons from the van to the two wings which had borne almost all of the fighting.

● Fireship attack in Dover Strait showing Armada beacons.
NATIONAL MARITIME MUSEUM.

The following morning, which was Tuesday, both fleets were off Portland Bill, and the wind came from the southeastward, giving the Spaniards again the weather gage. Throughout the morning the English ships attempted to beat around the Armada's flanks to regain it, while the Spaniards attempted to prevent them and force a close action. In the first object they succeeded, but in spite of heavy firing on both sides, the English still kept their distance and avoided any risk of boarding. During a day of heavy and confused fighting the wind shifted back to the westward, and by nightfall the two fleets were in much the same position as before: the Armada creeping ponderously eastward, the English dogging its heels. Once more the English ships had expended a prodigious quantity of powder and shot and Howard's anguished pleas for fresh supplies were redoubled. Once more they had completely failed to break the Spanish formation. The two ships taken had both

been crippled by accidents, and if, as the English were sure, several Spanish ships had been severely handled, it did not seem to have had any effect on the cohesion of the Armada as a whole. For real victory it was essential to break that formidable order, and the English were no nearer breaking it.

For the next three days, from Wednesday to Friday, the two fleets moved slowly up channel before very light breezes. The Spaniards held to their purpose of meeting Parma, to whom a stream of messages was despatched, warning him to be ready to embark as soon as the Armada appeared. The English concentrated on preventing the most immediate peril, a landing on the south coast. Both sides seized every chance of action, but neither was able to bring on a decisive battle. On Wednesday morning the English surrounded a Spanish straggler, the *Gran Griffon*, and fought a hot action with the Spanish ships which came to relieve her. That afternoon the wind fell away completely, and Howard took the opportunity to hold a council of war which addressed the question of tactics. The previous day the English fleet had split into at least three uncoordinated parts, while once again the Spaniards had been saved from serious

damage by their unity and discipline. Beyond what seems to have been a general custom of attacking in something like line ahead to deploy their broadside guns to best advantage, the English captains had shown themselves innocent of tactics or fleet organization. The contrast with the Spanish performance was glaring, and that afternoon it was decided to break up the English fleet into four squadrons, commanded by Howard, Drake, Hawkins and Martin Frobisher, the well-known Arctic explorer. The new organization does not seem to have extended to any sort of formation beyond the line ahead, or any but the most informal coordination between the squadrons, but at least it gave some prospect that the ships might be handled more effectively than was possible with a fleet of a hundred sail in a body.

The next morning, being Thursday, the two fleets were off the Isle of Wight, and in light airs, part of the day almost flat calm, there was further confused fighting. The moment was, or might have been, critical, for the Spaniards had already identified the Isle of Wight as their best prospect of a landing on the south coast, and if they could enter Spithead with their formidable discipline intact it might have been extremely diffi-

cult for the English to have dislodged them. At the time when they would have had to haul up for the anchorage, Drake's squadron was pressing hard on the seaward wing of the Armada and tending to drive it further eastward and inshore. Whether this was deliberate or not, it forced the Spaniards towards the Owers, the shoals which stretch out from Selsey Bill and form the eastern perimeter of the broad entrance to Spithead. It was essential for Medina Sidonia and his admirals to make a quick decision; either to haul up close and commit themselves to trying to get into Spithead, there to land their troops in the presence of the English fleet and establish a bridgehead on the island, or to alter course to seaward, follow their orders and continue down channel to where the Duke of Parma awaited them with his invincible army. Disobedience might possibly have gained a famous victory, but it would have been extremely risky to have attempted a landing with an undefeated fleet at their back, and neither Medina Sidonia's character nor his orders encouraged recklessness. The Armada stood away south-easterly, leaving the Isle of Wight and the English coast behind them.

For the English this was something

like a victory at last. The Spaniards were still undefeated, but at least Howard had managed "so to course the enemy as that they shall have no leisure to land". On Friday morning he knighted Hawkins, Frobisher and several of his captains on his quarter-deck. But though they had something to celebrate, the situation remained very grave. There was now no hope of preventing Medina Sidonia's junction with the Duke of Parma. The greatest fleet would be joined to the finest army in the world, and if the English navy could not defeat the former, it was hardly to be hoped that the English army could face the latter. Only the difficulties of geography which the Spaniards would have to overcome, and the powerful reinforcement of Sir Edward Seymour's squadron waiting in the Straits of Dover, gave the English any confidence.

For the Spaniards the crisis of the campaign was approaching. Undefeated and undaunted, they now approached the decisive rendezvous with Parma's army, the object towards which King Philip's orders directed them with such finality. What they did not say was how the junction was to be achieved. Ahead of them lay the coast of Flanders, protected by banks which the great ships of the Armada could not cross. Most of that coast was in the hands of the Dutch rebels, and Parma's only deep-water port, Sluys, was far too small to take the great fleet. It seemed certain that the Armada could not come to him, and he would have to come to it. How he would or could do so when the Dutch squadrons of Justin of Nassau controlled the shoal water which divided him from Medina Sidonia was a question to which the Duke urgently needed an answer. None of his despatches had returned from Parma, the weather was breaking up, and the Armada could go no further without hearing from him. So on Saturday evening (27 July by the English reckoning), the Spaniards, disciplined as ever, anchored in formation off the French port of Calais, and the English anchored just to windward of them. Late that evening Sir Edward Seymour's squadron from the Downs joined the English fleet, bringing it to its greatest strength of about 140 sail.

It was predictable that the Spaniards would have to anchor somewhere if they were to make rendezvous with Parma, and it was equally obvious what to do about it. Orders had been given some days before to prepare fireships, but they had not joined the English fleet by the

Sunday morning when Howard once more summoned his council of war. Something had to be done at once; the Armada was only 30 miles from Parma at Dunkirk, off a port nominally neutral but believed to be friendly to Spain. Whether he came overland or by water, Parma would doubtless come soon, and the Armada had to be driven off first. The English decided not to wait for the arrival of the intended fireships, but at once to improvise them from some of the smaller ships of the fleet. Drake and Hawkins each offered a ship of their own, others were found, and that Sunday night, with the wind freshening and the spring tide assisting, they were loosed on the Spanish ships.

Medina Sidonia had foreseen and provided for just such an attack. A screen of pinnaces was in position to grapple and tow off the fireships, and if any should nevertheless get through, the Spanish ships had orders to slip and buoy their cables, to drop to leeward only so far as was essential to avoid the fireships, and to be ready to return to their anchorage in the morning. Unfortunately the memory of the explosive fireships used by the Dutch at Antwerp, which had nearly killed the great Duke of Parma himself and whose inventor was known to be in England, was fresh in the Spanish fleet. For the first and last time, when the fireships bore down the Spaniards panicked and the discipline of the Armada disintegrated. Two of the fireships were grappled and towed aside; six swept down on the anchorage. Medina Sidonia and four other galleons only followed his orders; the rest cut their cables and fled in a disorderly mob towards the Zealand Banks. Not one was actually burnt by the fireships, but they had nevertheless gained what the English had never yet achieved; they had broken the formidable Spanish formation. At dawn the English saw what they had done, and at once they weighed anchor to attack. Only Medina Sidonia's five galleons were in sight, plus one damaged galleass in shore. This ship the Lord Admiral took for himself, leaving the other four divisions of his fleet to attack the galleons. This was a mistake, which he undoubtedly would never have made had he known that he was missing the Spanish admiral, for the boarding and looting of the galleass, driven ashore under the guns of Calais, wasted several hours and prevented Howard rejoining the main battle until the afternoon. Meanwhile the other English ships had at last an open battle, a fleeing enemy among whom they could pick their targets. Medina Sidonia stubbornly fought a rearguard action, giving time for his scattered ships to rejoin him, but with its formidable discipline, and most of its ammunition, gone, the Armada began to suffer severely for the first time. It seems that the English realized that they would have to close the range to achieve results, and with the Spanish formation broken up they were at last able to do so. Moreover the weather was worsening, with rising winds and falling visibility. In spite of all that weather and gunfire could do, however, the discipline of the Spanish fleet and the dauntless courage of their commander gradually reformed their formation, so that by afternoon the English once more faced a regular line of fighting ships. But at really close range, with many Spanish ships completely out of round shot and replying only with small arms, the English were able for the first time to inflict real damage. At least two Spanishs ships were sunk, and two more were driven on the shoals and taken by the Dutch. All the while the wind was driving the two fleets towards the Zealand banks — and there was no doubt which of the two would be able to claw off to windward.

All through the night the English followed the Spaniards as they drove into shoal water, waiting for their inevitable destruction. From this peril the battered Spanish fleet was saved, as they believed, by a miracle. At the last possible moment, soon after dawn on the Tuesday, the wind shifted suddenly to the southward, allowing the Spaniards to haul off to the northwards and once more restore their formation. By this time the English too were almost out of ammunition, and could not renew the action. So the two fleets sailed northeastwards into the North Sea, the English, as they put it, "putting on a brag countenance" and hoping that their bluff would not be called before they received fresh powder and shot. No one believed that the fighting was over: Howard's own estimate was that "their force is wonderful great and strong, and yet we pluck their feathers little by little". The English resolved to watch the Spanish fleet until it was certain that they would not land in England or Scotland.

For their part the Spaniards were in a difficult if not desperate position. Short of food, water and ammunition, with many ships badly damaged, they were in no condition for a long voyage, but they

had no hope of returning to southward and resuming their mission unless the wind shifted. Damaged as they were, they could not hope to beat against the wind. Given the chance they resolved to renew the fight with what means they had, make contact with Parma if God should make it possible, and somehow complete their task. If the wind should hold there was nothing to do but attempt to return by a voyage north about Scotland and so home to Spain — a voyage for which they were in no condition. The wind held. On 2 August by their reckoning, past the latitude of the Forth, the English turned away in search of victuals and ammunition, leaving the Spaniards to hold on northwards.

Though no one realized it, this was the last time the two fleets were to be in contact, and the last contribution of the English fleet to the campaign. About one-half of the ships, and perhaps as many as three-quarters of the men of the Armada were eventually lost, but very few of them to English guns. The English could and did rejoice that their country and their religion had been saved from the power of Spain, but sober observers were appalled at the narrowness of the victory and at the risks which had been run. For public consumption, especially abroad, Elizabeth's government stressed that the victory was God's alone: "the wind blew and they were scattered" on the coasts of Ireland. For the naval men, even the most devout, it was in a sense all

too true. A Protestant God, they had confidently expected, would have favoured their arms and not simply struck down the enemy's. As it was, all those who had fought the Armada down the Channel were haunted by the memory of that compact and unbroken formation, repelling all their efforts, and for many the lesson of 1588 was simply that "our parsimony at home hath bereaved us of the famousest victory that ever our navy might have had". They learned from the experience that it was essential to come to close quarters with heavy guns to achieve victory, and essential to sail with much greater reserves of ammunition than they had had in 1588, but it was not until long after Elizabeth's reign that ships and tactics were developed which could achieve the sort of crushing victory which the English hoped for in that year. Both sides entered the campaign with quite unreasonable expectations of what might be achieved with the novel weapons and novel enterprises they were engaged on. The English, or some of them at least, overestimated their own fighting efficiency and underestimated the Spanish. The Spaniards for their part had a much soberer realization of the difficulties which they were to face, and most of the best-informed seem to have been frankly pessimistic, but the one crucial figure, King Philip, launched his great enterprise with orders which made its success virtually impossible. So long as the Armada

● OPPOSITE: Charles Howard, Lord Effingham and Earl of Nottingham, by an unknown artist.
NATIONAL PORTRAIT GALLERY, LONDON.

ad to make contact with Parma's army, nd so long as that contact was prevented by the Dutch ships which conrolled the coastal waters of Zealand, it would have been impossible to carry out he proposed plan even if there had been o English navy at all. The first essential or this plan was for Parma to capture a eep-water port, preferably Flushing which alone was large enough to shelter fleet the size of the Armada. Until he ad done so he could not in any circum-stances have invaded England. The only hope of Spanish success in 1588 was for the Armada to ignore Parma and trust to the troops it carried to mount an invasion somewhere on the south coast. It would have been extremely risky to attempt to land with the English fleet undefeated, and difficult to conquer England with no more than 17,000 men, but it was certainly the best hope available.

For their part the English adopted, or tried to adopt, a strategy almost equally unwise, and were only saved from it by chance and poverty. If Drake had had his way the Armada would have been met off Lisbon or Corunna rather than in the Channel. For historians like Sir Julian Corbett, steeped in the careers of Nelson and his contemporaries, this was a brilliant anticipation of the strategy of blockade employed two centuries later, but it is hard to believe that it could have worked in 1588. Even in the 1790s it was recognized that blockade required a large superiority in ships (to allow for reliefs and refits) and an immense apparatus of supplies. Howard had at best, with the addition of Seymour's squadron, about equal numbers, and his ships were victualled month by month, at the crucial period week by week. Most likely, even if the fleet could have been got off the enemy coast at the right moment, it would have encountered the Armada already at sea, and had no more success than in the Channel in breaking up that formidable order. Then their ammunition was almost exhausted in a single day's fighting, and there would have been no friendly shore to appeal to for more. The few weeks the English fleet was at sea in July and August was enough to spread disease rapidly through the ships, as was almost inevitable in the conditions of the age. A long voyage to the enemy coasts would no doubt have had the same effect, and might well have half-crippled the English fleet before the decisive moment, as it did the Spanish. Queen Elizabeth's ships faced King Philip's with such slender logistical margins that a forward strategy, however attractive, would have been exceedingly risky. The cautious and defensive strategy which events forced on Howard was probably the most economical possible use of his forces. With them he won a notable victory, and if all the Spanish ships had reached home safely he would still have had the credit of decisively defeating the greatest expedition ever mounted by the greatest power of the day. But Spanish losses owed more to the weakness of Spanish naval administration and the impossibility of carrying out the King's orders than to the English navy.

Dr Rodger is an historian at the Public Record Office.

THE INVINCIBLE ARMADA

Not all the gold of the Indies nor all the excellence
of Spanish seamanship could bring England to its knees.
Ian Thompson exposes the incompetence that led to
the defeat of the Armada

WITH THE benefit of hindsight, the Enterprise of England seems to have been inevitable. One modern scholar has written, "The preparations for the Armada campaign may be said to date from the accession of Elizabeth to the Throne". From 1558, differences over religious, political, and colonial interests convinced many contemporary observers that a Spanish conquest of England was the only likely outcome. After Philip II's annexation of the Portuguese empire in 1580, rumours of an invasion of England, expectant, fearful, or merely curious, were everywhere, London, Paris, Lisbon, Madrid, Rome, Venice, Constantinople. The year 1580 was seen as confirming the King of Spain's thirst for hegemony in Europe and so strengthening his power, particularly his naval power, as to make that hegemony a real possibility. For modern historians, too, the conquest of Portugal has seemed to mark the beginning of a new, aggressive phase in Philip II's foreign policy, of which the Armada of 1588 was the logical culmination, a turn from the Mediterranean to the Atlantic made possible, diplomatically, by a truce with the Ottomans in 1578 and, financially, by a great increase in remittances of silver from the mines of Mexico and Peru.

The truth is rather different. The Armada was not a mature, long-planned, well thought out, strategic enterprise, but a hasty, rushed, and underprepared expedition with vacillating and uncertain objectives. The apparent continuity between 1580 and 1588 is false. The Enterprise of England marked not the culmination of long-prepared imperialist ambitions, but the end of what the French historian, Pierre Chaunu, has called "the military tranquility during the years 1582-1585". The proposal by the Marquis of Santa Cruz, the Captain-General of the Ocean Sea, in a letter of August 9, 1583, that his fleet, victorious over the Portuguese dissidents and their English supporters in the Azores, should be kept in being and sent against Elizabeth, was ignored. If the words of Philip II's reply seemed to leave the option open, his actions did not. The military apparatus that had conquered Portugal and the Azores was dismantled. The last 3,000 German and Italian troops in Lisbon were finally sent home in March 1584. A reform of the munitions industries, notably the reopening of the shot factory in Navarre that had been negotiated with an Italian entrepreneur on various occasions between 1578 and 1584, was suspended in 1585 and the matter not revived until July 1586. A contract for 10,000 cwt of Hungarian copper for gunfounding was negotiated some time before 1584, but only 4,000 of it was ordered to be taken up. The programme for the construction of 15,000 tons of shipping in Guipuzcoa and Vizcaya to serve as a kind of naval militia which had been first put forward in 1581, when the pacification of Portugal was still uncertain and it was feared that the French, the English, and the Dutch were planning attacks on Spain, was abandoned in October 1584 only a third completed. At the same time, the Crown was contemplating selling off the nine galleons that were being built for the Indies Guard to private buyers. It is clear that at the end of 1584 not only had Philip II no immediate plans for naval action in the Atlantic but that he so little anticipated any such action that he was in the process of reversing a policy that had been intended to begin the creation of a permanent, Spanish high-seas fleet.

The policy decision to do something about the English problem was made only after Philip became aware of the Treaty of Nonsuch of August 1585 which committed Elizabeth to provide aid to Philip's rebellious subjects in the Netherlands, but not until the spring of 1586 was any administrative action taken to put the Enterprise in train. A

● OPPOSITE: Title page *La Felicissima Armada que el Rey Don Felipe . . .*

LA FELI
CISSIMA AR-
MADA QVE ELREY
DON FELIPE NVESTRO
Señor mandó juntar enel puerto
de la Ciudad de Lisboa enel
Reyno de Portu-
gal.

El Año de mil y quinientos y
ochenta y ocho.

fr.si.tis. A. Jacques
Goullain fils Dr. fru-
Guille. lequel. fist lachat de
mey. en la ville deliseboine. 1588

HECHA POR
Pedro de Paz
Salas.

DESEMBARCACION DE SV M EN LISBOA

● Departure of the Armada from Lisbon.
Engraving J.B. Lavanha's *Viage* (1622).
FOTOMAS LIBRARY.

the end of January, the King had asked Santa Cruz for his estimate of the forces that would be needed to send against England. Santa Cruz's plan reached the King at the end of March, and on April 21 a "Purveyor-General of the High-Board Fleets to be assembled in the Kingdom of Portugal on the account of the Crown of Castile" was appointed. On May 1, the secretaryship of war, vacant since early February, was split into two, with one office for land and the other for sea — a move that had not been contemplated as late as November 1585 when the post had last been filled, and one that was clearly geared to the new administrative requirements of the war at sea.

These appointments, but perhaps first of all a Royal letter of April 4 to all the bishops of Castile asking for prayers throughout their dioceses for "the affairs of Christendom and good success for public matters", were the first real signs that the Enterprise of England was going to happen. Almost immediately, however, it was recognized that it was too late to do anything in 1586, and at the end of May, the Venetian Ambassador was reporting that everything was being suspended for a campaign the following April. Provisions began to be assembled after the harvest, a good one as it happened, and in September a special purveyor, Antonio de Guevara of the Council of Finance, was sent to Andalusia,

where much of the wine and grain was to be procured. But by early December, it was decided that preparations were still insufficiently advanced for an April expedition, and the target date was shifted to August - April and August being thought the best months for the weather. Then Drake's activities cost Spain the summer, not so much because of his attack on Cadiz and the destruction of ships and stores there — the Spanish documents give that episode far less importance than English historians have done - as because Santa Cruz, with his squadron in Lisbon, was forced to put to sea from July 16 to the last week of September to protect the fleets returning with silver from America, "and on that alone to waste the greater and best part of the summer". By the time Santa Cruz returned, Phlip II was desperate that the whole year not be lost, hoping to take advantage of what seemed like a brief Indian summer and fearing that over the winter Elizabeth would have time to strengthen her defences, negotiate foreign help, or organize a diversionary attack on the Indies.

Every day was wasting resources and costing Spain money and reputation, and the entire credibility of the operation was being put in doubt, not least because the delicate military and diplomatic balance that was temporarily neutralizing France and Turkey and on which the Enterprise depended, might well not survive into 1588. A succession of increasingly intemperate October and November deadlines was sent to Lisbon

ordering Santa Cruz to sail immediately with whatever forces were ready and rather to leave ships behind than lose another day. But after their late-summer voyage, a number of the vessels needed careening, there were shortages of sailors and artillerymen, Miguel de Oquendo's squadron of seven ships from Guipuzcoa could not be put to sea for lack of cables, anchors, and sails, the troops were sickening and had to be put ashore to recover while their shipboard quarters were sanitized, rain held up the transshipment of victuals, and a violent storm on November 16 damaged 17 fighting ships and 10 storeships, and another 15 days had to be spent on repairs. By November 9, Philip II was reconciled to the impossibility of any departure before the end of the month.

On November 30, Santa Cruz was ordered to put to sea within six to eight days with 48 fighting ships and the storeships, but on December 12 the Marquis estimated that he still needed 28 to 30 days before the fleet could sail. In another sudden change of plan, the King ordered the detachment of 35 ships to leave immediately to transport 6,000 picked troops to Flanders. What the object of this exercise was is not clear, whether to reinforce Parma for an independent invasion from the Netherlands, or simply to do *something*, to show that something could be done, regardless of the dangers of the season. In the event, information about the strength of the English fleet posed too many risks for any such limited exercise, and having

● Recruiting table; detail from a Sixteenth Century view of Cadiz.
NATIONAL MARITIME MUSEUM.

failed to meet another series of winter deadlines in January, Santa Cruz died suddenly on February 9, 1588. It is difficult to know how far Santa Cruz was personally responsible for delaying the expedition over the winter, as many in Madrid suspected. He was cautious — perhaps excessively so considering the size of his force, probably justifiably so considering the dangers of a winter campaign — and he was unhappy with the strategic role he was to play, and it may be that his death was a disguised blessing for the Armada. The new commander, the Duke of Medina Sidonia, appointed on February 14, though not a sailor, was a capable and experienced naval administrator, and by no means the poltroon that for so long he has been portrayed. Within three months of his arrival, the Armada was at sea, and in much greater strength and in much better shape than it had been at Santa Cruz's death.

The Armada that sailed out of Lisbon water on May 30, 1588 was a very much more substantial force than it had been at the beginning of the year. Between January 4 and May 28, 7,920 soldiers and 2,622 sailors had been added, and since September 30, 1587 the number of ships had been increased by 35 and the tonnage by 18,758. In the last three months, the guns on board had been increased by up to 200, and munitions supplies by 2,000 cwt of powder and about 50,000 shot (20 per gun). Detained by contrary winds for two weeks off Cape St Vincent and hit by a gale off Finisterre on June 19-20, Medina Sidonia was forced to put into Corunna in Galicia to refit and reassemble, and when he left again on July 22 he had lost 10 ships, 600 seamen, and 1,500 soldiers. He nevertheless still had at his command incomparably the largest force ever seen in Atlantic waters. The last full muster of the fleet, dated Lisbon, May 28, 1588, gives it 141 vessels, 62,278 tons, 7,666 seamen, and 18,529 soldiers. The ships were divided into six front-line squadrons with a total of 63 or 64 fighting-ships, plus four great, oared galleasses from Naples, each carrying more than 600 men on board, and four light galleys.

● Galleass: detail from *A Discourse concerning the Spanish Fleets*, by Petruccio Ubaldini, 1590.
BRITISH LIBRARY.

They were headed by the two élite squadrons of Royal galleons, apart from the galleasses and the galleys, the only specialist warships in the fleet, the flag-squadron of the Crown of Portugal with nine of the largest galleons, and the Castilian Squadron, under Diego Flores de Valdés, consisting of the nine galleons of the Indies Guard completed in 1584, and five privately owned ships. Almost all the other ships were privately owned. Two squadrons were composed of ships from the northern province of Guipuzcoa, that under Miguel de Oquendo with nine ships and a hulk, and that under Juan Martinez de Recalde with 10. Though private vessels, many of these ships had been built with government subsidies as part of a long-standing programme for the encouragement of domestic shipbuilding in Spain. The 1,000-ton *San Salvador* in Oquendo's squadron, costing over 13,000 ducats, had been built with a loan from the Crown of 1,000 ducats, and its original owner received a bounty of 10,000 *maravedis* (c.27 ducats) a year for every 100 tons, as long as it remained in his possession.

To some extent, therefore, the Armada was a vindication of the efforts the Crown had made since the 1560s to build up a merchant marine in the Cantabrian provinces capable of serving when needed in the Royal service. The other two squadrons were the Andalusian, with 10 ships under Don Pedro de Valdés, so called because the ships had been requisitioned there in the spring of 1587 while preparing for a trading voyage to New Spain; and the Levant Squadron of Don Martin de Bertendona, composed of 11 ships, most of them very large, originating from different parts of the central Mediterranean, Ragusa (the present-day Dubrovnik), Venice, Naples, Sicily, and one a galleon belonging to the Grand Duke of Tuscany. They had all been requisitioned in Iberian ports, mostly in mid-1587, having arrived with grain and troops from Italy. In addition, there were the storeships, 23 hulks, mainly from the Baltic, and 11 small caravels, averaging 100 tons or so, a squadron of pinnaces, with their flagship and storeships (there were 32 of them in all, averaging less than 80 tons each), and 11 feluccas. The Armada was a spectacular and impressive sight, even to men such as the secretary of the navy, Andrés de Alva, who had spent his whole life at sea. Even so, it is worth pointing out that Medina Sidonia had fewer ships than the English were to assemble against him,

only 25 per cent greater tonnage, and only one-third the men carried in the Christian fleet at the battle of Lepanto in 1571 against the Turks.

The despatch of the Armada has often been, and is now again in Spanish circles increasingly being, presented as a triumph of planning and organization, one of the wonders of the world of early-modern administration. Such an assessment, however, depends very much on how far the Armada of May 1588 conformed to the Armada that was planned two years before, and that we simply do not know. Although military preparations began in April 1586, it is by no means clear at this stage what it was precisely that Philip II was preparing.

There were, broadly speaking, three military options canvassed. One was a direct assault on England by sea from Spain. This was the approach advocated by Santa Cruz in his reply to the King's request for a plan of operations in January 1586. Another, favoured by Philip's governor in Flanders, the Duke of Parma, was a surprise invasion across the Channel by the army in the Low Countries, with the Armada from Spain following up to protect the rear and bring

in reinforcements. The third was a diversionary landing in Ireland, Scotland, Lancashire, the Isle of Wight, or some other peripheral area, to support or to incite a Catholic rising and compel Elizabeth to recall her forces for her own defence. Some combination of any of these was also possible, and as many as 15 different plans were floated in the 20 months or so before the Armada sailed. No firm decision on which strategy to employ seems to have been reached until the autumn of 1587, over a year after the military preparations had been put in train. Not until after the Spanish capture of the Belgian port of Sluys in August 1587 was the final plan, involving the despatch of the Armada to join up with Parma's forces in the Netherlands, reinforcing him with 6,000 soldiers from Spain, and covering the crossing of his troop-carriers, resolved upon. Even so, other options remained open. As late as December 1587, an independent assault direct from the Netherlands was still being contemplated and, according to one report, had the Armada been held up in July 1588 for another fortnight, it would have made not for England, but for Ireland.

It looks, therefore, as if for a year and a half, military preparations went ahead without any firm decision having been made about what the Armada's role would be and without relation to any fixed strategic objective. In the event, the strategy of the Armada was to be determined by the state of its preparations.

Cutting through the secrecy, the deliberate misinformation, the desire to keep all options open, and the sheer indecisiveness of Madrid, the evidence suggests that until the autumn of 1587 some sort of independent action was envisaged for the Armada, if not alone, at least as part of a larger strategy. The adoption of the 1588 plan, announced to Lisbon in an Instruction of September 14, 1587, has all the appearance of a sudden, if not precipitate, decision which radically altered existing expectations. It certainly came as an unwelcome shock to Santa Cruz, who was only just persuaded from resigning in protest against the merely passive role now attributed to his command in covering Parma's crossing and neutralizing the English fleet. That decision of Philip II's, fatally flawed as events were to prove, was the key moment in the history of the Enterprise,

and it is worth considering why he took it. The reasons were clearly set out in the Instruction. "Not having been able to assemble this year everything called for in the estimates", and having lost the summer, the King had ordered his fleets in Andalusia and Lisbon to join up "in order that, as the forces of the two fleets were not as great as had been projected or were to be desired for the principal objective (*la empresa principal*), they should be employed this year to conquer Ireland, as had been discussed with the Marquis himself before he left, wintering there, and going ahead next year with new strength." The capture of Sluys, however, had opened up the prospect of a combined Hispano-Flemish operation that would eliminate the dangers of deferring the main attack over the winter. As the Instruction put it, "the forces that His Majesty has there and here, although neither by themselves sufficient, together, if we are capable of uniting them, will win the game".

The point is that after a year's preparations, Spain had simply not been able to mount *la empresa principal*. Why this should have been so cannot be understood without a closer look at the

● Spanish map showing the Channel, c. 1555-60.

state of Spain's military forces and supply services at the moment when the Armada began to be organized.

In the middle of 1586, there was not a single branch of military organization that was adequate to the task. The preparations for the Armada took place against the background of a prolonged and serious run-down of the entire Spanish military machine. With the conquest of Portugal, Philip II had acquired a high-seas fleet of a dozen powerful galleons, but the nine galleons built for the Indies Guard and delivered in 1584 were nearly sold off, as we saw earlier, and the plan to increase Spain's naval strength by contracts with Basque outfitters was aborted. The galley fleets in the Mediterranean, about 150 vessels in 1576, had fallen to 88 by 1587. The 40 galleys of the Spanish squadron, based in Andalusia in 1580, had been dispersed and in November 1587 only 24 remained, and those were recognized to be very few and very ill in order - "fishing boats not galleys", Cardinal Granvelle had called them. It was also becoming increasingly difficult

165

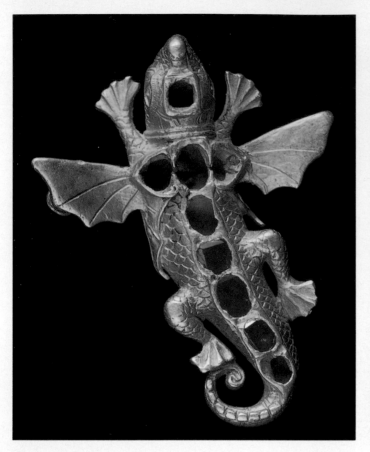

● Salamander pendant.

ULSTER MUSEUM.

● Cross of a Knight of Santiago.

ULSTER MUSEUM

to recruit soldiers or sailors in Spain. The refusal of mariners to join the Royal service was a chronic problem, and in 1581 the King had had to attempt a form of conscription in the Cantabrian provinces to man the Indies fleets, without, however, much success. The persistent difficulty of raising soldiers voluntarily, on the other hand, was relatively new. Between 1571 and 1578 the average recruiting captain was raising 256 men; in the decade after 1580 the average slumped to 161, and even this was achieved only at the cost of inordinate expense to the Crown and intolerable suffering and humiliation to the villages through which the rapacious and licentious soldiery passed. Indeed, in the years after 1580, with the Crown unable to pay its soldiers and with the consequent breakdown of discipline, the entire recruiting system was falling apart. Serious attempts at reform and alternative methods of recruitment were beginning to be undertaken in 1586, precisely to meet the demands of war in the Atlantic, but by 1587-88 they were still largely untried.

A similar breakdown is apparent in the supply services. Again this was the result of a combination of insufficient funds and inadequate administrative control, brought to a head by the logisti-

cal demands of raising an army for Portugal and maintaining a substantial garrison there after 1580. Just as in recruiting, the 1580s were a period of constant complaint by the Cortes on behalf of peasants and artisans whose goods were requisitioned without payment and in excessive quantities by insensitive and unscrupulous purveyors. The problem of supply, particularly of grain and other agricultural produce, was made worse by the increasing difficulties of Castilian agriculture, reflected in a series of unreservedly bad harvests between 1580 and 1584, and by the reduction of imports from Northern Europe resulting from the Spanish embargo on English and Dutch shipping in May 1585, and the growing danger from piracy in Spanish waters.

It was the Spanish munitions industries which were in the worst position to meet these new demands. With the breakdown of the negotiations with the Prince of Salerno there was no cannon shot made at all in Spain. The Royal cannon foundry at Malaga had never been sufficient for Spain's needs, and the country's gunpowder manufacturing capacity, for reasons still not entirely clear, was on the decline. The only one of the war industries that was expanding in the 1580s was the small-arms industry in

Guipuzcoa and Vizcaya, but this, like all the other munitions industries, was crippled by lack of money. The gunsmiths and pike-makers were owed 40,000 ducats in 1584, at least 31,000 in 1586, 48,000 in December 1587, 45,000 in May 1588. Repeatedly, the immediate cessation of production was threatened, and work did stop for a period in 1587. It was the same with gunpowder manufacturing. Between November 1580 and May 1587, there was not one grain of saltpetre worked at the saltpetre plant at Lérida (Catalonia) because there was no money to buy it. There was nothing unique about Lérida. An account of 1587 stated baldly, "in 1586 powder manufacturing ceased in all parts for lack of money". In November 1587, the casting of 30 guns was suspended and all ordnance work brought to a halt for lack of 10,000 ducats, and in 1588 the carpenters and iron-workers employed by the King in Lisbon stopped work because they had run out of materials. It was, therefore, against the background of an almost total collapse of the administrative and supply system that the decision to embark on the invasion of England was taken.

Coming when it did, the Armada and the means to equip it (with the exception of the 18 galleons of the Portu-

● Forks.

● Sole of a shoe.

guese and Castilian squadrons) had to be created more or less from scratch and this, as it turned out, in something less than two years. The consequences of this were fundamental. Spain at sea was lacking in all the intensity factors necessary to fight the English on equal terms, and these were not things that could be produced in a summer — the nine galleons for the Indies Guard, for example, first ordered in February 1581, were not completed until April 1584, three years and three months later. The disadvantages of the Spaniards in ship construction, seamanship, and gunnery, and the realization that the English would seize the wind, lie off, and batter the Spanish fleet from long range, without allowing them to close sufficiently to board, meant that the strategy of the Armada had necessarily to be a strategy of mass. The Armada had to be as large as possible. It had to be too big to be defeated. It had to intimidate and overawe, even if its sheer mass actually meant that its effectiveness as a fighting force was even more impaired. Nothing better exemplifies this strategy of mass than Santa Cruz's fantastic blueprint of March 1586 asking for 510 ships of 110,000 tons, 46 galleys and galleasses, and 94,000 men, more than in the entire Christian force at Lepanto and twice the number that had conquered Portugal in 1580. This gargantuan armada was to conquer England on its own by a direct assault in overwhelming and irresistible force. It was a simple and uncomplicated plan. It was perhaps the only strategy that could have succeeded, but it was a logistical impossibility. How seriously anybody took the plan we do not know. It is certain that nobody acted on it. By the end of 1586, it is clear from the financial allocations and procurement targets that we have that any scheme on that scale, if indeed it had ever been contemplated, had been abandoned. The inventories of the purveyors in Andalusia and Lisbon indicate that the numbers that were being catered for were barely one-quarter of those envisaged by Santa Cruz, and much smaller than all other proposals for the direct invasion of England were calling for. Already by that date it is clear that the Enterprise of England was not to be a purely Spanish enterprise. The allocation of funds shows that the strategic effort was to be divided between the Armada of Spain and the Army of Flanders. A special *junta* set up late in December 1586 was instructed to find 7 million ducats for the following year, one-third was to be for the Armada and two-thirds for Flanders.

From the summer of 1586 and throughout 1587 and 1588, there was a rush of reforms - the division of the

168

secretariat of war, the expansion of the Council of War, the appointment of military governors in Galicia and Andalusia, the creation of a new office of *comisario general* to co-ordinate and supervise recruiting. New biscuit baking ovens were put up in Lisbon and Malaga. Surveys were begun to discover new mineral deposits; the privately owned sulphur mines at Hellin in Murcia were taken over by the Crown; the Lérida saltpetre plant was put to work again (May 1587); the cannon foundry in Lisbon was brought into production; negotiations were resumed to open the shot-works in Navarre, and the agreement with the Basque shipbuilders seems to have been taken up again at the beginning of 1587.

But it was all too late. The first cannon balls, for example, were not cast in Navarre until the end of 1588 at the earliest, and, as with so much else that was used in the Armada, the shot had to be got from abroad. Fifteen thousand cwt of copper that the Council of War had wanted brought from Milan in May 1587 still had not arrived in Spain by September

● Broadsheet: A Thankful Remembrance of God's Mercy.
MANSELL COLLECTION.

1588, and although the Captain-General of the Artillery claimed that he could produce 4,000 cwt of gunpowder within six months, in April 1588, the Armada had less than half the powder it was thought to need and 550 cwt had to be bought from German merchants in Lisbon at more than double normal prices. To the last, the Armada remained critically short of munitions of all kinds. It was short also of biscuit and wine. The harvests of 1585 and 1586 were abundant; that of 1587 was expected to be equally good, and it may be that this favourable prospect helped with the decision to go ahead with the Enterprise. In fact, the harvest of 1587 failed to live up to expectations and this undoubtedly played a part in delaying the Armada in 1587 and contributed to the depletion of its reserves of biscuit and wine the following year.

In only one respect was the situation favourable for the Enterprise, and that was the financial. The trade difficulties that hindered the procurement of supplies meant that the Crown's Genoese bankers were looking for outlets for their capital and anxious to recover the debts and the specie export licences that had been suspended after the Crown "bank-

ruptcy" of 1575. At the same time, increased taxes in Castile in the late 1570s, substantial revenues from sales of land and offices, and a doubling of bullion imports from the New World in the decade after 1578, bringing in 4 million ducats for the King in 1587 alone, provided the securities against which the financiers proved happy to lend. During 1586-88, the Crown was able to conclude a series of very large asientos on remarkably good terms, which left a considerable part of current revenues available for use.

The extraordinary cost estimated for the Armada for 1587 was a shade under 2 million ducats, 529,000 for the pay of the soldiers, 310,000 for the freightage of ships and seamen's wages, and more than 1,000,000 for provisions. The cost of artillery and munitions was accounted separately. In January 1587, Philip II appointed a small, select junta to raise 7 million ducats, "for the things which are in train and to be put in train this year"; 2-2½ million were to be for "costs of the naval expedition" and 4½-5 million for the recurrent and extraordinary requirements of Flanders. The junta met for the first time on the 31st, and at the end of a week had organized the funding of the

continued on page 172

It's an anniversary
for communications, too...

The conflict with the Armada
began with swift communications
– from beacon to beacon across
the hills of Britain.

400 years later, the Royal Mail
leads in communications; and the
anniversary of the Armada is
being marked by a special stamp issue,
together with First Day Covers,
postcards and presentation packs
of the stamps.

Colourful, exquisitely designed,
superbly printed, this special
issue will make a beautiful gift you'll
want to keep. From 19 July it's on
sale at The Armada Exhibition
and main post offices.

For details of all British Stamps,
please write to the
Marketing Department,
The British Philatelic Bureau,
20 Brandon Street,
EDINBURGH EH3 5TT

Royal Mail Stamps

The Post Office will issue a set of special stamps on 19 July 1988 to mark the 400th anniversary of the Armada. The set will consist of five first class stamps in the form of a 'se-tenant' strip; that is, the five stamps will be printed side by side on the sheet and it will be possible to buy a strip of all five joined together by the perforations.

The stamps, designed by Graham Everndon, will be officially unveiled on 13 April and it is therefore not possible to say what they will actually depict. However, the British Post Office has promised a very exciting and colourful set of designs which will be greatly popular and a fitting commemoration of one of the most decisive battles in the history of Europe.

The events that led up to the battle are described elsewhere in this publication but perhaps a word or two about the selection of stamp subjects and designs would be interesting to readers. The number of special issues each year is limited to eight because of production and distribution constraints and also to keep down the cost of collecting.

There is never any shortage of suggestions and requests for special stamps which are received from members of the public, Members of Parliament, Government departments and organisations and institutions of various kinds. The Post Office also carries out its own research to ensure that the list of subjects from which the final choice is made is as comprehensive as possible, will have popular interest, good marketing possibilities and be suitable for translation into attractive stamp designs.

Once the programme has been decided and the Stamp Advisory Committee, comprising experts in design and philately, representatives of public opinion and a nominee from the Department of Trade and Industry, have discussed possible design interpretations, the Post Office Design Adviser commissions and briefs designers, usually two or three for each subject. One set is chosen for further development and after the final artwork is produced the printer is asked to prepare stamp sized proofs or essays. Once the Queen has seen and approved the essays, the printers can begin production.

The Armada set would have passed through the same stringent process. The stamps to be issued on 19 July 1988 will be available at all post offices for two weeks. They can also be obtained by post from the British Philatelic Bureau, 20 Brandon Street, EDINBURGH EH3 5TT for a period of one year from date of issue and at special philatelic counters.

In addition to the Armada stamps the Post Office will also bring out three highly colourful and desirable products to complement them. A special First Day Cover will be on sale at all post offices from 4 July to 19 July inclusive, price 16p. Also available from 19 July will be a Presentation Pack containing all five stamps in a transparent sleeve mounted on an attractive card folder which is packed with interesting background information on the issue. Price £1.12.

Equally popular and with a special appeal for tourists will be a set of postcards showing an enlargement of the Armada stamps. They will go on sale from 4 July at 15p each or 75p for a set of five.

The stamps and associated products will be on display at the Armada Exhibition at the National Maritime Museum, Greenwich, and later Belfast and will also be sold from the Exhibition shops from 19 July 1988.

The Post Office is also promoting the Armada stamps through an on-pack offer with Kelloggs Cornflakes. In return for tokens from the Kelloggs packs, respondents would be able to obtain a souvenir cover bearing all the five Armada stamps together with replica Armada coins. The promotion is expected to commence in April.

The products described in this article and other philatelic items illustrated can be obtained at philatelic counters and by post from the British Philatelic Bureau. Special stamps are also obtainable at all post offices for two weeks from the date of their issue.

For information about philatelic services please write to:

British Philatelic Bureau
Dept 88 – ABA
20 Brandon Street
EDINBURGH
EH3 5TT

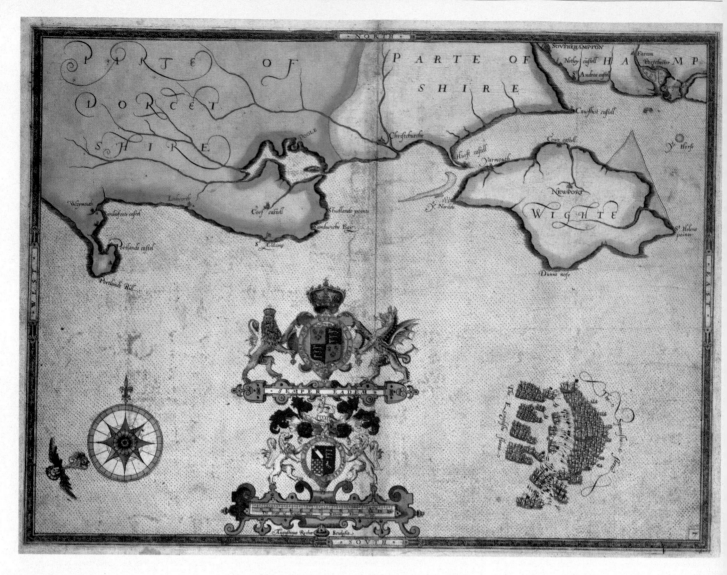

● Adams chart (no. 7) showing the English and Spanish fleets in the Channel.
NATIONAL MARITIME MUSEUM.

continued from page 169

million for the purveyors with two Spanish financiers, the Marquis of Auñón and Juan Ortega de la Torre, and was confident that cash and other assignations on revenues would meet the rest of the budget for the fleet. It had also arranged 2 million for Flanders, enough to last until May. On February 7, it was able to report, "as a result of all this, the Junta believes Your Majesty can rest greatly satisfied and content, and cease to worry that these funds will not be available when they are needed".

The Armada was, of course, to cost a good deal more than 2 million ducats. The figure bruited at the time, 900,000 ducats a month according to the President of Finance, was 10 million ducats, more than a year's revenue of Philip II, and something like seven years' of Elizabeth's. For the entire cost of the Enterprise between 1586 and 1588, including additional funding for the Netherlands, that figure might be possible. For the

Armada alone, a nominal 4 million ducats is probably nearer the mark. From the roughly 70,000 a month budgeted in January 1587, the wages of ships and men had risen to 115,000 a year later, and to a peak of 166,600 in May 1588, 73,200 ducats for ships and seamen, 82,000 for the infantry, and 11,500 for the high command and staff officers. Provisions were costing another 100,000 a month. When it sailed, the Armada was costing Philip II £2,350 a day, four times as much as the English fleet was costing Elizabeth. From the financial point, it was as well that it left when it did, and it was fortunate that it did not all return. The financial provision of January 1587 could not last for ever. The bankers had been prepared to wait for repayment until the arrival of the silver fleets of 1587 and to take assignments on taxes due in 1588, but that meant that those revenues were now pledged. By the beginning of the year, the financial situation of the Armada was becoming serious. At the end of January, the soldiers, sailors, and shipowners were owed 440,000 ducats, nearly four months' pay. Some of these

debts were outstanding for years, and in the case of the men who did not return, were perhaps never paid. The widow of Captain Andrés Felipe, the owner of the Gran Grin, was owed 9,000 ducats in 1591, four-fifths of what her husband should have been paid for the $15\frac{1}{2}$ months his ship was in the King's service, before ship, crew, and captain were all lost on August 28, 1588. The previous owner had foreclosed for the 8,000 ducats credit he had advanced for the purchase of the ship, and Felipe's widow had had to sell even the bed she slept in to pay him off. The bill for the Armada was picked up by a host of people like her, and by the population of Castile as a whole, whose representatives in the Cortes granted the King 8 million ducats to "wipe out the stain which this year has fallen on the Spanish nation".

The fact is that a strategy of mass posed insuperable problems for 16th century administrations. The greater the Armada, the more the ships and men, the more provisions and supplies that were needed, the longer the time it took to prepare and assemble; the longer it

● Alvaro de Bazán, first Marquis of Santa Cruz.
MUSEO NAVAL, MADRID.

with Parma was essential if for no other reason than the need to restock with provisions and water in the Netherlands. When, after Gravelines, this hope of succour vanished and the Armada was reduced to its own resources, the men were living on one-third rations, 8 ounces of biscuit a day, $\frac{1}{2}$ litre of water, $\frac{1}{4}$ litre of wine, and the only way of saving them was to get back to Spain as soon as possible. That was three weeks after leaving Corunna.

There was a second reason why a direct invasion from Spain was out of the question. There were not enough soldiers available, either in Spain or in the Italian *tercios*, for such an undertaking, not only in numbers but also, and even more importantly, in quality. The soldiers were, as Philip II himself put it, "the marrow of the Armada and that which matters most for the execution of its purposes". Santa Cruz had wanted 55,000 soldiers, one for every two tons of shipping. Medina Sidonia thought the Armada should have at least one man for every ton so that troops could be landed without weakening the fleet. To have raised such numbers would have required the recruitment of 28,000 in Spain and Portugal, according to Santa Cruz's proposals. In light of the experience of the early 1580s that was a patent impossibility. The inability to recruit men was already holding up the despatch of the Indies' fleet in the summer of 1586, and it was apparently the lack of soldiers on board that prevented Santa Cruz from going out to intercept Drake off Lisbon and Cascaes in May 1587.

Throughout 1587, the shortage of men continued. Even at the end of March 1588, the Armada was desperately undermanned, with perhaps only 9,000 or 10,000 soldiers in all. It was only the arrival of 3,000 men from Extremadura, the withdrawal of some troops from the garrison of Lisbon, and the late recruitment of 2,000 Portuguese in April and May that gave it a degree of numerical respectability — and even then there were only one-third of the men per ton that Medina Sidonia had thought essential the year before.

Moreover, all were agreed that the troops to be put ashore for any assault must be an élite of trained and hardened veterans, gente vieja. Santa Cruz had

took to prepare and assemble the greater the wastage, the deterioration and the decay, and the more that was consumed merely to keep it in existence. There were soldiers being maintained on the Armada's account well over a year before it finally set sail. By November 1587, 1,400 of 5,000 who had already been embarked on their ships for six months had fallen sick. In the 11 months it was in Spain, between July 1587 and May 1588, the *tercio* of Naples (squadron) lost 25 per cent of its effectives. The same thing was happening with the troops in the Netherlands, but to an even greater degree. Provisions also began to be assembled in Andalusia and Extremadura after the harvest of 1586, and large quantities of biscuit were sent from Naples and Sicily. But with 43,000 tons of shipping already in being in September 1587 and never less than 16,000 mouths to feed, by May 1588, the Armada had already used in normal rations alone half as many victuals again as it was to carry with it out of Lisbon, in addition to all the wastage that we know to have occurred. Some of the food was already inedible by the begin-

ning of 1588, and in June considerable quantities "in bad condition, stale, and rotten", had to be dumped into the sea. By July, the eight months' provisions that had been taken aboard in January had fallen to 60 days', as the Armada was delayed week after week fitting out the ships, increasing stocks of munitions, and awaiting the arrival of new recruits. Fresh victuals were taken on at Corunna, but even before it left Spain, the Armada was on short rations and sailed with biscuit for only 57 days. But it was all very haphazard. Some ships got back to Spain in September still quite well stocked; others were near exhaustion within a month. When, at the beginning of August, the English captured the Rosario, they found stinking fish, bread full of worms, leaky casks, and sour wine. By September, the biscuit that had been taken on in Lisbon only four months before was "in such a state that neither the pigs nor the dogs would eat it, even when it had been dunked in broth". In these circumstances, the Armada from Spain could not possibly be an independent force. A rendezvous

● RIGHT AND FAR RIGHT: Plans for shipbuilding from *Instrucción Náutica para Navegar*, by Dr. Diego García de Palacio, 1587.
BIBLIOTECA DEL MUSEO NAVAL, MADRID.

wanted 27,000 professional mercenaries from Germany and Italy, 11,000 experienced Spanish infantry from the *tercios* in Italy, the garrisons in Portugal and the Azores, and the Armada of the Indies Guard, and 17,000 new recruits from Spain and Portugal. The Armada in May 1588 had only 19,000 soldiers, and none of them Germans or Italians. Of these 19,000, 104 companies of the *tercios* of Pimentel from Sicily, Luzón from Naples, Toledo from Portugal, and Isla from the Indies galleons, with a total of 10,479 men, would seem to correspond to the 11,000 veteran Spanish troops that Santa Cruz had asked for, leaving the remaining 67 companies with something over 8,000 Spanish and Portuguese *bisoños*, but a closer examination reveals that it is impossible to regard all these men as experienced veterans. Luzón's *tercio* of Naples, for example, is listed in the Lisbon muster as having 26 companies with 2,889 men. Yet we know that when the *tercio* arrived in Spain in July 1587 it had only 10 companies with 1,864 men, and that by May 1588 there were only 1,396 of them left. In fact, a very substantial proportion of those four *tercio* is known to have been new troops raised in Spain during 1587 — at least 12 companies in Luzón's *tercio*, at least five in Pimentel's, at least four in Toledo's, and at least eight in Isla's. Pimentel himself declared that only 15 of the 32 companies of the *tercio* of Sicily were old soldiers, *infanteria vieja*. At an absolute minimum, some 2,500 of the 10,500 men who at first glance look like experienced, trained, veteran Spanish infantry turn out to be raw recruits, and the real figure could very well be double that. Moreover, even the "veterans", that is those not newly raised in 1587, were far from being battle-scarred warriors. At least four of the original 10 companies of the *tercio* of Naples had been initially raised in Castile no longer ago than 1584 (three in June 1585, one in March 1584) and a further five, at least, of the companies from the garrison in Portugal had been raised between 1584 and 1586. It is unlikely that any of them had ever fought. At the most conservative of estimates, no less than 60 per cent of the Armada's soldiers (11,000 of the 19,000), and maybe as many as 75 per cent of them, were raw recruits who had, in all probability, never been to sea, never

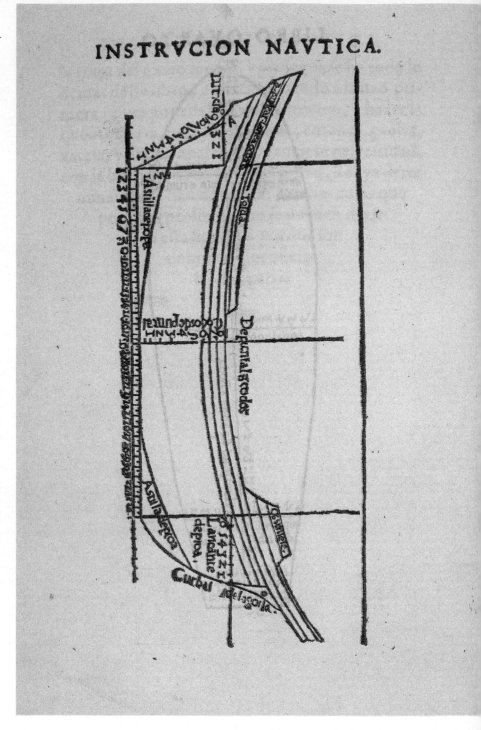

INSTRVCION NAVTICA.

fought, and knew no more about military manoeuvres, discipline, or the handling of their weapons than what they had picked up in a few months of training in their billets. Their inexpertness is all the more likely when one remembers that maybe half of these recruits were not volunteers, the *guzmanes* who had made the Spanish *tercios* famous throughout Europe, but conscripts levied by the lords and cities of Andalusia and Extremadura. This was the legacy of the collapse of voluntary recruiting after 1580. The Armada was the first time that Spaniards were conscripted for service overseas in this way. One can only guess

at the morale and fitness of the men involved. The troops in Seville, levied for the fleet to flush Drake out of the Indies in 1586, were described as "poor, all raw recruits, from the scum of the people, raised by force and kept by force, prisoners in monasteries". The 400 Galicians sent by the Counts of Lemos and Monterrey to join the Armada were so old and decrepit, so underfed, and so ignorant of arms, that even their captains did not want them, and Medina Sidonia, rather than have them drop dead on board ship, sent them back home to their despairing wives and children. These were not men to conquer kingdoms.

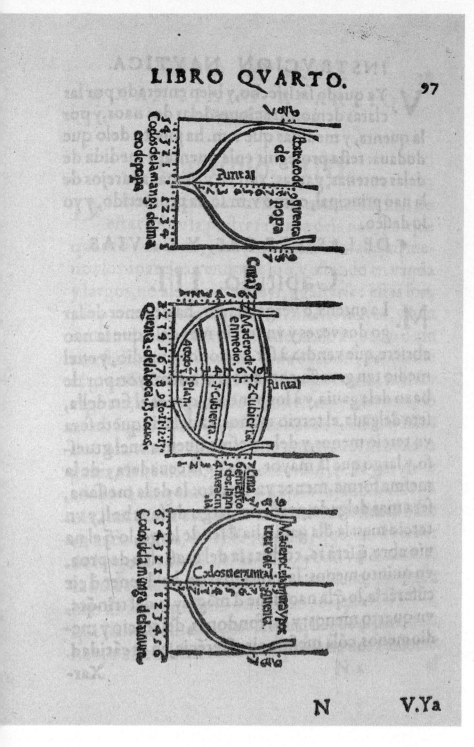

It was apparent fairly soon, therefore, that there was no possibility of making Santa Cruz's ambitious project a reality. A comparison of the 1586 plan with the final Lisbon inventory of May 1588 reveals that on almost all counts the 1588 fleet was not only absolutely smaller (half the size in tonnage and capital ships, a third the size in manpower), but proportionately weaker as well. For every 100 tons, there were to have been 40 soldiers in 1586, there were 33 in 1588; in 1586, 15 sailors, in 1588, 13.9; for every man there were to have been 402 lbs of biscuit and 244 litres of wine in 1586, there were 357 lbs of biscuit and 217 litres

of wine in 1588 — and that on the basis of the May 1588 inventory which, with hardly any doubt at all, was a gross and fraudulent inflation of the provisions laden. Even in guns, the 1588 fleet failed to reach the standards of 1586 with, on the most favourable calculation, only one gun for every 23.8 tons, as against one for every 23.4 tons in 1586, and if one takes only the armed sailing ships into account, the 1586 figure rises to one for every 16.1 tons and the 1588 figure falls to one for every 26.2 tons. Only in cannon balls was the 1588 fleet at an advantage, and even that was negated by the failure to provide a proportionately grea-

ter supply of powder. Indeed, if one includes all the powder available in the fleet, there was only half as much per gun in 1588 as had been planned in 1586 (213 lbs and 406 lbs).

Philip II's realization that he was incapable of launching the empresa principal was the decisive moment in the long and uncertain evolution of the Enterprise of England. The dilemma was clear. The strategic requirements of a direct invasion made impossible demands on the supply system, and in turn the inadequacies of supply contributed to the adoption of a less demanding strategy, but one that was in other ways even more fundamentally unworkable. The course resolved upon in the Instruction of September 14, 1587 required that some means be provided by which Parma's soldiers in the Netherlands could be brought out across shallows dominated by the Dutch, which could not be navigated by the great galleons of the Armada. Having opted against Santa Cruz's plan for a direct invasion of England, this was the problem that had to be solved. That it was not solved might, tentatively, be associated with another and apparently unrelated change that took place between 1586 and 1588, the disappearance of the galleys. Santa Cruz had wanted 40 galleys. Only four sailed with the Armada in 1588 — not Portuguese galleys, as is often stated, but Spanish galleys based in Lisbon. The disappearance of the galleys has been seen as a modernization of the Armada, a conscious change of policy consequent upon the lessons of Drake's raid on Cadiz in April 1587, and a belated recognition of the new technology of naval warfare. It was nothing of the kind, and there is no substantive evidence whatever for such a belief. Even after Cadiz, Philip II believed that the galleys had demonstrated their effectiveness by checking the attacks of the English fleet on the Portuguese coast in May 1587, and everybody who had anything to do with the Armada in 1587 and 1588 wanted more galleys, not less, more than the four of 1588 — that is, eight or 12 at least. The galleys, they believed, had proved their ability to operate on the high seas in the Azores and in the Indies. They were invaluable not only in a calm, when they could manoeuvre independently or be used to tow the fighting galleons into position, but also in shallow waters, particularly for embarking and disembarking soldiers.

One can only speculate about

whether the galleys could have been that last crucial link to cover Parma's egress and to bring the army and the Armada together. The four galleys that sailed with Medina Sidonia did not last a week. Would it have been different if there had been eight, or 12, or 40? Could they, in any case, have held off the 25 Dutch cromsters standing off Dunkirk? Before and after, Spanish opinion certainly, and Dutch also, it would seem, did not doubt that the galleys were a match for the rebel coasters. Indeed, one of the last things the Marquis of Santa Cruz had said before his death was that had galleys been sent to Flanders the war would have been over long ago. Whatever lessons the Spaniards learned from the Armada, it was not that the galleys should be abandoned, and in subsequent armadas in the 1590s there were far more galleys than in 1588. The absence of galleys in 1588, therefore, was not a policy decision, but a logistical one. With the run-down of the Mediterranean galley fleets, the renewed activity of the Algerian and Moroccan corsairs, and the breakdown of the truce with the Turks, it was impossible to release any more galleys for the Armada, and without the galleys whatever hope there was of making the new invasion plan work had gone.

With the rejection of Santa Cruz's plan and with the impossibility of uniting the Flanders army with the Lisbon galleons, there could be no landing in England. The only success the Armada could achieve was at sea. But the general procurement situation in which the Armada was prepared meant that it lacked many of the essential ingredients for success in battle, also. The restricted number of specialized warships in the Royal fleet forced Philip II to make up his Armada by the seizure and requisition of whatever Spanish and foreign merchantmen were to hand. Inevitably, many of those vessels were unsuitable for the tasks that faced them in northern waters and their masters unused to the disciplines of sailing in naval formation. On the evidence of the dimensions of 12 new warships built in Ragusa, Venice and Naples for the King of Spain's service in the early 1590s, the Mediterranean galleons were all deeper in the hold and even broader in the beam than almost all contemporary pundits, even Spanish ones, recommended. The unseaworthiness of such ships, suggested by the high mortality of the Levant Squadron in 1588, is confirmed by the dismissal of eight of the 12 new

Ragusan galleons in 1596 because, in the opinion of the Council of War, "past campaigns had shown them to be ill-suited for those seas". Witnesses on both sides were unanimous that the English fleet was far superior to the Spanish in design, rigging and handling, and able no only to gain and keep the weather, but so manoeuvrable that they were capable of getting off two broadsides to the Spaniards' one.

No less important were the deficiencies of morale that were only to be expected in a force whose ships, sailors, and soldiers were largely conscripted from all corners of Europe. The Armada was a marine Babel. There were ships from Dubrovnik at one end, and from Danzig at the other; there was one, at least, from Scotland. There were Dalmatians, Italians, Portuguese, Germans, Flemings, Frenchmen, Dutchmen, even Englishmen on board, whose commitment to the success of the Enterprise was by no means uniform. Ships captains, like Andrés Felipe, who had invested 20,000 ducats in his ship only two months before it was requisitioned, in the expectation of making a handsome profit in the Americas, were unlikely to be the most enthusiastic of participants, or to want to expose their capital to avoidable risk. The *maestre de campo*, Don Francisco de Bobadilla, in one of the most revealing assessments of the action, asserted that, apart from some 20 ships which conducted themselves with honour, the rest of the fleet simply took flight whenever they saw the enemy attack. The collapse of morale was related also to the unhappy relations within the high command and between the seamen and the military. The admirals of the squadrons were all northerners from the Cantabrian coasts and all men of immense experience whose seamanship could not be faulted. Unfortunately, there was a good deal of discord among them and with the predominantly Castilian, military officers and their Andalusian commander-in-chief. Diego Flores de Valdés, deputed to be Medina Sidonia's chief naval aide, was clearly a difficult man, and Don Pedro de Valdés seems to have clashed with Medina Sidonia and his other colleagues early on, disagreeing about tactical dispositions and protesting that the Captain-General was disgracing him by insisting on vetting his disbursements. Don Pedro also complained bitterly about another problem in the Armada's command structure, the division of

authority between the captain of the ship and the captain of the troops on board, and the disparagement of the sailor, and in particular of the sea captains of his squadron with years of experience in the Atlantic on the Americas run, by haughty and overbearing officers who knew nothing about ships or the sea. Valdés went so far as to claim that it was the demoralization of the sea captains that had been in part responsible for the dispersal of the fleet off Finisterre in July. It was perhaps no accident that one of the first disasters to strike the Armada was the crippling of the Andalusian flagship and the abandoning of Valdés to the English by his chief.

If the ships of the Armada were no match for the English, neither were their guns. An appreciation of the state of the munitions industries in Spain on the eve of the Armada, such as has been described above, must cast considerable doubt on the capacity of the Spaniards to have carried out the coherent, late change in gun policy that the naval historian, Professor Michael Lewis, attributed to them. Some guns were being cast by the Captain-General of the Artillery in the last months before the fleet sailed — the Venetian Ambassador spoke of 200 — but most of what was got was got haphazardly by purchase or by requisition from foreign ships in Iberian ports. The marine archaeologists have dug up not only obsolete but also ill-cast guns, not necessarily Spanish made.

Michael Lewis argued that the Spanish fleet was weaker than the English in long-range, light-shotted guns, but considerably stronger in heavy-shotted, medium-range guns and medium-shotted, short-range guns. According to Lewis, the average Spanish broadside, when it was within range, was nearly double that of the English fleet. There was the possibility, therefore, that in the right circumstances, the Spaniards could have done the English a great deal of damage. New documentary evidence from the Spanish archives now makes this seem very much less likely. Information on 1,841, or 76 per cent of the total guns in the Armada, itemizing gun types and weight of shot fired, reveals that not only was the Armada even worse off at long-range than Professor Lewis thought, with only 172 "countable" guns of 4 lb shot or more, compared with the English fleet's 497, but that even within the heavy and medium gun range the Armada was markedly weaker as well, with only 162 guns throwing shot of 15

● Seventh Duke of Medina Sidonia. Artist unknown. This painting from among the family portraits at San Lúcar de Barrameda, shows the Duke in his sixties, wearing his collar of the Golden Fleece.
BY KIND PERMISSION OF THE DUCHESS OF MEDINA SIDONIA.

bs or more, as against 251 on the English side. Indeed, the Spanish firepower far from being double, was only about three-quarters of that of the English, as regards the total firepower of the two fleets and the average broadsides of their front-line fighting-ships. We have with these comparisons the beginnings, at last, of an explanation for the inability of the Spaniards to dominate the English even at those moments during the campaign when the opposing fleets were within arquebus, or even hailing range.

By August 8, there were other factors adding to this disadvantage — a shortage of powder and a shortage of shot. It had been pointed out before the Armada sailed that, even with the increases in the powder supply during April and May, it was carrying less than three times the

amount that had been used in one day by a much smaller fleet in Santa Cruz's victory in the Azores. What may have compounded this deficiency was the notoriously poor quality of Spanish-made gunpowder (probably three-fifths of the total). A ship's pilot resident in Seville blamed the ignorance and the shoddy workmanship of the powder makers, who, he thought, ought to take an examination. The General of one of the Indies fleets in 1586 thought the gunpowder made in Spain "the worst in the world ... pure mud", that had to be double charged before it gave any response. If this was happening in the Armada, the effect on its gunnery and powder supplies must have been catastrophic. By the end of the day-long battle of Gravelines there was hardly a front line ship

with any powder or shot left, and the galleon San Mateo was lost precisely because it was left without munitions and defenceless.

Don Francisco de Bobadilla's informed, yet little-known report, sent on August 20 to Philip II's minister of state, Don Juan de Idiáquez, is the best contemporary statement that I know of the deficiencies of the Armada as a fighting force. "You need to have been here to see and believe what has happened in

177

● Detail of the Spanish galleon appearing in the watercolour by Rafael Monléon: *Galeones del siglo XVII según gravados, dibujos y descripciones.* (c. 1885).
MUSEO NAVAL, MADRID.

order to recognize what a deception this great machine has been. You will now not find anyone who is not saying, 'I told you so', 'I predicted it', as always after the horse has bolted ... We found the enemy with a great advantage in ships, better than ours for battle, better designed, with better artillery, gunners, and sailors, and so rigged they could handle them and do with them what they wanted. The strength of our Armada was some 20 vessels, and they fought very well, better even than they needed, but the rest fled whenever they saw the enemy attack. Of that I will say nothing in my account to save the reputation of our nation. Furthermore, we brought so few cannon-balls that I hardly had a fighting ship that had anything to fire. Thus, the San Mateo, having run out of powder and shot, was caught and destroyed, and if the enemy had attacked us one day more after we made to the north, the same would have happened to the rest of the ships."

The Armada then was sent off undermanned and under-equipped. It had neither the quantity nor the quality of the soldiers it needed to make a direc assault on England, and it had not th means of effecting a junction with th veterans of the Army of Flanders; it wa encumbered by a hotchpotch of slow crank, and unweatherly ships, many o them structurally unsuited to the north ern seas; it was armed with guns tha could give it an advantage neither a extreme nor at point-blank range, fire by powder that was in great part ineffi cient and unreliable, and that was no expected to last more than three day and it was provisioned with mouldin biscuit, souring wine, and putrescen fish which was becoming inedibl almost before the ships left port an which, despite all the pious hopes and false relations, was in such short supply that within a month it had contributed materially to the decision to abandon the Enterprise and bring the Armada back to Spain. There was almost nothing in this catalogue of woes that had not been brought to the attention of Madrid and the Escorial over and over again in the months and the years before the disaster. By the time he reached Corunna, the commander of the Armada, the Duke of Medina Sidonia, was so disheartened by the sysiphean task of trying to improve the condition of his fleet and by the inadequacy of the means at his disposal that he wanted, even at that late hour, to call the whole thing off.

What then was the point of sending the Armada to sea in such a condition? Had the decision been a purely military one, perhaps the answer would have been, none, but by July 1588 the Armada had long ceased to be solely a military venture. Maybe Englishmen have too readily assumed that the only thing that mattered about the Armada was whether it conquered England. Yet as far as Philip II was concerned, the invasion of England was only a means to an end, and, in the opinion of many of his advisers, not by far the most desirable of means. The basic aim of the Armada was not the conquest of England, but to shift the burden of war from Spain to England, to transform an immensely costly, passive and demoralizing, defensive war into an aggressive war in which the Spaniards would have the initiative and the English would have to pay the economic and psychological costs of eternal vigilance. Philip II's purpose was to put a stop to English interference in his affairs, to get Elizabeth out of the Netherlands, to make her abandon her support for the Portuguese pretender, and to drive the English pirates out of the Indies by compelling them to concentrate their forces at home for their own defence. To do this it was essential, not necessarily to conquer England, but to appear to be able to do so. The King of Spain had to show that he could put an Armada to sea. He had failed to do so in 1586, and even Drake was surprised. He had failed to do so in 1587, and Drake had sacked Cadiz. By 1588, men were beginning to laugh at the King of Spain and his Armada. It had already cost millions of ducats and was costing a further 900,000 ducats a month. It was a massive burden on Portugal and Flanders. It was interfering with commerce and with the Indies trade. Further

delay could only allow the English to strengthen their defences or again take pre-emptive action as they had done the year before, and increase the chances of a collapse of that delicately balanced diplomatic stalemate that was keeping the French and the Turks temporarily out of action at the critical moment. Further delay must finally destroy Parma's invading force and do who knows what harm to Philip II's cause in the Netherlands. If the Armada did not sail, the English would be completely unrestrained and Spain would be exposed to the "intolerable disgrace" of even more daring and more damaging outrages on its shipping, its ports, and its Indies. If Elizabeth went unpunished, what credibility would be left to the bubble reputation of Spanish power, either in Europe or in its empire. By July 1588, with half a dozen deadlines already passed, there could be no worse defeat than to leave the Armada rotting in port.

Besides, it was by no means certain that the Armada would have to fight at all. Ideally, it would not need to, and Medina Sidonia's orders were to avoid battle as long as his purposes were not thwarted. The very size and reputation of the huge fleet — its unheard-of numbers exaggerated by the flood of official propaganda broadsheets that flowed from the presses — the awe-inspiring sight of its towering ships, that would be enough. Elizabeth dare not risk her fleet and her kingdom against such a force. She would have to make peace and the Armada would be vindicated. This curious mixture of fantasy and desperation is nowhere better manifested than in the admonition sent in reply to Medina Sidonia's defeatist letter from Corunna on June 24, 1588. The ships of the Armada, Medina Sidonia was told, despite all reverses, were still newer, larger, and stronger than the English, and their soldiers more numerous, more experienced, better trained, and disciplined. Reserves of victuals would be sent after the fleet from Lisbon and more could be taken on in Flanders. Parma's morale was high and his troops raring to go. With only six days of good weather it could be all but over. Furthermore, and this was the rub, "for our fleet to remain in Corunna is so far from strengthening our position (giving reputation to, literally) in any peace negotiation, should this be intended, that it would more likely give the enemy extra incentive for hostile action, thinking it a weakness ... Even if our purpose were solely to make peace, this could not

be done on honourable terms without the fleet's going ahead and joining with the Duke of Parma, clearing from its path whatever might cross it". In short, "the shame of finding our fleet bottled up and ineffective" would merely be to "exchange offensive war for defensive, by which we would lose both advantage and reputation".

The Armada did not conquer England, it did not prevent English assaults on Spanish territory or English attacks on Spanish ships; it did not force England to abandon the Dutch or the dissidents in Portugal; but did it do any harm? Was Spain any worse off with the Armada a failure than if it had never sailed at all? Financially, of course, it was — though we must not forget that one way or another there would have been massive defence costs. Santa Cruz, for example, in 1586, argued that it would cost in other ways three times as much if nothing were done. Materially, and in human terms, the losses were enormous. By November 19, only 7,486 men of 98 companies of infantry had returned; 60 per cent of those who had left on May 30 had not come back. The loss of ships is less exactly recorded, but half the total (63) is probably the upper estimate, one-third (44) probably the lower. Politically, there is obvious scope for argument about the effect of the Armada's failure on the fate of the Guises in France or the war in the Netherlands. Yet, in one way, the Armada succeeded. If the emphasis in this chapter has been on the structural and accidental inadequacies of the Spanish Armada, we should not forget that by contemporary lights it was a fearfully impressive looking force, and that despite everything, it reached its objective off Calais almost unscathed. That long-running fight up the Channel with its four battles, each one far exceeding what those who had been in both campaigns had experienced at Lepanto, did not destroy the reputation of Spanish naval power, it made it. Lord Howard of Effingham said it: "Some made but little account of the Spanish force by sea; but I do warrant you, all the world never saw such a force as theirs was". Within two years, Spain again had a fleet of 100 ships and 43,000 tons, and with the memory of that week in August 1588 behind them, no Englishman could feel confident that there would not be other Armadas and that the next one might not succeed.

*Dr Thompson is lecturer in History
at the University of Keele.*

THE GREAT SOCIAL DIVIDE

The differences between the rich man in his mansion and the poor man at the gate were enormous. John Pound explains why

*I*N 1558 ENGLAND'S population stood at about three million, with perhaps another quarter of a million in Wales. It was essentially a rural population. London's inhabitants totalled some 100,000 in the 1580s and may have increased to 200,000 by the end of Elizabeth I's reign, but no other English town contained as many as 20,000 people. Norwich alone among the big provincial towns had a population of 18,000 or so before the disastrous plague of 1579 reduced its numbers by a third, but it owed much to a vast, and unprecedented, influx of alien refugees to the city in the previous decade when as many as 6,000 Dutch and Walloons were admitted. This was unusual. Bristol may have reached 10,000 by the turn of the century, Newcastle and York between 7,000 and 8,000, but other towns were decidedly smaller. It has been estimated that no more than 8 per cent of the people lived in towns of more than 5,000 by 1600 and London alone accounted for 5 per cent of this figure. The larger towns were walled, at least 146 English and Welsh boroughs being fortified by as early as 1520, and many were concerned with overseas as well as internal trade. The smaller towns, in contrast, relied even more than their larger neighbours on servicing their immediate hinterlands through markets, fairs, and shops. The countryside, in turn, contained many people engaged in industrial as well as agrarian pursuits.

At the beginning of the reign, the country had still to recover from what has been described as the worst population crisis of the century, the years 1555-7 witnessing widespread starvation in the provinces and in London itself. The disastrous weather not only ruined the harvests, but led to cattle murrain as well, the poor being especially affected, and the harvest crisis was followed by a severe outbreak of influenza. In some places, the population was reduced by as much as 20 per cent and in England as a whole the decrease was at 5.5 per cent.

The people of Elizabethan England lived in conditions of great uncertainty, at the mercy of the weather, disease and, less predictably, inflation. While really bad harvests occurred only in 1586 and 1596-7, the latter led to starvation in some parts of the country, notably in the north. Plague, however, occurred with much greater frequency, though usually affecting different parts of the country at different times. London, for example, experienced severe outbreaks in 1563, 1578-9, 1582, 1592-3, and again in 1603. Norwich, the largest provincial town, suffered even worse, plague being responsible for the deaths of at least 6,000 people out of a total population of some 18,000 in 1579-80. The city was given little chance to recover. In contrast to the national picture, deaths exceeded births for the next decade and beyond,

with plague being present in 1584-5 when deaths were five times as numerous as births, 1589-92, and again in 1603-4 when one-quarter of the city's population perished.

Nevertheless, appalling though these scourges undoubtedly were, the population of the country as a whole continued to grow steadily and by the end of the reign stood at about 4 million.

The people of England were loosely divided into a number of well-defined categories, succinctly described in William Harrison's description of the country which was first published in Holinshed's Chronicles in 1577:

> We ... divide our people commonlie into foure sorts, as gentlemen, citizens or burgesses, yeomen, and artificers, or laborers. Of gentlemen the first and cheefe (next the king) be the prince, dukes, marquesses, earls, viscounts, and barons: and these are called the nobilitie; they are also named lordes and noble men; and next to them be knights and esquires, and simple gentlemen ... Citizens and burgesses have next place to gentlemen, who be those that are free within the cities, and are of some substance to beare office in the same ... Our yeomen are those, which by our lawyers are called Legales homines, free men borne English, and may dispend of their owne free land in yearlie revenue, to the summe of fortie shillings sterling ... The

fourth and last sort of people in England are daie labourers, poore husbandmen, and some retailers ... copie holders and all artificers.

The lay peers were similar in number at the beginning and end of the reign, 57 in 1558 and 55 in 1603, figures which disguise the fact that few of them were peers of the first or second generation. When Elizabeth came to the throne 46 per cent fell into that category. At her death, the proportion had fallen to less than one-fifth. She created or recognized only 18 peerages and none was created duke after Norfolk's execution in 1572.

Immediately below the peerage came the knights who may have numbered no more than 300 at the beginning of the reign and still less than 400 at the end, even allowing for the large numbers created by the Earl of Essex in Ireland at the end of the century.

Esquires and gentry were much more numerous, the terms embracing a variety of people. Harrison adequately describes contemporary opinion:

Who soever studieth the lawes of the realme, who so studieth in the universitie or professeth physicke and the liberall sciences, or beside his service in the roome of a capteine in the warres, can live ydlely and without manuell labour, and thereto is able and will beare the port, charge and countenance of a gentleman, he shall be called master, which is the title that men give to esquiers and gentlemen, and reputed for a gentleman...

Gentry of all classes may have numbered 16,000 or so by the end of the reign. Quite apart from the county gentry, the aldermen of the larger towns, as well as those aspiring to such status, were invariably described as gentlemen. This was not simply a case of aping their betters. Many were younger sons of existing county families, apprenticed to prestigious trades, such as grocer, mercer, or draper and who, in the fullness of time, would themselves retire to manors bought from the profits of commerce and establish yet another line of a particular family.

Yeomen and husbandmen — broadly speaking, the larger and smaller farmers — came next in the rural hierarchy, a contemporary, Thomas Wilson, estimating the former at 10,000 in 1601, the latter at four times as many. Their urban counterparts were the common councillors, or ruling group below the aldermen, and those other freemen, or master craftsmen, who never aspired to, or could afford, the delights of civic service.

Inevitably, the various categories overlapped, but as a rule of thumb a man's status was defined by his wealth, a definition as true for the towns as it was for the country districts. In Norwich, for example, the 24 aldermen were nearly all superior in wealth to the 60 members of the common council, although those common councillors who were waiting in the wings for an aldermanic vacancy were invariably men of substance as well. Choice of occupation was equally important, some being considered infinitely superior to others. In a city where

● Sir Henry Unton.
NATIONAL PORTRAIT GALLERY, LONDON.

some 100 trades were practised, little more than two dozen were considered suitable for aldermen and twice that number for aspiring common councillors.

Under normal circumstances, the bulk of the husbandmen and the less wealthy freemen in the towns lived in conditions of reasonable comfort. It was the poorer labourers or tradesmen, whether in town or country, who formed the broad base of the social pyramid and it was from their ranks that the Tudor poor were inevitably drawn.

The disparity in wealth among the various classes in Elizabethan England was enormous, even among the peerage whose income from rents at the beginning of the reign ranged from less than £500 to the £6,000 obtained by the Duke of Norfolk. For those below the peerage, the subsidy (tax) assessments of the 1520s provide the clearest guidelines, their broad details being as valid for the reign of Elizabeth as they were for that of her father, Henry VIII. Virtually everyone was taxed on goods, the items which provided the greatest revenue. Many, however, owned or rented land in addition to this, a proviso which is especially

important where the relatively poor are concerned. In Babergh Hundred in Suffolk, for example, 30 per cent of all those named in the military survey, which preceded the subsidies, were landowners in their own right, apart from those who were renting or leasing land. All classes from the labourers upwards were included among the freeholders, most of whom had holdings ranging from five to 30 acres.

Everywhere a minority of wealthy individuals owned a majority of the moveable goods with a substantial majority owning little or nothing. In Norwich, about 6 per cent of those taxed owned some 60 per cent of the property; at Exeter, an upper class of 7 per cent were in possession of two-thirds of the town's goods. Men of the same social standing in Bristol, Salisbury, and Canterbury, never numbering more than 7 per cent of the taxable population, all owned more than half of the property in the town concerned. In the relatively small, but extremely wealthy, cloth town of Lavenham, Suffolk, an unusually large upper class of 12 per cent had more than four-fifths of the town's property in its hands. At the other end of the scale, the 570 Norwich wage- earners owned less than 4 per cent of their city's wealth. At Lavenham, where men of the same

class made up more than half of the population, the wage-earners' share of the wealth was less than 3 per cent. The proportions were similar elsewhere, ranging from 2 and 3 per cent at Stamford, Lincs, and Thetford, Norfolk respectively to 7 per cent at Bury St Edmund's, Suffolk. The only exception to this was at Lincoln where a wage-earning class of 5 per cent owned about one-eighth of the moveable goods.

Subsidies continued to be levied, at intervals, throughout the 16th century but they were never again as all-embracing as those of the 1520s. As early as 1525, some men succeeded in getting their assessments drastically reduced and by the reign of Elizabeth they were derisory. The Crown, of necessity, relied on voluntary co-operation and this was seldom forthcoming to any reliable degree. Thus, in 1559, the subsidies brought in almost £440,000. In 1601, in contrast, they produced no more than £80,000 which, taking into account inflation, was a fall of more than one-half in real terms. The main culprits were the subsidy commissioners who refused to make realistic assessments. By 1594, the government was so exasperated that it ordered that any commissioners who were justices of the peace and assessed themselves at less than £20 were to be

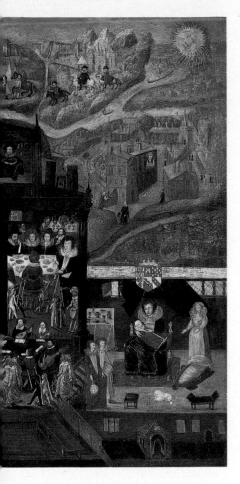

put out of the commission, a disgrace for local gentry who regarded the position of justice as one of supreme importance and a distinct status symbol.

The figure of £20 tells its own story and is a clear indication of how the situation had deteriorated over the previous 60 years. In 1524, for example, the mayor of Norwich had been assessed on £1,100, with 32 of his colleagues taxed on sums of £100 or more. In 1576, the wealthiest Norwich alderman was assessed on a nominal £28, his 23 fellows on sums varying between £14 and £25: they were quite as wealthy as their forebears. Thomas Wilson, writing at the end of the 16th century, said that he knew 24 Norwich aldermen worth at least £20,000 apiece, some much more, and several lesser men worth half as much. He was obviously generalizing about the aldermanic body as a whole, and the "lesser citizens" may well have been the common councillors. Apart from lands, plate, and jewels, more than one Norwich alderman was able to bequeath in excess of £1,000 in cash, with several disposing of between £300 and £500. Similar examples could undoubtedly be quoted for most of the cities, and for most of the country gentry.

The wealthy, whether gentry, yeomen, or merchants continued, in a majority of cases, to maintain a high lifestyle, but before considering this we need to look at least briefly at the whole question of inflation and how individuals responded to a situation which they barely understood.

Inflation had its beginnings in the 1520s and was a European phenomenon. A growing population stimulated the production of goods of all kinds and created an increasing demand for money. This, in turn, made mining for gold and silver more profitable and the output of European silver alone increased fivefold between 1460 and 1530, reaching its peak in the latter year. By whatever means, and much more significantly, Spanish silver from South America also entered Europe in great quantities, trade, war and piracy, among others, all contributing to the influx. While this had obvious effects on this country, as well as others, they were exacerbated in England by the costs of war and the currency debasements of the middle years of the century. Agricultural prices had begun to rise from the beginning of Henry VIII's reign, with those of industrial products following in the 1540s, and all prices and wages rose sharply in the next decade. After a pause in the 1560s, inflation continued its upward course for the rest of the century. The famine of the 1590s saw another huge rise in agricultural prices, possibly by as much as one-third, and by 1603 grain prices were four times what they had been in the last years of Henry VIII's reign. In the same period, the prices of livestock and industrial products had doubled. By 1603, the wages of builders and their labourers were twice what they had been in 1547, with those of agricultural labourers a little behind.

While there is no doubt at all that some, perhaps many, people were adversely affected by inflation, it is generally recognized that its effects were not equally disadvantageous for all classes.

The peerage and upper gentry, essentially the same grouping, relied on land for the greater part of their income. As all landowners from the 1540s onwards had relatively fixed expenses and were able to increase their selling prices, it was possible to profit by increasing prices for farm produce, especially as these tended to keep ahead of the wages they paid and of the industrial products they bought. Some had problems with long leases, but as far as possible they maintained their real income from increased annual rents, increased entry fines on their manors, or both. Others partly replaced cash rents by food, bought more land or substituted direct farming for leases. Collectively, they more than held their own as is evidenced by their lifestyles discussed below.

Almost without exception, the yeomen gained from inflation. They had sufficient land to maintain their families and to provide a surplus for the market where they were able to sell at enhanced prices. They were in an excellent position. The main difference between them and the husbandmen was that the yeomen tended to be primarily freeholders, while the smaller farmers were essentially leaseholders. Freeholders were protected from adverse conditions. Leaseholders, in contrast, were heavily dependent on whether rents were raised, although they could, and did, profit in the intervening period.

The labouring classes who might reasonably be expected to have suffered the worst were, in fact, cushioned against inflation in a variety of ways. The Reformation, for example, had reduced the number of holidays, or holy days, available, enabling labourers, whether rural or urban, to work on a greater number of days than before. Many demanded their wages in kind which helped to offset the declining purchasing power of their money wages, while the price of manufacturing products rose more slowly than food and made correspondingly fewer demands upon their pockets. As industry expanded, too, more job opportunities became available for women and children, so that a family's purchasing power, as distinct from an individual's, might not suffer to the same extent. It was also possible to cut nonessentials and substitute cheaper for dearer food, and processed products, such as bread and beer, rose more slowly than grain and malt. It was only a minority, and those mainly in the towns, who depended wholly on wages. For others, with smallholdings and common rights, the effects of inflation were easier to offset.

Broadly speaking, the possession of land and especially the possibility of producing a surplus for the market made the difference between those who were able to combat inflation and those who were not. The gentry, using that term in its widest sense, tended to maintain as high a lifestyle as ever, as did many of the yeomen. This is evidenced, above all, in the building carried out by these people, whether in erecting palatial mansions, as

continued on page 186

183

San Miguel

Premium beer

Gets everywhere · En todas partes

SAN MIGUEL CONQUERS THE ENGLISH PALATE

Kaye Watson

Bound for Britain . . . UK Marketing Manager Lance Brown (left) and Export Sales Manager Antonio Claramunt inspect the first newly designed case of San Miguel as it reaches the end of the Burgos Brewery's production line.

Four hundred years after King Phillip II's Armada set sail, San Miguel — the Spanish lager — has successfully landed in England, spreading its conquests as far afield as Scotland, Ireland and Wales.

Although this famous Spanish lager was well-known amongst British travellers to the Far East, its surge in popularity did not begin until the sixties, when thousands of British holiday-makers started invading the Spanish coast in search of sun, sea, sand and cool beer to slake their thirsts.

Such was the insatiable appetite for this high quality Spanish lager — which currently accounts for 15 per cent of the total Spanish beer market — that San Miguel had no alternative but to expand its brewing operation and in 1965 they built their Malaga brewery, the first sight to greet the eyes of the tourists as they leave the airport.

Today 42 million tourists, including seven million Britons, visit Spain each year and the Spanish economy has never been healthier. The visitors' increasing demand for San Miguel to be more than a sunshine drink has also resulted in worldwide escalation in the lager's exports.

Unlike their competitors who spend untold sums keeping their products before the eyes of the British public, San Miguel did nothing to promote their premium lager in the United Kingdom until the beginning of last year. Without warning, they suddenly awoke from their long siesta and began to unfold a clever programme of low-cost, promotional activities to woo the British lager drinkers.

First, San Miguel brought their product into the homes of 17 million television viewers who unwittingly switched on at regular intervals to see a more credible form of product exploitation than straightforward advertising. For, in this instance, the familiar San Miguel bottles featured strongly on set of the popular series, *Auf Wiedersehen Pet* when four episodes were filmed in Spain.

San Miguel then made a successful attack on the main population areas of England, Scotland and Wales with a £·25 million advertising campaign which couldn't fail to gain the stamp of approval from the jazz and rock music fans. This involved two catchy, hard selling commercials, one featuring Georgie Fame which capitalised on the jazz revival, the other by rock singer Joe Fagin to appeal to the younger market.

In a concerted effort to maintain San Miguel's quality image their next move was to launch a major annual event for golf club stewards in the United Kingdom. This proved to be a very welcome event on the stewards and club masters calendar as it was the biggest activity ever held for members of the Golf Club Stewards Association in their 100 year existence.

Over a three month period more than 400 golfers tee'd off in regional tournaments, staged throughout the country, to find eight finalists to take part in the San Miguel UK Golf Club Stewards Championship, which was held in Torremolinos over a five-day period last November, and won by David Lithgow, representing Great Barr Golf Club, near Birmingham.

Needless to say, this event proved so popular that many golf clubs are now stocking San Miguel and the stewards are already practising their swings to qualify for this year's event.

Throughout the year San Miguel also began wooing Britain's sports and social clubs by inviting small groups of club owners and stewards on three-day hospitality visits to their Burgos Brewery in Northern Spain. Many were surprised to see a high-technology operation which produces 1,300 cases of San Miguel an hour, and half a million kegs a year.

In the first year of actively promoting their premium lager, there was not an avenue left unexplored. In keeping with their strong support of the Arts in Spain it seemed an opportunity not to be missed when they were asked to support and encourage young English talent by sponsoring last summer's San Miguel Fringe on London's South Bank — one of many events staged during the annual Capital Music Festival. This was the first time they had made a direct approach to the UK's main premium lager market, the 18-35 year olds, and during the three week event one particular performance attracted an audience exceeding 10,000 who, undoubtedly, enjoyed the taste of Spain for they consumed more than 30,000 cans of lager.

This year with UK sales confidently forecast at more than half-a-million cases, San Miguel's promotions to selected audiences continues. The golf club stewards are already testing their strength on the fairways and throughout the country snooker clubs are taking their cues for the regional rounds leading up to the first San Miguel UK Snooker Pairs Championship.

For further information: Kaye Watson, Press Officer — San Miguel Telephone: 01-458 2104

● Shepherds and Harvesters: a woodcut from *The Shepheardes Calendar*, 1579.
BBC HULTON PICTURE LIBRARY.

continued from page 183

was done by some of the rich, or in the rebuilding and refurbishing of existing buildings by the yeomanry.

As late as the mid-16th century, most nobles were housed as they had been in the Middle Ages. In the north and west, in particular, they tended to live in castles, notable chiefly for their cold, damp, and draughty conditions and inadequate lighting. Elsewhere, such buildings had ceased to be inhabited and were in ruins or being converted into more comfortable dwelling places. The former included Liskeard Castle in Cornwall which was being used as a cattle pound when the antiquarian, John Leland, visited it in the 1530s; Rockingham, Northamptonshire, which retained its keep and outside walls while the rest of the buildings were in ruin; Worksop, Nottinghamshire, where the old castle was "clene downe" and Redde Castle, near Whitchurch, Shropshire, which was "now al ruinus". In contrast, Belvoir Castle in Leicestershire had been transformed from a place with rotten roof timbers and elders growing between the walls into a grand house where even the dungeon had been converted into "a fair round tour " (tower) ... "as a place to walk yn, and to se the coun-

trey aboute". A garden had been placed within the walls.

The dissolution of the monasteries heralded the change of attitude. Most of the nobles were able to obtain at least some monastic property, and after the uncertainties of Mary's reign they could feel secure in its retention. Although few, for a variety of reasons, felt comfortable about converting monastic property for secular use they had fewer scruples about dismantling it and using the building materials for their own use. Of those who were prepared to convert the original buildings, Lord Russell "mad hym a fair place" of a house belonging to the Black Friars; Sir William Sharington converted Lacock Abbey; and Sir Richard Grenville turned the nave of a former Cistercian monastery into a great hall with a splendid plaster ceiling. The first house built at Longleat and burned down in 1567 also had its origins as a Carthusian house.

As Elizabeth's reign progressed, a combination of ambition and a determination to outstrip their rivals led an increasing number of noblemen to embark on what amounted to an orgy of house building. In Hertfordshire alone, 78 houses were built or rebuilt between 1540 and 1580, while in the counties of Derbyshire, Essex, Shropshire, and Somerset more houses were built in the period 1570-1620 than in any subsequent

half-century. The wealthier nobles built sumptuously. Thus Hatton had Holdenby, modelled on Burghley's house at Theobalds, and Kirby. Lord Burghley had Burghley House, begun while he was still plain William Cecil, and the much larger Theobalds. Lesser men contented themselves with one sumptuous palace and several lesser country seats. Costs soared, not least those involved in the decoration of the buildings. Whereas Losely in Surrey cost £1,600 in 1560, Longleat cost £8,000 a decade later, with both palling into insignificance compared with the £40,000 invested by Robert Cecil in the building of Hatfield between 1607 and 1612. Audley End in Essex, built, like Hatfield, just after the reign of Elizabeth, was even more expensive whether one accepts the Earl of Suffolk's own estimate of £200,000 or the more conservative £80,000 of contemporaries.

The great houses built by the ministers, courtiers, civil and political servants of Elizabeth were in a class of their own. As Sir John Summerson has pointed out, "no architectural effort has ever originated more decidedly in the prestige and personal influence of a sovereign. Much of Elizabethan architecture is the expression — conscious and deliberate — of a cult of sovereignty". They were built specifically to receive the Queen and altered or enlarged at her slightest whim. Per-

● Vagrants, from *Liber Vagatorum.*
BBC HULTON PICTURE LIBRARY.

It would be wrong to imagine that building was confined to the nobility, however. The lesser gentry and yeomen farmers were building, or rebuilding, on an unprecedented scale from the middle years of Elizabeth's reign onwards, and Hoskins and Barley have drawn attention to the housing revolution which began about 1575 and continued until well into the 17th century.

The term gentry, by its very nature, is a wide-ranging one and the houses built by these people varied in size from those scarcely discernible from the richer yeomen to those which were almost comparable with some of the nobility. Navigable waterways allowed at least some people living in Bedfordshire, Cambridgeshire, and even parts of Norfolk and Suffolk, to take advantage of the excellent building stone available in Northamptonshire. Most, however, had to rely on local materials. Thus those of mid-Wales, the West Midlands, Lancashire, and Cheshire were invariably built of timber, with their equivalents in the limestone and sandstone area being built of stone. Timber-framed houses tended to be built in modules, dictated by the maximum usable length of timber that contemporary practice allowed. They were rarely of more than one module in depth, although one could be piled on top of another to give an impression of height. Houses of this kind reflect an extended, rather than a compact, plan and, in many cases, were added to by succeeding generations. For some at least, such houses were built or extended for show, to impress their neighbours, or to maintain their position in society.

The wealthier yeomen undoubtedly had the same object. The majority were concerned with more practical reasons and for most this meant altering existing housing stock, rather than completely rebuilding it, and having altered it seen that it was furnished in an appropriate style. Most yeomen houses originally possessed a hall open to the roof with storeyed bays on either side for specialized services or storage. The addition of a fireplace meant that staircases could be added and upper rooms provided, in many cases allowing families to sleep "upstairs" for the first time.

Even below this level, building was considerable. It has been suggested that cottage building, in particular, reached its peak between 1580 and 1630. In the

aps the most incredible example of this ccurred when the Queen visited Sir homas Gresham's house at Syon in 577. She complained that the courtyard as too long and would be better divided y a wall. Gresham called in workmen hile she slept and the alteration was ompleted by the following morning.

The Queen's retines were always rge and had to be accommodated. With is in mind, the so-called prodigy ouses had a much larger number of dgings than those provided for houses mply designed as family seats, a lodg-g being a suite of two or three rooms r people of quality. The two long sides the courtyard were designed specif-ally for this purpose, the side opposite e entrance comprising the hall, kitchen d other rooms so necessary for the rger house.

Limitations of space prevent any etailed descriptions of these houses, it a few may be mentioned briefly.

Longleat, rebuilt in 1568 after the fire of the previous year, was essentially outward looking, a four-sited palace with light and shade regulated by carefully spaced bays. Hardwick Hall, built in the space of seven years between 1590 and 1597, was similarly many windowed, described by contemporaries as being more glass than wall. It had square towers with very exaggerated bays rising a storey above the mass of the building, giving it a castle-like appearance. The largest of all of those built in the Elizabethan period was Burghley's house at Theobalds, destroyed like Hatton's Holdenby during the Commonwealth period. It took just over 20 years to build (1564-1585) and at its completion extended across five courtyards with huge three-storeyed towers capped by ogee-roofed turrets stretching towards the skyline. It was essentially a royal palace erected for the occasional use of the monarch as and when she chose.

187

● Little Moreton Hall.
NATIONAL TRUST.

enough to occupy the towers around the city walls, hardly commodious dwelling places as those surviving today make perfectly clear.

The "building revolution" was accompanied by a general rise in the living standards of those fortunate to combat inflation. Harrison, as so often, has described it in words that are worth repeating, emphasizing that he spoke "not ... of the gentry and nobility only, but likewise of the lowest sort in most places of our south country... " He noted that:

> ...In noblemen's houses it is not rare to see abundance of arras, rich hangings of tapestry, silver vessels, and so much other plate as may furnish sundry cupboards to the sum oftentimes of a thousand or two thousand pounds at the least, whereby the value of this and the rest of their stuff doth grow to be almost inestimable. Like wise in the houses of knights, gentlemen, merchantmen, and some other wealthy citizens ... their great provision of tapestry, Turkey work, pewter, brass, fine linen, and thereto costly cupboards of plate, worth five or six hundred or a thousand pounds ... But ... so in times past the costly furniture stayed there, whereas now it is descended yet lower even unto the inferior artificers and many farmers who ... have, for the most part, learned also to garnish their cupboards with plate, their joined beds with tapestry and silk hangings, and their tables with carpets and fine napery...

manor of Epworth in Lincolnshire, 100 additional cottages were built in that period, and there is similar evidence for Rockingham Forest, Northamptonshire and Oxfordshire. Most of the Oxfordshire examples are cottages of one bay, measuring 10 feet by 12.

These were still houses of people of some substance. By the very nature of things, there is little surviving evidence for the housing of the very poor. From the information we have, it seems that many of them built one-roomed hovels of the kind which were still commonplace in the Leicestershire and Lincolnshire countryside in Elizabeth's reign. As late as 1680, houses of turf were still visible in Staffordshire, while others in Northumbria were described as "mean beyond imagination ... without windows, only one storey". The Spanish

entourage of Philip II, who married Queen Mary, were appalled at the low standard of some of the English housing, describing the dwellings as "made of sticks and dirt", although they were suitably impressed with the diet of the people concerned.

Rather more information survives for the urban poor, much of it derived from the great Norwich census of the poor, taken in 1570. While housing conditions, as such, are not described, some of the poor lived in houses that they owned and others were in the process of buying them. Most lived in rented accommodation, much of it being the property of the city's aldermen and common councillors, with a small number of women and even some of the poor themselves providing accommodation for their less fortunate fellows. Although there were exceptions, few appeared to live in unduly crowded conditions, with the exception of those unfortunate

Apart from the increasing number of chimneys which had appeared in so many houses, old men in Harrison's village continued to be amazed at the general improvement in living conditions. In their day, they had slept on rough mats covered with a sheet with a "good round log" to rest their heads on, pillows being considered "meet only for women in childbed". Servants were lucky to have a sheet above them, for they seldom had one below to protect their bodies from the pricking straw that ran through the canvas of the pallet. Now mattresses, flock beds — even feather beds — were relatively commonplace, with sheets and pillows for everyone, or nearly everyone for, as Harrison was careful to note, such improvements, although great, were "not general". They also commented on the change in household utensils, notably the replacement of wooden spoons for silver or tin, and the great increase in pewter.

For the fortunate, general improvements of the kind outlined above were matched by the infinite varieties of food available and the seemingly endless changes in fashion. The variety available to the rich can best be illustrated by examples of specific meals, with general guidelines about what was available to their less wealthy fellows. It should be emphasized that people were not expected to eat every last thing that was provided for them. They could, and did, elect only what pleased them at a particular time and it was not uncommon for dishes to be returned untouched. They would then be passed successively down the social scale to be finally given away as scraps after lesser gentry, officials, and servants had had their share.

It was commonplace for noble households to entertain frequently and at great expense. In a household of 150, for example, food would, of necessity, be served in more than one apartment. Thus two tables would be provided in the dining-room, three in the hall, one in the private apartment of the chaplains, and two more in the housekeeper's room or the ladies-in-waiting. Cloths would be placed on the tables, with trenchers, napkins, and spoons at every place. Wine, ale, and drinking vessels would stand on the buffet, with clean goblets or Venetian glasses available for drink as required. Bread would be squared before being set on the board. The great salt-cellar would be placed on the table, with basins, ewers, and damask towels for the guests. Any silver or gilt not in use would be set to view on appropriate cupboards.

The nobleman, his family, and most important guests would be served at the first table in the dining-room, the second being reserved for knights and gentlemen. The steward presided over the high table in the hall, where the principal officers of the household would sit. The second table was set for the gentlemen waiters and pages and the third for the inferior officers of the household. The various servants also fed in the hall, but at a separate sitting. The cooks, if Harrison is to be believed, were frequently "musical-headed Frenchmen" and strangers, or other foreigners. Huge quantities of meat were consumed, with beef, mutton, veal, lamb, kid, pork, rabbit, capon, and pig being served as frequently as the season allowed, supplemented, on occasion, by red and fallow deer. At Lent, or on other fish days, the variety of fish was equally startling — salmon, plaice, whiting, flounder, and so-called mud-fish

being commonplace. The main meal would be followed by a variety of sweetmeats, tarts of different colours, conserves, and jellies, described by Harrison as being:

> of all colours, mixed with a variety in the representation of sundry flowers, herbs, trees, forms of beasts, fish, fowls, and fruits, and thereunto marchpane (sweet almond paste) wrought with no small curiosity, tarts of divers hues, and sundry denominations, conserves of old fruits, foreign and home-bred, ... marmalades, marchpane, sugar-bread, gingerbread, florentines (a pie with no crust beneath the meat) ... and sundry outlandish confections, altogether seasoned with sugar...

Foreign observers, not surprisingly, accused Englishmen of over- eating and asserted that their consumption of meat was far in excess of that eaten elsewhere in Europe, although Harrison implied that among the well-to-do food and drink was taken in moderation and frequently in relative silence. No doubt, the £629 spent on the wedding feast of Lord Burghley's daughter in 1582 was exceptional, but as Professor Stone, who provides the information, says, "it makes splendid reading". Among other things, the guests consumed 1,000 gallons of wine, 6 veals, 26 deer, 15 pigs, 14 sheep, 16 lambs, 4 kids, 6 hares, 36 swans, 2 storks, 41 turkeys, over 370 poultry, 49 curlews, 135 mallards, 354 teals, 1,049 plovers, 124 knotts, 280 stints, 109 pheasants, 277 partridges, 615 cocks, 485 snipe, 840 larks, 21 gulls, 71 rabbits, 23 pigeons, and 2 sturgeons. This vast quantity was consumed over three days, but it has been estimated that in large households, between five and eight pints of beer a day were consumed by each person and, in addition, between 750 and 1,250 gallons were drunk, mostly claret, white wine, and sack.

The Saturday fish-day had been reintroduced in 1548, to be followed by a similar stipulation for Wednesdays in 1573. The so-called "Political Lent" was intended to give a boost to the English fishing industry as well as making additional vessels available in times of emergency, and they were to be of some use when the Armada finally set sail. Whatever the reason, they did little to reduce the size of meals. On June 7, 1594, the 10 judges of Star Chamber were provided with ling, green-fish, salmon, pike, gurnard, dory, carp, tench, knob-

berd, grey-fish, plaice, perch, sole, conger, barbel, flounder, turbot, whiting, lobster, crab, and prawns, supplemented by eggs, capons, chickens, rabbits, artichokes, peas, strawberries, apples, gooseberries, oranges, lemons, quinces, and barberries.

Meals such as this were unusual and provided a greater choice than was sometimes available to the Queen herself. Nevertheless, she had variation enough. Details have survived of her entertainment on 17 November, 1576, the anniversary of her accession. The dinner menu provided two courses, the first of which had a choice of beef, mutton, veal, swan or goose, capon, rabbits, fruit, custard and fritters, with "cheat", manchet (the finest white bread), ale and wine. The second offered lamb or kid, herons or pheasant, cocks or godwits (bird of the plover family), chickens, pigeons, larks, tart, butter, and fritters. Supper was again a two-course meal. For the first session, boiled and roast mutton, capon, herons, "chicken-bake", conger, beer, ale, cheat, and manchet were available; with lamb or kid, cocks or godwits, pigeons, larks, partridges, and plovers being provided for the second. The Queen preferred beer to ale or wine, and drank little of the latter.

We must move from the specific to the general. The varieties of meat and fowl available as well as those of fish on fish-days have been outlined in some detail, as has the Englishman's predilection for beer and wine. These apart, the 16th century saw an upsurge of interest in fruit and vegetables, and new species were introduced for the first time, notably by alien refugees from Flanders who set up as market gardeners. By the reign of Elizabeth, Thomas Tusser was able to draw up a list of 27 different fruit trees and bushes for the gardener. They included those as familiar as gooseberries, grapes, mulberries, bilberries, and strawberries as well as relatively recent arrivals, such as the apricot and raspberry, either introduced or still rare as late as 1548. Red and black currants and melons also became more common, and the orange was grown in this country for the first time sometime before 1562 on the Beddington estate of Sir Francis Carew in Croydon. The sweet potato first appeared in print in a recipe of 1596 and was evidently eaten after being roasted in ashes, or sopped in wine.

Dr Pound is lecturer in 16th century social history at East Anglia University.

189

In 1993, we'll be taking o

Just five years from now, Eurotunnel's shuttle trains will get you
and your car across the Channel in thirty-three minutes flat.

different sort of Armada.

That's nearly three-quarters of an hour quicker than today's quickest ferries. Another game of bowls, anyone?

EURO TUNNEL

A breakthrough for Britain.

STATE OF EMERGENCY

Queen Elizabeth's captains scoured the
gutters and hedgerows for men to defend the realm.
Joyce Youings describes the English Militia

EW PEOPLE today, unless they have sailed in the English Channel, can imagine what it was like in July 1588 to be with Howard and Drake pursuing the Spanish Armada towards the Straits of Dover. But, especially for those old enough to have lived through the 20th century Battle of Britain, it is easier to comprehend the preparations made by the subjects of Queen Elizabeth I to meet the Spaniards on land. It is possible to appreciate the problems, social, topographical, and logistical, and even to hazard a guess at the probability of success. Compared with the seamen, an increasing proportion of whom were now full-time professionals, the men of the Elizabethan militia, like the Home Guard of the 1940s, were almost entirely part-time amateurs.

Philip of Spain's instructions to the commanders of his troops aboard the Armada regarding the place and manner of their landing in England are still a matter of debate. Had any thought been given to what opposition, if any, they were likely to encounter? Were they promised a triumphal march to London? Philip's own reception as Queen Mary's husband in the 1550s had hardly been warm, but it was many years since he had been in England. It is ironic that the statutory provisions in force in 1588 about the formation of a nationwide defence force were two acts passed 30 years before in the last year of Mary Tudor's reign, known officially as "4 and 5 Philip and Mary, c. 2,3".

NATIONAL DEFENCE

The English monarchy had never poss-essed a standing army, that is a permanent, paid, professional force, and it was nearly a century after the defeat of the Spanish Armada that the first regiments of the modern British Army were founded. A suggestion in Henry VIII's reign that a standing army should be financed out of the proceeds of the Dissolution of the Monasteries had found no support in high places. Only very rarely had foreign mercenary soldiers been used on English soil, the last time in 1549 when troops intended by the Protector Somerset to be used against the Scots had been diverted to quell a rebellion in the south-west. Their commander had been John Lord Russell, later first Earl of Bedford, the first to be appointed Lord Lieutenant of that apparently dissident region. It was his son, Francis, the second Earl, who was to be one of the chief architects of Elizabeth's citizen army.

But the Earl of Bedford would not be building from scratch. The principle underlying Queen Mary's militia statutes was of immemorial antiquity, embodying the obligation of all able men between the ages of 16 and 60 to be available to defend the realm against internal disorder or foreign invasion. Well known to the Anglo-Saxons, it had only been reaffirmed in the Statute of Winchester of 1285 and more recently by Henry VIII's Parliament of 1511. By then, there had been added the obligation placed on persons of substance that they should provide, according to their means, horses, armour, and military weapons. Musters had been held somewhat irregularly and lists of men and gear compiled, the latter with varying degrees of efficiency. However, musters were held with some success in 1539 when a newly-Protestant England prepared to defend itself against an expected invasion by the Catholic powers of Europe, including Spain. The crisis passed, but at its height, the City of London delighted Henry VIII, and is said to have impressed the French Ambassador, by providing a magnificent procession of some 20,000 able citizens, clean shod and dressed all in white, including their hose, their officers in silk. Indeed, even in times of greater national emergency, the musters never quite lost the air of popular pageantry. In Elizabeth's reign, it was seriously suggested that to help pay for the militia, it should itself mount public displays which people would pay to see, rather in the manner of a modern royal tournament.

FEUDAL OBLIGATIONS

By comparison with the militia, the military service in the field once required of feudal tenants by their landlords, and by the King himself as the ultimate lord, was relatively new, virtually an invention of the Normans, and also long since outdated. To some extent, its place had been taken in the later Middle Ages by what historians call "bastard feudalism", a system whereby men of wealth, largely landed magnates, formally "retained" other men to render them service, including accompanying them to war, in return for a regular fee, or some other

● OPPOSITE: Francis Russell, second Earl of Bedford (d.1585)

● An English army on the march. Engraving in J. Derricke, *An Image of Ireland*.
BRITISH LIBRARY, C.21, b.32.

consideration. Retaining of private armies had been made illegal long before the accession of the Tudors, except by royal licence, but Queen Elizabeth, though she granted fewer licences than her predecessors, could not do without the retinues of her nobility, especially their tenants, many of whom, unlike the militia proper, wore their lords' badges and even uniform.

More important, what had survived out of all these feudal and *quasi*-feudal relationships was a deeply-ingrained feeling that in times of emergency, the natural leaders of any defensive army were, according to their status, the owners of land. The history of the English militia cannot be properly understood unless the remnants of medieval feudalism are taken into account. Indeed, the use in Tudor times, even at Westminster, of the Anglo-Saxon word "manrede", meaning rather more than the modern "manpower", exemplifies these archaic survivals.

MUSTERS

The militia was traditionally county-based, being therein divided into the ancient "hundreds" (or "wapentakes" in northern England), in which were grouped the parishes or "tithings". No one was required to muster except in the

city, town, or village where he had his principal residence, irrespective of where he owned or occupied land, or earned his living. To prevent the lending of arms, and even of able men, all musters were supposed to be held on the same day, but modern historians, especially those interested in population studies, probably scrutinize the lists of names which have survived more carefully than did the Tudor muster commissioners, and they find much to puzzle them.

Only in the event of an enemy landing, or a serious civil disturbance could the militia be asked to cross county boundaries and it could not be sent overseas. But the real difference between armies royal and the militia was who paid. Those who went abroad, voluntarily or as pressed men, had to be paid maintenance by the Crown, but all strictly militia, that is local, expenses had to be met by the parishes, whose constables levied a rate for the purpose on the more substantial householders.

Traditionally, musters had simply involved calling all those eligible to present themselves, with their horses, armour, and weapons, for the checking and updating of old lists. From these, brief certificates were prepared to be sent to London. County commissioners were appointed who in turn delegated the task to local gentlemen, and they in their turn left most of the business to the parish constables. The commissioners would

usually include the current sheriff, but he was no longer *ex officio* leader of the *posse comitatus*. Until the appointment of lords lieutenant, the county militia had no commanding officer. All the muster commissioners would be justices of the peace in the county, a great convenience as statutory obligations had to be enforced, when necessary, at Quarter Sessions. But JPs were exempt from mustering in person.

Immediately after her accession, Queen Elizabeth issued commissions for a general muster throughout the kingdom. Excuses flooded in from the counties. The 11 Devon commissioners pleaded that some of them were aged, some were too sick to travel far, and some had been in London for the Queen's Coronation. But gradually, anxiety not to be found wanting in loyalty overcame inertia. The certified totals have a spurious air of authenticity. In 1559, Devon returned a total of 6,742 able men. The following year, the commissioners had found more than 28,000, which they reduced in 1569 to well under 20,000. Such vagaries are not to be explained either by population history or by migration, important as both of these undoubtedly were in determining the base line from which the Elizabethan militia could be drawn.

After the muster of 1569, called for against a background of alarming developments in the Netherlands and made doubly necessary by the internal crisis

caused by the Rebellion of the Northern Earls, lists of names were called for and supplied, most of which have survived in the state papers. These tell us who were assessed that year to provide horses, armour, and weapons as well as who were "abled" to serve in person, the latter neatly categorized as archers, billmen, pikemen, and Harquebusiers. Later certificates also included pioneers, that is labourers capable of wielding picks and shovels, and even carters.

ARMS AND ARMOUR

Besides an assortment of swords and daggers which all Tudor men carried for self-defence, all able men were expected to be proficient in the use of a particular military weapon. There seems to have been an assumption, especially about horses, that those assessed to supply military equipment would also provide men able to use it. The first Militia Act of 1558 laid down in great detail what was required. Reputed income, based on the most recent tax assessment, of more than £1,000 a year from land carried an obligation to provide, first of all, six "horses for demi-lance", that is cavalry suitable for men-at-arms carrying the shorter lances used in battle, rather than the longer ones used in tournaments. In addition they had to find 10 "light horse" (geldings), fully "furnished" (equipped), with "harness" (armour) and weapons; 40 corslets, these being the hip-length suits of armour worn by pikemen; 40 "almain rivets", the now somewhat old-fashioned, German-style, flexible body-armour worn by foot-soldiers; 40 pikes; 30 longbows, each with a sheaf (24) of arrows; 30 "skulls" or steel caps; 20 black bills; 20 "hackbuts" and 20 "morions" or "sallets", which were the common man's visorless helmets. It was no light obligation, but few men who were not nobles enjoyed an income of such magnitude. The hackbut, which had been virtually unknown in 1539, was still the only firearm widely used in England. A light, matchlock gun, held in the hand, it was to be replaced, though never totally, in Elizabeth's reign by the caliver, a somewhat larger gun which needed a rest, and finally by the musket, a firearm which could penetrate armour. The lowest band included in the Act of 1558 comprised those with reputed landed income of between £5 and £10 a year. They were required to supply one almain rivet, one

195

bow with arrows, a steel cap and a bill, no more than was needed to equip one foot-soldier. A similar tariff applied to those assessed on their movable goods. These rates would encompass all gentlemen, including knights and esquires, and the more substantial yeoman farmers. Whether many of the rest, husbandmen and craftsmen and their sons, who served in person, owned serviceable weapons is not clear. The situation probably varied from parish to parish. To some extent, they could be supplied from the communal parish armouries which were obligatory and were also listed in the 1569 returns. The nobility were exempt, their military service being drawn upon by other means.

In 1577, the rates for the provision of arms and so forth were extended below the £5 level to include:

> such persons as by keeping of taverns and alehouses do gain highly by resort of persons more for pleasure than necessity.

Being unable to prevent the multiplication of what were regarded by the Queen and her ministers as socially undesirable establishments, they had no compunction about taxing their owners. Nor was it a Puritan parliament but one of Henry VIII's which provided that any man whose wife wore:

> any gown of silk ... any French hood or bonnet of velvet or any chain of gold about her neck or in her partlet ... any velvet in the lining or other part of her gown ...

should provide an additional light horse. The obligation ceased in the event of divorce. Despite tremendous efforts by the government to encourage the breeding of war horses, they remained in short supply throughout the century. But this seemingly desperate "sumptuary" provision is echoed in an instruction to the muster commissioners in 1570 that they should not be satisfied with people's rating for the subsidy, but should take note of their "open doings in the world" to discover those "of secret wealth and never charged with service as the gentlemen be". Gentlemen, almost by definition, were, of course, those who displayed their wealth.

Too willing a response to the government's unending reproaches about the possession of arms inevitably sent up prices. Efforts to peg these were no more effective than in the case of other consumable goods, especially those necessarily imported. Sir Thomas Gresham managed to buy and bring over quantities of arms and armour from the continent, but not all which reached the Tower of London, whence it could be purchased by the public, was serviceable. Town corporations in particular found that they could buy better on the open market. The government never attempted to claim a monopoly.

BOWS VERSUS FIREARMS

All over Europe, firearms were gaining ground, in use if not in efficiency, but Queen Elizabeth and her ministers were in no particular hurry to make the bow obsolete. Indeed, an Act of Parliament of 1571 declared the longbow to be "God's special gift to the English nation". Continental soldiers now effected to despise English bowmen and it is true that they were not what they had been in the days of the Hundred Years' War. The bow required considerable physique, but above all long and regular practice. Some contemporaries blamed enclosures for the decline, too many gentle shepherds, and too few sturdy ploughmen. The powers-that-be seemed to be convinced that muscular flabbiness went hand in hand with moral degeneration and that instead of practising at the butts which every village was required to provide, young men in particular spent their leisure time playing cards and gambling with dice, especially in the taverns and alehouses. Continual admonitions to practise archery were accompanied by instructions to the bowyers to make smaller and cheaper bows for boys of seven and upwards to use. The bowyers, who were still numerous among the occupational groups in the towns, ridiculous as it seems, persuaded the government that unless more work was found for them they would take their skills abroad.

For rapidity of fire and reliability, especially in wet weather, the bow could still more than match the gun. Arrows were much less expensive than powder and match and, in practice at least, could be retrieved and used again. Moreover, not all Elizabeth's subjects possessed sufficiently nimble fingers to insert the powder into the pan and strike the match so that the resulting shot did more damage to the enemy than to the handler. But had the militia been put to the test what would have mattered as much as individual skill would have been

● 'Jack' or padded jacket. Probably worn by harquebusiers.

discipline, the ability to create that hail of arrows which had been so terrifying in the battles of long ago.

However, even by 1569, almost every parish had its small contingent of harquebusiers and their number crept up proportionately over the years, though rarely outnumbering even the bowmen by the end of the century. There were still military pundits who thought that firearms would be a nine days' wonder and gentlemen feared for their game. Parliament limited the possession of firearms to those with income from land of at least £100 a year, but there is little evidence of the law being put into force. It was an offence to carry firearms on the highway, though the introduction of training camps for the militia made nonsense of this. But a great deal of thought, if little action, went into the establishment of county armouries. The trouble was that there would have to be custodians, and who would pay?

SOCIETY DISPLAYED

The muster rolls, especially those of 1569, provide a splendid series of local social tableaux. Of the able men listed to serve in person, the better sort appear largely as pikemen, ordinary husbandmen, and artisans as archers, and the labourers in town and country as billmen, using a short-shafted, stubby weapon not unlike that which they regularly used for such agricultural tasks as cutting hedges. Altogether, a large country parish would muster 50 or so able men, keeping up the early-Tudor proportion of about one in 10 of the population,

26

excluding vagrants. Only settled men were regarded as suitable. In 1577, the county commissioners were instructed to include only "meet and able husbandmen and farmers' sons that are likely to continue in the place" and not "such artificers as commonly are removing". "Masterless men", especially those of no fixed abode, were best sent overseas, including Ireland.

Some men no doubt were only too willing to be mustered, if only to prove their free status, for legal bondage was not entirely unknown in Elizabethan England. But most regarded it as an unwelcome chore. For the more well-to-do in particular, it represented, with taxation, twin coils within which they felt enmeshed, and this even though neither for her military nor for her financial needs could Elizabeth be said to have exploited her subjects. The statutes provided for a fine of 40 shillings or 10 days in prison for any who failed to turn up or to produce his quota of arms. But it was widely believed that those who could afford to do so could buy themselves out of mustering. What is certain is that many escaped by being retainers of great landowners. Others were exempted from ordinary musters as members of such privileged bodies as the Stannaries, the organization of the tinners in Devon and Cornwall. Wealthy widows could not easily avoid being assessed to supply arms, but the clergy enjoyed, if that is the right word, the privilege of being assessed by their own diocesan officers.

MILITARY TRAINING
Early in 1569, Elizabeth's right-hand man, William Cecil, convinced that the

Duke of Alba would soon break the Dutch resistance and that the Catholics would soon regain total power in France, advised the Queen that,

> The realm is become so feeble by long peace as it were a fearful thing to imagine, if the enemies were at hand, of what force the resistance would be.

The muster rolls soon to be in hand showed that the realm had many thousands of able men of military age, but did they know how to put up a fight?

As it happened, Cecil's long peace was to last for more than another decade and the 1570s provided a breathing space in which to prepare for whatever conflict would ensue. What was lacking in the militia statutes was an obligation to be more than reasonably competent in the use of one's appointed weapon, to have learned military discipline, to be familiar with basic military drill and manoeuvres, and, above all, to know and to obey one's officers. Fearful, no doubt, of its chances of getting further legislation through Parliament, from about 1573 the Privy Council proceeded by proclamation and by circular letters to the justices of the peace, to insist on the holding of regular training camps. There was much resistance, especially on the grounds of cost, because men were entitled to be paid 8d a day for loss of earnings when absent from home, even if the camp ran over a public holiday. The cost had to be borne by the parishes, in effect the more substantial householders. There were also fears about the assembling of men, with arms, in large numbers lest some hotheads start a commotion. Camps

● Harquebusiers, from engraving in Thomas Lant's *Roll of the Funeral Procession to St. Paul's of Sir Philip Sidney.*
BRITISH LIBRARY, C.20, F12.

would be attractive to Puritan preachers, with great potential for trouble. One suggested precaution was to let the harquebusiers practise getting their eye in without the issue of powder and match until shortly before they departed for home.

The new emphasis on training found the gentlemen who had hitherto only been called upon to take a mild interest in the musters almost totally unprepared. How to defend themselves in single combat would have been an essential part of their education as boys, but warfare was an entirely different matter. Their battlefields as adults were more likely to be the courts of law. Sir Humphrey Gilbert's elaborate proposal in 1570 for the establishment of a military academy in London to serve as an alternative to the Inns of Court as a finishing school for young gentlemen fell on deaf ears. He, together with his younger half-brother, Walter Raleigh, was exceptional in his considerable experience as a soldier - in France, in the Low Countries, and in Ireland. Indeed, in a schedule of "martial men" drawn up for a dozen counties in June 1588, Devon headed the list with 16 names, even though so many of the county's young men were sea captains.

A chorus of appeals for help did not in this case go unheeded. As early as 1570, instructions drawn up for the Earl of Bedford as Lord Lieutenant of the south-western counties recognized the lack of enough "gentlemen of knowledge" of military matters and promised the appointment *at the Queen's expense* of "certain chosen honest captains" as peripatetic "trainers" of the militia. This would mean that camps could be smaller and thus less hazardous. There was also the carrot that they would be less expensive, though it was reported that sending their men to camp still cost the Cornish parishes between £4 and £5 a year. Exactly how many of what were later called "muster masters" were appointed is not clear, but certainly most of the "maritime counties" along the south coast did receive some outside help. The trainers even received unsolicited testimonials from the gentlemen. In Cornwall, a certain Captain Horde was such a model of tact as well as efficiency that it was reported that some men who had hitherto been prepared to pay large sums for exemption were keen to buy more weapons and to put in more practice with them. How far the gentlemen themselves took advantage of the opportunity to be instructed does not emerge. But the trainers' visits were few and far between and in 1573 Cornwall was dependent on its resident gentlemen, "the best that could be got". By 1580, it was admitted that despite the holding of twice-yearly camps,

> it is manifest that the soldiers profiteth little, as is seen in that they neither know readily how to put their match into their sock or take their mark to annoy the enemy, or [even] to stand soldierlike in their pieces.

In 1569, some Cornish parishes had included men able to use slings. Theirs was an art perfected in early youth and it was said that they could project stones, and even lead bullets, with great rapidity and accuracy over distances of up to 250 yards. Met with these, the Spaniards might well have imagined that the English (for they would not know the difference) had devised yet another secret weapon.

SELECTION

It was quickly realized that to attempt to train every militiaman was quite impractical, if only on grounds of cost, and not really necessary. Moreover, as Sir Walter Raleigh and others were to argue, too large an army for local defence would be unwieldy. The greatest single advance in the 1570s was the acceptance of the principle of selection for training, this

being now added to the older rule of selecting as far as possible only settled householders and their resident sons and servants. Indeed, some counties had already numbered their soldiers in tiers, certifying, besides their able men, those merely "willing", or, as in the case of Devon in 1560, those "unable but to keep the country", meaning, presumably, those who would protect the homesteads. The Earl of Bedford as early as 1558 drew up a scheme whereby mobile units would be responsible for the defence of certain strategic points along the coasts of the south-west, mostly the ports and harbours. As a boy, he may well have accompanied his father when he surveyed those same coasts for Henry VIII.

By the early 1580s, instructions came thick and fast from Westminster to maintain what were now called the "trained bands" and also the reserves, to be adequately furnished with arms and armour. Back went protestations of loyalty and good intent laced with excuses, usually about lack of funds, the decay of the local economy, poor harvests, and so on. But there also emerged delineations on paper, and even on parchment, of armies, it was claimed, existed in the flesh. Some counties expected special commendation for having exceeded their quotas and in others sharp rebukes often produced quite extraordinary improvement. A promise made to the militia of Wiltshire in 1578 that arms provided voluntarily would not be taken away from their owners except in a dire emergency resulted in an increase of one-third in the number of harquebusiers. The Crown would have been quite helpless in the face of wholesale recalcitrance and the Queen knew better than to push her subjects too far. In December 1580, she reminded the inland counties of the need for "some convenient number of able men well furnished and sorted with armour and weapons", but only "in such sort as should not be overchargeable to her subjects". However, she added, nothing should be considered too costly if "public safety" demanded it, and she reminded people of their long freedom from "the great and excessive burden and charges of wars". It was against the tyranny of rulers too much addicted to war, she might have added, that they were being asked to defend themselves.

OFFICERS

By 1580, most counties, besides selecting part of their able manpower for training,

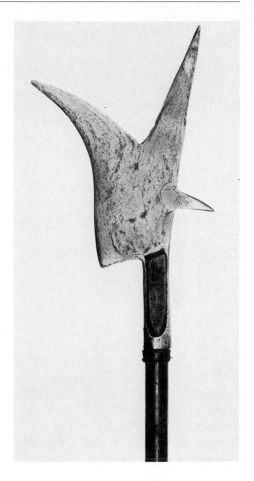

● Bill, 16th century.
BOARD OF TRUSTEES OF THE ROYAL ARMOURIES

had also divided their forces vertically into units. The larger counties used the "divisions" long familiar to their justices of the peace and below these groups of hundreds. It is likely that the parishes were becoming less important, except as suppliers of cash. There begin to appear in the certificates the term "regiment", though with little agreement on its size, and the designation of certain officers as Italianate "coronells".

But what appears to have been missing, at least on the evidence of the certificates, were named junior officers, captains of companies. It would appear that the deficiencies of the county gentlemen as trainers also extended to their aptitude for leadership. And yet any alternative to the gentlemen was unthinkable in Tudor England. What emerges from the certificates for Devon is that the few local knights and gentlemen who were named as officers were in charge of units whose very size was determined by their captains' social status. Indeed, in 1589 the Lords of the Queen's Privy Council decreed that "every knight that has charge should have the leading of 200, every esquire 150, and every gentleman 100".

This was flexibility of a kind which

● Gentleman's field armour, as worn by Sir John Smythe, soldier and diplomat.

an efficient fighting force could have done without. Drake and others at sea were slowly but surely cutting the gentlemen down to size. But the real problem continued to be the lack of gentlemen with military experience. They were certainly rising in wealth and numbers, but were not rising to it as far as the defence of the country was concerned.

LORDS LIEUTENANT

At county level, however, certainly by 1580 and in some cases much earlier, there was a local military *supremo*, the Lord Lieutenant. The office dated from the reign of Edward VI, but was intended to be filled only in times of emergency. Queen Elizabeth held out on this point as long as she could, having no desire to create provincial princedoms. In 1570, when the internal and external crises were thought to have receded, the lords lieutenant were thanked and stood down. But by the early 1580s, external threats were continuous and appointments were more or less permanent, as they have remained ever since.

Most lords lieutenant had charge of several counties and in the North of England, the Earl of Huntingdon, already chief commissioner for musters, became Lord Lieutenant of Yorkshire, Northumberland, Cumberland, Westmorland, the bishopric of Durham and the cities of York, Hull, and Newcastle. He kept himself on his toes by being President of the Council of the North. Most of those in command of the militia in the southern, including the maritime, counties were noblemen who were also members of the Queen's Privy Council and few can have spent much time in their counties. Most had local landed property, but few were experienced soldiers.

For most practical purposes, they relied on their deputies, a handful of whom made their appearance in each county during the 1570s. They eventually became, along with their chiefs, part of the local administrative scene. Nearly all were knights, that is members of that local élite of men who had been honoured thus, usually on account of their administrative service. Few were experienced soldiers, but they held most of the divisional commands in the militia. Like the lords lieutenant, and indeed also the justices of the peace who attended the camps or acted as militia commissioners, they received no pay or even out-of-pocket expenses. The Queen expected her officers to recoup themselves as best they could from the exercise of patronage and such other opportunities as presented themselves. It was all an accepted part of the Tudor system.

THE SOUTH-WEST

As the day of reckoning with Spain approached, the concern of the Queen and her ministers was focused less on the country's land boundaries to the North and West and more on what were known as the "maritime counties" in the South of England. These stretched from Cornwall eastwards along the Channel coast and around to Lincolnshire, and also included those next in line, from Somerset to Cambridgeshire, 17 in all.

Until what seems in retrospect extraordinarily late in the day, most direct government expenditure was devoted to the defence of the coasts of Hampshire, including Portsmouth, and the Isle of Wight. Here there were two lords lieutenant in 1587, the Marquess of

Winchester and the Earl of Sussex. This was an area long regarded as the likeliest "place of descent" by the enemy, but by the mid-1580s there was growing a conviction that Philip of Spain would want to establish a supply base with the shortest possible sea crossing from the Continent. This pointed to the south-west, even to Cornwall where, as Raleigh was later to point out, Falmouth provided one of the best deepwater havens available. But a landing west of the Tamar (the boundary between Devon and Cornwall) was unlikely because of the long and difficult land communications between east and west Cornwall. The county of Devon, with its ports of Plymouth and Dartmouth, and to a lesser extent that of Dorset, were clearly in the front line. But perhaps because the Earl of Bedford was now ageing and carrying less weight in high places, or because the Queen decided to lean on the Hawkins tradition of self help in Plymouth as long as she dared, no Royal cash was made available for the fortification of Plymouth, or indeed Dartmouth. Between 1585 and 1588, principally in the last of those years, the corporation of Plymouth spent

nearly £1,000, most of it on ordnance, which may have been in response to suggestions made the previous year by Sir Richard Grenville. If all the guns had been in place in July 1588, and the evidence on this point is inconclusive, Spanish ships entering the Sound could have been subjected to a considerable battering. But did the town possess a sufficiency of gunners? Very little of the town's expenditure was in support of the militia. Was there a single trench on Plymouth Hoe? Had Plymouth been captured, it is difficult to know who would have been more to blame, the Queen herself or her representatives in the counties of Devon and Cornwall. There were no militia officers nearer than the Champernon brothers at Modbury, a dozen miles away, and they had only 300 trained men.

Throughout the 1570s and the early 1580s, the Queen had put her whole trust in the Earl of Bedford to look after the south-west, including its public order, much as her father and brother had depended on his father. The second Earl, although a committed Protestant who had spent the early part of Mary's reign

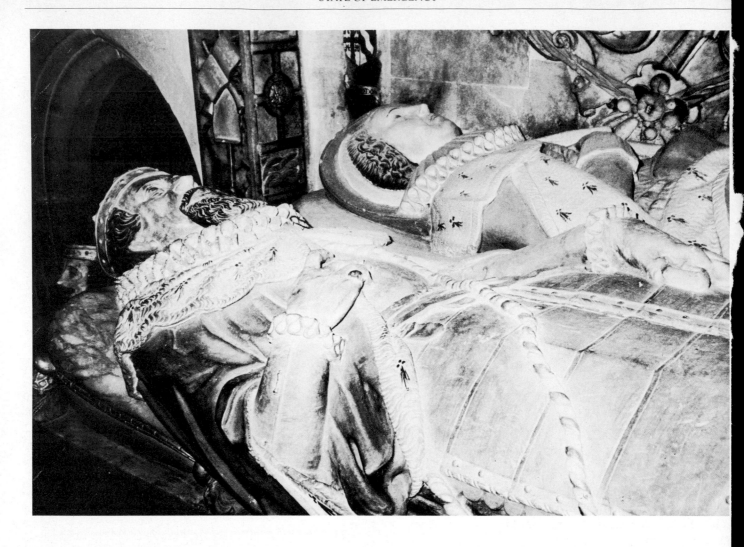

● Tomb of the Earl of Bath. Print by Joyce Youings.

in exile on the Continent, held the Lord Lieutenancy of all three south-western counties during Mary's last year. Queen Elizabeth deprived him of Dorset, but that left him with Devon (including the city of Exeter) and Cornwall. In 1585, the year when England at last broke off relations with Spain and when Sir Walter Raleigh and Sir Richard Grenville were preoccupied with their colonizing project on the eastern seaboard of North America, the Earl of Bedford died. The previous day, his son and heir had been killed in a skirmish on the Scottish border and the next in line was a boy of 14. To a certain extent, the Queen may have been glad of the opportunity to end what was beginning to look like an hereditary office in the south-west, but who was to succeed Bedford? The Queen delayed. Not until February 1586 did she renew the commissions of the deputies, only to lose two of those for Devon who died from gaol fever caught from prisoners awaiting trial at Exeter Assizes. Corn-

wall, besides the frantically busy Grenville, had the indefatigable Sir Francis Godolphin and in Devon there was Sir John Gilbert, elder brother of Sir Humphrey, the deceased soldier and would-be colonizer of Newfoundland. Gilbert's letters to Westminster suggest a certain helplessness. What was he to do about musters at Exeter? Whereas Devon had once been able to supply 700 horses, he could now find only 200.

One of Bedford's offices, that of Lord Warden of the Stannaries, was quickly bestowed on Sir Walter Raleigh, putting him in charge of the many thousands of militantly-independent tinners of Devon and Cornwall, from working miners to gentlemen owners of tinworks, many of them resident in the immediate hinterland of Plymouth. It was virtually a private army. Raleigh did not hesitate to put in his elder brother, Carew, as his deputy for Devon, for which county he was also made Vice-Admiral, a judicial office. Was this the beginning of a new family empire? In fact, Bedford's lord lieutenancy was eventually divided, that of Cornwall only going to Raleigh and for Devon the Queen's choice fell on William Bourch-

ier, Earl of Bath, the only nobleman with a residence in the county. At 29, he was about the same age as Raleigh, but had none of the latter's experience. Except for a short spell in the Low Countries with the Earl of Leicester, his career so far had been that of a scholar, mostly in Cambridge. He was told by the Privy Council to lean on his deputies, which he proceeded to do, from his newly built mansion at Tawstock, near Barnstaple, in North Devon.

Sir Walter Raleigh continued to bask in the Queen's favour. In December 1587 he was sent on a special mission to the south-west. He reported from Exeter to Walsingham that he found the Earl of Bath, Gilbert, and Grenville active and loyal, but he expressed doubts about others whom he forbore to name. Was he perhaps suspicious of one of the deputies for Devon, Sir William Courtenay, one whom Philip of Spain had been promised would "ensure the possession of Plymouth"? But then Raleigh himself at about this time was also being described by a Spanish agent as the Queen's favourite and Philip's friend. Who knows? Courtenay was certainly a religious conservative at heart, but only a degree more so than the majority of his fellow Devonians. He must have attended his parish church at Powderham on the River Exe or he would have been in trouble. He was to die a Catholic many years later but, a matter perhaps even more important to him, without having regained for himself or his heirs the title of Earl of Devon forfeited by the Marquess of Exeter in 1538.

THE CRISIS DEEPENS

Sir Walter Raleigh's mission in 1587 was part of a final rethink about the size and disposition of the militia. Raleigh was in favour of the appointment of a General of the West with a small force of a mere 2,000 foot-soldiers and 200 horse, selected from Devon and Cornwall in a ratio of two to one. Besides a general, he provided for a lieutenant-general, a marshall, four colonels, and two treasurers, all to be unpaid. Each of the 20 bands of 100 men would have a hierarchy of eight "NCOs" and a drummer, all of them paid wages. The total cost for 16 days, including the purchase of powder, match, and lead (so all were presumably to be gunners) was £2,163.5s. Raleigh mentioned the decay of local trade and suggested that the Queen might meet half the cost. The Queen provided no cash, but she did lend the county nine big guns which arrived quite late in the day and were stored at Ashburton in the charge of Sir John Gilbert and Mr George Cary of Cockington.

During the early months of 1588, the Earl of Bath was bombarded with inquiries and instructions from Westminster. Back went guarantees that all likely landing places had been identified and had been provided with trenches as cover for the defenders and with pits and stakes to hinder an invader. Bath did complain about a lack of experienced men to instruct the pioneers. No doubt he could have made good use of the tinners, but they did not even muster until the Armada was in sight. Had he enough carts? No, he replied, somewhat wearily, because Devon roads were unsuitable for wheeled traffic, but he had arranged for every village to provide sufficient nags for the carriage of shot. Should the enemy land and his forces be compelled to carry out an orderly withdrawal, he was told that the country should be "driven", that is cleared of all supplies of food, in the fields or in store.

This last tactic might have been very effective for, as we now know, the victuals aboard the Armada ships were spoiled. But if the enemy was to be starved, not so the English militia. At Blandford, in Dorset, in May 1588, the deputy lieutenants agreed on a daily ration per man which included $1\frac{1}{2}$ lbs of bread, $2\frac{1}{2}$ lbs of meat, and 2 quarts of beer. Many Dorset men must have prayed that the Spaniards would come, and those in the parishes who would have to meet the bill that they would soon be sent packing.

The Earl of Bath did his best to convey to the Privy Council an air of calm assurance. Everyone was doing his duty and Devon was in a state of "orderly readiness". So it would appear from the splendid certificate engrossed on parchment which he sent to Westminster in April 1588 and which survives among the state papers. Each of the county's three divisions was divided into several units, each with a named captain and lieutenant, some of the latter being professional soldiers. There were no divisional commanders, however, except for the horse and for the powder and match which was stored in a number of corporate towns in each division. As predicted, there were only 150 light horses, plus 50 "petronells", that is unarmed beasts, but each unit was said to have what seem like suspiciously round numbers of horses for carriage of arms and armour.

It is the extraordinary symmetry of the whole splendid tableau which strains credulity, each of the companies in each division being made up of exactly the same number of shot, pikes, bows, bills (meaning men furnished with the same), and pioneers. The trained and furnished companies numbered 3,650 in all, the untrained reserves 2,550, the latter also neatly categorized, but lacking shot. All the trained shot were said to have calivers or muskets. Among the untrained men, billmen were still in the majority, but bowmen were still numerous among the trained, more so than among the untrained. Are we to believe that all the "defaults" noted the previous year had been rectified?

A certain mystery, however, surrounds the mobile units which were supposed to be ready to cross county boundaries to relieve hard-pressed neighbours. Those at Westminster were most anxious that everyone detailed to this duty should know exactly what he had to do. Whether they did so is not revealed by the records and may not have been entirely clear at the time. Years later, Sir Walter Raleigh was to point out how much easier it would be to relieve the militia of Devon from Somerset rather than from Cornwall which, as he quite rightly pointed out, was effectively an island, communications across the Tamar being very easily cut off by an enemy.

Whether in July 1588 there was anyone in Devon or Cornwall sufficiently decisive to put all these preparations into effect may well be doubted. There is no evidence that the Earl of Bath ever visited the Channel coast. His deputies were men of experience in giving orders, but were only too apt to quarrel, as did Sir John Gilbert and Mr George Cary in the early 1590s about their respective recruiting territory. This was clearly an old sore. However, enormous advances in training and selecting the militia had been made since the beginning of the reign. Even the order, anticipating one of 1944, that the soldiers should not rush madly to the coast at the first rumour, but remain at home until ordered to march to wherever it had been established that the enemy had landed might even have been obeyed for fear of the justices. It is only too likely that the line of armed men which the seaborne Spaniards reported seeing all along the clifftops of Cornwall and Devon were in fact no more than sightseers from the coastal parishes, drawn there out of curiosity and no doubt in the hope of a Spanish wreck. The people of Torbay were not disappointed, the great *Nuestra Senora del Rosario*, her mast broken by accident, being escorted to the Devon shore by Sir Francis Drake himself. Was it not with his tongue in his cheek that Sir John Gilbert later claimed that he alone, from his headquarters at Greenway on the River Dart, had conducted 1,000 men to the coast of Torbay, implying that Mr Cary had stayed at home?

An historian may be forgiven for regretting that the Elizabethan militia was never put to the test, or at least not in 1588. From what is known of the weapons carried by the Spanish soldiers, the two sides would probably have been well matched, the greater professionalism of the Spaniards being more than offset by their ignorance of the English terrain. One can even imagine a mutual disinclination for battle and an outcome as dependent on the weather as that at sea. Whatever their place of descent, however, the Spaniards would not have made a triumphal march to London such as was the good fortune of the troops of William of Orange exactly a century later.

AMOR ET VIRTUTE.

ÆTATI
A

THE BEACONS

The news of the sighting of the Armada was undoubtedly relayed to Howard and Drake at Plymouth by spy ships and by men riding on horseback. It was carried thence to the Earl of Bath at Tawstock and more importantly to London by the fastest post horses available. What then of the beacons which Macaulay has convinced posterity flashed the news to England that its hour of destiny had arrived? The beacons were there all right, many of their locations dating from Roman times. There were supposed to be three at each coastal site, two on nearby hills, and single ones at more distant vantage points. There was a very complicated code which all concerned were supposed to understand. Their building and their maintenance - and some were quite elaborate stone structures - as well as their watching, at least in summer time, were the responsibility of the nearest village, and it was one of the duties laid on the lords lieutenant to ensure that it was performed. Those who watched were required to be men of trust and sobriety. But official instructions were also very precise about what was to happen if the enemy was sighted. No beacon was to be lit without authorization by two JPs (and by no means every village had even one in residence) and they were not to give the word "until they have found out by speedy and trusty messengers why the previous beacon was fired". Clearly, the powers-that-be feared false alarms more than lack of intelligence. Is it not possible, then, that like the church bells which rang out their message in 1945, the beacons were fired in 1588 only when the time had come to rejoice? The parish records are strangely silent. In any case, it would surely have been too much to expect of the weather gods that they should provide clear skies ashore as well as the storms so damaging to the Armada at sea.

TILBURY

The failure of the Queen and her ministers to contribute to the fortification of Plymouth will not really have come as any surprise to provinces long accustomed to playing second fiddle to London and the Court. Royal purveyance and even the ensuring of adequate supplies of food for the capital's ever growing population had long been a thorn in the flesh of distant counties. The call to each county to provide a contingent of trained soldiers to be ready to proceed to London to protect the Queen and her capital was just another of these demands. More men were required of the maritime counties on the grounds that they were likely to be better trained. In the event, the Queen left the summonses until the last moment and before the majority of detachments reached the assembly point at Tilbury all were sent back home, a great financial saving to the Queen. Hence it was that few county militiamen can have been part of the largest audience to be addressed by a reigning monarch until the days of radio and television. With luck they clattered home in time to get in what remained of the harvest.

Joyce Youings is Professor of History at Exeter University

● A detail from the Muster Certificate for Devon, April 1588.
PUBLIC RECORD OFFICE.

● OPPOSITE: Sir Walter Raleigh, in the year of the Armada.
NATIONAL PORTRAIT GALLERY, LONDON.

ARMADA

1588–1988

THE OFFICIAL EXHIBITION CATALOGUE

Introduced by Dr Mia Rodriguez-Salgado

- A lavish and unique pictorial record for all the family – over 450 photographs, maps and illustrations.

- Comprehensive and authoritative guide to *all* the items and galleries of the exhibition at the National Maritime Museum, Greenwich.

- Brilliant, scene setting, introduction plus 30 expert contributions covering different important Armada topics.

 £12.95

Duff Hart-Davis, Deputy Editor of The Sunday Telegraph, contributor to the Independent, and biographer, is also the author of Armada, published by Bantam Press, (cover price £15.95). The book is reviewed here by Richard Hough, publisher and managing director of Hamish Hamilton who is also a national press contributor and naval historian.

The Spanish Armada of 130 ships was intended to pick up the army of the Prince of Parma which was operating in the Low Countries and transport it to England, where it would crush all opposition, capture that tiresome and arrogant woman, Queen Elizabeth, and reinstate the Catholic faith. This admirable book by Duff Hart-Davis tells us just why, and how, it failed.

The first reason was that the Spanish, for all their colonial and maritime supremacy, failed to distinguish between a naval battle and a land battle fought at sea. Their ships were packed with troops and the rela-

tively few sailors were mere drivers, to sail their galleons to within grappling distance of the English enemy in order that the soldiers could board and kill in hand-to-hand combat. The Spanish ships were big and high-sided, as intimidating and almost as un-manoeuvrable as castles. Hart-Davis calls them "floating garrisons", an excellent analogy.

Lord Howard of Effingham commanded a smaller mixed fleet of sailor-gunners trained to fight a naval battle. His ships were faster, leaner and infinitely more manoeuvrable so that he could choose how and when to fight. From the start, the English held the initiative. Their "race-built" galleons, as the author calls them, with a total complement of some 400 men and around 40 guns were no more than 140 feet overall with a beam of a mere 36 feet. Thanks to the unique co-operation of the National Maritime Museum, the reader learns more about these nation-saving vessels than ever before.

Duff Hart-Davis's narrative is crisp, authoritative and a delight to read. He gives us the facts and passes few judgements, allowing these facts and events to tell their own tale — and, oh what a tale it is! For example, while Garrett Mattingley in his fine 1959 account treats Francis Drake's suspiciously opportunistic night capture of the treasure-carrying Spanish ship and Drake's justification for it the next day as "a straight-faced tale" and "a very odd story indeed", Hart-Davis allows readers to draw their own conclusions.

This is an objective formula that works well, even if it is far from Henry Newbolt's vision of Drake:
Call him on the deep sea,
    call him up the Sound,
Call him when ye sail to meet the foe;
Where the old trade's plyin'
    an' the old flag flyin'
They shall find him ware an' wakin'
    as they found him long ago.

Well done, Duff Hart-Davis! This is a great read.

MACDONALD CHILDREN'S BOOKS

THE SPANISH ARMADA

*T*HE SPANISH ARMADA (6.95 hardback/£4.95 paperback) is written by David Anderson, head of education of the National Maritime Museum, and is the official Armada book for children. The book sets the Armada in the broad context of 16th century Europe and relates the full story of the campaign. The author, with the help of full colour illustrations, focuses on individual items of background, the design and bulding of ships, what life at sea was like, navigation, and how sea battles were fought. He also recounts the stories of shipwrecks suffered by the Spanish fleet and aims to dissolve the prejudice and myth that surrounds the Armada in the final section which reveals the distortion of truth about events over the last 400 years.

BATTLEGAME ARMADA!

*H*ISTORY records a resounding defeat of the Spanish Armada in 1588. But suppose things had been different ... Battlegame Armada! combines a factual account of the English victory with an intriguing board game that allows children to replay the English Channel battles.

The full colour board (320mm x 470mm) reflects the realities facing the opposing sides. For example, English ships have longer-range cannon, but the Spanish can fire heavier shots. Both Fleets are at the mercy of changing and unpredictable winds, though the game allows for the superior manoeuvrability of the English ships. Unlike reality, either player can win; Spain can reverse history by using new strategies, or history can repeat itself with an English victory. Available in the souvenir shop at the National Maritime Museum.

MODEL GALLEON

*A*N EASY to assemble, full colour model of an English galleon of the sort that took part against the Spanish Armada in 1588. Based on Matthew Baker's detailed and accurate drawings (the only ones that exist from this period), this is a realistic model that stands about 30cm high. Accompanying text includes illustrated information about the lives of ordinary seamen aboard ships of this period. Comprehensive instructions with the help of scissors and glue will help you create this fantastic model galleon in a matter of hours. Available in the souvenir shop at the National Maritime Museum.

THE SPANISH ARMADA HAS ARRIVED!

David Anderson, Head of Education at the National Maritime Museum at Greenwich, has written the official children's book **THE SPANISH ARMADA** (Price £6.99 hardback/£3.99 paperback), an accurate history which debunks many of the myths surrounding the event, to complement the NMM's ARMADA Exhibition.

BATTLEGAME ARMADA! Two players can change the course of history with an exciting boardgame in a book whose accompanying text briefly outlines English Naval warfare. A challenge at only £3.50!

MAKE A MODEL GALLEON in a matter of hours. You need only scissors and glue to make your own realistic galleon with the help of easy instructions. A snip at £3.50.

Read about the swashbuckling adventures of Sir Francis Drake, one of England's greatest seafarers, in Fiona Macdonald's **DRAKE AND THE ARMADA** (£4.50).

You'll find them in all good bookshops.

Macdonald Children's Books